'Man is born free, and everywhere he is in chains. One man thinks himself the master of others, but remains more of a slave than they are.'

Jean-Jacques Rousseau, *The Social Contract*, 1762

'Everything is awesome . . .
It's awesome to win and it's awesome to lose.'

The Lego Movie, 2014

After graduating from the London School of Economics, **Jacques Peretti** became an investigative journalist whose award-winning television series include *The Men Who Made Us Fat*, *The Super Rich & Us* and *Trillion Pound Island*.

JACQUES PERETTI

THE DEALS THAT MADE THE WORLD

HODDER

First published in Great Britain in 2017 by Hodder & Stoughton
An Hachette UK company

This paperback edition published in 2018

1

A CIP catalogue record for this title is
available from the British Library

Paperback ISBN 9781473646421
eBook ISBN 9781473646414

Typeset in Plantin Light by Hewer Text UK Ltd, Edinburgh
Printed and bound by Clays Ltd, St Ives plc

Hodder & Stoughton policy is to use papers that are natural, renewable
and recyclable products and made from wood grown in sustainable
forests. The logging and manufacturing processes are expected to
conform to the environmental regulations of the country of origin.

Hodder & Stoughton Ltd
Carmelite House
50 Victoria Embankment
London EC4Y 0DZ

www.hodder.co.uk

For Esme and Theo

CONTENTS

INTRODUCTION

What if the way we understand the world is wrong? What if it is not politicians and world events that have fundamentally transformed our everyday lives, but business deals? Deals made in secret: high up in boardrooms, on a golf course, or over a drink in a bar.

These deals changed everything: money, work, why we buy what we buy. They changed our attitude to wealth and inequality, even how we define illness. Deals that taught us to embrace financial risk and a world of perpetual upgrade. Transformed the power balance between business and government; even rewrote the rules on what constitutes news and the 'truth'.

These deals often had far-reaching consequences the protagonists did not foresee: triggering the Arab Spring and fourth-wave jihadism by 'shorting' the price of wheat on Wall Street; using 'risky' loans to AIDS patients to create the financial mechanism that became sub-prime; harnessing the science of food to fatten up the planet and then using the business opportunity created to thin humanity down.

These deals changed our collective mindset, rebooting society to think in a different way, even redefining who we think we are. And each sprang from a single brilliant idea with a profound psychological insight at its core.

When planned obsolescence – manufacturing consumer goods to break – began being rumbled by the public in the 1950s, it was kept on track by just such an insight. Instead of simply making things that stopped working, manufacturers reprogrammed consumers to want the newest new thing. A seed of doubt was planted in every purchase we made: that it was already out of date. The plan had a name: 'engineered dissatisfaction' and the 'upgrade' was born. Today the never-ending upgrade defines consumerism.

A similar insight led to the transformation of medicine in the 1980s, from the treatment of illness to the medication of modern life itself, by vastly expanding the number of nebulous psychological conditions and syndromes available to be 'diagnosed'. Overnight, hundreds of new 'illnesses' appeared, with prescription drugs to alleviate the symptoms. At a stroke, we had in effect all become patients, and modern life was the illness.

These deals were ambitious in scope. They turned tax from a duty to pay into a global avoidance industry, with government incentivising criminality by setting up the offshore tax haven system, then blaming companies for using it.

In the twenty-first century, cash is fast being eradicated, making the data about you and me the newest and most valuable currency on earth. In 2020, China will launch 'social credit': monitoring every person's data 24/7 to create a score rating based on how good or bad a citizen they are.

At the same time, the deals now being cut by the Silicon Valley tech giants to weave big data, Artificial Intelligence, block chain and algorithms into an all-encompassing digital blanket is breathtaking in its scope. Nothing short of a controlling system over life itself: glibly termed 'singularity'.

We have habituated so fast to this new world, we barely remember it being different. But these deals did not happen by chance. They were hard-edged business decisions made by people who reconfigured the way we live with a business plan, and at the heart of this plan was one simple conceit: invent a problem and then sell the solution.

It is inevitable that as business became not simply a way of making money, but a machine with the potential to reshape society, its influence over elected government increased vastly, shifting the power balance between the two.

President Eisenhower first warned the American public in 1961 of a 'military-industrial complex' taking over the hushed corridors of the White House and the threat this posed to democracy.

In 2016, we saw the completion of 'corporate capture' with the election of a businessman as President, who appointed the CEO of one of the world's largest oil companies as his Secretary of State. Trump's most significant legislative action in his first year was to create the biggest tax cut to business in US history.

This incremental occlusion of politics, power handed piece by piece from elected officials to global corporations, had been a long time coming, but was not as straightforward as it might seem. The mechanism that first enabled it was put in place over half a century ago.

In the 1950s, the power struggle between politics and business was a straight shoot-out and evenly matched. But as business began to globalise with the postwar recovery of international trade and gain the upper hand, its ascendency over government was formalised in the creation of a special court, where global companies can (and frequently do) sue entire nations for failing to look after their business interests.

ISDS (Investor-State Dispute Settlement) courts were established in secret in 1964 by the World Bank and are a legal version of black sites: places that do not exist on a map, outside the jurisdiction of national law, where corporate lawyers interrogate government lawyers on the mismanagement of a company's assets by the countries they represent.

The decisions made in these courts affect millions of people, unaware their lives are being determined by a room full of lawyers. ISDS rulings have allowed companies to drill, mine, pollute, price-fix, tax dodge, overrule public opposition to power stations and toxic waste facilities, ignore environmental laws, and even siphon off scarce drinking water. If governments oppose these rulings, they can be fined the equivalent of their entire health budget for one year, as happened recently to one Latin American country.

When anti-capitalist protestors campaigned against TTIP/ TTP in 2015, believing corporations would henceforth 'run the world', they seemed unaware that exactly such a system had formally been in place for over forty years.

So how did this shift to the deal makers happen? In the early 1990s, I began working as a journalist for the BBC. At that time, there was an assumption that 'high politics' – the practice of government on Capitol Hill, in the Kremlin or Downing Street – is where real power lies. Reporters and commentators pored over the tiniest actions or utterances of politicians, imbuing them with the utmost significance. Even interpreting their body language at conferences – an overly strong handshake or domineering arm on the shoulder – as proof of a nuanced shift in the geopolitical power balance.

Thanks to Brexit and Trump, we witnessed a seeming collapse of belief in high politics and its accompanying 'elites'. In 2015, I was interviewing three investment bankers in the Cayman Islands when Donald Trump announced his candidacy for president. 'He could do it,' I said. They laughed dismissively and sipped their Mojitos. Trump was elected against the odds in 2016 (very good odds I now wish I had put some money on) as a formal anointment of this implosion of the political 'elite' and crowning of business.

In truth, not only had business run the show for forty years, according to the Washington-based Pew Research Center that monitors levels of public trust in politics, there had been a steady decline in this trust since the early 1970s, beginning with the Watergate Scandal. This was the other side of the coin – business had not only taken over politics, politicians had lost all credibility and potency. Trump had been a long time coming, too.

His election seemed the apotheosis of this slow death of high politics: The End. Apparent proof of the final implosion of the governmental machine. Many of those who voted for Trump did so because he seemed to be the opposite of a politician (one commentator observed that the media took him literally, not seriously, whilst the public who elected him took him seriously, but not literally). Trump was in 'business', though he wasn't in truth a self-made businessperson. He said he was a 'deal maker', though it was unclear he had ever made a successful deal in his life.

One thing we knew for sure, Trump – or rather, his team of king makers: Steve Bannon, Roger Ailes et al – was against 'the swamp': the murky world of pleading special interest groups and lobbyists perceived to be working on behalf of 'global corporations'. To this extent, the Bernie Sanders Left and the Alt Right shared the same hatred of Washington as a servant of big business: the Left hated polluting oil companies telling successive presidents what to do and the right hated Silicon Valley's 'liberal' billionaires having had free reign over two terms of Obama.

On the election trail, Trump deliberately played into public anxieties about corporate capture, indulging the fantasy that they were coiling themselves round politicians and bending them to their will behind closed doors. In reality, business gets its way without needing to go to such brutal effort.

When UK construction giant Carillion collapsed in January 2018, it was still being handed contracts by government as the company imploded. The only people who seemed oblivious that Carillion was going down were the politicians throwing more work at it worth billions of pounds. The Swamp – the bureaucratic soup that allows this structural incompetence – is itself filled with a miasma of competing interests that have swirled round every government since time immemorial. The Swamp is simply a fact of government, and the problem with promising to drain it is that it will refill as quickly as it has been drained. Unsurprisingly, all talk of draining the swamp evaporated within weeks of Trump's election: indicative of its indestructability.

How does this swamp operate?

I experienced it for myself firsthand. Before working for the BBC, I worked as a researcher in Parliament. I saw close-up how the political process works, and it was very far from what I had imagined. The majority of politicians did not appear to do very much. They made speeches, went for lunch, and got interviewed on TV (or spent a lot of time trying to be). Westminster politics was memorably described at the time as 'show business for ugly people'.

The Palaces of Westminster are themselves a huge architectural exercise in political impotency. When Charles Barry and Augustus Pugin rebuilt Parliament in the 1830s, augmenting James Wyatt's earlier design, their intention was to make it look even more of a neo-Gothic Hogwarts. Pugin was famously annoyed by the resulting mess ('All Grecian, sir; Tudor details on a classic body,' he told a colleague), but it was successful as a construction of kitsch *mise-en-scène*. A stage set designed to convey solemnity and political gravitas.

The reason was simple. Power was draining away from Parliament. The clamour for reform created by the seismic upheaval of the Industrial Revolution could not be contained by Parliament. We think we are living through profound change now, but it was no different in the 1830s. The population was exploding (doubling between 1815 and 1870) and work was being revolutionised by automation, threatening the livelihood of millions. It was being resisted by direct action groups such as the agricultural 'Swing' rioters, who smashed their own threshing machines and the Luddites, who burned down mills, not because they were against technology *per se*, only the way it was being implemented.

In the face of this turmoil, the subliminal message conveyed by Pugin and Barry's imposing faux-medieval makeover of Parliament was clear: we are in charge. Parliament is sovereign, even if 'The People' outside claim sovereignty for themselves, just as they did with Brexit.

Power in such dramatic flux made Parliament nervous. And the response to the human collateral created by industrialisation was brutal. The 1834 Poor Law Amendment Act made the starving and destitute ineligible to receive food unless they entered a workhouse. Conditions were deliberately inhumane to deter anyone – to use today's terminology – 'claiming benefits', unless bereft of hope or close to death.

In his 1859 bestseller *Self Help*, Presbyterian evangelist Samuel Smiles famously promoted the idea that poverty was the fault of the poor: the outcome of their 'laziness'. By 1861, 35,000 children under twelve lived in workhouses: the direct result, as the prevailing orthodoxy had it, of their 'laziness'.

Parliament used the stick of 'self-help' with unflinching force, and it failed. Organised labour regrouped and changed tack. It had learnt a lesson from the deportation of the first would-be trade unionists – the Tolpuddle Martyrs – to a penal colony in Australia, and devised a new strategy. To shift authority away from Parliament by seeking an accommodation with business. A new axis of power: workers and bosses, with Parliament suddenly peripheral to the needs of both. Parliament could go back to doing what it did best, managing the Empire and avoiding any more wars with the French.

By the mid-1800s, organised labour no longer sought to overthrow capitalism, but to cut a deal with it. In 1868, the Trades Union Congress was created for this specific purpose. The great social reforms of Gladstone and Disraeli that followed were framed by this co-option of the worker as a player; in effect, another member of the Establishment, with boots under the negotiating table.

The huge, potentially combustible force of an urbanised working class, conjured and then radicalised by the Industrial Revolution, was gone. It had been neutered and made part of the power play. Parliament's authority was restored. We had avoided the fate of Europe: revolution and dictatorship. High politics has drawn the sting of the working class and made Parliament relevant once more. Barry and Pugin's job had been to make the Palaces of Westminster appear the real hub of power – not the mills and cotton factories of Lancashire. Neither the bosses nor the workers. And it worked.

When I moved from Parliament to reporting in the early 90s, I witnessed in my first week how power operated 150 years later, revealed in a single moment in the hospitality room. I had produced a report about an oil company alleged to be polluting a large section of the Canadian coastline. There was a furious argument between a representative of the oil company and a member of a prominent environmental pressure group lobbying to stop the oil company. In the studio, they had practically come to blows.

In the hospitality room afterward, they were having a drink. The oil company exec turned to the environmentalist. 'That was very good,' he said. 'You were excellent.' 'Thank you,' the environmentalist replied. 'You know,' the oil exec continued, 'we could really do with someone like you. Give me a call.' They exchanged cards, and three weeks later, the environmentalist was working for the oil company.

They had cut a deal and the bargain was this: the oil rep understood what the environmentalist could do for his company and the environmentalist spotted an opportunity. But what kind of opportunity? To 'sell out' and make money for himself? Or the chance to influence a multinational company from within, to make the kind of changes he might not have been able to action from outside?

This was real politics in operation and it was complicated. There was no easy moral position to take on that hushed conversation between the environmentalist and the oil company exec because it was far from obvious who was playing whom, or what the true motivations or strategic outcome would be for either. What was clear was that there were no politicians present.

Of course, politicians cut deals behind the scenes as well, but the macro-picture for politicians has profoundly weakened in the last thirty years. The Industrial Revolution did not make high politics redundant: quite the opposite. The Palace of Westminster continued to oversee the management of the British Empire. Following the Second World War we had thirty years of planned corporatist partnership between business and government resulting in growth and full employment. But following the seismic economic schism of the mid-1970s, this pact between government and business altered irreversibly.

Governments became increasingly powerless with the collapse of the Bretton Woods agreement on fixed exchange rates in 1971, after which corporations began to wield ever greater transnational power without recourse to needing to cut a deal with government. Corporations now run the global show not so much through evil Machiavellian design but as a geopolitical inevitability.

This is evident from any cursory look at a map of the world. To a child, the world appears neatly ordered; countries have borders marked by pretty-colored lines. In one respect, the map is correct. Governments govern vertically within the narrow parameters of their borders. Corporations work horizontally across the planet with scant concern for the little colored lines.

That's why the anti-globalist rhetoric of Donald Trump the candidate disappeared when he became president. Because the reality of government means not just accepting the swamp, but accepting globalisation as well. We know we live in a globalised world but continue to wrongly frame our understanding of that world in a pre-globalised way: with politicians and nation-states as the units of power. To understand how power really operates, we need to shake the snow globe and see things differently. Corporate power has not merely been wielded to make business more profitable: the deals in this book show how it has profoundly altered the way we live our lives.

It is not politicians who choose when you upgrade your phone, which breakfast cereal you ate this morning, why you take prescription drugs for a nebulous anxiety that thirty years ago didn't have a medical diagnosis. Politicians do not make you feel fulfilled – or worthless – in your job. Or decide that an algorithm should dictate your work load. Politicians did not make the world obese. They did not decide that you should use contactless payment and stop using cash.

Business did, with government looking on: powerless and uncomprehending before the tidal wave of the Third Industrial Revolution.

Business is less uncomprehending. It sees the responsibility that comes with the power to determine what it means to be human in the second half of the 21st century. It will show its cards – what it chooses to do with this responsibility – as these deals pan out. Deals that were no shadowy conspiracy but just brilliant ideas conceived by gifted businesspeople who observed human behaviour, and simply found a clever way to change it.

Very few of the people I interviewed ever imagined the huge ramifications of what they had come up with. They had a eureka moment – a blinding insight into how to re-wire the way we behave – they put it into motion, high up in a boardroom, and we did the rest.

CHAPTER ONE
CASH: WHO IS KILLING IT AND WHY

The Deal: Peter Thiel, Elon Musk and Max Levchin sell PayPal to Pierre Omidyar of eBay for $1.5 billion
Aim: To create the first billion-dollar platform for online transactions
Where: eBay Headquarters, San Jose, California
When: Monday, 12 August 2002

In 2014, we tipped into a new world. It happened without fanfare, a mention on TV, a spike on Wall Street, it did not even trend on Twitter. But for the first time in history, card and contactless payments overtook cash transactions.

By 2025, even drug dealers will not take cash. South Korea plans to have no cash at all by 2020.[1] In Sweden, the European country going cashless first, buskers use contactless machines. A new app, BuSK, lets Londoners do the same thing. In Holland, a coat developed for the homeless allows people to give money by swiping a card on their sleeve.[2] Physical money in your hand – a system of payment that began 600 years before the birth of Christ – is coming to an end. Apple's CEO Tim Cook says the next generation 'will not even know what money was.'

Coins first began circulating on three continents in the sixth century BC. A technological innovation every bit as far-reaching as the iPhone. Small metal discs were exchanged for a desired trade. Coins were a physical embodiment of trust, a simple way of doing something astoundingly complex: creating an agreed value between two strangers. Vikings and textile manufacturers in Southern India could cut a deal over a shipment of silk. Cash created 'globalisation' two thousand years before it became a term of abuse on a placard.

By the 1860s, there were over eight thousand separate currencies in operation in the US alone. Different banks, railroads and retailers all had their own form of money: bonds, exchange systems and numerous forms of credit. The National Bank Act of 1863 tried to end this fragmented chaos and unify the United States under one currency: the dollar.[3]

With the end of cash, the world of eight thousand currencies is returning. Mobile money, bitcoin, digital vouchers, Apple Pay, iTunes, exchangeable shop credits, everything from overseas currency transfers to billion-dollar deals with the digital handshake of blockchain. All of it is money.

But the death of cash is not simply part of the natural evolution of payment, making it ever more seamless and consumer friendly. The death of cash is the result of a plan – to cede control of money away from the banks, and even governments, and place it instead in the hands of the new players: tech companies.

And this plan was hatched as the result of an experiment proving something blindingly obvious to anyone who has ever used cash, but it is also an observable neurological process: paying causes actual pain.

THE DEAL AND THE EXPERIMENT

When we pay with cash, neural pathways light up like a Christmas tree. This is the flinch moment we experience when our hands are forced to part with money. In that instant, the brain is telling the hand not to let go. We are torn between wanting to buy an object we desire and avoiding the neural pain, and this creates the flinch.

Having cash in your hand is not, as we might assume, a licence to spend irresponsibly. In fact, cash does the opposite: it stops us spending. So in creating a payment system that eradicates cash, we remove the neural pain – the flinch moment – and open the brain to limitless spending. Which is exactly what two men decided to do in 1998.

Max Levchin and Peter Thiel, two strangers, met in an empty lecture hall at Stanford University. The meeting was not by chance. 'I basically went there,' says Levchin, 'to see this guy Peter Thiel, who was giving a free lecture about currency markets. I figured it would be a filled auditorium, but actually it turned out to be a lecture with six people. So it was fairly easy to make contact afterwards ... I came up and said: "Hi, I'm this guy Max. I've been in Silicon Valley for the last five days and I'm going to start a new company and how are you doing?"'[4]

Levchin was a wild, directionless ball of energy. He had run a few start-ups that had 'sort of blown up in catastrophic ways where people started the company and it was sort of like marrying the first person one met at the slot machine in Las Vegas. You might hit the jackpot, but chances were things would just blow up.'

Thiel was different. Now one of the overlords of Silicon Valley and part of President Trump's original inner sanctum, Thiel is reported to inject the blood of eighteen-year-old girls to keep himself looking young (he doesn't). In 1998 he was already legendary in Silicon Valley for a different reason. Thiel believed he was the future, even though he did not know how. Levchin wanted to do a deal with him, because Thiel was one of the few people on the planet that shared his limitless ambition, and with whom he could get a meeting.

Thiel grew up in South Africa and was sent to a strict boarding school where pupils were struck for the pettiest transgression of the rules. As a teenager, Thiel had already identified himself as a libertarian with a hatred for what he considered to be mindless conformity.

In 1998, when Thiel met Levchin, he was clear on one thing: he wanted to change the world. Thiel is a follower of the mimetic theory of French philosopher René Girard, and the idea that imitation destroys genuine innovation. Only by stepping outside the mimetic prison of trying to be like other people do you truly succeed. Be yourself, however strange that might appear to anyone else.

When the sub-prime crash began in 2007, Thiel told the *Washington Post* we had put too much trust as a society in science and technology and been let down. But in mimetic terms, our confidence was misplaced. The technocratic elite had told us to believe in ever-increasing wealth creation, when the truth was that only those in Silicon Valley were going to own the future. We should have seen all of it for ourselves long before it happened. To this degree, the crash was our own fault.

When Levchin approached Thiel in that empty lecture theatre in 1998, Thiel had the mimetic mindset to take over the world, but did not have the vehicle. A couple of venture capital failures under his belt, but with nothing promising on the horizon. No idea.

In 1998, the internet had just arrived as a platform for the world to communicate with. Since 1969, the Pentagon had been using a closed version called the Arpanet and since the very beginning, fears of hacking had dogged it. In 1976, encryption technology called TCP/IP (Transmission Control Protocol/ Internet Protocol), developed by computer scientists Vinton Cerf and Robert Kahn, did not manage to prevent the first ever computer virus being created: the 'Morris Worm', by Cornell graduate Robert Tappan Morris.

In 1988, a dozen lines of code took down thousands of computers across the planet. In November 1989, Tim Berners-Lee made the first successful communication between a Hypertext Transfer Protocol (HTTP) client and server using the internet. The World Wide Web for everyone was here, but one very obvious thing was still waiting to happen.

No one had figured out how to monetise it yet. The holy grail in Silicon Valley was finding a secure online payment system. Whoever created it would own the coming century. Something both Thiel and Levchin were keen on doing.

Levchin was an encryption genius, but it was Thiel who knew finance, and for Levchin to ensure his out-there ideas on encrypting an online payment system did not bomb like all the others, he needed Thiel. Which is why he turned up at that empty lecture. Thiel and Levchin only talked for minutes, but it was enough. They did a deal to start a business called Confinity.

'Max and I spent a lot of time brainstorming different ideas on different types of markets,' Thiel explains. 'We finally decided that we wanted to try something with encrypted money on PalmPilots. We thought this was going to be the future of the world.'[5]

The truth was that for all their ambition, Thiel and Levchin were like all the thousands of other tech entrepreneurs standing in queues in various coffee houses across California: prospectors sifting through pans in the great internet gold rush. There was no reason they should succeed first. Except for one thing. In PalmPilot, they saw something no one else saw: a proto-iPhone, and one that could be used for buying and selling.

Three thousand miles away, an experiment was being carried out by a Serbian neuro-psychologist at MIT into what happens to the human brain when we pay in different ways. Drazen Prelec was fascinated by the irrational behaviour people demonstrate towards money: why do we buy lottery tickets and insurance at the same time? Because we do not have a consistent approach to spending.

Instead, Prelec says, we accumulate random rules and ideas about money throughout our lives which then co-exist irrationally in our heads, such as buying the cheapest brands at the supermarket, but insisting on getting a cab home because we do not like the bus. Or using cheap cosmetics, but having a monthly spa massage.

Prelec wanted to know how that irrationality towards money manifests itself when we use cash and decided to measure the brain's response to paying with cash versus credit.

Prelec asked five hundred students on the MIT campus to make sealed bids for a silent auction for a sold-out basketball match. Half were asked to use cash; and half, cards. Prelec had an instinct that the credit card bids would be higher, but the degree to which they were higher blew him away. The credit card bids were on average twice as high as the bids made with cash. Some were six times higher. The cash bidders simply refused to part with their money, whereas the card bidders saw no limit on what they should spend.

Prelec was stunned. 'That's got to be crazy, right? It suggests the psychological cost of spending a dollar on a credit card is only fifty cents.' This is because credit cards give the pleasure of buying with none of the pain. 'The moral tax gets blurred. When you're consuming, you're not thinking about the payments, and when you're paying, you don't know what you're paying for.'

The psychological self-delusion that credit cards are a free lunch is so strong, Prelec said, it is the reason most debit cards carry a credit card logo. 'The logo alone is a powerful inducement to spend. Consumers get excited just seeing the logo. It's like waving a hamburger in front of a hungry person.'[6]

So the appeal of credit cards is clear, but Prelec wanted to know why we had such a problem paying with cash. Is this resistance to spending cash hardwired? Prelec set up an MRI scan with the students who had bid in the silent auction with cash and what he found out next was to change the future course of money.

When we pay for something with cash, Prelec realised, a specific neural pathway lights up. Prelec had discovered the 'flinch moment', the nanosecond in which we feel measurable neural pain as the brain registers the hand parting with money. The moment we literally feel the loss.

Those bidding with cards in the experiment had felt no such pain. Only the pleasure of shopping. Prelec's discovery was to have far-reaching implications. Cash, he concluded, does not enable but actively hinders spending. By removing it, and making payment instantaneous, the brain has no time to register pain. We are released to spend without limit, because it is simply too fast for the brain to catch up with the transaction.

Peter Thiel and Max Levchin were working on cracking the holy grail of Silicon Valley: an encrypted payment system. But Prelec had discovered the real holy grail: pain-free shopping for the consumer. Deliver that and you owned the internet.

STAGE LEFT: ENTER IRON MAN

In 2000, a year into Confinity, Levchin and Thiel met with an entrepreneur who understood the significance of Prelec's work on the neural pain of payment. Elon Musk. Musk, like Thiel, was a visionary open to the visions of others. Twenty years on, he is known as the man who will do whatever it takes to colonise Mars and save humanity from global warming with a planetary exodus. He is serious, too. Musk was the inspiration for Tony Stark in the *Iron Man* movies.

Like Thiel, Musk had grown up in South Africa, and like Thiel, Musk forged a fiercely ambitious and anti-authoritarian spirit from childhood trauma. In Musk's case, bullying at school was so bad, he was once hospitalised after being left unconscious from a beating.[7]

Back in 2000, Musk used the money he had made from his first venture, Zip2, to propose a merger with Thiel and Levchin's Confinity. He recognised their vision. If Confinity could crack secure encrypted payment, Musk said, they held the keys to the kingdom of limitless spending. But to sell this to the consumer as a way of removing neural pain – in other words, to turn it from a clever but small Silicon Valley tech innovation that could be stolen by other clever, small Silicon Valley tech companies, into a globally recognised brand that would take over the world – they needed to do something very important. Promise the consumer that payment would be instantaneous: 'one click away'. So they called their new company PayPal, and one click away was their promise.

Thiel brought in a money guy from Wall Street, Jack Selby. We met in their huge offices in San Francisco, right next door to

George Lucas's offices. Thiel and Selby's office is decorated in mid-twentieth-century Scandinavian furniture and with rows of bookshelves filled with philosophy: Kierkegaard, Ayn Rand, Marx, and the collected works of Donald Trump. Jack swanned in looking like the title character in *The Great Gatsby* with slicked-back hair and smashed-up boating shoes, as if he had just parked his yacht (in fact, he had just parked his plane).

'You make it sound like it was all going to happen – a fait accompli,' says Jack, 'but these stories get made up. The truth was, it was touch and go we'd survive. At one point we had a burn-rate of over a million dollars a month. It was tremendously hairy.'

But they knew they were onto something and needed to hold their nerve.

I met Eric M. Jackson, hired as PayPal's vice president of marketing. 'It was a very funny place. When you arrived, you were given this task, which was literally to build your own desk from scratch. It was like a test of your ingenuity.'

But behind the quirky makeshift offices, something amazing was going on that no one, least of all those at PayPal, could quite believe: their growth. 'It was phenomenal,' says Eric. 'It went from a million dollars a week to a million dollars a day to a million dollars an hour, just like that.'

PayPal's meteoric success put it on a collision course with two huge established money players: the banks and the regulators. Jack Selby recalls the bafflement of the established money players at PayPal's arrival. 'Were we a bank or a payment system? They didn't know. We didn't fit into any neat regulatory box, and because we were still relatively small compared to the banks, we were like this little speedboat that could dart around and run rings around them.'

Thiel said PayPal wasn't a bank in the traditional sense, because it didn't engage in fractional-reserve banking. But the banks saw it as a threat, Jack says, and they had ammunition. PayPal had been taken up enthusiastically by online gambling, and this allowed PayPal's enemies to tarnish its growing reputation as a trusted mainstream payment system with the taint that it was illicit with dubious connections.

It seems laughable today, but PayPal was feeling the heat as a fly-by-night purveyor of vice. Moreover, financial regulation is a minefield and PayPal had a problem, because the financial laws differed hugely from state to state. What was okay in Arizona was not necessarily allowed in California. Because PayPal was not a bank, it was forced into state-by-state agreements, not only across America, but in Europe and its new territories across the world.

It was expanding at ferocious speed, and the problems were expanding with it. In short, it was a nightmare. Selby recalls one politician in particular who had it in for PayPal and made it his mission to try and make life difficult at every turn. And because PayPal did not have the muscle of the banks, it could be easily thwarted by someone with the right connections on Capitol Hill, which the PayPal Mafia, as they quickly became known, did not. Yet.

If that weren't enough, the company was losing millions of dollars a month to online fraud. Because it was still unclear what PayPal actually was, the FBI could not march in and treat it as straightforward bank or credit card fraud. It was a crime, but what kind? PayPal itself was forced to find risk management solutions to fraud: another huge drain on cash, as well as massively stressful.

At several points, they were close to folding the whole thing, not least because the powers arraigned against them were bearing down with all their might. But Thiel held his nerve.

'Peter was brilliant,' Jack says, 'because he realised we needed to get into business before the whole dotcom bubble burst. When that popped, it cleared away the dead wood and Peter knew the guys left standing were going to be huge. We made sure we were those guys.'

Thiel also made a simple but very important observation to his business partners. The world has a few Palm Pilots, but millions of email addresses. If PayPal could access those email addresses, then the potential business was infinite.

The four men who created PayPal now had the key that would unlock the internet. But if PayPal was to grow, it needed a big-time partner. In 2002, only a year after launching, PayPal did a deal with eBay for $1.5 billion.

'By today's standards, it was a paltry sum,' Jack says. The deal was bittersweet. On the one hand, it secured PayPal's future and took it out of the regulatory hell it had been in, by getting some muscle on board. But it also sold PayPal short.

'You could have held on,' I tell Selby. 'You could have been Google if you'd only held your nerve.'

'People say that,' he responds, 'but they don't understand the pressures we were under. When you know those, you'll see that it was a pretty good deal.'

The internet now had a marketplace with which to trade through PayPal, and PayPal was now accepted in over seventy per cent of all eBay auctions. The PayPal founders were legendary in Silicon Valley: the 'PayPal Mafia' had gone legit and were not running scared of the banks anymore, because they were the new law. They appeared in a Rat Pack-style photo spread in *Fortune* magazine, looking mean in sharp suits and smoking cigars. There were stories of wild excess and crazy extravagant nights out, at odds with Silicon Valley's main reputation as a dull place filled with nerds on bikes in T-shirts. Selby smiled his Gatsby smile when I asked him if even half the stories were true.

Back at MIT, Drazen Prelec's research into the neural pain of cash should have served as a warning that we were about to enter a fathomless, glittering new world of untethered online spending. Instead, his work unwittingly signed the death warrant on cash.

Cash, he says, is the one thing that firmly tethers us to spending within our means.

'You want to know how out of kilter we are with our spending?' he asks me when we meet. 'Try using only cash for one week. Buy everything with it. Pay your mortgage with it. Look at a thousand dollars as a mountain of cash. You will never treat money the same way again.'[8]

GIVING THE PUBLIC CREDIT IS 'LIKE GIVING SUGAR TO A DIABETIC'

Prelec was not the first to warn of the dangers of moving away from cash for the 'convenience' of credit. In the 1950s, credit cards moved out of the exclusive domain of business and began being marketed at the general public. They were sold as giving greater speed and efficiency to a transaction than cash. Their true appeal lay in giving the illusion of wealth, magically conjuring whatever you desired – a new sofa, fur coat, car – but without a genie and a puff of smoke, merely the wave of a signature.

In early ads for American Express, a card was taken coolly from the pocket of a suave businessman and flashed impressively like VIP ID to a breathless air stewardess. Credit cards turned failing middle managers into James Bond. Here was something too good to be true, and it was.

Concerns were soon raised at the highest levels of government. President Johnson's special assistant for consumer affairs, Betty Furness, believed the aspirational dream the credit card offered was a mirage. In 1967, she said pushing credit cards on a general public of 'compulsive debtors' was as responsible as 'giving sugar to diabetics'.

But were the public 'compulsive debtors'? The great myth of the masses and especially the poor is that they cannot manage money or budget and therefore demand new technologies that 'help' make precarious lives more 'manageable'.

The truth is the opposite. The poor have a tighter rein on money than anyone else. With each new payment innovation – from credit cards in the 1950s to digital and mobile money now – technologies arrive doing the complete opposite of what they claim. Instead of 'helping' the masses 'manage money', they make them even more indebted.

In 2016, the average American family owed $16,061 on credit cards.[9] Seventy per cent of Americans own at least one card, but fifty per cent have two and ten per cent more than three, with the average American family carrying $40,000 of debt. Debt in Britain is at the same level, and is increasing. In the last quarter of 2016, the average British family accrued more debt in the last three years than in any other period in history.

When the economy boomed in the 1950s, debt was encouraged, but tethered to paying it back. In the mid-1980s, credit cards replaced hire purchase, and by the 1990s they were given to anyone who could sign their own name (dog owners could even get credit cards in their pet's name, because no one bothered to check to whom the card was going). Any notion that debt should be paid off was gone. Instead, debt became a way of life.

Each time credit has become easier and faster, we have normalised ever higher levels of debt. And every time the economy goes into recession (the early 1980s, the early 1990s, post-2007) credit cards take on a new role – enabling people to survive.

Credit cards are now a tool for subsistence: paying for heating, food shopping and the monthly mortgage. Debt is also the *modus operandi* for governments claiming 'growth' by factoring credit-fuelled consumer spending into GDP. Debt provides a politically expedient role, window-dressing a stagnating economy by faking a healthy balance sheet.[10]

ENTER EBAY: TURNING THE WEB INTO A MACHINE FOR SELLING

When PayPal did the deal with eBay in 2002, the aim was quite simple: to define what the internet was for. Up until that point, Web 1.0 had been a static page forum for the circulation of ideas within academia, the government and the military. By transforming into Web 2.0, the internet became a living thing, fed, cultivated and grown by every human on earth with a connection.

Beneath the grand promises that this new living internet would deliver 'empowerment', 'decentralisation', 'connectivity', even a new kind of 'democracy', was the hard-nosed reality: PayPal would turn Web 2.0 into a giant machine for selling.

When the deal was done with eBay, the first true behemoth of Web 2.0, the internet clicked. On a beach in Honolulu, eBay's reclusive founder Pierre Omidyar now wiles away his time funding the *Honolulu Civil Beat*, an online investigative journal. In 1998, aged thirty-one, Omidyar set up eBay. The apocryphal story is that it was a speculative punt trading Pez dispensers. The truth is that he knew exactly what he was doing.

With eBay, Omidyar consciously recreated the bustling marketplace in which coins were first traded two thousand years ago. A space in which everything is up for barter and value is infinitely fluid and market-driven.

Now every tech platform is a marketplace: Google is a marketplace for information, Uber for cabs, Airbnb for space, Deliveroo for food. But the first of these big digital souks was eBay. An empty space to be filled with the detritus of Planet Earth: shoes, furniture, concert tickets, vacuum cleaners, holidays, sex, old cameras, spare human organs, an unwanted husband.

eBay is capitalism in its purest form: one giant peer-to-peer trade in which the buyer, not the seller, controls the market and value is determined entirely by what someone is willing to pay. $1,209 for a Dorito shaped like the Pope's hat (bought by the same buyer as a grilled-cheese sandwich with the face of the Virgin Mary); Kurt Cobain's chair; Britney Spears's chewing gum; $55,000 for a ghost in a jar; ad space on someone's forehead; and perhaps most poignantly, the meaning of life, which was worth just $3.26.

Entire countries are signed up. Sixty per cent of all Australia's online shoppers use eBay, but Australia is also the prime eBay trader with Jan Mayen, a tiny Norwegian island in the Arctic Circle with a population of eighteen, who bought twenty-six items in 2014 from Australian eBay sellers – just over one Australian export item per person.[11]

eBay offered something that cash did not: the addictive thrill of the online auction. The endorphin rush of gambling. In comparison, cash was boring. Online shopping exploded in the early 2000s at the same time as online gambling, and both shared the binge quality of an addiction without constraints that could now be indulged in privately behind closed curtains.

Online shopping opened up, according to social anthropologist Benjamin Barber, a 'candy shop of instant gratification'. It re-infantilised the adult consumer, turning us back into children.

'When a child says, "I want that! And I want it now!" there's an adult there to say no, but when an adult demands the same shopping online, they can have whatever they want.'[12] The neural pain we experience parting with cash is gone and there is nothing to stop us shopping without boundaries. The parent figure is removed.

YOU ARE THE NEW CURRENCY

If I hand you a ten-pound note or a dollar bill, no one is making money from that transaction. It is cash from one hand to another. But if I make the payment digitally, someone has to facilitate that payment. The space between you and me becomes the place where money can be made.

This is the space the big tech giants – Facebook, Apple, Google, Amazon and Microsoft – all want to own, and it is a race to own money itself, and thus redefine what it is. Which is to make you the currency.

The value in that space is not even the charge for the transaction. This service is now given away free. It is the data on you that can be mined. Data is the hidden price tag in any transaction we make. It is a price we are willing to pay, because we are not handing over our cash. What we hand over instead is every last detail of our lives: from the euphoric or mournful playlist chosen to suit our mood to a preference for Chinese over Indian food, whether you are straight, gay or Mormon, surf or knit, have

Attention Deficit Disorder, go on holiday to the Caribbean or Canvey Island.

In 2016, data was used to hone the profiles of potential swing voters in both the Brexit referendum and the US presidential election, and it proved decisive. In 2017, the UK's privacy watchdog launched an investigation into how personal data is affecting political campaigns. The company that supplied the Leave campaign, Cambridge Analytica, targeted voter intention in a sharper way than was ever possible before. Without it, any political campaign – especially one run on tight margins – is sunk.

Critics describe such data mining by businesses as a privacy issue, but the public are less alarmed. As the *Harvard Business Review* pointed out in 2015: 'Our research shows that consumers are aware that they're under surveillance ... (but) consumers appreciate that data sharing can lead to products and services that make their lives easier and more entertaining, educate them, and save them money.'[13] We simply do not care that we are handing it over. We are more concerned when data mining strays into the realm of our health, which is the space the tech giants are coincidentally most interested in.

In 2007 came the moment of crystallisation: year zero for this new world. The banking system began to crash, and the iPhone was launched. Subprime set explosives beneath the banks that had controlled the ebb and flow of money for centuries and were now about to implode like derelict tower blocks.

These financial institutions had ridden the epic cycles of boom and bust for over a century: through the Wall Street Crash, Glass-Steagall and regulation, Reagan and deregulation, the 1990s recession, the longest bull market in history, and the hidden time bomb of subprime. They were momentarily vulnerable and someone else was poised to move in: the tech giants.

These giants call themselves 'tech' companies, but tech is a stepping stone – they want to become the new banks. And with the implosion of the old banks came their chance to take the first step.

In 2008, the iPhone propelled shopping off the laptop and onto the phone – the first stage in moving money away from the old institutions and shifting power to the tech companies. First, they would own shopping, then money management and financial services, and finally they would become the new banks. But first base was shopping and for this, they had a new weapon: the app.

Initially, Steve Jobs did not get it. It took a venture capitalist called John Doerr and the activities of a group of 'jail-break' hackers breaching the defences of the phone to turn Jobs on to third-party apps and what they could truly do for the potential of the iPhone.

In just days following the launch of the iPhone, these jail-breakers developed a refined copy-and-paste system. One that far outstripped Apple's. Jay Freeman, the Godfather of jail-breaking, created Cydia – an app marketplace where phones could be jail-broken and freed up to use powerful software to customise outside the rigid control of Apple.

Apple could not believe it and needed to act fast. Within weeks of the iPhone's launch, Apple decided to create the App Store to claw back control. It was the best thing Apple did from a business point of view, yet it was prompted not by the company's own programmers, but a bunch of hackers.

I arrange to meet Jay on a park bench in San Francisco. A tall man with shoulder-length hair, in a wide-brimmed hat and a leather coat, appears from behind the trees and strides purposefully over. Jay is sanguine about his achievement: that he inadvertently handed Apple a model for turning the iPhone into the world's most successful platform for selling.

'Sometimes I wish I hadn't done what I did, because if I hadn't, who knows what else Apple would have invented? On one level it opened things up, but also closed things down.' Did Apple ever offer you a job? 'They reached out to me, though I wasn't aware they were. I kind of turned them down, which you shouldn't do. Other hackers went to work for them: classic poacher turned gamekeeper.'

All of this happened behind the scenes. When Steve Jobs announced the launch of the App Store, Apple was a platform for third-party apps: a platform for selling, and with the potential not just to transform payment systems, but ultimately replace banks.

Third-party apps justified the Apple boss's claim that once in a while a technological advance comes along that 'changes everything'. They proved pivotal in propelling the iPhone from merely attaining phenomenal success to becoming the defining invention of our time.

Apple was first to plant their flag on a new moon: the space in the middle of a transaction where everything now happened. If you prised this space open, you would walk out onto an infinite plain of information – the data on one specific purchase connected by digital threads to millions of other purchases made by you, your family and everyone you know. And beyond these dead purchases, the living purchases yet to be made as the result of algorithmic suggestion: the things you, your family and everyone you know – and don't even know but should know – will buy in thirty seconds' time.

The race was on to own this space, and to give an example of how fiercely this space was fought over, here is what happened when Apple did the deal with Chase over Apple Pay.

In the summer of 2013, Apple embarked on a highly confidential new project. The tech giant may have wanted to own the future of money, but knew the only way to get there was to partner with the big existing players. Apple approached the five major banks, as well as American Express, Mastercard and Visa. Apple couldn't go it alone, because it needed their infrastructure.

At the time of the deal, Nathaniel Popper of the *New York Times* analysed the rationale for both Apple and each of the players in wanting to cooperate. 'For the banks and credit card networks, Apple Pay could threaten some revenue streams as the technology giant looks set to assume a more central role in the financial universe,' he surmised. 'But the eager participation of banks and credit card companies suggests both Apple's clout, and the recognition among financial institutions that they face broader challenges from upstart technology ventures, many of which are not as eager or willing as Apple to work with the incumbent financial industry.'

The banks and credit card companies may have perceived Apple as a threat long-term, but Apple could be an ally for now, and help shore up the industry against new tech innovations such as iZettle, the mobile contactless payment system launched in Sweden in 2010, or even Bitcoin, which in spite of its inherent volatility was gaining ever more traction and legitimacy with the markets.

In 2015, the New York Stock Exchange launched a bitcoin price index, and in December 2017, the cryptocurrency formally arrived on Wall Street and began trading, immediately jumping twenty-five per cent in price and causing a five-minute halt in trading. Both Apple and the old money institutions could see the future of money fragmenting fast and needed to collaborate on Apple Pay before it happened.

By way of explanation for the Apple Pay deal, JPMorgan CEO Jamie Dimon told investors that the companies in Silicon Valley 'all want to eat our lunch.'[14]

In spite of the fact Apple was partnering up with every big player in the financial industry to maximise the ubiquity and presence of Apple Pay on its launch, only those at the very top of each organisation knew the full extent of the plan.

According to a *New York Times* account of what happened behind the scenes, 'from the beginning, the project was top secret, with what one person involved called a "code name frenzy".' In London, I asked one of the key people involved in the deal, James Anderson, vice-president of Mastercard, what these code names were. 'I think our code words were superheroes or types of metal. I'll be Krypton, you can be Zygon, that type of thing.'

The *New York Times* described the level of secrecy involved at another key player, JPMorgan, which 'set up a war room in a windowless conference room in San Francisco, where the most sensitive work was done. Only about 100 of the 300 JPMorgan employees working on the project knew that it was a partnership with Apple.'

I asked James Anderson how difficult it was to maintain secrecy and coordinate the multiple participants with the single goal of launching Apple Pay. 'It was really a huge logistic task. Getting all the ships – the different organisations involved – to cross over the horizon at the same moment . . . it was very difficult.'

According to the *New York Times* account, when launch day came – 9 September 2014 – a smoothly choreographed pincer movement was carried out by Apple and JPMorgan Chase on the West and East Coast simultaneously. As Apple's Chief Executive Tim Cook made his announcement in California, Marianne Lake (JPMorgan Chase's chief financial officer) addressed the media in New York.

'When Apple's chief executive, Tim Cook . . . finally brought up Apple Pay in California . . . one of Ms Lake's deputies in New York took a green apple out of her bag and put it on the table on the stage, signalling that Ms Lake was free to discuss the service. "So, we are very excited . . .".'[15]

I asked James Anderson, who was there, about the apple on the desk story and he smiled. 'Huh. I didn't know that.' No one told him.

Even though this was an accommodation between Apple and the old money institutions, it wasn't a marriage of love, but convenience. The future was not 'disruption', but an earthquake, shaking the businesses that had run money for a century to the core. Mastercard's vice president, James Anderson, said the Chase Apple Pay deal did not 'respect and honour the payment networks.'

What he meant was that Apple Pay did not respect and honour the revenue stream of the big banks and credit card companies.

Apple and Chase had parked their tanks in the middle of the prime real estate of America's oldest financial institutions.

More importantly, Apple was going to give away its service for free. The space in the middle of a transaction where the money was, was no longer where the money was. Apple was stealing a march on its competitors by deliberately vacating it. Why? Because Apple saw value simply in facilitating a transaction to become a major money player. But to Apple's competitors, like Google and Facebook, the value of this space was not just about becoming a player, but about a new type of money that wasn't money at all: data. The new currency.

AFRICA, NOT SILICON VALLEY, IS WHERE IT IS TRULY AT

In December 2016, Facebook CEO Mark Zuckerberg wanted in on this new world of data as money. His jet touched down in Kenya. Zuckerberg, like Apple, knew that information, not charging to facilitate a transaction, was the future. But also that the plains of central Africa, not Silicon Valley or Wall Street, might hold the key to winning.

In 2007, M-Pesa, a mobile money system allowing Kenyans to transfer money directly from one phone to another, was launched across the country. Not through an app or a complex encrypted payment system, but by text.

M-Pesa was a revolutionary exercise in the democratisation of money, using an entire nation as the laboratory. It not only cut out transfer fees, but made banks – as well as cash – extinct. It did not require an iPhone or a bank account, all it required was a twenty-year-old Nokia.

Within a year of its launch, M-Pesa had seventeen million users in Kenya. Forty per cent of the population. By 2010, more people used M-Pesa than had a bank account. It proved that Kenyans did not need one.

I visited Twiga Foods, the same banana-storage depot outside Nairobi that Zuckerberg visited months earlier. Twiga have used M-Pesa to become one of the fastest-growing companies in Kenya and Zuckerberg wanted to find out how. He met with Edna Kwinga, head of HR, and Kikonde Mwatela, the COO.

'We didn't even know we were meeting Zuckerberg until ten minutes before he came in,' Edna told me. 'We were told it was the regional head of Facebook, and then in walks Mark Zuckerberg.' What did he want to know? 'He was very interested in how we'd used M-Pesa to grow. He was very nice. He'd been in West Africa the previous day and was off to South Africa in the evening.'

Mwatela is under no illusions that the big tech companies are muscling in on M-Pesa's innovation and sensing an amazing opportunity. 'Silicon Valley often looks up to the top of the pyramid to see where money can be made, but Zuckerberg is incredibly clever. He's facing the other way and seeing that it's at the bottom of the economic pyramid that far more money is to be made.' Hoovering up the poor of the world and sticking them on Facebook in the process.

Twiga pay everyone through M-Pesa. On a banana plantation near Mount Kenya, farmers pay their employees not with cash, but through their mobile. People who do not have a mobile get a lesson from the boss into how to use one. Did he foresee a time when he wouldn't use cash? I asked him. 'What? We don't use cash now. No one does. It's heavy and difficult to transport, it's unsafe, you can be robbed, you can be extorted. That is gone. I might use cash to buy a tea.'

M-Pesa has allowed Kenya to leapfrog the standard twentieth-century stages of development: infrastructure and banks. Once you needed a bank account to get a business. Not anymore. M-Pesa loans money and so it is making banks irrelevant, too.[16] M-Pesa has genuinely disrupted money, and has done it with the most basic technology available.

But Zuckerberg can take it to the next level with Facebook, opening up the poor half of the planet to a money revolution. And if it has worked in Kenya, it could work across the world.

M-Pesa offers the gateway to digital consumerism. Selling money transfers, payday loans, credit, food, cars and holidays, even alcohol and online gambling.

But these money transfers using text garner as much information about someone as their online shopping footprint. In 2016, a group of Kenyan police officers were arrested for making huge M-Pesa money transfers. They were not using bitcoin as drug cartels do, or banks to launder cash, they were using text. Zuckerberg realised that M-Pesa offered micro-data surveillance on transactions in much the same way Facebook can, but it could also potentially access billions of people that Facebook cannot.

When digital money arrived in 2000, the likeliest scenario seemed to be the cementing of global inequality. The wealthy half of the planet would use digital and mobile money, while the poor would continue with cash. In fact, M-Pesa proved the complete opposite. M-Pesa both empowered the poor and netted them. Exactly as debt did.

IS CASH AS IRRELEVANT AS WE ARE TOLD?

The subtext – and in many cases the text – of the drive to kill cash is the eradication of the black economy. Kenneth Rogoff, former chief economist at the International Monetary Fund (IMF), says the global end of cash is both an inevitability, and a good thing.

We met in his office at Harvard and Ken showed me his extraordinary mountain range of a graph detailing the boom and bust cycles of Western capitalism for the last two hundred years. The tax revenue generated, coupled with the devastation of the black economy – an economy fuelled by cash – would make a cashless world the greatest leap forward in fiscal management since the end of fixed exchange rates. It would also provide, he said, a far more effective policing of illegal immigrants than building walls or banning entry to the country at passport control.

But something perplexing is going on, said Ken. He demonstrated with his hands, crossing in mid-air. 'As governments attempt to decrease the availability of cash and phase it out, there has never been more cash in circulation. People just keep using it, and it's not apparent who or for what.' To governments wanting to kill cash, it has become Hydra. A multi-headed gorgon: they chop off one head and it simply grows another.[17] The black economy – the cash or 'shadow' economy – is really a euphemism for the livelihoods of the poor. Freakonomics economists Ceyhun Elgin and Oguz Oztunali, using a dataset for 161 countries between 1950 and 2009, estimated the shadow economy to account for over twenty-two per cent of the world's GDP.[18]

Nearly a quarter of the planet's entire wealth is cash in hand. Cash provides an essential mechanism of survival for billions of people across the planet. Criminals use the shadow economy, but so does someone cleaning an office, working on a building site or keeping a business afloat waiting to be paid. For those on the cusp of paying tax, cash can be the difference between surviving and going under. And if they pay tax, they are finished.

Scooping up the poor quarter of the globe that use the shadow economy, by forcing them to use digital money instead of cash because tax has so far failed to net them, is a strategy that governments are embracing around the world, especially with their failure to collect revenue at the other end of the wealth spectrum: from corporations and the super-rich.

'Aren't you simply seeking to use cash as a Trojan Horse to collect revenue from the poorest, because you can't collect it from the richest?' I asked Rogoff. He shrugged. 'Cash isn't going to disappear as quickly as anyone might want it to, and I'm not saying it should. It serves a purpose for sure.'

In 2016, the Indian government suddenly and unexpectedly withdrew 500 and 1,000 rupee notes (the rough equivalent of a

$7 and $15 note) from circulation. Their explicit aim was to cut
the legs away from the huge Indian shadow economy. The results
were disastrous.

Cash shortages lasted for weeks: twenty-five people collapsed
and died after queueing for hours outside banks. The legitimate
economy suffered a stock market crash, there was an agricultural
crisis and road haulage stopped. The black economy, the
intended target, remained untouched.

WHEN DRUGS MONEY BAILED
OUT THE BANKS

India is still a significant cash economy, but Western economies rely on cash, too, and especially when there is a crisis. In
August 2007, one of the world's largest multinationals, the
French bank BNP Paribas, did something unprecedented in
their history. They terminated withdrawals from three hedge
funds citing 'a complete evaporation of liquidity'. The major
banks of the US, Europe, Asia and South America followed
suit. In a matter of hours, an entire banking system built on
liquidity – one bank being able to borrow from another bank
based on the cash in the system – ground to a halt. No one was
prepared to lend to anyone else, and capitalism was about to
stop. It was like that scene in *Reservoir Dogs* when everyone
draws a gun and stares at each other, waiting for someone to
make the first move.

But there was one place the banks could still borrow from.
An entire global network flush with cash running in parallel to
the world's banks: the drug cartels. Antonio Maria Costa was
head of the UN Office on Drugs and Crime. A year after the
crash, he says evidence began to emerge that as liquidity seized
up in the legitimate banking system, the banks turned to the
cash available in the drugs economy to keep the Western banking system afloat.

'Organised crime was the only liquid investment capital available to some banks on the brink of collapse,' he explains. Cash had stopped flowing, but drugs money would save us. It may have been earned from heroin and cocaine deals carried out on street corners from Los Angeles to Reykjavik, but this was money the banks now needed to stay alive.

So Western banking effectively laundered drugs money to keep the cash flowing. In the days following the crash, as governments bailed out the banks and liquidity came back into the system, normal service was resumed. But for a crucial period of time, the hours when capitalism teetered on the brink of collapse, you could only draw cash from a cashpoint machine because the world banking system was being propped up with the help of drug cartel money.[19]

The IMF estimate that large US and European banks lost more than $1 trillion on toxic assets and from bad loans between January 2007 and September 2009, and more than two hundred mortgage lenders went bankrupt. Profits to gangs from the drugs trade in the same period are estimated to have been worth $352 billion, according to the UN. These drug cartels had traditionally kept proceeds in cash or moved them offshore to hide them from the authorities, so moving the money discreetly back above radar – giving it to the banks to reboot their liquidity – was not a problem.

Costa says the evidence that this drug money flowed into banks came directly from bank officials working in Britain, Switzerland, Italy and the US, and he claims, 'That was the moment when the system was basically paralysed.' We may view what happened as immoral but if we use a bank as I, and I assume you do, we are also complicit. Drugs money pumped into the system allowed us to keep paying our mortgages.

However, it is what happened next, according to Costa, that was most disturbing. 'The progressive liquidisation to the system and the progressive improvement by some banks of their share values has meant that the problem of illegal money has become much less serious than it was.'

Banks became far more willing to turn a blind eye to laundering criminal money post-2008, because banks recognised that they owed crime. The quid pro quo of banking and criminality has a long history – moving money discreetly offshore and aiding criminals in investing in legitimate businesses to launder money – so when banks needed to borrow some cash from the drug cartels, they were more than happy to oblige.

BLOCKCHAIN – THE NUCLEAR KEY

In April 2014, the SSL encryption protocol providing watertight security for millions of online transactions carried out every second, and used by millions of businesses across the globe, was hacked. SSL was generally regarded by security experts to be the most secure payment system yet devised.

So how does it work? SSL is a new generation of 'blockchain' payment. Blockchain was originally developed as a way of allowing huge corporations to do billion-dollar deals securely. It now works for everyday transactions carried out by you and me, and is based on the principle of the nuclear key.

In a nuclear submarine, with missile capability to destroy an entire continent, control does not lie with one person but with a number of individuals, each of whom has a separate key. These keys need to be inserted in the control panel in the right order and at the right time for the missile to go off. The crew do not know who has the keys, and thus there is theoretically no way of overriding the system.

With a financial transaction carried out using blockchain, computers take the role of crew members. Each algorithm is primed to play its role inserting a password at the correct moment. No one party can override the system. It is an interlocking process with layer upon layer of security. It appears impregnable. Blockchain is so trusted that the Pentagon are researching the use of it to encrypt nuclear weapons.[20]

Yet in 2014, SSL was hacked. Millions of people all over the world were told to change their passwords – the first nuclear key. After millions of passwords were changed, Walmart in America and the Chinese restaurant chain P.F. Chang's both reported a further security breach. The very act of changing passwords had made the system easier, not more difficult to hack.

In 2015, a year later, the entire TalkTalk mobile network went down, because a teenager in a bedroom in Northern Ireland figured out the company's key passwords. The hack destroyed TalkTalk's credibility, resulting in thousands of customers leaving and the stock value of the company collapsing. When PayPal launched itself as a secure online payment, the deal seemed done on security. But twenty years on, with cybercrime and malware on the rise, the inherent fragility of this security is now a given.

When coins were first created two thousand years ago, their value was dependent on mutual trust between the two parties involved in the transaction: the buyer and seller. Today, in killing cash, trust is one way. We have no choice but to put our faith in the tech companies, and hold no cards of our own. Yet the belief we are supposed to have that they can securely hold on to our money is seeping. Forty per cent of bank fraud now goes uninvestigated, because banks simply write it off.

Police have neither the resources nor the expertise to deal with fraud; the number-one crime to get away with. Lax security checks, and an ocean of easily accessible current accounts with ever faster payment systems, allow fraudsters to move money nanoseconds after a fraud has been committed. This is the truth of online security.

Yet a parallel can also be drawn with terrorism: for every large-scale event you hear about, there are hundreds of thwarted attempts that you do not. On this basis, the battle with fraud could be argued as well fought; the write-off, simply the unavoidable collateral.

THE EMPTY BANK VAULT

In Sweden, where cash is set to disappear in the next five years, a debate rages over the dangers of embracing its extinction without first pausing to think about it. A debate no other country is openly having.

In 2016, cash made up less than two per cent of all payments in Sweden. Cards are the main payment method: an average of 207 swipes per year. Three times more than any other European country. Mobile phone apps, primarily Swish, developed by the country's four biggest banks, are fast taking over from cards: the final nail in the coffin of Swedish cash.

Nine hundred of Sweden's 1,600 banks do not even keep cash on hand, or take cash deposits. In April 2013, a bank robber found this out the hard way.

At 10.32 a.m. on a Monday morning, CCTV footage picked up what police described as 'a single culprit, male, entering a bank in Östermalmstorg, central Stockholm, with a gun-like object.'

After demanding the staff open the safe, a woman behind a screen informed the robber that the bank held no cash. The vaults were empty. CCTV footage captures the moment the robber exits the bank less than two minutes after going in, penniless.

In 2012, there were only twenty-one bank robberies in Sweden. Half that reported in 2011, and the lowest level ever recorded. Yet as physical bank robberies become all but extinct, online fraud in Sweden is at a record high.

Björn Eriksson, former president of Interpol, now runs Cash Uprising – a pressure group lobbying to keep cash flowing to stop fraud. The end of cash will, Eriksson says, marginalise the poor and hand over economic power to the new tech giants, who cannot and do not know what to do about fraud.

However bad the banks have been with fraud, Eriksson declares, they will prove to be paragons of vigilance next to the tech giants. Eriksson is no anti-capitalist protestor. He ran the biggest anti-fraud police force in Europe.

The cash divide is generational. The older generation trust cash and the young trust digital money. 'Cash-free' businesses like coffee shops across Sweden are run by young entrepreneurs who use a sole trader app called iZettle.

The watershed for this divide between the young and the old in Sweden is the banking crash of 2008. The old remember a time before the crash when the banks could be relied upon. The young believe the banking crisis fatally holed the banks beneath the water. Instead, they put their faith in the new tech giants, who wish to replace the banks.

In 2007, with the invention of the iPhone, a device was created for the passing of trust from the banks to these tech giants. They were now the new custodians of money. But are they any more secure than the banks? Critics of digital money like Björn Eriksson say a digital crash is inevitable and will be far worse than the last.

The risks managed by banks in 2007 were spread bet, but one breached blockchain is enough to wipe digital money off the face of the earth with the single press of a button. We could live without a Lehman Brothers, but we cannot live without Google and Facebook, because they are the infrastructure.

Beyond the technological deficiencies of a secure payment system that was never secure to begin with, a crash is made far more likely by the sheer amount of money being created by fractional reserve banking. The key element fuelling economic growth is consumer spending. But this spending boom depends on consumer prices staying low. When the price bubble eventually bursts – as commodity prices go up and inflation follows – the whole house of cards comes crashing down.

THE CONTAGION

We are now about to embark on walking the high wire of an entirely digital capitalism, with another crash potentially encrypted in the system. The glitch. The ostensible reason is greater speed and efficiency for the consumer, but the truth is the eradication of the black economy and the control of money in the hands of five tech companies.

A decade ago, as the digital revolution got under way, a mountain was drilled through in order to produce a high-speed internet connection that increased the speed of transactions on Wall Street by one thousandth of a second. This extra thousandth of a second translates to a billion extra dollars transacting through Wall Street every hour. But as speed becomes the god of new money, the dangers of an entirely digital economy being wiped out because a rogue algorithm decides to sell instead of buy, or a cyberattack is launched, becomes ever more likely.

In May 2017, an unprecedented 'ransomware' attack was launched simultaneously across the globe on the same day. A cyberattack like none ever seen before. The WannaCry malware aimed at extracting ransoms from its victims and wreaked havoc on four continents at the same moment. Operations were cancelled as the NHS in Britain became paralysed. FedEx and Telefónica in Spain watched powerless as their operating systems crashed. The ransomware spread like wildfire across Asia, the US, South America, Europe and Russia. 150 countries were affected. And it was only down to a 28-year-old called Darien Huss inadvertently activating a 'kill switch' hardcoded into the malware by registering a nonsensical domain name that the whole thing stopped.

Because the ransoms involved were relatively small, various culprits were fingered: North Korea? Russia (attacking itself as well as everyone else)? Islamic fundamentalists: the cyber-Caliphate? A dark-web crime syndicate avenging the closing of the Silk Road?

The day before the attack, I was in the research lab of a major credit card company being shown amazing new prototypes for payment systems such as hand and body swipe and augmented reality shopping. I asked about cyber crime. This is all great, I said, but couldn't the whole system go down with a single attack? 'Oh, don't worry,' I was told. 'We're ahead of the game.' They were winning the fight with cyber crime and malware, they said, because they were trialling new defences on the criminals themselves. The *Catch Me If You Can* approach.

It's a battle and both sides are arming up fast, but as the events of 12 May 2017 showed, the cyberattacks are getting bigger and potentially more catastrophic each time.

I went for a sandwich to Pret A Manger the other day. The card machines had mysteriously stopped working and they were taking only cash. Staff politely asked customers to take money out from the ATM machine next door, but no one did. Because it took a minute out of their day. It took too long.

Instead, people preferred to queue for the card readers to come back online. Staff said it could take up to half an hour – but people preferred to wait, because they had habituated to a new way of paying.

My Pret experience perfectly played out the irrational behaviour we demonstrate to paying that Drazen Prelec discovered at MIT. A few days after, supermarket chain Asda made customers wait up to an hour to pay, and that sixty-minute delay cost the company £10 million.

When the system crashed, cash was the speedy and logical thing to use. But we consider cash to be dirty. Visa have carried out research on how much bacteria is carried on a bank note. Contactless payment companies are demonising cash by drilling into our fears that cash is dirty.

The psychological contagion cash carries is fear of poverty, and this is the true success of the digital revolution – to make us believe cash is synonymous with social inferiority, and using it, even coming into contact with it, could mean contracting the contagion of failure. One of the reasons young Swedes prefer digital money to cash is that they believe, as Visa researched, that cash teems with germs. To the socially aspirational, digital equals clean, and clean equals success.

Cash is over, but we should seriously question why, and who truly benefits from its demise. In 2017, police discovered $20 million hidden under a mattress inside a wooden frame bed in Massachusetts.

A Brazilian man called Cléber Rene Rizério Rocha was charged with laundering money to Brazil via Hong Kong on behalf of a defunct internet phone company. Rocha's defence was that, in the scheme of things, the amount he was laundering was tiny compared to the billions being laundered by banks online. Cash was small fry. It was a nice argument, but did not stop him being convicted.

In 1989, something similar happened in Britain. Comedian Ken Dodd was charged with tax evasion after his bank account was discovered empty, but £336,000 was found in cash, stashed in suitcases in his attic and under his bed. When asked by the judge, 'What does a hundred thousand pounds in a suitcase feel like?' Dodd replied, 'The notes are very light, m'lord.'

Dodd was acquitted, but had only gone on trial because it was assumed that if he was stashing cash under his bed, he must be doing something criminal. That is because cash is inherently criminal. It is guilty of being cash, and for that it will never be forgiven.

When it finally disappears, the question of whether it was a good idea to get rid of it will be academic. Cash will be gone, and all as a result of a meeting in an empty lecture hall between two men who wanted to erase the pain of payment, and succeeded.

CHAPTER TWO
RISK: HOW CHAOS CAME TO WALL STREET

The Deal: The OPEC oil states Saudi Arabia, Syria, Egypt, Iran and Tunisia meet and agree to an oil embargo on the United States
Aim: To use the Yom Kippur War as political leverage for a massive hike in oil prices
Where: Vienna, Austria
When: 16 October 1973

SHORTING AND THE ARAB SPRING

On 16 December 2010, a twenty-six-year-old Tunisian street vendor called Mohamed Bouazizi did something he knew was risky. He borrowed money. Bouazizi needed to buy fruit and vegetables to sell at market the following day. As a result of an astronomic rise in food prices, brought about by a single decision made thousands of miles away, Bouazizi, like every other street trader across North Africa, had no choice.

Bouazizi woke early the following day. He was saving for an Isuzu pick-up truck to move his produce, but did not yet have enough. He was at his usual spot at Sidi Bouzid market by 8 a.m., but by 10.30 a.m., according to eyewitness accounts, local police began harassing him to move on, ostensibly because he did not have a vendor's permit.[1]

An argument ensued over money. Officials had extorted bribes from Mohamed in the past, but this time he refused. As he stood his ground, a forty-five-year-old municipal officer called Faida Hamdi slapped him in the face. She then spat at Bouazizi and confiscated his electronic weighing scales. Two unnamed men with Hamdi then overturned Bouazizi's cart into the alleyway.

In court, months later, Hamdi denied all charges.[2] Not in dispute is the fact that as Bouazizi tried to recover his overturned cart, officials kicked and punched him. His goods were then confiscated. He now had no means of making a living.

Bouazizi, a quiet man who did bookkeeping and accounts for other traders, was enraged. He and his uncle attempted to retrieve the cart from the municipal office. He asked to see the governor – Hamdi's superior – but was ignored.

Bouazizi then left and bought a large container of paint thinner. On the pavement outside the governor of Sidi Bouzid's office, he poured the paint thinner over himself. Onlookers gathered and took out their phones. Bouazizi is alleged to have shouted, 'How do you expect me to make a living?'[3] He then set fire to himself with a match and a revolution began.

Forty-two years earlier, a Czech student called Jan Palach set himself alight in Wenceslas Square, Prague, in protest at the Soviet invasion of Czechoslovakia. A month after Palach burned himself alive, another student, Jan Zajíc, did the same thing in exactly the same spot. Seven more followed, burning themselves to death to keep the protest alive.

Days after Bouazizi set light to himself, a one-thousand-strong funeral procession was forbidden by the Tunisian government from passing the place where he died, for fear of inspiring copycat acts. But it was too late. The Arab Spring has begun. The crowd chanted, 'Farewell, Mohamed, we will avenge you,' and on social media people were mobilising.

The Arab Spring is often described as a 'Twitter Revolution', but there were only two hundred active Twitter accounts in Tunisia on the day Bouazizi committed suicide. There were, however, two million Facebook accounts, and it was the handful of Twitter posts shared with these millions of Facebook users across North Africa that fuelled the uprising. One image in particular went viral; not of Bouazizi, but a woman in a hijab holding her BlackBerry aloft to film the growing mob. The fact that Bouazizi's act could be communicated was as important as the act itself.

The Arab Spring erupted in days over the whole of North Africa, toppling governments like dominoes: first the Tunisian government of Ben Ali, then Mubarak in Egypt and Gaddafi in Libya, then Saleh in Yemen. In Syria, Assad was challenged by pro-democracy rebels, erupting into a complex civil war that drew in Russia, the US and Europe.

In a strange twist of fate, Faida Hamdi, who first confiscated Bouazizi's goods and later said she blamed herself for the Arab Spring, was arrested and imprisoned for 'civil offences'. She was made a scapegoat for the government and had become another victim of unfolding events.

The political vacuum created across North Africa was filled by Islamic State, who, unlike their predecessor Al-Qaeda, saw territory gain in the crumbling regimes as an opportunity to create a continent-wide Caliphate. A borderless Islamic State from the Atlantic to the Red Sea, wrapped in a black flag. When IS rolled into town, they didn't just use terror, the first thing they did to win hearts and minds was to bring down the price of wheat.

Mohamed Bouazizi's death sparked the most dramatic reconfiguration of the Middle East since the Sykes-Picot Agreement of 1916 carved up the map of North Africa to create French, British and Russian 'spheres of influence'. Sykes-Picot enshrined religious conflict by promising homelands to both Jews and Arabs in exchange for support in the First World War.

A century on, the Middle East is reshaped by a humiliated street vendor pushed over the edge by a sudden rise in food prices. Sykes-Picot fuelled religious fundamentalism, and in 2010, the ramping of wheat prices fuelled the rise of Islamic State and fourth-wave jihadism.

The Arab Spring was portrayed in the West as a spontaneous outpouring of anger to bring freedom and democracy. But that was not how it started. The Arab Spring was the direct result of a decision by four big food companies to begin gambling with the value of wheat on the international markets.[4]

Bouazizi set fire to himself because a chain of events in Sidi Bouzid market led him to a place where he could not make a living, and this desperation was the result of the most basic food-stuff on earth becoming financialised. Global wheat was now a chip in a casino thrown on the roulette table. If the bet went wrong, millions of people starved.

AS SIMPLE AS ABCD

ADM, Bunge, Cargill and Louis Dreyfus are the biggest food companies on earth, known by their initials, ABCD. They collectively control ninety per cent of the world's wheat. In essence, ABCD feed the planet and decide how much the world should pay to be fed.[5] In the early 1970s, President Nixon tried to win the Cold War by suggesting the food giants hike corn prices to Soviet Russia and starve communism into submission. They refused and Nixon backed down.[6] That is how powerful they are.

SOAS professor, Jane Harrigan, has extensively researched the control these companies exert on food prices and their influence on the Arab Spring.[7] In doing so, she made a startling discovery. Sub-Saharan Africa is the most 'food insecure' region on earth: the gap between what is needed to feed the population and how much is imported to fill that gap is greater than anywhere else on the planet. Fifty per cent of food is imported and thirty-five per cent is wheat. In short, the entire region lives on bread and if the price changes even slightly, people starve.

But in 2005, the food giants ABCD faced a crisis of their own.

Because harvests are unpredictable, pricing cereals is notoriously volatile and in 2005 profits were down. So ABCD made a fateful decision: they decided to start betting against their own crops on the international markets. If a crop went bad, they actually made money. If it did not, and they bet the wrong way, they simply raised prices. It was a win-win. They had shorted the world's wheat.

In sub-Saharan Africa, this was devastating. In Egypt, bread is known as *aish*, meaning 'life'. In Yemen, there are over twenty different types of bread. As Rami Zurayk, professor of agricultural and food sciences at the American University of Beirut points out,[8] 'the fertile crescent, stretching from the Egyptian Nile to the mouth of the Tigris and the Euphrates, is where agriculture began, where wheat, lentils, chickpeas, sheep and goats and olives were first cultivated.'

In spite of the fertility of the region, it is also one of the poorest on earth. Forty per cent of Egyptians and Yemenis live in poverty. Why? The richness of the soil should on paper make it one of the most self-sustaining regions. Since the 1980s, when the IMF and World Bank introduced policies that reduced farming subsidies and encouraged the export of fruit to the West, rather than investment in local grain production, the region became increasingly dependent on the imported wheat of US food giants ABCD.[9] And as a result of wildly fluctuating prices, life for millions of people barely able to afford a loaf of bread began to be lived on a knife edge.

In 2006–7, there was a bumper harvest, which would logically mean a price drop, but ABCD did the opposite. They hiked the price of cereal across the planet. In Africa, where a tiny price rise has catastrophic consequences, a food crisis ignited across the continent.

There have always been 'bread riots', but this was different. 'The first protests of the Arab Spring in Tunisia were quickly dismissed as another bout of bread riots,' Zurayk says. 'Arab regimes responded by making adjustments to food prices and offering more subsidies. Increasing the subsidy slightly relieves the popular, pressure, but also increases the profit margins for importers and manufacturers. But this time round, truckloads of flour did not do the trick.'

In 2010, weeks before Bouazizi set himself alight, President Obama went to war with ABCD. Under pressure from the World Health Organization, UNICEF, British prime minister Gordon Brown and French president Nicolas Sarkozy, Obama attempted to pass legislation curtailing a food conglomerate's ability to short on grain prices in the poorest parts of the world. Obama called the behaviour of ABCD 'immoral' and politically destabilising. He failed.

Obama was not afraid to go toe to toe with the food industry. At the same time as he attempted to fight ABCD shorting the price of wheat, he was simultaneously trying to impose a sugar tax on sodas in the United States to deal with childhood obesity. The climb-down by the Obama administration on both fronts was indicative of the food industry's power.

In spite of this, there remains fundamental disagreement between economists over the genuine culpability of ABCD in destabilising food prices. As researchers Sophia Murphy, Dr David Burch and Dr Jennifer Clapp observed in an August 2012 report by Oxfam on the volatility of wheat pricing, 'there has been a particularly heated debate among economists over whether ... agricultural commodities futures markets via new financial derivatives is [the] main driver of recent food volatility.' They noted, however, that ABCD had not taken a hit to profits post the 2007–2008 crash requiring the kind of price recalibration that occurred.

The authors also point to the fact that Obama did manage to pass legislation curtailing ABCD's ability to short prices in the wake of the crash – primarily the Dodd-Frank Act passed into law by Congress in July 2010, calling for a regulatory agency to police commodity derivatives markets. This policing of their manipulation of pricing, the Oxfam report concludes, was the real anxiety for the food giants, not a few bad harvests.

In its 2010 annual report to shareholders, Bunge (the B in ABCD) singled out the potential problems the Dodd-Frank Act could create for them: 'While it is difficult to predict at this time what specific impact the Dodd-Frank Act and related regulations will have on Bunge, they could impose significant additional costs . . . and could materially affect the availability, as well as the costs and terms, of certain derivatives transactions.'

But before the Dodd-Frank Act could curtail ABCD's capacity to manipulate pricing artificially, the price of wheat went through the roof across sub-Saharan Africa, including Bouazizi's market in Tunisia, the Arab Spring erupted and Islamic State's 'fourth-wave' jihadism rolled across border after border. In ancient Rome, the poet Juvenal described *panem et circenses* ('bread and circuses') as a strategy that politicians use to buy the contrition of the masses. As Islamic State marched forward, they understood the importance of 'bread and circuses' to winning over the people they advanced on. A lesson the West had failed to learn.

ABCD were playing a risky game, and the people who lost that game were those that did not even know they were playing: the people of North Africa. They could now be 'liberated' from the colonial West, and the black-flagged advance of the Caliphate had leverage with the people they 'liberated' when it came to food prices.

As North African states collapsed, refugee ships began sailing across the Mediterranean sparking a crisis on mainland Europe. This in turn fuelled fears of a migrant invasion, which in turn propelled the rise of anti-immigration parties across Europe. And all because some food companies thought they could win a bet on Wall Street.

At the heart of the food companies' gamble was the idea that risk was the way to do business. And risk as an all-encompassing business philosophy was sold to Wall Street by one man.

I INVENTED THE BOMB. I DIDN'T DROP IT.

In New York, overlooking Central Park, is an anonymous apartment block. On the fiftieth floor, Robert Dall is being moved from his bedroom to the chintz living area by a nurse. Dall uses an oxygen canister to move around the flat, but when I arrive, he greets me with a strong slap on the back.[10] Back in the 1980s, Robert Dall was the man who changed the world by teaching it to embrace risk, and in so doing, invented the mechanics for shorting. In *Liar's Poker*, Michael Lewis says that Dall shaped the world to come because 'he began to think thoughts years into the future.'

Robert Dall's light-bulb moment was 'securitisation'. It was a conceptual shift in the very idea of trading. Instead of trading with physical assets and their value now, Dall said you should be able to trade in what something would be worth in the future, but secure it against something that existed now, like a mortgage policy.

Dall was the man who turned capitalism into gambling, and risked trillions of dollars on the roll of a dice in the casino of the trading floor. Dall inadvertently placed the first bricks on the road that would lead to subprime, ABCD shorting wheat, and the Arab Spring.

At Salomon Brothers, Dall loomed over the trading floor, a giant in a pinstriped suit, who by his own admission 'worked hard, partied hard, did everything hard.' He was 'a down-and-dirty brawler. But I was coasting for a while there in Wall Street.' Till something changed. Dall discovered Black and Scholes. Two Harvard economists with a formula that could magic money from thin air.

Fischer Black and Myron Scholes were the Copernicus of stocks and shares. In the early 1970s, they took economic wisdom and turned it on its head. Everything you know about the way the market works, they said, is wrong. To risk everything is not bad but good. Do not avoid risk, embrace it. They encapsulated risk in a single equation, known as the Black-Scholes formula:

$$\frac{\partial V}{\partial t} + \frac{1}{2} \sigma^2 S^2 \frac{\partial^2 V}{\partial S^2} + rS \frac{\partial V}{\partial S} - rV = 0$$

This equation was to become the basis for options and deriva-tives, today worth \$1 quadrillion. Ten times the value of all goods produced on earth. ABCD took a risk with wheat prices in North Africa in 2010, because Robert Dall read Black and Scholes in the late 1970s and then taught Wall Street how to put risk into practice in the 1980s.

This is how the Black-Scholes formula works. Say this book has a physical value of £10 today. That's fine, because it is there in black and white on the cover, but no one can predict what the book will be worth in a year's time. It might be £12, it might be £16, or it might be worth only £8. It could be worth nothing. The genius of the Black-Scholes formula is to get rid of any ambiguity in what the future value will be by pinning it down to a fixed amount. When this happens, the future value of the book then becomes its price as a stock option, which crucially means it can then be traded. Black and Scholes had upended Marx's dictum that 'all that is solid melts into air'. They had taken air and turned it into something solid – a stock option – with a fixed value.

So how is this future value worked out? The price of a stock option for this book, Black and Scholes said, would be the differ-ence between the expected share price for the stock option on the book set for a year's time (£12) and the actual price when the option comes due (£16). That difference is the value – in other words: the stock option on this book is worth, alas, just £4.

The more you think about the Black-Scholes equation, the cleverer it gets. Value resides not in the innate book-ness of a book. That value is an illusion, since people will continuously disagree on that true value and so it will fluctuate from minute to minute, second to second. The important thing is not to chase the tail of the market and second-guess what people will think at any given moment, but instead to embrace this inherent volatility and make that the underlying law.

Black and Scholes looked to the molecular particle theories of Albert Einstein, Jean Perrin and Marian Smoluchowski for inspiration: theories that studied the random movement of liquids and gases, and attempted to create a unifying principle that could explain, even predict, this random movement of particles.

Black-Scholes was first adopted on Wall Street by the US company Bankers Trust under the chairmanship of Charles Sanford, who was enthusiastic about what the formula could do for his company to transform its pricing approach into something dynamic and risky. 'Successful people,' Sanford said, 'understand that risk, properly conceived, is often highly productive rather than to be avoided.'

Bankers Trust used a quantified measure of risk called RAROC, or 'risk adjusted return on capital', to give precise numerical value to the potential risk on any trade. Californian economist Hayne Leland then created a formula for insulating against the risk. It was an early form of 'shorting'. Pricing was speeding up at a meteoric rate in the early 1970s, and Leland had cleverly worked out that there was as much money to be made in providing a service for insulating Wall Street against risk as in risky trading itself. The genius of Black-Scholes was that it encouraged risk as a fundamental dynamo of business, but also provided the tools for mitigating the dangers of risky trading by calibrating the level at which a business was prepared to risk.

But Wall Street, though toying with Black and Scholes, had recently received a breathtaking real-world lesson in taking risk to the very edge.

On 3 October 1973, an Arab coalition of states led by Egypt, Syria and Iraq invaded Israel on the holy day of Yom Kippur. OPEC, the oil producers of the Middle East, used the resulting instability to hike the price of oil overnight. It was a massive gamble, dependent on the United States dithering over what to do about the invasion of Israel. With the eyes of the world on

Arab tanks rolling through the desert, the price of oil smashed through the roof and, more to the point, stayed there.

The strategy was brilliant. The ostensible political reason OPEC gave for the 1973 price hike was solidarity with their Arab neighbours when Israel counterattacked, but the reality was pure economic opportunism.

Six days after the Arab coalition invasion, the Nixon administration supplied weapons to Israel to support Israel's counteroffensive into Syria. OPEC's leaders, meeting at its headquarters in Vienna, decided on 17 October to strike, using oil price increases as their weapon against Israel and its Western allies.

Initially, OPEC decided to raise prices seventy per cent. But in December, OPEC met again – this time in Tehran – and prices were raised 130 per cent. OPEC also imposed a total oil embargo on the United States, Canada, Japan, the Netherlands and the UK, industrialised countries heavily dependent on the Arab export of oil. OPEC had attempted an embargo before as a response to the Six-Day War in 1967, and it failed. But this time it believed it would work. The United States, Britain and the countries supporting the Israeli counteroffensive were some of the heaviest oil consumers on earth. These countries could not afford a prolonged embargo from OPEC, and OPEC knew it.

OPEC's was a double-edged plan. On the face of it, turning the tap off for Israel and its allies provided evidence its behaviour was motivated primarily by political solidarity with the Arab nations. But this masked the economic opportunism beneath: grasping the moment to ramp prices without any need to moderate the hike, and then keeping prices at this new astronomically high level. It was risk pushed to the limit. The Shah of Iran told the *New York Times*, 'Of course the world price of oil is going to rise ... certainly! And how! Let's say ten times more.'

OPEC then offered what looked like an olive branch. It gave conditions under which it would end the embargo: a negotiated settlement favourable to the Arab combatants. It created a Catch-22 situation for President Richard Nixon. If he negotiated peace under these terms, the embargo would end but the price of imported oil to the United States, quadrupled from $3 to $12, would remain irreversibly high. A drop in price was not on the table, and Nixon would also be seen to be capitulating to OPEC's demands.

Yet the other option for the US government was no more appealing. If Nixon refused to entertain a negotiated settlement, the political crisis would escalate, and oil prices with it. Either way, oil prices went up. Nixon initiated multilateral talks and on 18 January 1974, US Secretary of State Henry Kissinger negoti-ated an Israeli troop withdrawal from the disputed Sinai Peninsula. OPEC lifted the embargo, but not until March. And the price of global oil was now set at an unprecedented $12 a barrel.

The OPEC price hike was pure Black-Scholes in action. The riskiest gamble imaginable, and it paid off. The received wisdom on business decisions prior to Black and Scholes was that they were finely calibrated judgments based on minimising risk, not maximising it. OPEC's gamble was the opposite. They had put everything on black – risked big – and won.

It was a wake-up call for Wall Street and Western governments. The OPEC oil crisis demonstrated perfectly the Black-and-Scholes view that the coming world was volatile, not controllable, and business needed to harness this volatility, like a skilled sailor harnessing a storm. And risk did not only make you money, if you did not risk big, you would not survive in the new cut-throat business climate. From now on, a company that stopped taking risks was like a shark that stopped swimming. It was dead in the water.

The Black-Scholes formula spread like wildfire through Wall Street. They were hailed as economic prophets, heirs to Adam Smith and David Ricardo. But one man in particular took their equation and turned it into banking reality – Robert Dall.

Dall homed in on one target: the mortgage. By taking a safe asset like a mortgage and using a complex series of 'financial instruments' to turn it into a risky 'liquid asset', that house could now be traded as a 'security'. An ironic name, because there was nothing secure about it.

Wall Street was no longer trading real things, but promises 'securitised' or underwritten by real things owned by real people.

'Securitisation' was Dall's creation, but it was really Black and Scholes on the trading floor. You were Jesus and they were God, I told Dall. And you were doing God's work on earth. He rasped in agreement, laughing.[11]

By the early 1980s, Dall would walk into a downtown restaurant and brokers would come up to him and shake his hand or buy him bottles of champagne. 'I'd turned them into multimillionaires. Of course they thanked me!'

Securitisation dropped like a bomb onto the financial markets. If you could securitise a house, why not a bank? Or a supermarket chain or global corporation? Why not securitise a whole country? In 2000, the European Union shoehorned Greece into the Eurozone, taking a risk on the balance sheet of an entire nation that had flagged how risky it was as an asset. In doing so, the European Central Bank was risking the entire stability of Europe.

What the world did not know was that Goldman Sachs had been tasked with massaging Greece's accounts in order to make them 'eligible' for entry into the Eurozone.[12] An entire country became liquid on the promise of a better credit rating sometime in the future. Goldman Sachs warned that it was risky, too, but we were now in a post-Black and Scholes world. Risk was good.

I wondered what Robert Dall thought when he woke on the morning of 9 October 2007 and heard that the entire banking system of the West had collapsed, built largely on a system of risk that he had conjured.

His nurse fusses about him. He rearranges himself in his penthouse apartment, and takes a brief hit from his oxygen mask. 'I always knew it would go too far. That they'd push it too far.' But don't you have to take some blame? You created this thing. Dall thinks about the possibility that he might be the man that lit the fuse that nearly brought down the entire banking system. 'I was like Robert Oppenheimer,' he answers. 'I invented the atomic bomb, but I didn't drop it.'

In 2010, that bomb dropped on North Africa, as food prices exploded for no apparent reason on the people on the ground. The decision of ABCD to short wheat prices had the same catastrophic consequences as dropping a bomb. More people have been displaced from the region in the seven years that followed the Arab Spring than during the whole of the Second World War. The geopolitical impact – the rise of ISIS, the Syrian civil war and the displacement of millions of people across Africa and into Europe – is ongoing. But to the food giants, a simple decision to short wheat prices was a risk worth taking.

HOW AIDS INSPIRED SUBPRIME

In 2007, the Jenga pyramid of subprime mortgage bundles built on Black-Scholes risk-taking was pushed to the edge. But years before this financial cataclysm unfolded, Wall Street had already been given a tantalising glimpse of the Jacuzzis of cash to be made from bundling risky loans, not in the housing market, but with AIDS patients.

In 1982, as Robert Dall's securitisation revolution was coursing down Wall Street, a health insurer down on his luck was sitting on his porch in Florida reading his local paper. Tucked inside was a story that piqued his interest – about gay men dying of a mysterious disease in San Francisco.

Peter Lombardi ran a small Florida-based health insurance company called MBC. And in 1982, things were not looking good. But when he read this story, he had an idea. One that would light a separate fuse from securitisation, but lead all the way to the same powder keg of subprime.

Lombardi discovered that gay men dying of AIDS could not

access their life insurance when they needed it. While they were still alive. This was money that could buy them better health care, pay off a mortgage for a partner, or they could blow on a holiday. Money that would massively improve the remainder of their life, but they were not able to get their hands on.

So Lombardi had a deal to put to them. I will give you the money. Well, not give you the money. I will loan you the money you need now. And in exchange, I will collect on your life insurance when you die. You win now, I win later. Lombardi came up with a name for his weird new loan: he called it a 'viatical'. He had created the death futures market.[13]

It was a genius idea. The insurance policies of a few men dying of AIDS amounted to little in themselves, but when thousands were bundled together into a viatical, suddenly you were looking at hundreds of millions of dollars. Money that could be used as leverage to make far bigger loans and deals. Which is exactly what Lombardi did. Without knowing it, the first handful of gay men dying of AIDS that Lombardi signed up were going to make him a major player on Wall Street.

But viaticals depended on one crucial element to work: the men dying quickly. The quicker they died, the quicker he collected and paid back whomever he had borrowed from. The only reason Lombardi could loan all this money in the first place was because he himself had borrowed it at extortionately high interest rates. It was a pass-the-parcel of debt, just as subprime would be.

If these men died fast, he collected promptly, and could pay back his loan and pocket the difference. The quicker they died, the more money he made. Lombardi's viatical pyramid was colossally risky, but Lombardi could handle it. What could go wrong?

In 1985, it did. An AIDS drug was discovered. Clinical trials on an HIV inhibitor called AZT began at Duke University, led by a Burroughs-Wellcome virologist, Marty St Clair.

To the rest of the world, from the millions of HIV-positive

people in sub-Saharan Africa to the men in San Francisco and their families, it was a miracle. But to Peter Lombardi and his business partners at MBC, brothers Joel and Steven Steinger, it was a disaster. MBC were loaning out hundreds of millions of dollars to people who were now going to renege on their end of the deal by living.

The money started slowing down and Lombardi got frantic. MBC were no longer collecting the life insurances fast enough to pay their creditors. They had forked out over $100 million to more than 28,000 people with terminal AIDS, but now it was no longer terminal, they needed a new strategy: they needed terminally ill people with other diseases.

Lombardi and his associates widened their net, seeking out ill people with other terminal diseases. People who had an immediate need for cash up front, as Lombardi now did.

By the early 1990s, AIDS had dried up, but MBC had found new, deep wells into which to drop their bucket. Between 1994 and 2004, the company raised £1.2 billion from 30,000 new 'investors' across the globe.

They were back on track, but then disaster struck again. The IRS came calling. In 2003, the Securities and Exchange Commission swooped, accusing MBC of the largest health fraud in US history.[14]

Lombardi was bullish in his defence. His behaviour could have been interpreted as a public service to people who could not access money any other way – a kind of cash Dallas Buyers Club. But the court did not see it that way. The 'MBC 3' were imprisoned for twenty years each.[15]

Lombardi's story, and the story of the thousands of people he signed to his extraordinary Ponzi scheme, would be a curious historical footnote, were it not for what happened next.

The gay men whom Lombardi had been targeting were high-risk customers – they were people that no one would lend to, but when their insurance policies were bundled together, they were worth a fortune.

In 2004, the year Lombardi went to jail, viaticals got a surprise resurrection as Lehman Brothers, ACC Capital Holdings, Merrill Lynch, Wells Fargo, Countrywide Financial, HSBC, Loan Star, JPMorgan Chase and the twenty-five other biggest lenders in America looked at new models of bundling risky loans.

Imagine. Just imagine, if you could bundle a viatical for the home-owning market, and call it a 'subprime mortgage'? Robert Dall had embedded risk in the psyche of Wall Street, but thanks to Lombardi, Wall Street was about to take it to the next level with subprime, risking the entire global economy.

Just as OPEC had bet everything on black and won, the banks bet it all on red and lost. Wall Street failed in – or should I say learnt a lesson from – the banking crash and in 2016, subprime was back. Wells Fargo, Bank of America and the very same banks responsible for the first crash began again offering mortgages with less than a three-per-cent down payment. All you needed to do was 'state income' without any proof of that stated income whatsoever.[16]

Wells Fargo had a new deal with the consumer. If you had no savings, you could be eligible for a lower interest rate. All you needed to do was sign up to a government-sponsored 'personal finance class'. A tutorial on debt so you could get into more. Bank of America had a special low rate that could only be accessed if you could prove to them your income was below the national average.[17]

In 2016, the biggest economy on earth got in on risk. Chinese banks began using complex financial instruments to disguise risky loans as 'investments'. Chinese lenders began using shadow banking – shifting loans off the balance sheet through partnerships with non-bank institutions such as trust companies and securities brokerages – to disguise the fact they were now in the game of risking everything, like everyone else.[18]

China's central bank governor, Zhou Xiaochuan, warned in 2016 that the world should not underestimate the levels of toxic debt being created in China. It mattered, Xiaochuan said, because China was underwriting the world's debt. China was the economy that the US turned to when it sold $700 billion of bonds to bail itself out in 2008.[19] China had effectively granted a giant overdraft extension.

A back-of-the-envelope calculation in 2016 by Dallas-based short seller Kyle Bass, of Hayman Capital Management, estimated Chinese debt at $10 trillion,[20] dwarfing anything even Western banks managed. If this toxic debt went belly-up, who would bail them out? The Bank of Tomorrow, otherwise known as more debt.

Yuan Yang and Gabriel Wildau of the *Financial Times* have investigated how difficult Chinese debt is to penetrate and quantify. Lenders use 'assets that are in effect loans but structured to appear as holdings of investment products issued by a third party. Such financial alchemy allows banks to evade regulations designed to limit risk.'

In June 2016, regulations designed to curb banking risk were blamed for encouraging greater risk-taking. The Basel Committee on Banking Supervision was criticised by lenders for proposing safety regulations on banks aimed at making it harder for banks to cheat the rules.[21] These new measures might encourage banks to lend more, not less, to their weakest lenders.

Like the sorcerer's apprentice, who destroys the enchanted broomstick by chopping it with an axe, only to discover the pieces rising up into hundreds more broomsticks, any attempt to curb debt simply multiplies the debt infinitesimally.

Risk is at the heart of the banking system, but we too have become encouraged to be risk takers. In the 1980s and 1990s, as securitisation drew in Wall Street, the 'shareholding democracy' attracted the high street, with ordinary people encouraged to see themselves as players on the stock market.

Prudent, hard-working savers trotted off to financial advisers offering schemes that prised their savings from them. Of course, the financial adviser would say, there is always a little risk involved – but you have to risk a little, sir or madam, to win. If savers wanted any convincing, all they had to do was look at their bank balance – low interest rates wiping out any attempt at sensible, incremental wealth accumulation.

We have now normalised risk to such an extent that it is synonymous with the financial system. It is the system. But the biggest risk of all is the sheer amount of debt that has been sucked up by every household in the Western world. This ever-burgeoning debt is the iceberg beneath the surface of our lives, accruing more heft by the hour.

CHINATOWN

Risk is seen as a daredevil high-wire act played out by clever traders, but the only people actually taking risks are real people with real houses and jobs, who lose everything when the markets gambling on our behalf get it wrong.

In accepting risk as good, we have accepted the gravest risk of all: the extinction of the planet. According to Maria-Helena Semedo of the FAO, the UN Food and Agriculture Organization, the world has only sixty harvests left in it.[22]

Intensive farming has leached the soil, which is fast turning the planet into a global dust bowl. We are putting ourselves out of business as a species by 2080, when the food stops growing.

The UN estimate that to keep up with global food demand, six million new hectares of farmland will be needed every year.

We currently lose twelve million hectares a year through soil degradation. In 2014, scientists analysed the sediment at the bottom of a French lake, undisturbed since the eleventh century.[23] By measuring the nitrate quality of the sediment, they concluded that as a result of the intensification of farming over the last century, the rate of soil erosion had increased sixty-fold.

In other words, we are over (unless vertical farming takes off with a newly invented soil substitute). But on the bright side, the end of humanity is an unprecedented chance to make money, offering investment opportunities unlike any other in history.

Elon Musk's SpaceX programme plans to have two super-rich space tourists orbiting the moon by 2019, but Musk's long-term plan is planetary exit and life on a new biosphere: the *WALL-E* escape ship for real, a giant shopping mall floating in space inhabited by the wealthiest 0.01 per cent.

As the sixty harvests begin running out, the trading endgame begins. And the new shorting gold rush is not even depleting food, but the planet's most basic resource: water.

'It is intuitively appealing to talk about water as a traded asset,' says Deane Dray, a Citigroup analyst heading up their global water-sector research.[24]

Oil, wheat and gold are all traded on the futures market but, Dray says, 'if you look at projections over the next twenty-five years, you'll see that global water supply and demand imbalances are on track to get worse. The majority of the world population is living in water-scarce and water-stressed regions of the world.'

Water is disappearing and as it does, its value as a commodity escalates. Researchers at Aarhus University in Denmark estimate that the world shortfall in water need will be forty per cent by 2030.

Shortages of water due to global warming, and increased demand to produce energy, are turning it into a political weapon.

In the Middle East, the Euphrates and Tigris Rivers have become a focus of resource conflict between Turkey and Syria. On these huge rivers, critical to the water supply of the whole region, Turkey are building two of the biggest dams on earth. The two rivers supply not only Syria and Iraq, but Iran as well. All three countries fear they could find themselves at the mercy of Turkey, which has already used controlled water shortages as a weapon against Kurdish villages in Northern Syria.

In 2014, Turkey turned off the supply, affecting the lives of millions of people in Syria and Iraq. The same is going on with the Nile. In 2017, Egypt and Ethiopia began protracted talks about Ethiopia's Grand Renaissance Dam on the Nile, which Egypt fears could cede control of their water supply to their upstream neighbour, shifting the balance of power by controlling the tap.[25]

We are now entering a *Chinatown* scenario. In 1975, Robert Towne's script for the Roman Polanski movie about the control of the water supply to a drought-ravaged Los Angeles, and the nexus of corruption it creates between business and government officials, won an Oscar. But we are now embarking on an era in which a thousand similar storylines are created across the globe. Wherever supply dwindles to a trickle, the shortage will be engineered to hike prices.

In 2015, Los Angeles got a taste of *Chinatown* for real. An investigation by the San Bernardino *Desert Sun* discovered Evian owner Nestlé had been allowed to siphon water from some of California's driest areas on permits that expired nearly thirty years ago, in order to produce premium crystalline products like Arrowhead, sold across the world.

In March 2015, protestors at Nestlé Waters' North American bottling plant in Sacramento forced a one-day closure. They brandished plastic Evian bottles as batons and even made plastic pitchforks out of them.[26] The US is the world's second biggest consumer of bottled water behind China. Nestlé, like Coca-Cola and Pepsi, have cut deals with isolated rural communities, taking a percentage of the local water supply, but with the incentive of keeping municipal local rates lower for local residents, so they will agree.

As water runs out, global companies are able to buy up the supply through such locally negotiated deals, just as oil companies bought up land rights in the twentieth century. I met a lawyer a couple of years ago, whose job consisted of flying round the world and persuading indigenous peoples to sign away their land rights to the global oil company for whom she worked.

This job is now being carried out by water companies, and the deals that are cut over the heads of communities by municipal governments in North Africa, Australia, South America, China and India, will mean local people suddenly find themselves without access to the water that comes from their own village.

In 2006, Coca-Cola were accused of 'drinking India dry' by opening a bottling plant in Rajasthan that left local farmers unable to irrigate their fields.

But in Australia, where water shortage is historically acute, a solution has been attempted. The Murray-Darling Basin provides the life blood of New South Wales – the two rivers stretching thousands of miles and providing water, not only for millions of people in cities such as Canberra and Murray Bridge, but for the hundreds of farms that lie adjacent to the rivers, and rely upon this water to survive.

By the mid-1990s, seventy-seven per cent of the Murray's average annual flow was being consumed by humans. The resulting reduced flow, combined with silting and increased run-off from saline soils churned up by farming, were killing the river. So in 1995, the state and federal governments capped extraction, meaning that if you wanted to use more, you had to pay. Rhondda Dickson, chief executive of the project, explains that, 'one of the most significant reforms we have made in Australia is to separate water property rights from land rights and cap water use, so water can be traded on the market.'

Australia had done something seemingly impossible: squared the circle of need and price. A water user could sell their allocation of water for a year or hold on to it. Supply and demand, and transparent. But it did not solve the bigger picture – water is drying up across the planet as demand for water explodes. In 1992, governments from across the globe convened in Ireland to produce the 'Dublin Principles' on water: recognising it as an economic good. But little has happened to produce a coordinated strategy for the global crisis.

The *Desert Sun* investigation in California unearthed what happens at micro-level: government oversight of water falls between the cracks of under-resourced agencies like the Forest Service and local community groups. Nestlé's pumping operation at Strawberry Creek in the San Bernardino National Forest, sixty miles east of Los Angeles, took advantage of the fact that the site had been unlicensed since 1987.[27]

Companies can exploit the fact that water is a natural phenomenon – a 'common pool resource'. Rights are often in conflict, and therefore can be negotiated their way. Water is easy pickings.

When they do, the money to be made is phenomenal. The average price of water piped into a home is approximately $1.50 per 1,000 litres. At $3 to $4 for a litre of bottled water, that is a price increase of 280,000 per cent.[28] But you do not have to drink bottled water to feel the price hike from the commoditisation of the water shortage. Ratings agency Fitch polled seventy-eight per cent of the forty-six retail water utilities in California in 2015 and estimated a coming price rise over the next decade in piped water to the home of potentially up to thirty-one per cent.[29]

The result of shortages of water in drier parts of the world, which also happen to be the poorest, will be to move production of food to the richer, wetter parts. Rather than carry the water elsewhere – which is heavy and costly to move, like oil – acute shortages of water will be the catalyst for widening global inequality. Not only will the poorest in the driest places pay the highest premium for useable or drinkable water, they will suffer the most from highly volatile jumps in food prices: food imported because there was no water to grow food where they lived.

The money to be made is not in water's transportation but in betting on price – on the water futures market. On risk. Michael Burry, the one-eyed visionary trader who shorted subprime and was made famous by *The Big Short*, moved swiftly on from betting on a mortgage crash to trading on the price of global water. A man always ahead of his time.

BETTING ON THE END OF THE WORLD

This is the dawning of the Anthropocene age – a new epoch in which humanity decides the fate of the planet. It began in the

1950s with the dispersal of radioactive elements from nuclear tests such as Mururoa Atoll and marked the end of the Holocene, twelve thousand years of stable climate since the last Ice Age.[30]

The Anthropocene age has initially at least been defined by humanity exercising total power over the planet with full extractive force: global warming, deforestation, pollution and the toxification of the oceans, rivers, lakes and soil; the mass extinction of species and the bio-manipulation of the ones we choose to keep – the battery-bred chicken is now the world's most common bird,[31] outnumbering sparrows and starlings, even though it should not be in evolutionary terms.

The Anthropocene age cements the fact we are bigger than God, but even now, we cannot let go of risk, because risk is what propelled us here. And now phase two of the Anthropocene begins: the end game.

Professor Chris Rapley, a climate scientist at University College London, believes we should drop our addiction to economic risk when it comes to saving the planet, or the end game will soon be game over. 'The Anthropocene marks a new period in which our collective activities dominate the planetary machinery. Since the planet is our life-support system – we are essentially the crew of a largish spaceship – interference with its functioning at this level and on this scale is highly significant. If you or I were crew on a smaller spacecraft, it would be unthinkable to interfere with the systems that provide us with air, water, fodder and climate control. But the shift into the Anthropocene tells us that we are playing with fire.'[32]

We are doing so because we have a planet constructed, and now spiralling to destruction, on an economic model of risk. But the risks that need to be taken now should be in saving us, not destroying the planet further.

That tipping point could already be coming, as business discovers there is more money to be made from saving the planet than either killing it or using the futures market to bet on its imminent demise. This is where the Anthropocene has taken us.

The end of the planet in sixty harvests' time. But on the bright side, this ticking clock has given humanity the focus of an end date, and business has not been slow to see the money to be made from forging earth's rescue plan.

In the past, earth's demise seemed too far off to be taken seriously by anyone other than those already converted to believing it was happening. As a result, earth became the proverbial frog in water, boiling to death so slowly it didn't notice its own demise.

The question is: is noticing it now, too late?

With US withdrawal in 2017 from the Paris Climate Change accord, it became clear governments acting in concert will be hard, if near-impossible. Paris offered each signatory the opportunity to monitor their own progress in reducing emissions from 2020 onwards. To police themselves. Because there is no external stick holding any nation to a target – as there has been none for obesity targets – these accords are essentially goodwill gestures.

Yet in January 2017, Chinese President Xi Jinping called the Paris accord 'a hard-won achievement'. A measure of how difficult it was to get even this goodwill gesture to reduce emissions, let alone a concrete plan of action together.

President Trump's withdrawal from the treaty in 2017 was widely interpreted as the ceding of world leadership for the battle on climate change to China. Trump wilfully set up the US in opposition to the whole idea. And China is the key to everything. The country with both the highest projected energy demands of any nation on earth over the next two decades, so becoming the biggest polluter. But the country simultaneously enacting the biggest, boldest solutions.

In December 2017, Xi announced the long-awaited carbon trading scheme for China's biggest energy suppliers, capping their emissions. In January 2018, China pledged to ban all imported plastic packaging. The clearest signs yet, according to environmentalists, that China is genuinely committed to a sustainable future, and setting a benchmark for the rest of the world.

OWNING THE RESCUE PLAN

At Paris, the protestors chanted '1.5 to stay alive' in the street outside the talks. But scientists predict a global temperature increase over the next century closer to five degrees centigrade: over 300 per cent higher than the 1.5C Paris target. In the meantime, business is getting on with the plan to save us. Not because it feels bad about what is happening to earth, but because the end also represents the biggest business opportunity in the history of the planet. One venture capitalist explained Silicon Valley's changing priorities to me in very simple terms: 'twenty years ago it was tech and today it's the planet.'

Thousands of ideas that a decade ago would have sounded like distant sci-fi fantasy are now serious commercial propositions being put together with millions of dollars of seed-funding.

Everything from synthetic soil and vertical farming to gene-edited crops, sea bins, iceberg dragging, asteroid mining, moon farms; even bio-printed models for the draining of smaller landlocked seas such as the Mediterranean, which could have the water removed and be turned into nutrient-rich farmland to fight the coming food crisis (a plan first suggested by Mussolini in the 1930s).

No plan is too big or insane when it comes to saving the earth – and if it is not too big or insane, it is not deemed investable or of sufficient scale. Some companies look at turning the movie *The Martian* into reality: growing crops in pods in space; others work on staying put on earth, taking to city-sized rafts: aquatic domes floating on the rising oceans of a fast-submerging world.

Business has a stick or twist moment: exploit the hell out of the last sixty harvests or come up with the rescue plan. And cracking the latter is not framed as a moral question – business does not see itself as the custodian of Gaia. It is just better business to save earth than let it die. Questions of what is right for the planet and its inhabitants are not of interest to shareholders or investors.

What is turning business on to rescuing the planet is its potential resource as a commodity to be owned. Forever.

Once upon a time – Anthropocene 1.0 – earth was a commodity to be exploited, but now it's a commodity to be saved. Because when you have a monopoly on the rescue plan, you have the ultimate monopoly. On life itself.

Yet this gold rush created by End Game Earth is also beginning to create new ethical questions. In 2017, deep-sea mining company Nautilus Minerals unveiled three huge crawling titans: machines moving slowly over the seabed 1600 metres below the surface of Papua New Guinea, grinding up everything they cross. The Nautilus plan is to extract copper, zinc and gold from the deepest recesses of the world's oceans, seventy per cent of which are unexplored.

In the process, seabed mining could destroy already fast-depleting ecosystems: not only the rapidly bleaching and increasingly lifeless coral reefs, but the undiscovered life that surrounds hydrothermal vents, rich in extractable minerals, where huge sulphide deposits are to be found. These sites are where some of the strangest and most extraordinary new species of deep sea life are routinely discovered. And where unimaginable riches are also to be found.

Interestingly, Mike Johnston, chief executive of Nautilus, says ripping up the world's sea beds is the green choice, because there is no other choice. 'It makes sense,' he says, 'to explore this untapped potential in an environmentally sustainable way, instead of continually looking at the fast-depleting land resources of the planet to meet society's rising needs.'

In other words, these huge machines will be tearing up the ocean beds to extract minerals to power green energy technologies, like solar power and electric cars, essential to earth's rescue plan. Minerals that cannot be mined on land at the extraordinary rate required to satisfy insatiable demand. This is the new cost-benefit analysis of Anthropocene 2.0: taking a risk on destroying the sea bed to save the planet, the first of many such uncalculated risks to that end.

It could well be that this second machine age has arrived just in time to save us from the first industrial revolution: can innovation and implementation of the craziest new ideas outrun the last sixty harvests? We shall see. In 2015, Nickelodeon launched their own take on End Game Earth. A $3,800 a night, SpongeBob SquarePants resort at Punta Cana in the Caribbean, where you can stay in a giant pineapple, designed with a sub-aquatic, coral-reef theme. A chance to experience a theme-world version of the undersea world fast disappearing for real.

The ridiculous thing is that we could have embraced a rescue plan long before we all realised we needed one. In 2015, Toyota produced a hydrogen-powered car that produces water as a by-product from the exhaust. But in 1946, more than seventy years ago, scientist Vincent Schaefer first discovered cloud seeding – the artificial creation of clouds using basic chemical agents. No one has yet decided to put an Evian or Coke logo on the side of a cloud, but when they do, then perhaps we will decide it is an idea worth pursuing.

Instead of continuing to follow the Black-Scholes formula for risk, perhaps we should be utilising $2H_2 + O_2 = 2H_2O + Energy$. The formula for the creation of water. It is actually pretty simple.

CHAPTER THREE
TAX: WHY EVERYWHERE WANTS TO BE THE CAYMAN ISLANDS

The Deal: The creation of FINCOCO by Sir Vassel
   Johnson, financial secretary of the Cayman Islands
   Monetary Authority and the leading accountancy
   firms on the islands, including Coopers and Lybrand
   and Maples and Calder
Aim: To rebrand The Cayman Islands as a legitimate
   place to do business
Where: Nassau, Bahamas
When: November 1975

On 2 January 2012, a cash machine at the Blockbuster video
store in the Fallowfield Shopping Centre, in Manchester, was
robbed. The thieves had spent six months digging a 100-foot-
long tunnel under the car park, even fitting it with lighting and
roof supports. Once they had dug the tunnel, the gang needed to
cut through fifteen inches of reinforced concrete to reach the
cash machine, which held £20,000 on a normal business day.
But this was not a normal business day. It was 2 January and
there was only £6,000 in it.

The gang of four had worked seven days a week for six months
to dig a tunnel to rob a cash machine no one was using. By my
calculations, they had earned £8.33 a day for their labours.

There are far easier ways to make money. You could instead

become a global corporation and stick your profits in an offshore tax haven. According to the last two American presidents, Obama and Trump, this is one of the greatest ongoing crimes perpetrated on the taxpayer.

Yet it is a crime that governments are keen to enable. The twenty-first-century race to become the nation on earth offering the most advantageous tax breaks has replaced the twentieth-century race to become the most productive manufacturing economy.

Theresa May suggested in 2017 that by turning itself into a tax haven, Britain could forge a post-Brexit identity. In December 2017, Donald Trump announced his first legislative victory as president: mammoth tax cuts, the largest in thirty years, to the wealthiest one per cent and to corporations, adding a trillion dollars to the national debt.

Trump said he wanted to attract US businesses that had offshored jobs back to America, and reboot business. It was, he said, a 'Christmas present' to the American people. Democrat minority leader in the Senate Chuck Schumer called the cuts, reducing corporation tax from thirty-five to twenty-one per cent, a 'disgrace' saying 'the only champagne corks popping will be those in the boardrooms of corporate America, including Trump Tower.'

Opinion polls in the days following Trump's 'Christmas present' suggested the American public agreed. Billionaire Michael Bloomberg, in the one per cent of the one per cent richest people on earth, said it was a giveaway even he found embarrassing. 'We CEOs,' he said, 'don't need the money.' Senate majority leader Mitch McConnell conceded as the vote passed that 'if we can't sell this to the American people, then we need to go into another line of work.'

If you wanted proof that governments now see driving tax down as a key driver for growth, even if the public don't support the proposals, you need look no further than the frantic scramble to own the low-tax crown.

Yet politicians also claim to deplore tax avoidance. In *Casablanca*, when Captain Renault is confronted by gambling in Rick's bar, he is affronted. 'I am shocked, shocked to find that gambling is going on here!' he says, as the croupier hands him his winnings under the table. 'Oh, thank you very much.' Then he turns to the other tables. 'Everybody out!'

This is how politicians behave when they talk about tax avoidance. But how tax itself went from a duty to pay to a duty to avoid is a comical one. In truth, a ubiquitous business strategy that politicians claim to deplore was hatched and most enthusiastically promoted by government itself.

The lesson to be learnt by the hapless cash-machine robbers digging beneath Fallowfield Shopping Centre is this: save your energy and make sure the next crime you commit is legal. So how did it happen? How was business schooled into thinking that tax avoidance was not simply a justifiable tactic, but an entrepreneurial imperative?

No one knows how much corporations have hidden offshore. A 2012 study based on data from the IMF put it at between \$21 trillion and \$31 trillion. Not million or billion. Trillion.

The US Senate Homeland Security sub-committee claimed one bank, HSBC, was alone responsible for 'failing to monitor' £38 million going offshore. They turned a blind eye, just like Captain Renault.

It is not only Google, Facebook and Amazon who reroute their profits. Everyone from Burger King to Sainsbury's and Manchester United do it, too. Even bus companies. Passing through a labyrinthine system of subsidiaries around the globe before ending up in the Cayman Islands or Bermuda or Luxembourg or London or Delaware. (Appropriately nicknamed 'the small wonder', Delaware has over five thousand global companies 'registered'. More than the Cayman Islands. Prior to becoming a tax haven, Delaware's main earners were poultry and soy beans.)

HOW WE BENEFIT AND HOW WE DON'T

Tax avoidance is integral to the way the world does business. It is perfectly legal, yet has real-world consequences. An estimated $700 billion has left Russia since the 1990s, $305 billion from Saudi Arabia, another $300 billion from Nigeria. The money taken out of developing countries could have wiped out their entire debt at a stroke. In the UK, much is made of the fact that one in three benefit claims is fraudulent, costing £1.3 billion a year. The tax gap created by tax avoidance is thirty-five times greater than benefit fraud.[1]

This smooth-functioning system, oiled by an army of lawyers and accountants, is not merely taking advantage of the increasingly borderless, frictionless global economy, it rewrote the rules to make it legitimate in the first place.

It would not matter if it didn't impact directly on ordinary taxpayers, but it does. Every adult in Britain and America picks up the tab left by corporations, paying higher tax bills as a result of big companies not paying theirs. Tax avoidance is anti-capitalist: by squeezing small and medium-sized companies trying to grow, in order to make up the shortfall, governments cut off new business at the knees.

Yet the companies avoiding tax feel maligned by a world that does not understand what they do in terms of contributing to the economy, and are positively bullish about defending their use of tax havens – or 'financial centres' as they have rebranded themselves.

When I was invited to speak at an offshore tax event in Geneva in 2016, the hedge fund managers and representatives of corporations attending seemed genuinely baffled that the world sees them as villains. The consumer, they argue, gets a cheaper Amazon package, or packet of tomatoes from the supermarket, only because they avoid the full tax whack, and we benefit from that.

They have a point. The consumer is an inadvertent beneficiary of tax havens. But only a bit. If I weighed up a cheaper book from Amazon against the billions in lost tax revenue to fund the NHS or the education of children, the money lost to key services, or reinvestment in basic infrastructure of the state, I think I might be inclined to add 2p to the price of my book.

HOW TAX AVOIDANCE BECAME LEGITIMATE AND PAYING IT BECAME FOR 'LITTLE PEOPLE'

So how did tax avoidance become the mechanism by which the modern globalised world does business? Who rebranded it as business savvy and turned tax from something you had to pay, into – in billionaire Leona Helmsley's immortal words – something paid only by 'little people'?

Once upon a time, dodging tax was actually wrong. In 1975, Baron Alfred Ernest Marples, who had served as Postmaster General in the Conservative government, overseeing some of the biggest changes to British life – the opening of the first section of the M1 motorway, the introduction of premium bonds and the postcode system – did something very strange.

He boarded a night ferry, hours before the end of the tax year. According to a *Daily Mirror* account from the time, he had with him only 'his belongings crammed into tea chests, leaving the floors of his home in Belgravia littered with discarded clothes and possessions. He claimed he had been asked to pay nearly thirty years' overdue tax. The Treasury froze his assets in Britain for the next ten years. By then most of them were safely in Monaco and Liechtenstein.'[2]

Lord Marples was portrayed as a classic upper-class rogue – a cad who had skipped the country. He had defrauded the nation, but his night-time escape was also seen as a very British two fingers to the establishment, and magnificently sneaky. The press and public response to Marples – that he was a cad – illustrated the wider attitude at the time that avoiding or evading tax was wrong. But at the very moment Marples was boarding the night ferry, two accountants in London were setting about changing the British mindset on tax avoidance – from criminality to clever accountancy.

JOHN LENNON: PATIENT ZERO

Their story begins in London. It is 1969 and John Lennon is at a drinks party in Mayfair. He is introduced to two men in suits called Roy Tucker and Ron Plummer. They stand out, because everyone else is a rock star or a groupie, but these men have a very enticing proposition for Lennon.

Tucker and Plummer had worked for the big accountancy firm Arthur Andersen, but now wanted to go it alone and believed that they had a new way to attract business: be creative with the accounts and magic a tax bill to zero. When the Labour government under Harold Wilson began taxing the rich at an unprecedented ninety per cent, they saw their chance.[3]

The fact they targeted John Lennon at the drinks party was not a coincidence. When taxes rose, the Beatles were livid. George Harrison wrote the song 'Taxman', even name-checking Harold Wilson fleecing hard-working, international rock stars:

Let me tell you how it will be
There's one for you, nineteen for me
'Cause I'm the taxman, yeah, I'm the taxman.
Should five per cent appear too small
Be thankful I don't take it all
'Cause I'm the taxman, yeah, I'm the taxman.[4]

Tucker and Plummer saw pound signs when they began chatting to Lennon. They were in the process of creating a 'bank' called Rossminster in discreet Mayfair offices. But this one was very different from the banks used by 'little people'. This bank would have a discreet entrance with a small gold nameplate. They would deal only with super-rich clients. If Lennon came on board, they could potentially get Roger Moore, Led Zeppelin, maybe Mick Jagger. And in return, they promised Lennon a tax bill of £0.00. In fact, they said, the Inland Revenue will be paying you money.

Lennon signed up and Rossminster had its first big-name client. Two men were going to change the British attitude to tax, but first they had to content themselves with merely creating the first orchestrated tax dodge of the 1970s.[5] Tucker and Plummer found all kinds of cunning places to spirit away large sums of money for their clients: charitable donations or shell companies with no evident business or board directors. Fellow Beatle George Harrison ploughed his royalties into the failing British film industry – a guaranteed money mineshaft – producing some great films like *Scum* and *Withnail & I* in the process.

Then Tucker and Plummer made their first mistake. They started getting cocky. As their fame in super-rich circles spread, their cavalier behaviour towards the Inland Revenue started to become a form of taunting. One morning in 1974, HMRC got its revenge. Twenty police officers and seventy-eight tax inspectors swooped on their offices.

Tucker and Plummer were shut down, but not before having set the template for a whole new tax specialism: creative accountancy. Instead of breaking the law by outright evasion of tax, you sailed to the very edge of criminality, twisting the rules to within an inch of prison, thus avoiding it. Thanks to Rossminster, that is what you pay a creative accountant to do.

Tucker and Plummer were prosecuted, not because they had broken the law, but because of what they represented: a wilful exploitation of the loopholes of the system. In this respect, they were a precursor of insider trading in the City in the 1980s. If Lord Marples had hung around, rather than sneaking off to Monaco, Tucker and Plummer could probably have got his bill down to zero.

Their message was profoundly subversive to a post-war society predicated on 'doing your bit'. They upended the duty of wealth creators from paying their way in society to doing their utmost to avoid it. Rules, they said, were no longer there to be followed, but broken. When they were arrested, Tucker and Plummer may have been over as accountants, but they had changed the morality of Britain.

TURNING A MOSQUITO-RIDDEN SANDBAR INTO A TRILLION-POUND ISLAND

All tax avoidance needed now was to go legit. And for that, the British government was on hand. In the late 1960s, the British Empire was being dismantled, and the colonies were faced with a choice. Some, like Jamaica, went fully independent. But for others, Whitehall had another plan.

In 1969, a civil servant called John Cumber was called into the Foreign Office. He was shown a map of the Caribbean and a circle was drawn round a small mosquito-ridden sandbar called the Cayman Islands. Pack your bags, he was told, because next week you are going to be the Governor.

So-called 'treasure islands' such as Switzerland and Monaco had long provided the rich with tax-haven status, but now the British government saw an opportunity to muscle in on the act with an actual physical island, surrounded by sea. Why, they surmised, could not ex-colonies like Cayman be retooled for the same purpose? Remain under British sovereignty, guaranteeing political stability, but acting independently, so they can write their own rules.

The reason Cayman could rewrite the rules was down to two little words: common law. Economist Jan Fichtner has analysed the importance of common law to Cayman's success as a tax haven in a 2016 report for the University of Amsterdam:[6]

The key difference between common law and civil law is that common law only stipulates what is prohibited, whereas civil law, as practised in Japan, Germany or France, identifies what is permitted. The consequence is that new financial innovations such as hedge funds or CDOs (collateralised debt obligations) can be set up easily, because strict regulation is only put in place with conspicuous misconduct or strong pressure from powerful foreign actors – governments.

In other words, they can do what they like, until someone stops them. And no one, least of all the British government, wanted to do that. Until Cayman was retooled as a tax haven, places such as Switzerland and Monaco were exceptions to the global financial system. Not the model for how it should work. But one man in Whitehall saw Cayman as a way of making tax havens the norm: the place where all business is conducted.

George Bolton was a director of the Bank of England and on 28 February 1958, he noticed something very weird going on. The Midland Bank were handling a transfer of $800,000 on the trading floor that had not been flagged. These were not dollars at all, they were eurodollars, normally used to keep large sums of US money secure outside the States by holding it in trustworthy banks across the world.

Trades with eurodollars were always traceable, above board and relatively small. This transfer was different. It was huge. So big that it looked like laundered money. Except it appeared it was being laundered in broad daylight through one of Britain's biggest banks. When George Bolton saw the Midland Bank deposit, he had a choice: do something or turn a blind eye. He turned a blind eye.[7]

In that moment, Bolton saw a whole new potential for eurodollars: as a parallel trading system in its own right, not simply a way of safeguarding assets. This could be a way of doing deals between companies and moving huge amounts of cash around the globe free of government and currency controls. Why be a criminal doing it illegally, when you could do it legally? The key was for these transactions to happen 'offshore'.

Eurodollars were an offshore market before offshore banking even existed.

The plan for making offshore real – a physical place, not just a concept – was to create a wheel.[8] At the centre was London, where legitimate deals could be carried out. But the spokes would extend far out to offshore havens thousands of miles away, where deals of a shadier nature could be transacted, and dirty money laundered. No one would be scrutinising these deals too much. London could turn a blind eye.

Civil servant John Cumber arrived on Cayman in 1969 and became the island's first governor. It was sparsely populated: only fishermen, their families, the Cayman crocodiles that give the islands their name, and the mosquito-ridden swamps. A huge programme was undertaken to spray the lagoons with insecticide and prepare the island for a new purpose. Tax avoidance.

However, Cayman's first clients were not big business as the British government hoped, but drug dealers. The idea of offshore coincided with the Labour and Democrat governments in London and Washington suddenly ramping up corporation tax, and refusing to allow companies to exile their profits abroad by maintaining restrictions on capital flow. Cayman was hamstrung.

But there was business: from Miami and Cuba, Colombia and El Salvador. Cessna planes would fly over the beaches dropping suitcases of cash to be deposited and laundered on behalf of the emerging drug barons of Central America, flush with cocaine money and with nowhere to put it. In years to come, Pablo Escobar would become one of Cayman's most loyal customers.

Then there was a further stroke of luck for Cayman. The Bahamas, their neighbour and one of Cayman's leading offshore rivals, descended suddenly into political turmoil, becoming independent in 1973. The Bahamas' accountants fled *en masse* to Cayman, bringing their business with them.

The Bahamas had benefited hugely from the collapse of the Bretton Woods agreement in 1971, a system of monetary management signed up to by the world's biggest economies. Bretton Woods lasted forty years, strictly controlling exchange rates and capital movements. But now it was gone, controls disappeared overnight. Currency was suddenly free to flow across the globe unscrutinised, exactly as George Bolton had imagined it would in the 1950s. And now all the accountants had moved from the Bahamas to Cayman, it was Cayman that would benefit from this big bang.

Cayman was all set to open its doors to the world's corporations. Yet in spite of the gonzo accountancy of Tucker and Plummer in the late 1960s, tax avoidance was still not widely accepted as best practice by the public, let alone government policy. That was all about to change.

In 1979, there was a revolution, and it was led by the two most powerful leaders of the free world: Mrs Thatcher and Ronald Reagan. They did not trust government with money, least of all with taxpayers' money, and both wanted to break the regulatory shackles that tied big business down. Markets, not government, should henceforth decide what was best for the economy, and at the heart of this revolution was low tax.

For forty collectivist years, taxation was seen as necessary. The price paid by citizens and business to have a functioning civil society. We would all do our bit by paying for roads, hospitals and battleships. But if business was freed from this burden, it was now argued, we would all benefit in the long run. Lower taxes would mean greater productivity and profit margins, and the economic benefits to business would 'trickle down' to the rest of us.

Capitalism was about to change course. After forty years of broad agreement on the need for taxation, it was now perceived as a stone around the neck of big business, and one man was to provide the evidence, with a single stroke of a pen.

THE DOODLE ON A NAPKIN

Arthur Laffer was an economist from the Kennedy era who had fallen out of favour. Laffer's ideas about tax were framed by the classic Kennedy position that low (or no) taxes would create a 'rising tide that lifts all boats'. In 1974, he had the first of what would prove to be a series of very important lunches at the Two Continents Restaurant at the Washington Hotel, in Washington DC, with two rising stars of the Republican party, Donald Rumsfeld and Dick Cheney. Jude Wanniski, a *Wall Street Journal* writer, was also present, invited by Laffer.

Rumsfeld and Cheney were part of the team managing the transition from the Nixon to the Ford administration. According to Rumsfeld, 'the country faced a number of serious economic problems and what was coming up through the system was not what I felt the direction the country should go.' America had just gone through the OPEC oil crisis of 1973 and felt the axis of global economic power shifting to the Middle East. Fixed exchange rates set by the Bretton Woods agreement were also coming to an end. Floating exchange rates were ushering in an era of globalisation and a shift in business priorities from the national to the world stage. Business could no longer be dictated to about where it should invest.

To woo business to one country over another, governments believed they could use low tax incentives as the carrot. A race was on. But no one had yet created a precise economic model for how low taxes worked, nor at what level low tax worked at an optimal level for both business and government. In other words, how low should you go?

Ford was proposing a five per cent increase in tax, but as Laffer explained to Rumsfeld and Cheney at the Two Continents lunch: 'Look, you're not going to get a five per cent increase in revenue from a five per cent increase in tax surcharge.'

Laffer got out a Sharpie pen and began drawing a graph on his napkin to explain. On one side was the level of taxation and on the other, the level of revenue collected from that taxation. If you tax people at zero per cent, Laffer said, you collect zero taxes. And if you tax people at one hundred per cent you get zero taxes, because there is no motivation to work.

But there was a sweet spot of low taxes, he said, incentivising greater productivity and thus generating more revenue as a result. Laffer drew a curve to illustrate his point. High taxes created a vicious cycle for business, he asserted, while lowering them did the opposite: it created a virtuous cycle in which growth and incremental reductions in tax worked in tandem, for the benefit of government, business and the public. If one followed the curve, one could determine the optimum level of taxation.

Rumsfeld turned to Cheney and said, 'Arthur Laffer is absolutely brilliant.' It was, Rumsfeld later told Bloomberg News, 'so simple and compelling and contested the liberal and conservative view.' It was brand-new thinking, but it dovetailed with the neoliberal thinking of the Chicago School of economists at the time, led by Milton Friedman. It was neoliberalism plonked right on Rumsfeld and Cheney's plate, and they liked what they heard. Wanniski, the journalist at the table, left and penned an article: 'Taxes, Revenues and the Laffer Curve.' The 'Laffer Curve' was born.

Laffer's instinct to look for an optimal level of low tax had another impulse. Even though his economics fitted the new neoliberal thinking, Laffer – the Kennedy-era Democrat – believed not only the rich but the middle class should benefit from the low tax revolution, and the middle class thought so, too. On 6 June 1978, two-thirds of Californians voted to pass Proposition 13, which cut and capped property taxes and mandated a two-thirds vote for any future taxes.

On 1 August 1978, the *New York Times* declared the revolt of the middle class on tax to be gaining momentum across America. If the middle class – hurting from rampant inflation – was not appeased by its own tax cuts and given the same benefits as higher earners, America faced a new kind of political crisis. A middle class who demanded the same treatment on tax as the rich.

In 1978, Laffer began lunching at the same restaurant he had met Rumsfeld and Cheney, but this time with the next president of the United States, Ronald Reagan. Reagan was as awed by Laffer's Sharpie pen curve on a napkin as they had been and Laffer was appointed Reagan's economic advisor. In 1980, Reagan sailed into office on a radical tax-cutting programme for this middle class. By 1982, under his leadership, it fell to fifty per cent, the top rate kicking in at an annual income of $101,000 or more. By 1988, the rate had dropped to twenty-eight per cent, triggered at $29,000.

The world was now prepped for a low-tax culture, but big business still needed a place to do business that was 'tax neutral'. A place to conduct post-Bretton Woods globalised transactions free of the burdens of tax. That place would be the Cayman Islands.

More than thirty years after his lunches with Ronald Reagan that changed the way the world did business, I meet Arthur Laffer in a bar a block away from the restaurant where they met. He arrives beaming from ear to ear, talking so fast and bouncing around with such manic energy, he could easily have become a talk-show host had he not become an economist. I can see why Rumsfeld, Cheney and Reagan were impressed.

Laffer is tremendous company and we get on like a house on fire, drinking away pretty much as he must have done in that restaurant forty years ago. Laffer relishes criticism of his theory. He defends the economics with a theatrical wave of his arm. At one point, he gets out a napkin and starts drawing his curve. I interrupt him. 'That's great Arthur, but what I want to know is, how you got away with it?'

'What do you mean, how I got away with it? Because it's true!'

'But it isn't. As a result of the low-tax doctrine, didn't business move offshore? Manufacturing collapsed in the US, and half the American population became disenfranchised.'

'No! No! This is so wrong! So wrong! We were proved right! Rich people are different from other people. The rich are the one group of people where if you lower their tax rate, you get more revenue. Taxing the rich would make society poorer. If you tax rich people and give the money to the poor, you're going to get lots and lots of poor people and no rich people. The dream is always to make the poor rich, not the rich poor.'

Laffer believes in his curve, and made everyone in government believe it, too.

And it certainly worked for big business, just not for everyone else. Tax havens are available only to companies that can afford the entrance fee, not start-up businesses or sole traders, and this means they contort markets rather than allow the market to work properly. Laffer argues the opposite.[9]

On both sides of the Atlantic, the reinvention of tax avoidance as entrepreneurial initiative meant government gave business a tacit nod and wink to ignore the rules the rest of us follow. When the Conservative chancellor Nigel Lawson was asked in the 1980s why his government were so keen on dropping corporation tax to next to nothing, he said that big corporations would no longer have a reason to avoid tax. Why would anyone bother, he said, when they did not pay anything anyway? It did not occur to him that government generosity can be pushed well beyond zero.

We have been programmed to think that low tax promotes enterprise. It does, when businesses are small and need to get off the ground. When global corporations scour the globe looking for the most 'tax efficient' place to register themselves, rerouting their money through numerous shell companies, then low tax has nothing to do with enterprise. In fact, it destroys entrepreneurialism by forcing small, growing businesses to shoulder the bill the corporations have dodged.

By the mid-1980s, the low-tax orthodoxy was so hegemonic, the idea of raising taxes was seen as far-left madness. The fact that German and Swedish right-of-centre governments kept taxes high to create corporate responsibility was conveniently ignored by those seeking to brand tax as a socialist dogma rather than a neo-liberal one. By maintaining reasonable levels of corporation tax for native companies such as BMW and Siemens (happy, by the way, to pay them), these countries also held on to their manufacturing base. Something Britain and the US destroyed by offshoring tax and jobs.

The US car industry collapsed, creating a rust belt from the very areas that had turned America into the number-one super-power. In Britain, the story was the same. Workers in traditional industries were deemed 'uncompetitive'. The reality was that the carpet under their feet had been ripped away and sent offshore. When Nissan opened a factory in Britain's North-East, workers were suddenly 'competitive' because they were cheap.

As financial services, not manufacturing, became the future, a huge creative accountancy industry sprouted in London servic-ing the tax-avoidance juggernaut, with a revolving door between the HMRC and the big accountancy firms. Richard Brooks was a senior tax inspector for the Inland Revenue, who became a whistle-blower after witnessing what he believes was the cosy relationship developing between tax inspectors and corporations.

'I saw people basically demoted or ignored for doing their job, which is collecting tax. But you were promoted for fostering relationships with the corporations and advising them on tax-efficient strategies.'[11]

Brooks thinks a two-tier system emerged at that time in the Inland Revenue. On the ground, stretched tax inspectors were struggling to do their best to chase tax evaders. But above these overworked inspectors at the coalface of avoidance, there was a cadre of senior officials who lunched and socialised with the big-time accountancy firms representing companies like Google and Facebook.

This upper echelon of the HMRC, Brooks believes, was fatally compromised by this association. They were 'in awe' of the very companies they should have been investigating, and were keener to impress than investigate. Not least, because they had an eye on their next job. Even if an individual had wanted to go after a big tax scalp, the culture prohibited it.[12]

Going easy on these big companies meant a shortfall in tax revenue and this shortfall could only be made up by coming down hard on small and medium-sized businesses. Easier targets, who pay up fast when a little brown envelope lands on the mat.

The revolving door between tax inspectors and the big four accountancy firms meant the rules on tax were now being written by people who six months later would be working for an accountancy firm, looking after a big corporate account and advising them on how to get around the very rules that they had written.

When the Cayman Islands Monetary Authority (CIMA) was created in 1997 to police wrongdoings and investigate the criminal behaviour of accountants and lawyers, it was not Whitehall or the Bank of England who drafted the limits of its powers, but Maples and Calder, the biggest law firm on Cayman. They wrote the rules on how to police themselves.[13]

Is it any surprise that the island's global clients, Google, Facebook, Starbucks and Amazon, are being asked to decide for themselves what tax they should be paying? No one else is going to. Ever since John Cumber was called into the Foreign Office and shown a circle on a map, the Cayman Islands waited twenty years to become useful to big business. But when they did, they became indispensable. So how did it eventually happen and what was the deal struck?

A STROKE OF GENIUS: MAKING CAYMAN LEGITIMATE-ISH

It was the Bahamas rather than the Cayman Islands that had initially benefited most from the collapse of the Bretton Woods agreement in 1971. Without it, currency was suddenly free to flow across the globe unscrutinised, and after all the accountants from the Bahamas had moved to Cayman, it was the Cayman Islands that stood to benefit. Tax avoidance was still not widely accepted by the public, let alone government policy, but that was all about to change.

Cayman had hoovered up criminal money, but South American drug barons were not the business the large accounting firms coming to the island wanted. They were keen on long-term relationships with the big corporations who could take advantage of Cayman's location and tax haven potential.

The first thing Cayman did to gain credibility with this kind of business was create its own currency: the Cayman Islands dollar, aligned to the US dollar.

Nevertheless, it was still difficult to attract legitimate business. Alan Markoff of the *Cayman Financial Review*, and author of *The Cayman Islands: From Obscurity to Offshore Giant*, has researched Cayman's switch to legitimacy in the eyes of global business and says it was achieved through a series of key meetings and decisions.

Truman Bodden served as Cayman's acting attorney general in the early 1970s. 'It was difficult getting people to have confidence in three little islands in the Caribbean. There was the stability of having Britain as the mother country, but people wanted to know if they go somewhere to invest, that there is a proper court system to deal with disputes.' In August 1972, Cayman gained a degree of self-governance from Britain with its own Privy Council as the final appellate body, strengthening the sense of an independent and legitimate judiciary in the eyes of potential clients.

Cayman now had legal and currency mechanisms in place that should have attracted bona fide companies from the United States and across the world, and yet still they did not come. It was down to two men to put Cayman on the map as the go-to tax haven location for companies that don't want to be seen to be doing anything wrong.

Marshall Langer was a US tax attorney who was one of the first in America to understand Cayman's potential to US business. According to Cayman accountant Paul Harris, 'Langer was the one who really promoted bank secrecy in those days.' Harris himself travelled to Los Angeles, San Francisco, Atlanta and Miami to give seminars for lawyers and accountants about the benefits of Cayman's 'financial services'. 'I'd tell them the people in the Cayman Islands don't live in thatch huts ... and try to instil a sense of security about the place.'

Cayman was trying to pull off a difficult conjuring trick in those days, simultaneously attempting to attract legitimate big business from the United States by playing up its credentials as a respectable place to invest, while also giving a sly nod that things could be done below the radar if required as well.

In short, it could be legitimate-ish.

One of the first bankers persuaded of Cayman's attractions by Marshall Langer was Montreal-based Jean Doucet, who moved to Grand Cayman to create the International Corporation of the Cayman Islands, later known simply as the International Bank.

According to Alan Markoff, Doucet arrived in Cayman and soon became evangelical in his promotion of Cayman to other American businesspeople. 'Doucet commissioned Marshall Langer and an attorney named W.S. Walker to write a booklet extolling the tax benefits of Cayman. He mailed twenty thousand copies of the pamphlet to potential investors. He spent about $250,000 on printing and mailing it out in 1973 and 1974 alone.' He even made a promotional film, shown to accounting firms and businesses across America, which he financed and distributed himself.

In July 1974, Doucet hosted a lavish party at the Holiday Inn Hotel, Cayman, celebrating the fruits of his labour, with one thousand business guests wooed to the island by his efforts. It was also the launch of his latest venture, Cayman National Bank Ltd. But on 16 September, less than three months later, Doucet's bank collapsed due to a liquidity crisis and his $50 million empire imploded overnight. However, Doucet was nowhere to be seen. He had left for Monaco with his wife on a private jet, three days earlier.

Cayman had only just begun to build its reputation with legitimate business and now faced a damage limitation exercise caused by Cayman's first high-profile scandal. In spring 1974, Cayman's governor, Kenneth Crook, convened a large conference on the island to offer a salvage plan. 'We must seek to convert the concept of tax haven into that of a purely financial centre ... and we must institute and keep under continuous review, the sort of control which is necessary, if we are to attract the right people and maintain the island's position.'

In November 1975, a plan was put into operation. Vassel Johnson, a prominent financial figure both in Cayman government and with the private banking sector, stood up at the Offshore Financial Centre conference in Nassau, Bahamas. Johnson is now widely regarded as the godfather of Cayman's offshore reputation as the number one go-to financial centre, largely as a result of what he was about to suggest.

'The Cayman Islands have never attempted to introduce legislation to attract the sort of business from highly taxed countries,' he said, 'which would tend to promote the local economy at the expense of foreign tax evasion, as we think this is unethical.'

A year before, Governor Kenneth Crook had spoken about developing a policy that would ensure Cayman's growth as a responsible financial centre, not one with a reputation as a haven for criminal activity. Vassel Johnson wished to create a bilateral partnership between the government of the island and the financial services industry called the Financial Community Committee – known as FINCOCO.

FINCOCO would provide a place for a tax strategy for Cayman to be agreed between government and businesses, meeting fortnightly and recommending legislation and refinements to the financial incentives industry, with the focus on turning the reputation of Cayman around. This was important, because Cayman was now in fierce direct competition with other tax havens across the world and needed to look credible with big business in order to win new clients.

Vassel Johnson's role in transforming the fortunes of Cayman is hard to overestimate. FINCOCO was a masterstroke, a deal at once giving a sense of transparency to Cayman's activities while protecting the island's clients from outside scrutiny. It developed mechanisms that would be adopted by other tax havens across the world, something other tax havens were slow to implement themselves. It was Cayman's bid to become top dog, and it succeeded.

SHADOWS BENEATH THE WATER

When I arrive on Grand Cayman, it is very different from the island John Cumber landed on half a century ago. Today, the place feels like an affluent suburb of Florida. Low-rise buildings run along the main road that provides the island's spine: white sandy beaches and turquoise ocean on either side. Mega-cruise ships from Miami arrive daily, dispatching thousands of tourists who buy T-shirts and conch shells with 'I Love Cayman' written on them, before reboarding their ship for a cocktail.

To look at the place, you would not think it was a hub of global finance. There are no gleaming glass towers, like London or Wall Street, but that is the point. Wealth here is hidden. Cayman has capital assets of a trillion dollars, well over 1,500 times Cayman's domestic economy. This single five-mile bar of sand in the ocean has more external assets than Japan, Canada or Italy. It is the number-one legal domicile of choice for the hedge fund industry (sixty per cent of the world's hedge fund managers operate from this one stretch of sand). It is also the number-one destination for asset-backed securities and collateralised debt obligations across the globe.[14]

In other words, Cayman holds all the profits, and all the debt, too, housed in anonymous low-rise banks and offices staffed by casually dressed accountants in Bermuda shorts and flip-flops, who avoid driving showy Ferraris in favour of a Toyota Prius. The thousands of corporations that are registered in Cayman – everyone from IKEA to HSBC, Starbucks to Vodafone, Pepsi to Disney – have no visible presence. Nothing.

I know, because the first thing I did was to look. There is, however, one building tucked away at the end of the beach in which more than twenty thousand companies are registered. In 2008, President Obama singled out Ugland House as 'either the biggest building in the world or the biggest tax scam in the world.'

There are no big gates or security guards. It is all hidden in plain sight. I walk up to the glass doors to have a look inside. A relaxed doorman eventually saunters out to see who I am. 'I wonder if I could have a look inside?'

I am politely told to leave the property, but not before looking though the darkened windows. A lot of desks, but not a single person from those twenty thousand companies sitting at any of them. Cayman euphemistically calls itself a 'financial centre', but this really means it is a giant deposit box with palm trees. A place to hold on to unimaginable sums of money, away from the prying eyes of the world.

It is very strange they have even let me in. After decades of secrecy, including a law forbidding journalists from even asking questions, let alone investigating anything, suddenly they want to open up and show they have nothing to hide. Why? The answer is simple, and it is all to do with business.

Because the race is now on between Western governments to offer the lowest corporation tax, Cayman faces fierce competition. Everyone is vying for attention by offering ever cleverer and more complex financial 'arrangements'. And looking even remotely shady to these global companies no longer cuts it. Cayman is hoping to stay ahead of the game by opening up and showing the world it is legit. In effect, laundering its own name.

Even though Cayman rewrote the rules on being a tax haven,

it comes in at number five on the financial secrecy index of least transparent tax havens.[15] Secrecy that takes the form of opaque financial structures enabling scams like Enron and Parmalat to happen.

Yet Cayman is only number five. That is less secretive than Switzerland (number one) or Singapore (number two). By stealing a march on their competitors through opening up, Cayman hopes to win their business. In 2009, the IMF said the greatest danger to Cayman's future as a tax haven was not governmental interference or even outside investigation, but 'reputational risk' – continuing to look dirty.

But if you ask Caymanians why they think their islands have such a bad reputation, it is not industrial tax avoidance or Pablo Escobar that is mentioned, but a 1993 movie starring Tom Cruise. I thought this was a joke until I had to stop counting how many times people kept mentioning it.

The Firm tells the story of a sharp attorney working for a law firm who comes to realise his bosses are laundering money for the Mafia through guess where. *The Firm* cemented a reputation that Caymanians say was unfair to begin with. Now they want to clean the slate. Hence my invite. Unfortunately, the week does not start well on the PR front. Google are caught siphoning eighty per cent of their profits through tax havens. Apple admit to moving $74 billion offshore, paying two per cent tax. I decide it is best to cough and not mention these headlines.

I am dutifully introduced to the island's governor, a polite woman in a pink hat who lives in a big colonial house, with whom I have tea. I am introduced to the elected premier, a polite if brusque man who clearly wishes he was not talking to me, and to various prominent business people, including John Cumber's grandson, who are all unfailingly charming. The message is clear: we are an open book, confident in the knowledge I will not find anything.

The place is a cross between a Caribbean island and Britain in the 1950s. I am given free rein to wander about asking anyone anything I want, as long as it is not about the corporations registering their profits here. I find out from a police officer that stealing a coconut from a neighbour's garden can result in a prison sentence. He doesn't explain why he is not downtown arresting the accountants responsible for laundering over a hundred million dollars for FIFA officials, and it seems rude to ask.

Once a year, the islanders put on ceremonial garb for the annual Queen's birthday parade, involving a brass band and prize giving. It is like being in a country fête in Somerset. Accountants turn out to the governor's garden party, where they eat cucumber sandwiches in a heat of 100 degrees.

I ask one of the accountants at the garden party about the FIFA revelations and he smiles. 'It's a bit old school, isn't it?' He is right. Nowadays, Cayman is simply the way business is done, and there is no need to go the criminal route, when the legal options for hiding money are so infinite. Yet criminality still takes place, and the world shrugs its shoulders.[16]

In the noughties, US, Dutch and British companies took advantage of Cayman because their governments enabled them to use it as a direct investment conduit, but now Brazil and China do the same. In 2000, accountancy firm PricewaterhouseCoopers devised a legal 'innovation' for Chinese corporations to list publicly abroad, so getting access to foreign capital and circumventing China's restrictions on foreign investments. It is called a VIE (variable interest entity), a variation on the holding company. And their number-one target was the US.

In 2014, Chinese e-commerce giant Alibaba raised a record $25 billion with its initial public offering (IPO) in the US, using PricewaterhouseCoopers' holding company innovation. The ICIJ (International Consortium of Investigative Journalists) have revealed that certain wealthy relatives of China's Communist Party elite also use VIEs to create shell companies in tax havens.[17]

Cayman is known to the world for tax avoidance, but its real function lies many layers beneath clever accountancy. And it is a big one. Cayman's biggest secret is that it provides the mechanism for foreign companies to buy up US companies and industrial infrastructure, without appearing to be foreign. And the magic euphemism is 'portfolio investment'.

In 2015, Cayman reported 'portfolio investment' assets to the IMF of $61 billion. Jan Fichtner at the University of Amsterdam drilled into the figures and put the real assets at $2,574 billion – forty-two times greater than reported. This huge discrepancy is down to one thing: reported assets exclude hedge funds. Derived liabilities (the real figures) do not. Hedge funds are at the absolute heart of below-the-radar Cayman, which explains why sixty per cent of the world's hedge funds operate here.

And their primary role is to buy up America, without America realising. On the face of it, the true 'nationality' of any portfolio investment is impossible to establish, because investment instruments cross-multiply jurisdictions, sometimes over dozens of countries. The only way to understand how they actually work is to look at two basic numbers: the money going in, and the money coming out.

This is called 'inward' and 'outward' investment and the biggest discrepancy in these figures on Cayman is with Japan: in 2015, $51 billion in, and $558 billion out. But mysteriously, less than a tenth of the Japanese portfolio investment of over half a trillion dollars went back to Japan.

Why? Because it was used in the US to make below-the-radar deals. Hong Kong and Japanese investors use Cayman as a conduit for portfolio investment into the huge American equity market. Cayman acts as a giant hedge, protecting Japanese investors buying into the US from being found out.

But these portfolio investments are also being used to hoover up opportunities in emerging markets, and politically sensitive China. Cayman is a hub for the buying and selling of the globe. Cayman 'intersects', Fichtner says, 'the nexus between Pax Americana, the Anglo alliance and Greater China sub-network.' Five countries alone are responsible for ninety per cent of

Cayman's portfolio investment: the USA ($1,206 billion), Japan ($558 billion), Hong Kong ($343 billion), the UK ($91 billion) and Luxembourg ($83 billion). But don't be fooled by the numbers. The companies that appear to operate through these countries do not. These jurisdictions are merely convenient temporary vehicles, like Cayman, till a better offer comes along.

And post-Brexit, post-Trump, two have come along. Britain has given up making anything. The former Chancellor of the Exchequer, George Osborne, said in February 2017 that the economy *per se* is clearly 'no longer a priority' for the government. By this, he means that low tax has become the main plank of economic survival in a post-Brexit world. Once we were a manufacturing economy. Then we became a service economy. Now we are a tax haven.

In the US, Trump faces two ways. Historically low interest rates provide a once-in-a-generation opportunity to rebuild the infrastructure of America *à la* Roosevelt's New Deal. But the temptation to provide the lowest taxes on earth to corporations in Trump's America and out-Cayman the Cayman Islands might prove too tempting to resist. Meanwhile the infrastructure of America is indeed being rebuilt. Just by the Chinese.

In 2016, two thousand jobs were created by Fuyao Glass in Moraine, Ohio. Eight years earlier, on 23 December 2008, the last General Motors truck rolled off the production line at GM's factory in Moraine. The very same factory now being resurrected by Fuyao Glass. When that last truck rolled out two days before Christmas, Moraine seemed finished as a town. The closure of the GM plant symbolised the end of American manufacturing. The rust belt was not simply a term for the death of the heartland of America, but shorthand for the end of the US as a global superpower.

Yet eight years on, the jobs are back. Moraine is heartland Trump country, yet those very same voters applaud the return of jobs through the Chinese glass giant. And there is no contradiction in their minds in holding both positions.

If Cayman becomes the instrument by which Chinese and Japanese companies are able to buy up America by stealth, but return manufacturing jobs in the process, then a simplistic moral position on the role of tax havens and the 'patriotism' of job creation becomes more difficult to sustain.

Railing against offshore is like railing at the ocean. It is there, and there is no changing it. Beneath that blue ocean, dark shapes move – the corporations waiting to come in. What started as a relatively simple mechanism for tax avoidance on a sandbar has mutated into an impossibly complex financial mechanism, with the moral complexities to go with it.

Offshore is how the world works, and this total global system operates beyond the control of any one government.

'How does Cayman benefit the British public?' I asked the governor of Cayman on my final day there. 'I'm sorry, I don't . . .' she was lost for words. 'I'm going to have to think . . .' The governor consulted with her press officer, struggling to find the right answer. It had clearly never occurred to her that such a childishly simple question would ever be asked.

It was a tough one to answer. How does Cayman in any way benefit Britain, taking billions of pounds in tax revenue out of the pocket of government and thus contributing directly to the under-resourcing of basic services?

I have an answer, even if she didn't. Cayman has shown us the way forward. If you reduce income tax to nothing you need to tax everything else. A packet of fish fingers costs £5. A monthly rent for a corrugated shack is more than a three-storey house in central London.[18] What you save on direct tax, you pay in indirect taxes. The only people who can afford these massively hiked indirect taxes are the wealthiest, for whom the cost of daily living is irrelevant. For everyone else, life is harder, so greater inequality is the price.

I asked the governor one more question. 'Could Cayman be shut down?' She looked shocked. 'What do you mean?' Could the British government shut you down? 'Good God, no. Cayman is an independent state.'

I put the same question to the premier. 'Ultimate sovereignty,' he told me, 'lies in London, with the British government.'

So, no one is responsible. Cayman operates in a very convenient no-man's-land, outside the remit of anyone. It is truly offshore in the way the entire banking system is offshore: operating somewhere out there in the middle of the sea, where dark shapes swim beneath the surface.

CHAPTER FOUR
WEALTH: INEQUALITY AS A BUSINESS OPPORTUNITY

The Deal: Tobias Levkovich and the Citibank
  presentation to the Bank's Biggest Clients
Aim: To show these clients why global inequality was
  widening dramatically and how to take advantage of
  this inequality to make money
Where: Citigroup Headquarters, 399 Park Avenue,
  Manhattan
When: 2006

Take a golf buggy that can carry eight people. Then put the eight wealthiest people on earth on that buggy. You would have Mexican telecoms mogul Carlos Slim (worth $75.5 billion) riding up front. Next to him, Bill Gates ($75 billion). On the middle seats, Zara founder Amancio Ortega ($67 billion), Warren Buffett ($60.8 billion) and Jeff Bezos of Amazon ($45.2 billion). A row back, Facebook's Mark Zuckerberg ($44.6 billion) and Oracle's Larry Ellison ($43.6 billion), with Michael Bloomberg (a mere $40 billion) in the bucket seat at the back.

These eight people now own the equivalent of fifty per cent of the planet's wealth with a combined worth of $451.7 billion. Eight people with as much money as 3.75 billion people, who also happen to be the poorest fifty per cent of the earth's population.[1]

This polarisation of global wealth has become human global warming. A seismic, irreversible process, widening and deepening like a tectonic fissure. Should we care? Overall global poverty is reducing and, as the Institute of Economic Affairs argues, the widening gap is the price you pay for the planet as a whole getting richer.[2] Whether you think it matters or not, the fact is that widening inequality is happening and to paraphrase Arnold Schwarzenegger, it doesn't give a damn whether you believe in it or not.[3]

The argument is nothing new. The first systematic attempt to understand inequality came from an Italian sociologist and statistician named Corrado Gini, who worked under Mussolini in Fascist Italy. Gini was a polymath intellectual and believed statistics, sociology, demography and biology could be merged to create a grand scientific understanding of human behaviour.

In 1908, he published a paper on natal sex ratios, presenting evidence that a couple may be more likely to produce a boy or girl depending on certain hereditary factors. Though he was initially a collaborator and friend of Mussolini's, they fell out as the Fascist regime began to lean on Gini's work as academic evidence of its ideology.

Gini was above all an eccentric follower of his own path. He was a eugenicist and firm believer in using eugenics to 'improve' the human race, as were many intellectuals of the left and right in the 1920s and 1930s. But he also had an insatiably inquiring mind. He led an expedition to study the Karaites in Poland, a sect of Judaism that holds the Tanakh alone as the supreme authority of Jewish religious law, because he genuinely wanted to understand Tanakh Judaism from the perspective of its scholars.

In 1912, as a way of measuring global inequality, he created the Gini coefficient, which he outlined in his famous paper 'Variability and Mutability'. A value of zero represents the most equal society – one in which every member owns the same amount – and the value of one the most unequal, one in which all wealth is controlled by a single person. The place a country falls on the zero to one scale is calculated by measuring the statistical dispersal of income of a nation's residents. The Gini coefficient became the standard by which inequality would be measured for the next century. While it is now widely criticised as an overly crude measure, it did make a reasonable stab at measuring relative and absolute poverty.

In 2017, Oxford University academics used the Gini coefficient to estimate global inequality trends in the twenty-first century and concluded that while overall global inequality was reducing – the poor were getting less poor across the planet – absolute inequality was rising dramatically.

Dr Laurence Roope of the Nuffield Department of Population Health at Oxford summarised their findings: 'Over the past forty years, over one billion people around the world have been lifted out of poverty, driven largely by very substantial growth in income in countries such as China and India. This rise has been accompanied by a striking rise in absolute inequality.'

As one of the report's authors, Finn Tarp, explained: 'Take the case of two people in Vietnam in 1986. One person has an income of US$1 a day and the other person has an income of US$10 a day. With the kind of economic growth that Vietnam has seen over the past thirty years, the first person would have now $8 a day while the second would have US$80 a day. So if we focus on 'absolute' differences, inequality has gone up, but if you focus on 'relative' differences, inequality between these two people would have remained the same.'

The world has never been richer, the wealth held in fewer hands, and the gap between the rich and poor wider. But in March 2006, long before inequality was on the wider public radar or viewed as a disaster by the IMF, UN and the OECD, a group of analysts saw the whole thing coming and did something quite mind-blowing: they decided to treat coming global inequality as a business opportunity to be exploited and widened.

These men were going to figure out how to make money from

the greatest divergence in history and in so doing, turbocharge inequality and make it a self-fulfilling prophecy. If the chasm between rich and poor was a seismic widening problem, that meant it was also a gift-horse like no other. Before 'the 99% and the 1%' became a slogan on the banners at Occupy, they had already coined the term in a boardroom.

THE HOURGLASS

Tobias Levkovich is a very smart man. He meets me in a board-room overlooking the Hudson River on the forty-ninth floor of the world's fourth-largest bank, Citi, where he also happens to run 'Global Strategy'. He tells me about a book he loves: *The Leviathan* by Thomas Hobbes. A political treatise based on the premise that human beings will do whatever they can get away with, unless strong rules prevent them from doing it.

When not reading seventeenth-century political philosophy, Tobias likes to think about the world deeply, differently and a lot. And in 2006, Tobias held in his pocket a photograph of the future that, if he chose to share it with his clients, was going to make them a lot of money. A very large amount indeed.

Tobias is one of the most important bankers on earth: he is responsible for identifying the plate-tectonic shifts in the way the global economy is moving, and advising Citi and Wall Street to invest not merely millions or billions, but trillions of dollars in whatever he thinks is going to happen next.

In 2006, Tobias spotted something big. Three Citi colleagues – Ajay Kapur, Niall Macleod and Narendra Singh – had written an internal equity strategy report entitled 'Revisiting Plutonomy: The Rich Getting Richer'.[4] In it they argued that global wealth was polarising, not merely a little or a lot, but in an unfathomable way that would eclipse anything seen in history.

'We talk about the one per cent, but to get technical, we're actually talking the zero-point-one per cent,' Tobias tells me.

'We've always had the haves and have-nots, but now we would have the haves, the have-nots and the have-yachts.'

Tobias predicted – to the incredulity of his colleagues – that by 2015, then a decade away, the one hundred richest people would own the same as half the world's population. It is actually eight: the guys sitting on the golf buggy.

Tobias dropped his bombshell in 2006 in the very boardroom where I meet him,[5] before a sea of stony-faced men and women in business suits. These people represented the biggest companies on earth: oil, steel, construction and hedge fund giants; food and chemical multinationals; supermarkets; aviation constructors; pharmaceutical companies and car manufacturers; mobile and internet providers on every continent.

'The coming decade will be marked by polarisation and social unrest,' Tobias said. 'A direct consequence of growing economic inequality.' The clients coughed and looked down at their notepads. 'Many will be worried by this. We at the bank worry less.'

I wondered why Tobias said that: 'We at the bank worry less.'

'You can't sit there and say, this doesn't meet everyone's social happiness criteria. I have to deliver results or they're going to take their money and give it to someone else. It's not cynical. It's practical. That is our job. We are supposed to make them money.' Tobias predicted correctly at that meeting that inequality between different countries in the coming years would lessen as inequality within each country grew, and this was where he gave his corporate clients a chillingly simple analogy: an hourglass.

Every country will come over time, he said, to look like an hourglass. At the top, the super-rich global elite, to whom you will be able to sell Learjets and Bentleys. At the bottom, the global poor, to whom there will be unimaginable new opportunities to sell poverty products: payday loans, zero-hour contracts, high-interest credit. As stress increases for the poor, gambling and alcohol will once again become boom industries. Pound shops and discounting will become huge, as people fail to make ends meet.

It was a breathtaking vision, but I was intrigued by the hour-glass. What was the deal with the tapered bit in the middle? 'Oh, that's the middle class. They will be squeezed out of existence. They will cease to have any purchasing power, and thus be over as an investment opportunity,' Tobias told me cheerily.

In fact, the middle class would be subsumed into the lumpen poor. They would sink into the lower globe of the hourglass, but continue to live for a period of time beyond their means, desperately clinging on to the tropes of being middle class (such as foreign holidays or a new car). Delusions of status.

To put it in context, an average Lamborghini costs £180,000 – the same price as the average British house. If you were one of Citi's clients faced with a dissolving middle class, would you flog a Lamborghini to the one per cent, who see £180,000 as loose change, or become a mega-landlord owning ten thousand slum properties? Both, but you would not bother with the middle class.

In Tobias's long-term view, the bottom orb of the hourglass would come to represent one giant, new global class: all of us, including the dissolved middle class. What we now know as the ninety-nine per cent, living one payday away from broke. The so-called 'precariat'.

As Tobias painted this brave new world to Citi's clients, he noticed something in the room. Total silence. 'You could have heard a pin drop.' At first Tobias thought this might simply be shock at the apocalyptic future he was predicting. 'It must be true if Citi are saying it, right?' But then he realised it was something else. There was an expression of awe on their faces as it began to dawn just how much money there was to be made.

In the two years between the Citi presentation and the 2008 crash, the companies in the room diversified their portfolios exactly as Citi advised, focusing on businesses at both ends of the hourglass: high-end luxury for the rich and poverty products for the poor.

But it was only when the crash happened that things really took off for Citi's clients. Tobias's prediction had come true faster than anyone could have dreamt.

THE *HUNGER GAMES* FOR REAL

The people on my golf buggy all think inequality is terrible. They say so all the time, as do the heads of the IMF, the World Bank, the Bank of England, the Fed and every other financial institution that spent the last twenty years putting in place the mechanisms that allowed inequality to open up like a chasm.

In 2015, I interviewed French economist Thomas Piketty, the author of *Capital in the Twenty-First Century*, who believes that selling to the rich and poor spheres of the hourglass is merely a by-product of inequality: the underlying process that drives its perpetuation is wealth extraction from the poorest to the wealthiest.

This, Piketty argues, is uniquely dangerous for society as a whole, because it tests society's reason for existing. It pushes the contract of shared rules to the edge, which is when society begins to break down. So, what can be done? Piketty shrugged his shoulders. 'Perhaps retool the IMF, so it has transnational jurisdiction to prevent multinationals escaping their legal obligations.' A kind of International Task Force like *Thunderbirds*, able to swoop on unsuspecting corporations and slapping them with a fine for tax avoidance. In short, as likely as wooden puppets saving the world.

Inequality is here to stay and we now live daily and acceptingly with its extremes. In London, it is possible to get a facial in a Knightsbridge beauty salon with a throwaway liquid gold mask and a caviar massage. A top-of-the-hourglass product. Treatments cost up to £30,000. Some clients come three or four times a month. The staff who apply the gold mask and caviar massage are sometimes on, or just above, the minimum wage. If they need a payday loan to make ends meet, they are using a poverty product from the bottom of the hourglass.

In Newham, East London, a group of single mums living in secure housing were evicted by the council in 2015 in order to make way for luxury flats.[6] When they went to see the mayor, they were told, 'If you can't afford to live in Newham, you can't afford to live in Newham. What do you want me to do about it?'[7]

They refused to leave and the police were called, yet the officers themselves baulked at the idea of forcibly removing women and children who had committed no crime. In the stand-off, the single mums began squatting in a disused community centre.

Less than a stone's throw from the centre, luxury glass-fronted flats have risen up, standing largely empty because they were bought off-plan by foreign investors to tie up huge amounts of surplus capital. These investors do not even see them as flats, but 'security boxes'. The mums watched these empty mausoleums of wealth being constructed as the power and water were cut from their own properties, forcing them out. They could see right into the luxury flats from their squatted building, but from the luxury flats you see only sweeping panoramic views across London, in which the grittiness of the unfolding poverty below is simply part of the brutalist, urban picaresque.

This cohabitation of the two orbs of the hourglass is nothing new. In 1845, Friedrich Engels wrote about Victorian Manchester in his *Condition of the Working Class in England*: 'The members of the money aristocracy can take the shortest road through the middle of labouring districts . . . without ever seeing they are in the midst of grimy misery.'[8] In Mike Davis's *Planet of Slums*, the eradication of the poor from view is catalogued across the globe – from slum clearances in Lagos to the displacement of 1.5 million people in Shanghai to make way for a reskinned city of glittering wealth.[9]

Extreme divergence is happening everywhere fast, but in London, it is acutely visible. If London were a separate country, it would be the seventh richest in the world. Yet twenty-eight per cent of Londoners live officially in poverty, and two-thirds are 'just managing' to survive. There has been £80 billion in austerity cuts since the 2008 crash – by neat coincidence, the same amount given to bankers in bonuses.[10]

For most people in Britain, wages have stagnated for ten years and remain at pre-crash levels. The average family earn £429 a week, as they did in 2006. But for the richest thousand people, their pay has more than doubled over the same period: from £200 billion to £500 billion.[11]

As the world's super-rich poured into London post the 2008 banking crisis to take advantage of 'quantitative easing' (money printed to save the banks, ninety-five per cent of which actually went directly to the bubble of the one-per-cent richest),[12] the fear for London was that it would become 'socially cleansed' of the poor.

London would become two cities. A mega-sprawl like Mexico City, Cape Town, Shanghai, Lagos, Los Angeles, or Capitol in *The Hunger Games*: an inner sanctum populated by the super-rich, living a gilded life of darkly lit exclusive restaurants, week-ends in Monaco on the super-yacht, skiing in Gstaad, shopping in Dubai for $100,000 handbags, and perpetual private-jet ('PJ') transit. This roped-off state of 'Richistan'[13] floats above and beyond the masses like a fluffy champagne cloud, but is uniformly identifiable as the same place, with the same brands and sched-ule, wherever you are on the planet.

And the other half of the city is an outer sprawl of the massed poor, bussed in to service these new masters. People living one payday away from destitution and so stressed by this precarious-ness, they die ten years before the rich. The *Hunger Games* anal-ogy is serious. In 2014, a report into global inequality part-funded by NASA's Goddard Space Flight Center concluded that a 'Hunger Games scenario of inequality is likely on current trends by 2030'.[14]

One can already see social cleansing in operation in every crevice of London. I live in the centre, and my local mini-super-market is a microcosm of inequality. Seventy-five per cent of the customers are fast-rising career people from Europe and the US

in their mid-twenties and early thirties working for big corporations such as Google, banks in the City, or digital companies
clustered round 'Silicon Roundabout'. They come into the
minimart wearing hoodies and tracksuit bottoms after a run, buy
some milk or quinoa salad, and leave.

There are eight staff members, who work twelve-hour shifts,
employed on zero-hour contracts. They are similar in age to the
customers, but their lives are very different. Three of them live at
least a ninety-minute journey from the minimart. One lives in Essex;
another in Luton – thirty miles away. They cannot afford to rent in
central London, but cannot afford to give up their job either. They
travel so far to and from work that they earn barely anything.

Yet my minimart is actually an aberration. In 2015, Hannah
Aldridge and Tom MacInnes of the New Policy Institute analysed
population movement in London in the wake of cuts to housing
benefit and discovered something unexpected.[15]

The *Hunger Games* two-city scenario understates what is
happening. The reality is a single city in which the rich and poor
coexist in the same space, but are invisible to each other. The
poor do not aggravate the rich, but defer to them – in public
spaces and wherever they intersect (like my minimart). The poor
have become transparent and instead of interacting, the rich
power-blank any awkward situation. It is *The Hunger Games* with
workers from the districts moving like ghosts among the rich.

So why aren't the poor moving out, if they cannot afford to
live in London? Moving means destroying everything. Key to
surviving on a low income with highly precarious work is a social
network of friends and family upon whom you can rely, allowing
you to juggle these precarious jobs. This cannot easily be recreated elsewhere. Neither can cobbled-together childcare, hard-
won school places, nor the cluster of casual, local, low-paid jobs
that together make up a barely survivable income. The 'working
poor' cannot afford to leave.

While better-paid people in offices hot-desk, the working
poor 'hot-bed'. This means sharing one room and sleeping in

shifts in the same bed. A childcare worker whom I met shift-slept in the same bed with another woman working nights. They each had their own sheets, and took eight-hour shifts. Childcare worker: 10 p.m. – 6 a.m.; woman working nights: 6 a.m. – 2 p.m. The maths would suggest they underutilised the potential of the bed by failing to monetise between 2 p.m. and 10 p.m. Perhaps there was a third woman they didn't tell me about.

The staff at my minimart are atypical. They moved out. The majority of the working poor living in London have to cut back on food and heating to meet the rent. They are trapped, holding on to a rising balloon of costs, but unable to move for fear it will be worse elsewhere. And they are growing exponentially in numbers in the centre of London, at the very moment they cannot afford to live there. As Aldridge and MacInnes conclude, the poor are being absorbed to service an insatiable machine of wealth, and it is a symbiotic relationship.

Notice how freely and unashamedly I use the words 'rich' and 'poor'. Thirty years ago, both were derogatory terms. No one worries about that anymore. Becoming rich is not shaming. It is not a term of abuse as it once was on the left. It is now a universal aspiration. And with rising household debt and low wages, the fear that poverty could tap you on the shoulder at any moment is real.

As absolute global wealth rises (very poor countries becoming slightly less poor and thus categorised as richer), widening inequality within each country is exploding, and the two are intertwined.

In *The Great Convergence*, Richard Baldwin at Harvard argues that a combination of free-flowing information technology and low globalised labour costs is making countries more equal: poorer countries growing as the richer ones stagnate, until eventually we are all the same. Between 1820 and 1990, the share of the world's income going to wealthy countries soared from twenty per cent to almost seventy per cent. But in the last twenty-five years, that share has fallen back dramatically to where it was in 1900.[16]

Countries across the world, regardless of their starting-gun wealth, are all in a race to become the same: Malawi, Spain, the United States, the UK, Uzbekistan. We are all morphing inexorably into the same kind of country with the same basic social stratification, defined by yawning divergence. We are all becoming equally unequal. If Corrado Gini were with us today, he'd be working on calculating the coefficient at which this machine breaks.

WHO STOLE THE PARACHUTE?

In 2008, the banks crashed. The answer was quantitative easing (QE). The US Federal Reserve, led by Ben Bernanke, bought bonds worth $3.7 trillion with money it had 'printed'. The Fed didn't print physical notes – it was electronically created – but 'printing money' became the colloquial shorthand for QE.

This is how QE works in principle: in a crisis, printing money increases the overall amount of usable funds in the financial system, helping to restore liquidity. This in turn allows banks to lend, businesses to invest and consumers to spend. It is CPR for the economy, kick-starting a recovery.

That's the theory. When interest rates are close to zero, as they have been for most of the last decade, there's an argument that some QE also serves a purpose in creating some limited upward pressure on prices, stimulating growth. But not too much upward pressure. Inflation is seen as one of the dangers of QE.

In October 2014, Janet Yellen, the successor to Bernanke at the Fed, called time on QE for the United States. It was seen to have done its job. In combination with low interest rates, QE had freed capital and encouraged a steady rise in risk appetite, helping US stocks rebound since 2009.

But growth had stalled, and stubbornly remained stalled. Even though interest rates had remained at an historic low, Yellen began entertaining the idea that interest rates might have to go below zero. In 2016, at the annual economic symposium at Jackson Hole, Wyoming, she outlined a plan for negative interest rates that could effectively force banks to lend money. With negative interest rates, banks would pay to park their own money in their vaults. Anything but lending and spending would not be an option.

Negative interests were discussed in relation to another economic crisis, like 2008, but continued economic stagnation is a slow-motion crisis. Negative interest rates have already been employed in Sweden, Switzerland and Taiwan.

So did QE in combination with low interest rates function as intended? In the immediate aftermath of the 2008 crisis, QE as CPR kept the system alive and prevented a deeper recession, but long-term, QE vanished. So where did it go? I ask Tobias Levkovich. 'Ninety-five percent of quantitative easing, sold as bailing out the whole economy, went to the top of the hourglass.'

QE covered a multitude of sins. But the biggest beneficiaries were the banks – with twenty or thirty times leveraged balance sheets. According to Marshall Wace, chairman of a London-based hedge fund, 'asset managers and hedge funds benefited, too.'

QE also enabled the one per cent to be able to invest in the poverty products from Citibank's hourglass that would widen inequality still further. In 2016, Scott Helfman, a Citigroup spokesman, said the bank does not comment on its relationship with clients, but *Bloomberg Businessweek* obtained a leaked copy of its favoured 'secret client list' kept on the equity research desk. At the very top is a handful of hedge fund giants: Millennium, Citadel, Surveyor Capital, Point72 and Carlson Capital. The kind of super-class clients who receive advanced models and analytics, such as Tobias's hourglass model.

In 2006, the investment advice to diversify into luxury brands and services catering to the top of the hourglass was complemented by poverty products for the bottom orb – extended loans on cars, furniture, holidays, property, and bridging loans to cover heating and food bills. And this market depended for its growth on the acceleration of debt.

'Debt is really the key to the whole thing,' according to London School of Economics economist David Graeber. 'The finance industry and the debt industry are really the same thing. To a large extent, "finance" really just means "other people's debts". They're simply trading our debts with each other.'[17]

But there was another option. Economist Anatole Kaletsky of the Institute for New Economic Thinking says QE was a fork in the road, and put forward a radical alternative that has gained traction on the left and right.[18] Had QE not gone to the banks but to everyone else in the form of a one-off payment, every household in Britain and the United States would have received a check for £22, 647.06p (or $30,600). This money would have been spent on holidays, fridges and cars, rebooting consumerism and a Keynesian boom.

Helicopter money was first mooted by the prophet of supply side, the Nobel-winning economist Milton Friedman in his 1969 paper 'The Optimum Quantity of Money'. 'Suppose one day a helicopter flies over this community and drops an additional $1,000 in bills from the sky, which is, of course, hastily collected by members of the community. Let us suppose further that everyone is convinced that this is a unique event which will never be repeated.' Friedman also believed money could be given directly to business rather than go through banks in order to maximise the 'potency' of money, especially at a moment when banks are caught in a liquidity trap.

Ben Bernanke revived the idea of helicopter money in November 2002 in a speech about heeding the lessons of deflation in Japan. 'Keynes once semi-seriously proposed, as an anti-deflationary measure, that the government fill bottles with currency and bury them in mine shafts to be dug up by the public ... essentially equivalent to Milton Friedman's famous helicopter drop of money.'

QE happened but the radical version, dropping money in people's accounts, was vetoed. Raghuram Rajan of the Reserve Bank of India said people would not spend the money. They would hold on to it. Claudio Borio of the Bank for International Settlements said there was 'no such thing as a free lunch' and helicopter money was legally problematic, blurring the lines between fiscal and monetary policy. Bundesbank president Jens Weidmann argued that it 'would tear gaping holes in central bank balance sheets.'

Parachuting money to families had been endorsed by economists across the political spectrum from neoliberal thinkers such as Deirdre McCloskey to Keynesians like Kaletsky, Eric Lonergan and Simon Wren-Lewis. But it was opposed by the big guns of the monetary mechanisms in the United States and in Europe. In a letter to parachute-money advocate and member of the European Parliament José Fernandes, the European Central Bank explained that 'legal complexities could still arise if the scheme could be seen as the ECB financing an obligation of the public sector *vis à vis* third parties, as this would also violate the prohibition of monetary financing.' The use of direct payments as a substitute for welfare payments was also vetoed. There was, however, a politically expedient solution: more debt, which – David Graeber argues –was the plan all along.[19]

'Our indebtedness, our addiction and entrapment by debt, fuelled London and New York as finance centres in the wake of the crash. It was at the heart of the recovery of finance, and our debt was the engine. So what you see after the crash are some fairly intentional government policies which are designed to guarantee most people are in debt.' Household debt in Britain now stands at a record £350 billion.

Tobias Levkovich's hourglass prediction back in 2006 is now a reality. But global inequality is about to go up several notches. Tobias admits even he could not have predicted some of the opportunities created at either end of the hourglass: pure Canadian oxygen pumped into super-rich apartments in Shanghai, or a debt collector in Newcastle who will extend your payment deadline in exchange for information on neighbours committing benefit fraud.

Citi's 2006 report was a prophetic document. No one outside that boardroom on the forty-ninth floor of Citi knew it was coming, but the deals it enabled were going to change the lives of millions of people walking the streets below.

WHY THE MIDDLE CLASS MATTER

One of the research papers mentioned in the footnotes of the Citi report was by a then unknown post-graduate student at the London School of Economics called Thomas Piketty, who was writing a dissertation on inequality – the dissertation that ten years later became *Capital in the Twenty-First Century*.

I asked Piketty, now the world's most celebrated economist, about the hourglass and the part of it that is fast tapering to extinction – the middle class.[20] Why does it matter that the middle class will cease to exist?

'The middle class is very important for the economy because they have been the means by which it's been possible to develop mass consumption and mass investment in construction.' The opportunity to become middle class in the 1950s and 1960s was what drove greater equality and distributed wealth evenly throughout society, reaching a high watermark in 1976. The year, according to opinion polls, when Britain was happiest.

'But the middle class has begun to shrink in the last twenty years,' Piketty says. 'And this is a major threat to democracies if it continues shrinking in the coming decades.'

Piketty thinks the death of the middle class will leave society as a whole with no way back. Between 1945 and 1978, wealth was more evenly distributed throughout society than at any other time in history. A thirty-year aberration of equality sandwiched between two periods of huge inequality: the 1930s and now.

And the reason for this was that the middle class had the means to own private property. Starting in the 1930s, interrupted by the war, but then vastly expanding in the 1950s, as a huge building programme by successive Labour and Conservative governments enabled millions of people to buy their own homes for the first time. It was the dream my immigrant grandfather followed as he moved out of the poverty of Kentish Town to the clean air and neatly trimmed hedges of suburbia.

Yet since 1996, that dream has dissolved as home ownership reversed. Widening inequality has coincided with the stagnation of wages and the consequent end of access by the young to the property ladder. If my grandparents aged twenty-five were looking to buy now, they would be stuck in the slums, lucky to cobble even a monthly rent together.

'Are we going to continue in the direction of a shrinking middle class?' Piketty asks. 'It's difficult to know how far this will go. What we know for sure is that in recent years, what we've observed in Britain and other countries is that the wealth of the top wealth holders – billionaires – is rising much faster than average wealth and much faster than the size of the economy. You can see that if this continues for several decades more, the share going to the middle class will decline.'

In years to come, renting – not ownership – will become the norm. The family that rents is £561,000 worse off over its lifetime than one that buys (it is £1.36 million worse off in London). In 2013, rents were going up five times faster than salaries.[21]

And this will make it virtually impossible to reverse inequality, because the middle class (and those aspiring to become middle class) will have lost their primary means of wealth accumulation. The reason there will be no going back for us as a society is because the hourglass will be structurally entrenched.

'How unequal will we become?' Piketty asks. 'On these trends, it looks pretty frightening.' But if you disenfranchise the middle class, you are also dealing with a highly combustible force. A contented middle class do nothing, but if they are either scared for their future security or growing greedy on a rising economic tide, they will drive revolution.

In Russia in 1917, an impatient and newly emboldened bourgeoisie drove the provisional government that replaced the tsar, which in turn was overthrown by the Bolsheviks. In Paris in 1968, middle-class intellectuals and organised labour nearly toppled President Charles de Gaulle (but famously didn't). In both cases, a disgruntled if ambivalent middle class was at the heart of the mobilisation.

Nick Hanauer lives in Seattle and was one of the first investors in Amazon. He is now worth $6 billion, and sees the hollowing of the middle class in the new hourglass model of society as a threat to capitalism. 'Capitalism, the greatest economic system ever created, does need some inequality, just like plants do need some water to grow. But in precisely the same way that too much water kills plants, too much inequality kills capitalism by drowning the middle class.'

Hanauer stands in a modest office with a spectacular view of Puget Sound, watching sailing boats darting across the water. 'In the middle ages, inequality was not a problem. You grew up expecting the world to be unequal. He's a peasant. He's a king. That's how it works. But when you live in a modern capitalist culture that encourages everyone to have more and to believe you can have it, then equality becomes a much bigger problem. You can't have what other people have and this is the cause of discontent. Capitalism has bred resentment, and the equality of opportunity it promised hasn't happened.' [22]

Hanauer has a personal stake. He is worried that when this happens, the massed ranks at the bottom of the hourglass will be coming for him. 'Are the pitchforks coming? Maybe not tomorrow, but for sure they will come. You show me a highly unequal society and I will show you either a revolution or a one-party state.'

NO ONE WOULD REMEMBER THE GOOD SAMARITAN IF HE'D ONLY HAD GOOD INTENTIONS. HE HAD MONEY AS WELL.

In 2007 the Ministry of Defence was worried, and asked Rear Admiral Chris Parry to write a ninety-page report on what a military response should be to mass civil disobedience.[23] The MoD had identified growing inequality as the fuel that would light the fire. In 2011, it came true as Britain's major cities erupted in the worst rioting since the 1980s. The MoD had gazed into a crystal ball and been right, just as Citi had been.

I met Rear Admiral Parry in Haringey, North London, where some of the fiercest rioting took place, and asked him what his report had predicted. 'That this was waiting to happen. When enough people say, "I don't have a stake in society," they will bust out. They'll reject capitalism and the market, and take action into their own hands.' Parry and the MoD's findings were not welcome in Whitehall, who were not interested in army people talking like angst-ridden social workers. The army were ignored, and only called upon by government when the riots actually started.

The deal Tobias Levkovich did with Citi's corporate clients in 2006 may have fuelled the inequality the MoD report predicted would ignite civil disobedience. Citi did not create it. But the chasm of inequality we face today has a founding stone, and 6 January 1980 at 12 p.m. was when it was laid, in a two-minute section of a forty-six-minute interview.

A deal had been just struck between Margaret Thatcher and the British electorate, and they were about to find out what this deal meant. The newly elected Prime Minister sat down for her first ever interview as premier with *Weekend World* presenter Brian Walden,[24] the sharpest political journalist of his time and as it would turn out, the most prophetic.

Mrs Thatcher's government were convinced that the solution to the recession they faced was to lower taxes dramatically for the richest one per cent. A strategy that depended for its success on wealth trickling down to the rest of society – as Arthur Laffer had predicted with his curve drawn on a napkin. But at what price? Walden asked:

Walden: Is the price, Prime Minister, for our economic recovery and prosperity greater inequality in this country?

Thatcher: You will get a more thriving society when people can rise to the limits of their talents, and out of the wealth they create, we shall all be better off.

Walden: So you think a more unequal society is actually better for Britain?

Thatcher: A more opportunity society (sic) that enables you to earn more.

Walden: But that does mean more inequality?

Thatcher: Yes, indeed. If talent and opportunity are unequally distributed, then allowing people to exercise their talent will mean more inequality, but it means you drag up the poor people. No one would remember the Good Samaritan if he'd only had good intentions. He had money as well.

This was the moment when twenty-first-century inequality was conceptualised and the fragmentation of our society became not a by-product, but integral to the plan. Mrs Thatcher was the most visionary prime minister Britain has ever had – her vision was so precise, stark and eviscerating, it was like a beam of light.

So did trickle-down, the theory Arthur Laffer sold to governments on both sides of the Atlantic, actually work? If anyone knows, Nick Hanauer should, one of the billionaires who benefited directly from the policies ushered in by Mrs Thatcher's Good Samaritan speech.

'Trickle-down economics is as old as civilisation. We used to call it Divine Right. It's simply the idea that I matter, and you don't. That what I do is indispensable and what you do is extra.

That's how we keep you in line. The great problem we face in the US and UK is we have formed our economic policy on essentially the idea of Reagan-Thatcherism. That if you make rich people richer, everyone will be better off. It's just not true, it's not how the economy works.[25]

'Use me as an example. I earn approximately a thousand times more a year than the median wage in the US. But I don't buy a thousand times as much stuff. I own three or four pairs of jeans, a couple of pairs of shoes. I have a big, beautiful house, but I don't have a thousand houses. So no matter how much money I have, I cannot sustain a national economy. Only a robust middle class can do that.'

At Cambridge University, economist Ha-Joon Chang has carried out an extensive comparative study of global inequality. We meet in the library where John Maynard Keynes first lectured on his *General Theory* and William Phillips constructed his famous 'water machine' to show students how money flows through the economy, using pumps, pistons and coloured water.

'In theory, trickle-down is not a stupid idea. But in reality, it has not been borne out. In country after country like the US and UK, investment as a share of national income has fallen. Economic growth has fallen. So where's the proof? The idea that if you give the richest more money, they'll create more jobs and more income for everyone else? It hasn't happened.'[26]

Twenty-first-century inequality is bookended by Mrs Thatcher's Samaritan speech at the end of the twentieth century and Tobias Levkovich's presentation at Citi at the beginning of this one, when he put his ear to the ground, heard the earth cracking in half, and told his clients to buy.

Perhaps the pitchforks are not coming for Nick Hanauer and his fellow billionaires quite yet. They may never. But the millennial cohort coming of working age now are the hollowed middle class with a loss of entitlement. They are utopian cynics, wanting everything the previous generation had, working as hard but reaping none of the rewards. As a result, they are potentially the most combustible force in a generation. Plus they have Facebook on which to organise.

The Ministry of Defence predicted this in their 2007 report: 'The middle classes could become a revolutionary class, taking the role envisaged for the proletariat by Marx.' Inequality would mean the middle class would 'unite, using access to knowledge, resources and skill to shape (outcomes) in their own transnational class interest.' [27]

A global precariat conjured by inequality would, according to the MoD, have fathomless potential power. Loss of entitlement + Facebook = X, whatever X turns out to be. As Edmund Burke said in 1777, 'those who have much to hope and nothing to lose will always be more dangerous'[28] than the dispossessed, who were at the bottom of the hourglass to start with. The tapered bit in the middle has the potential to shatter the whole thing.

CHAPTER FIVE
FOOD: OWNING FAT AND THIN

The Deal: The BMI index recalibrated by statistician Louis Dublin at Metropolitan Life Insurance is adopted by doctors and pharmacists across America
Aim: To create a scientific measure for obesity, in so doing inventing a health panic years before a genuine obesity epidemic existed, and a market for the diet industry
Where: Metropolitan Life Headquarters, New York
When: 1945

When you walk around a supermarket, what do you see? Walls of highly calorific, intensely processed food, tweaked by chemicals for maximum 'mouth feel' and 'repeat appeal' (food scientist speak for addictiveness). This is what most people eat. Pure science on a plate. The food, in short, that is making us fat.

And next to this? Row upon row of low-fat, light, lean, diet, zero, low-carb, low-cal, sugar-free, 'healthy' options, marketed to the very people made fat by the previous aisle and now desperate to lose weight.

What you see in a supermarket is the entire 360 degrees of obesity in a single glance. The whole panorama of fattening you up and slimming you down, owned by companies that have analysed every angle and money-making opportunity. They have made society fatter – we have not changed metabolism as a race – but they are now also making money from the obesity epidemic.

There is a deep, symbiotic relationship between dieting and obesity. Weight Watchers was bought in 1978 by Heinz, who in turn sold the company in 1999 to investment firm Artal for $735 million. SlimFast was bought in 2000 by Unilever, which owns Ben & Jerry's and Wall's sausages. Jenny Craig was bought by Swiss multinational Nestlé, which also sells chocolate and ice cream. In 2011, Nestlé was listed in the *Fortune* Global 500 as the world's most profitable company.

The story of how fat and thin became intertwined for the purpose of making money is a strange and remarkable one, marked by fierce battles between rivals, bizarre experiments, skewed data and dirty tactics; and in the middle of it all, scientists and businessmen who set out to alter the nature of what we eat. In the process, making deals that changed the shape of the human race.

INVENTING OBESITY AS AN INSURANCE SCAM

Long before we even had a real obesity epidemic, the idea of a weight problem was conjured from thin air. In 1945, a statistician called Louis Dublin at Metropolitan Life headquarters in New York was on his lunch break. He was down on his numbers and needed to impress his bosses. Dublin began looking at the health premiums being paid by Met Life's customers and realised that it was hugely influenced by their weight. Then he had an idea.

By lowering the threshold weight at which policy holders would move from the 'overweight' to the more health-critical 'obese' category, Dublin discovered that you could create tens of thousands more customers. And tens of thousands of 'normal' people could now be re-categorised as 'overweight'.

These newly 'obese' and 'overweight' customers would pay a higher insurance premium, because the health risks associated with their weight would be deemed greater. Dublin needed a scientific metric by which to make this happen, so he invented BMI (or 'body mass index'). A combination of weight and height. It seemed far more scientific than anything before, but it confused muscle density and fat. According to his BMI reading, Usain Bolt, the world's fastest man, is obese.

Overnight, half the American population were redefined as either overweight or obese and would now have to pay higher premiums. 'It wasn't based on any kind of scientific evidence at all,' according to Joel Guerin, an investigative journalist who has analysed Louis Dublin's methodology. 'Dublin essentially looked at his data and just arbitrarily decided that he would take the desirable weight for people who were aged twenty-five and apply it to everyone.'

Forty years before a real obesity epidemic existed, Dublin had invented one in his lunch hour. Met Life did a deal with grocery stores, doctors' surgeries and supermarkets across America, which began installing weighing machines with the Met Life logo on them. Concerned housewives and businessmen visited their doctors and were assured that, yes, the new BMI calculations did indeed show they were now a danger to themselves. There was a ticking time bomb inside Americans: fat, and it had to be dealt with immediately. Newspapers reported a nationwide fat panic. People with an especially high BMI were told they were at imminent risk of a heart attack or stroke. But help was at hand.

In 1960, the *New York Times* reported on a strange phenomenon sweeping America. Mothers were mixing up their baby's formula milk to drink themselves. They had discovered that a liquid diet made them lose weight. Chemical giant Mead Johnson & Co. spotted a gap in the market and launched Metrecal, the first powdered diet drink.

Johnson's head of marketing, C. Joseph Genster, had come up with the name by blending 'metre' and 'calorie'. Genster then did a deal with celebrity TV dietician Sylvia Schur to front Metrecal.

Like BMI, Metrecal sounded scientific, but it also needed scientific credibility with the public, gained by attaching a trusted name such as Sylvia Schur. But this infant diet industry already had some genuine science under its belt that it was less keen to share with the public.

THE MINNESOTA STARVATION EXPERIMENTS

Six feet beneath the centre circle of the Minnesota Golden Gophers football stadium is a network of underground cells and tunnels. In 1944, as Europe was being gripped by malnutrition, the US government wanted to find out what would happen if America was faced with the same kind of chronic food shortage. They decided to test what occurred to the human body when it was starved.

The esteemed nutritionist Dr Ancel Keys was tasked with experimenting on thirty-six conscientious objectors to monitor the effects of being systematically deprived of food.

During the Second World War, Keys had been responsible for creating the K-ration for soldiers: a highly calorific boost bar and in effect, the first energy snack. In the 1960s, he gained international fame promoting the 'Mediterranean diet'. He appeared on the cover of *Time* magazine and was hailed as the new guru of nutrition. But in 1944, he was working in secret for the US government.

Over a year, Keys kept his human guinea pigs in the underground cells beneath the Minnesota stadium, limiting their calorie intake to 1,500 a day. Three hundred calories more than the average woman on a diet in the US consumes today. They were given a relentless exercise regime, dropped into tanks of cold water, and forced to stare at food to see how they would respond.

The men quite simply went mad. In their diaries, they obsessed about food, fantasising about meals they would have when it was over. When allowed onto the grass pitch above the cells, some began trying to eat the grass; one of them bit a scientist; another chopped off three of his own fingers with an axe.

But Keys was most amazed by what happened when he began feeding them again. They began getting fat, and fast. Not just regaining their original weight in a matter of weeks, but surpassing their original weight and continuing to gain. Dieting, he realised, made them fat and had altered their metabolism, giving them a propensity to be fat where none had existed before.

Dr Traci Mann works for NASA at the University of Minnesota, studying the physiological effects of dieting on the body, only a stone's throw from where Keys carried out his starvation tests. 'The more and more I look at Keys's findings, the more remarkable I find them.' Keys had provided irrefutable evidence that diets do not work, Mann says. But he had also found that we steadily gain pounds each time we go through the yo-yo cycle of dieting, incrementally becoming fatter over time. Because we do not see this incremental gain, we keep coming back to diets as a quick-fix solution.

This science should have spelt the end of the diet industry before it even started. Instead, it provided the perfect business model. Before the war, diets had existed as fads, but never as a coordinated, multibillion-dollar business. Keys changed all that, giving the diet industry the science it needed to know that there was a returnable business here.

If you buy a car and it does not work, Mann says, you take it back to the dealer and get a new one, but if a diet fails, you tell yourself it is your fault and keep going back. It is the bullet-proof product.

Diets were a licence to print money. When Sylvia Schur did a deal with Johnson to front Metrecal in 1960, Keys was the science underpinning Mead Johnson's amazing new cure for obesity. Diets do not work, which is the very reason that makes them work as a business.

I JUST HAD THOSE TWO WORDS: 'SLIM' AND 'FAST'

Metrecal evolved into something huge, created by New Jersey chemist, Danny Abraham. Danny grew up above the pharmacy his dad owned and the antiseptic smell is one of his earliest memories. Danny became a chemist himself. Then one morning, everything changed. He woke bolt upright with two words in his head: 'slim' and 'fast'. Those two words were to end up earning Danny $2.1 billion when he did a deal to sell SlimFast to Unilever.

I meet Danny at his William Randolph Hearst-style castle residence in Florida, where he has a huge super-yacht parked on the lagoon – 'I always wanted a boat when I was a kid, now I've got one.'

How did Danny come up with SlimFast? 'I just had those two words. No product. But I figured anything called SlimFast is going to sell.' Abraham experimented at the development stage with Metrecal-type drinks, but they always wound up tasting chalky and medicinal. So instead he went down the milkshake route. Something all-American that should taste like an indulgence, but minus the calories. Slimming as if by magic.

Danny is now in his eighties, but looks fighting fit, taking me to his gym where he works out in front of me to show how much he can still bench press. He then theatrically takes out a SlimFast milkshake from the fridge and swigs it. 'Damn. Tastes as fine today as the day I came up with it.'

I put it to Danny that not only he, but the entire diet industry has made a fortune essentially peddling a lie. A miracle cure in a bottle. 'No, no, no,' he says, waving me away with his arm. 'Jack. Let me ask you a question. Who's in charge of you, Jack? Huh? You are. No one else. If people blame other factors for failing to lose weight, they're looking in the wrong place. Get on the scales, go to the gym, it's up to you, no one else.'

As I drive away, Danny waves goodbye and shouts: 'Remember Jack, you're in charge of you.'

Is this true when it comes to dieting? Are you 'in charge of you'? The diet industry was created as a conscious business decision to take advantage of a health panic that – at the time – was not real. But now obesity is a real health crisis, the diet industry cannot solve it. And it is not as if people trying to lose weight lack motivation: a few succeed, while the vast majority fail and keep failing. Over ninety-five per cent of dieters are returning dieters. Are these people simply weak-willed, or is something else going on?

Kelly Brownell is dean of the Sanford School of Public Policy at Duke University, and one of the world's leading epidemiologists in the field of obesity. I put Danny's point to Brownell. 'Of course we are in charge of ourselves, but when it comes to losing weight, it's not quite that simple.' Dieting is like playing poker. We are all handed a different set of genetic cards at birth. If you are starting with a weak hand, you are going to find it harder. The heavier you are when you begin dieting, the weaker you make your hand.

It is what we all know. Some people find it easy, others hard. But when you diet and you are already obese, your weak genetic hand is amplified exponentially. It becomes almost impossible.

There's something else, says Brownell. The body has its own thermostat. Once we go over a certain weight, our thermostat is reprogrammed. To lose weight once we have crossed this tipping point is doubly difficult, because the body's thermostat is fighting even harder against the diet.

The body thinks it is starving and wants to reset itself back to the new, heavier thermostat weight. So, the truism that 'in every fat woman there is a thin woman trying to get out' is the exact opposite of the biological truth. In every newly thin woman, there is a fat woman fighting to make herself fat again.

For a planet becoming obese at unprecedented speed, conventional diet products are not the solution. But the message of self-empowerment – you can do it, as Danny Abraham shouted to me – is key to the insulation of the diet industry from criticism.

If your diet fails, try again, because you did not try hard enough the first time.

SOMETIMES WE WOULD ASK OURSELVES THAT QUESTION: HOW ON EARTH DO WE GET AWAY WITH IT?

In New York, I arrange to meet Richard Samba, the finance director of Weight Watchers. Samba is a jovial man in his sixties with a touch of the Donald Trump about him – luxuriant hair and a relaxed swagger as he wanders over to shake my hand. From 1968, when he joined the company, to 1983 when he left, Samba transformed Weight Watchers from an $8 million a year franchise operation to a $300 million a year global brand.

Weight Watchers was begun at a New Jersey kitchen table in 1963 by housewife Jean Nidetch who, for years, had binge eaten chocolate-coated marshmallows and sugary snacks. She had tried pills, hypnosis and fad diets but nothing worked. One day, she saw some commonsense advice on a poster pinned to the wall of a local clinic run by the New York Health Department: cut out carbs, exercise a bit and form a support group to keep motivated.

Nidetch began following the first two pieces of advice, but they weren't working. Finally, she decided to focus on point number three, inviting six overweight friends to her home, where they had a group confessional about their overeating and problems. The friends invited more friends and within two months, the meetings had forty people attending. Al Lippert, a neighbour and fellow dieter, had seen Nidetch speak and was convinced there was a business model in utilising her motivational skills. Before long, Nidetch had become a polished, inspirational speaker, and it was time to go into business.

In 1963, Nidetch turned her following, now in the thousands, into an actual company that could be rolled out as a franchise across America, with lots of mini-Jeans using the franchise name to present their own weight-loss programmes. They called the brand Weight Watchers, with Jean and her husband Mortimer, Al Lippert and his wife Felice, all of whom had attended Jean's sessions and lost weight, the business's founders. Al would handle the operations side while Jean would be the face of the business. The idea of exploiting Jean's talents nationally, franchising out her inspirational message to thousands of other Jeans across America and charging these franchisees for the privilege to speak, was a brilliant one.

Al Lippert and Jean Nidetch had identified that the key to the success of each Weight Watchers group was the mutual support and encouragement the members gave each other. By making each group a self-help group counselling itself, Weight Watchers could maintain a home-spun, intimate feel. The group would not feel corporate and impersonal, but shaped by the people who turned up.

This business was an overnight success; by 1968, five million people had enrolled. In the same year, Richard Samba came on board as finance director. By the time he joined, the company was already America's number one weight-loss brand, offering not only a diet but an entire lifestyle: group support, weight-loss logs, all working toward an objective Samba described as a 'life-long commitment' to Weight Watchers. But how could a multibillion-dollar business, now the number one diet brand in China and India as well as the US and Europe, be constructed on a high statistical probability of failure, as Ancel Keys discovered all those years ago in Minnesota?

Samba smiled and shook his head. 'Well, you know. Sometimes we would ask ourselves that same question. How on earth do we get away with it?' Richard says they would see mothers bring their daughters, who would in turn bring their daughters when they became mums. Mothers who had spent a lifetime on yo-yo diets would be passing Weight Watchers on generation to generation, like a hereditary disease.

Weight Watchers point to their longevity as proof of their success, but the facts tell a different story. After five years on Weight Watchers, according to research by Carl Heneghan, Director of the Centre for Evidence Based Medicine at Oxford University, less than sixteen per cent of participants reach their goal weight. That leaves eighty-four per cent who have failed. And yet they still come back for more. Why? 'Of course they come back,' Samba says. 'Because the eighty-four per cent: that's where your business comes from.'

Ancel Keys was right. Diets fail, but for the diet industry this simple fact was all that was needed to turn it into a multibillion-dollar business. And the returning customers are that business. When Weight Watchers came to Britain in 1967, Bernice Weston, the UK head of operations told the BBC: 'When it comes to eating, the problem with fat people is they are very stupid.' The diet industry, as Richard Samba says, could not believe their luck.

HOW FOOD BECAME TOBACCO

In the 1940s, Louis Dublin redefined half of America as fat, fifty years before it was. But now obesity is real, there is a new game for the food industry. Denial.

In the 1960s and 1970s, the tobacco industry spent millions of dollars refuting the emerging scientific evidence that smoking caused lung cancer, and now the food industry seeks to do the same with obesity. The difference between cigarettes and food is that you don't need cigarettes to live. Food is not a lifestyle choice but a necessity: we need to eat.

Proving this causal link all hinges on 'satiety': the feeling of fullness. If the science stacks that the food industry did not simply alter the metabolism of the body by creating highly calo-rific processed food, but did so knowingly in order to short-circuit satiety, then we are in a new ballgame.

Culpability for obesity will move from the individual who ate too much and could not control themselves to the companies that took advantage of that individual's metabolic predisposition – the cards they were dealt – leading them to get fat. Blame will lie squarely at the door of the food industry. According to Kelly Brownell at Duke, the resulting class actions across the globe would make the tobacco industry payouts to thousands of lung-cancer victims seem tiny by comparison. This would be millions of people.

The United Nations have classified obesity as the fastest-growing threat to world health in the twenty-first century. In the UK, sixty per cent of us are overweight. In the US, it is seventy-five per cent. Ethiopia, stricken with famine in the 1980s, now faces an obesity crisis. In 2016, 14.9 per cent of urban Ethiopian women were classified obese.

This self-inflicted disease strikes the poor and rich alike: in the United Arab Emirates, the richest five per cent are the fattest. In Brazil and China, obesity has risen in tandem with the growing affluence of the middle class. To eat at McDonald's is an expensive luxury only the metropolitan elite can afford.

The creation of the diet industry was the result of a specific business decision to provide a solution to a health problem long before it actually existed. But once the real epidemic did exist, vast new opportunities were created for the companies that had made it happen. Opportunities they were quick to exploit.

THE FIRST OBESE MAN

Up a rickety staircase at the Newarke Houses Museum[1] in Leicester, England, hangs a portrait of Daniel Lambert,[2] painted in 1806. Lambert weighed 53 stone (335 kilograms) and was considered a medical mystery. Too heavy to work, Lambert came up with an ingenious idea: he would charge people a shilling to see him. Lambert was Britain's first documented obese man and made a fortune displaying his body across the country. His portrait shows him at the end of his life: affluent and respected. A celebrated son of Leicester.

Two hundred years on, specially designed vehicles called 'bariatric ambulances' pick up a dozen Daniel Lamberts round his home town of Leicester every week. Fifty-three stone is nothing special for these ambulance crews, it is at the lower end of the weight spectrum with only the 80-stone patient worthy of mention when a shift finishes.

The specially designed ambulance carries an array of bariatric gizmos including a 'spatula' to help with people who have fallen out of bed or, on one occasion for the crew I visited, an obese man jammed between the two walls in his hallway, whom they prised free by using the spatula.

As well as the ambulance, there is a convoy of support vehicles including a winch to lift patients onto a reinforced stretcher. In extreme cases, the cost of removing a patient to hospital can be over £100,000. One 62-stone teenager in Britain had to have her home partially demolished to take her to hospital.

But the morbidly obese are not where the heartland of the obesity crisis lies. On average in the UK we are all – every man, woman and child – three stone heavier than we were in the mid-1960s.[3] We have not noticed it happening, but this glacial shift has been mapped by bigger car seats, swimming cubicles, XL trousers dropped to L (L dropped to M). An elasticated nation with an ever-expanding sense of normality.

Why are we so fat? We have not become greedier as a race. We are not, contrary to popular wisdom, less active. A longitudinal study by the late Professor Terry Wilkin at Exeter University measured children's physical activity over twelve years. Wilkin discovered something completely at odds with the common assumption that kids are not as active as they once were. In fact, Wilkin found, their activity was pretty much the same as fifty years ago. But something has changed: the sheer amount of sugar in food.

Just as science in the 1940s proved diets do not work, so science in the 1970s began to examine the effect an unprecedented increase in sugar consumption would have on obesity. Unlike the first science, which provided the basis for the diet industry, the science on sugar was ignored.

PUTTING THE SUGAR INTO OBESITY

In 1971, Richard Nixon was facing re-election. The Vietnam War had eroded his popularity, but another central issue for his campaign was the soaring cost of food. Newsreel of housewives with placards demonstrating outside supermarkets was broadcast across America, sparking nationwide protests. To bring down food prices, Nixon needed the cooperation of the powerful farming lobby. He appointed Earl Butz, an academic from the farming heartland of Indiana and trusted friend of the farmers, to broker a compromise.

Butz opened up farms to start farming on an industrial scale, exhorting them to plant 'fencerow to fencerow' and one crop in particular: corn. The surplus corn was ploughed back into the feed of cattle, who in turn were fattened by the immense surge in corn production. Burgers got bigger. Fries fried in corn oil became fattier. Corn also became the engine for a massive surge in cheaper food supplied to American supermarkets.

Butz's strategy was twofold: supply food producers with cheaper corn, which could in turn be used in a host of supermarket products, and boost demand for this cheaper food with the consumer. The key was production: if it could not all be eaten, it could be exported.

In 1973, the USDA (Department of Agriculture) under the leadership of Butz secured a $700 million deal to export 30 million tons of grain to the Soviet Union. The deal was paid for with export credits, so Nixon's government effectively subsidised the Soviet purchase and kept Communist Russia fed.

Using food to fight the Cold War was not an option Butz or the farmers would entertain.

But there was another reason for this strategy. Butz wanted to open up foreign markets aggressively to American corn and if that meant subsidizing exports to capture the market, so be it. Subsidy would underpin both massive overproduction by US corn farmers as well as overseas sales. As a result of Butz's reforms, US farmers went almost overnight from smallholders to multimillionaire businessmen with a global market.[4]

In the mid-1970s, Butz flew to Japan to investigate a strange new scientific innovation that utilised the waste from corn. Called high fructose corn syrup (HFCS), it was an intensely sweet, gloppy syrup that was also incredibly cheap to produce. HFCS had been discovered in the 1950s by the Clinton Corn Processing Company in Iowa, but it was only in the mid-1960s that a process was found to harness it for mass production at a scalable level. The scientist who made the breakthrough was Yoshiyuki Takasaki at the Japanese National Institute of Advanced Industrial Science and Technology, who in 1967 created an acid-enzyme process for the corn starch extract derived from milled corn, making HFCS a commercial proposition for the first time.

In this process, high-temperature enzymes are added to metabolise the starch and convert the resulting sugars to fructose. To make the purified solution free of contaminates, a number of enzymes including alpha-amylase and glucoamylase must be added. The solution needs to be filtered continuously to remove protein and demineralised using ion-exchange resins.

The resulting HFCS, which is made up of twenty-four per cent water and between zero and five per cent unprocessed glucose oligomers, can be further processed into a variety of forms of varying sweetness for different processed foods.

HFCS 42 (so named because it has a forty-two per cent fructose content) is used in ready meals, breakfast cereals and bread. HFCS 55 is sweeter still, with fifty-five per cent fructose, and is used in sodas. These are the most commonly adopted HFCSs.

HFCS 65 is even sweeter, and was taken up by Coca-Cola for certain lines of Coke. But HFCS 90 is the sweetest and is used for niche super-sweet products like pancake syrup.

These myriad HFCS products, scalable thanks to Yoshiyuki Takasaki, were soon pumped into every conceivable food: pizzas, mass-produced baked goods, even meat. They provided that 'just baked' sheen on bread and cakes, made everything sweeter and extended shelf-life from days to years. In Britain, the plate of food on a family table became a scientific experiment – each processed milligram tweaked and sweetened for maximum palatability. The public was oblivious to the changes taking place to the foodstuffs they were putting in their mouths.

But HFCS was also packed with sugar. And it was one of the most sugary items in the supermarket, soft drinks, that HFCS would transform most profoundly, so making an obesity epidemic real for the first time.

Hank Cardello is a tall man with a hesitant manner, who greets me with a businesslike handshake at a diner in downtown Manhattan. In 1984, Hank was head of global marketing at Coca-Cola, which was about to make the decision to swap sugar for HFCS.

Coke was to use HFCS 55, an amalgam of HFCS 42 and the far sweeter HFCS 90 (ninety per cent fructose). It was supplied to Coke by CCBSS (Coca-Cola Bottlers Sales & Services), a limited liability company created, owned and authorised by Coca-Cola. With something as important as the key ingredient of their drink, Coke could not rely on an outside supplier.

As market leader, Coke's decision to endorse corn syrup sent an unequivocal message to the rest of the industry, which quickly followed suit. It was the papal puff of white smoke that they needed.

At the time, Hank says, there appeared to be 'no downside'. HFCS was two-thirds the price of sugar, and even the huge potential risk of messing with the taste (a slight metallic tang in their first test batches) was a risk worth taking when you looked at the margin. What could go wrong? In 1984, Hank says, 'obesity wasn't even on the radar.'

But another health issue was: heart disease. And since the mid-1970s, a fierce debate had raged behind the closed doors of the medical profession over what was causing it. Professor John Yudkin, a researcher at UCL in London, blamed sugar. But there was someone else keen to pin the blame on fat: Ancel Keys, the man behind the Minnesota starvation experiment.

In their fractious arguments, both in public and private, Yudkin began to become isolated. Keys was an internationally renowned nutritionist, a titan in his field, and Yudkin was an outsider with an unorthodox and unpopular view within academia: sugar is not only harmful, but potentially lethal.

Endocrinologist Professor Robert Lustig at the University of California believes there was a concerted campaign to discredit Yudkin, because his ideas threatened the bottom line of the sugar industry. Keys did research that aligned far more closely with the direction the food industry was intending to take in the future: to demonise fat and exonerate sugar of blame for heart disease.

Yudkin's colleague at the time, Dr Richard Bruckdorfer at UCL, remembers that 'there was a huge lobby from the industry, particularly from the sugar industry, and Yudkin complained bitterly that they were subverting some of his ideas.' Lustig puts it more simply. Yudkin was 'thrown under the bus.'

Yudkin's ideas were published in a book, *Pure, White and Deadly*.[5] It was a bestseller and became a key text for the growing health-food movement of the 1970s, but it was rubbished in academic circles and by Yudkin's peers.

Yudkin eventually became a pariah: ostracised and forgotten. But according to Lustig, Yudkin had predicted the future by identifying the potential dangers of sugar, not just in relation to heart disease, but in an obesity epidemic. He was silenced, according to Lustig, because too many people had too much at stake for him to be heard.

Ancel Keys, who had spearheaded the fight against Yudkin, was the same Ancel Keys who thirty years earlier had starved conscientious objectors under the Minnesota Stadium and discovered that dieting makes you fat. Keys not only lent his medical credentials to the food industry's defence of sugar, much of his research was funded by the food industry. He was a stakeholder.

And there was more at stake than simply protecting sugar as a commodity. Something new was brewing: an opportunity. The public was starting to get fat and keen to embrace a new product to fight the very obesity epidemic Yudkin had predicted. The food industry had the answer. A product in their research labs ready to fly onto the shelves: a brand-new concept in food called 'low fat'.

THE RATS GET FAT

Low-fat products were an industry dream: a new type of food forged in the panic around heart disease that could now be rolled out to deal with the coming catastrophe of obesity. But there was a problem. 'When you take the fat out of a recipe,' endocrinologist Dr Lustig says, 'food tastes like cardboard, and you need to replace it with something – that something being sugar.'

Overnight, miraculous new products arrived on the shelves that seemed too good to be true. Low-fat yoghurts, spreads, even desserts like Black Forest gateau. One low-cal biscuit, the oddly named *Ayds*, launched with disastrous timing as the AIDS epidemic unfolded, tasted far sweeter than its full-fat counterpart. And there was a reason: all these magical have-your-cake-and-eat-it foods had had the fat stripped out and replaced with sugar.

Nutritional wisdom in the 1980s became beholden to what food historian Gary Taubes calls 'the low-fat dogma', with sales of this incredible wonder-food rocketing across the globe.

And as low-fat took grip, so too did obesity, rolling like a glacier over the Western world. By the mid-1980s, doctors were being visited by patients who were getting fatter than any patients they had ever seen before. Neither the doctors nor the patients knew why. The food industry began stressing that individuals must be responsible for their own calorie consumption, but even those who exercised and ate low-fat products were gaining weight. Everyone was getting fat and nothing seemed to work.

In 1966, the proportion of people with a BMI of over 30 (classified as obese) was only 1.2 per cent for men and 1.8 per cent for women. By 1989, the figures had risen to 10.6 per cent for men and 14 per cent for women. And no one was joining the dots between the huge increase in sugar consumption and this explosion in obesity.

There was something else going on. The more sugar we ate, the more we wanted and the hungrier we became in the process. Sugar appeared to be a new kind of addiction.

A professor at New York University, Anthony Sclafani, began to investigate. Sclafani was particularly interested in the connection between appetite and weight gain, and began to notice something very strange about his lab rats. When they ate rat food, they put on weight normally. But when they were given processed food from a supermarket – sugared cereal or snacks – they ballooned in a matter of days. Their appetite for sugary foods was insatiable: they carried on eating and could not stop themselves, long after their bodies were physically full.

Sclafani had identified a paradox of obesity: the more you eat, the hungrier you get. Over time, the more sugar in a diet, the more malnourished the body becomes as it is slowly starved of essential nutrients, pushed out by an insatiable desire for sugar. In short, we cannot get enough.

This, Sclafani believed, was unlike any nutritional attack the human body had faced before: a three-pronged assault on the metabolism that alters our metabolism in the process. Sclafani observed his lab rats not only gorging on sugar, but on low-fat products, too. And if he put them on a diet, they got fatter when the diet stopped, exactly as Ancel Keys had observed with the conscientious objectors in those cells beneath the Minnesota Football Stadium.

The obese, Sclafani concluded, cross a line of no return. They reprogram their body thermostat to make weight loss a near-insurmountable challenge. It is like playing poker with that genetic hand of cards, and finding you have a two of clubs.

THE MONICA LEWINSKY BLOW JOB

Professor Jean-Marc Schwarz, Senior Lecturer at the Faculty of Biology, Medicine and Health at Manchester University, has been trying to understand the physiology of obesity for over a decade. Schwarz studies the precise way in which the major organs metabolise sugar and calls the momentum it builds in the body 'a tsunami'.

The effect this has on our primary organs is only now being understood. Around the liver, it coalesces as fat, leading to type-2 diabetes. Sugar may even coat semen and result in obese men becoming less fertile. But the organ of most interest is the gut. According to Schwarz, the gut is a highly complex nervous system – the body's 'second brain' – and this second brain becomes conditioned to wanting more sugar, sending messages back to the first brain that are impossible to fight.

There is growing scientific evidence that fructose can also trigger processes that lead to liver toxicity and a host of other chronic diseases. Men who drink sweetened beverages most often are twenty per cent more likely to have a heart attack than those who drink the least. Schwarz says this assault on the body is so comprehensive, it is analogous to an attack on the nervous system.

So, if the food industry was responsible, how did they get away with it? What the World Health Organization has called the most serious global health crisis of the twenty-first century? In San Francisco, I meet David Kessler, the former head of the US government's most powerful food agency, the Food and Drug Administration (FDA), and the person responsible for introducing warnings on cigarette packets in the early 1990s.

How was Kessler able to introduce warnings on cigarette packets and not on food packaging? Kessler sips his tea. 'Because at that point the science couldn't be refuted any more on the link between cigarettes and cancer, but more importantly, we were pushing at an open door. The tobacco industry had given up on the US and Europe. Their new markets were in China, India and South America, that's where the business lies. So they let it happen.'

Kessler believes the same will happen with the food industry when (and if) the science on culpability in the obesity epidemic becomes impossible to refute. The difference is that the tobacco industry is relatively weak compared to the food industry, which is tied into a complex matrix of other interests: drugs, chemicals, dieting products, and tobacco itself. The panoply of satellite industries that make money from obesity means the food industry's relationship to obesity is a net-profit one.

As one K Street lobbyist in Washington put it to me, the food industry is up there with oil and weapons in terms of access to the White House. 'When you can get the President of the United States on the phone in five minutes, then you don't need people like me to lobby.' The food industry has real power.

A joke, she said, that did the rounds in Washington in the late 1990s to illustrate the access of the food industry went something like this: How do you interrupt President Clinton when he's getting a blow job from Monica Lewinsky? Tell him Monsanto are on the line.

The reason the food industry is so powerful is simple. Food is an essential that has become a vice. And sugar has turned food into a vice by creating an unbreakable link between gut and brain. It is as addictive as cigarettes or alcohol. But unlike cigarettes and alcohol, the temptation cues are every ten yards, unregulated and unrelenting: vending machines, coffee shops, fast-food outlets, supermarkets, cinemas, even gyms, libraries, swimming pools, train stations. Everywhere.

'Sugar is hedonic,' Kessler says. 'Eating it is highly pleasurable. It gives you this momentary bliss. It takes over your brain.' And it has taken over our brain at the very moment that a 360-degree, obesogenic environment has been handed to us on a plate.

THE SODA SHARK ATTACK

At Hammersmith Hospital in London, Dr Tony Goldstone is mapping out the specific parts of the brain and neurological pathways stimulated by sugar, showing patients huge pictures of cream cakes and chocolate bars, then measuring the neural pathways that light up excitedly.

In so doing, he may have discovered a smoking gun. According to Goldstone, when you become obese, a hormone called leptin ceases to work properly. Normally, leptin is produced by the body to tell you that you are full. However, in obese people, it becomes severely depleted, and a high intake of sugar is a key reason. When the leptin does not work, your body simply doesn't realise you should stop eating, just as Sclafani's lab rats could not stop gorging on sweet snacks.

Leptin raises a big question: did the food industry knowingly create foods that were addictive and inhibited leptin? Kessler, back in San Francisco, is cautious in his response: 'Did they understand the neuroscience? No. But they learned experientially what worked.' Lustig agrees. 'Has a food industry whistleblower come forward yet? No. Does one exist? I haven't met them.'

If it is subsequently proved the food industry did knowingly inhibit leptin – and there is science behind the fact you still feel hungry after eating a Mars bar or a Big Mac – then those tobacco lawsuits will be sure to follow, and sink the industry that keeps us fed.

Kelly Brownell, dean of the Sanford School of Public Policy at Duke University and one of the world's leading experts on obesity, believes it will happen and we are only a couple of years away from the first successful lawsuit. On current obesity figures, half the planet would be able to sue the food industry for engineering the body's response to leptin in order to make us eat more. It is one thing to mess with the constituents of food, quite another to mess with the body.

The food industry's defence has always been, as was the tobacco industry's, that the science is not there. Susan Neely, president of the American Beverage Association, is a perky, smiling woman in a neat, coordinated trouser suit, who arrives for our interview in the ABA's New York office and briskly settles down as if to watch a movie. 'Very warm in here, don't you think?'

The ABA are a lobby group funded by the soft-drinks industry, and Neely's job is to routinely defend Pepsi, Coke, 7 Up and the dozens of brands signed to ABA from charges that they caused and continue to cause obesity.

'There's a lot of work to try to establish causality,' Neely says, 'and I don't know that I've seen any study that does that.' Does she think soft drinks contribute in even the smallest way to the obesity epidemic? Susan smiles at me. 'I think that when you swim in the sea, doesn't mean you are going to get bitten by a shark. Because you drink a soft drink, doesn't mean you are going to become obese.'

It is a weird answer, but also strangely apt. Neely knows that the science can be fought and if proof is ever established, they will fight it, just as they fought attempts to introduce a sugar tax by Mayor Bloomberg in New York, by the Obama administration, and by Chief Medical Officer Professor Sally Davies in the UK in 2015.

The food industry can tough it out and even if it eventually loses, the defeat would be no great loss anyway. Just like cigarettes,

Europe and America are small fry compared to the rest of the planet: a sustainable hit when the world is waiting to be conquered.

PROGRESS

It is dawn on the Amazon and the mist rises off still water. On a bend in the river, a ship sails into view covered in huge, painted hoardings for chocolate bars and milkshakes. It makes several short bursts on its horn and people emerge from the forest.

The '*Nestlé Até Você a Bordo*' ('Nestlé Takes You Onboard') boat is described on Nestlé's website as a 'floating supermarket'. Its mission is to sail up the Amazon stopping at remote villages and encampments, reaching a potential 800,000 low-income tribal people. The crew of the Nestlé ship hand out free 'starter packs' of ice cream, baby milk, milkshakes and chocolate bars to people who have never seen or eaten processed food before.

In Brazil, the collapse of the traditional Amazon diet and rise in obesity has coincided with the adoption of highly calorific, Western processed food. At the same time, urbanised middle-class Brazilians are adopting the 'Amazon diet' to lose weight and be healthy. This is twenty-first-century progress, just as it has been in India: urbanisation and rising obesity running in tandem. Is the arrival of highly processed, calorific food a new form of colonialism, or is the real discrimination denying people across the world the same opportunities that the West has had to get fat?

In San Juan Chamula, Mexico, the country with the fourth-highest consumption of Coke in the world, the walls of the town's church are studded in Coke bottles – Coke has been deified since its introduction to Chamula in the 1960s. It is both worshipped as a god and reviled as a health risk. In Mexico, as in Brazil, India and China, all working rapidly through the gears of economic change, obesity is the corollary. China is not only the world's fastest-growing economy, it is now Weight Watchers' biggest market.

Is obesity the inevitable price of growth? France has one of the lowest rates of obesity in the Western world and has maintained its indigenous food culture – it has held on to home-cooked food and a sense of pride in its national cuisine, just as urbanised Brazilians are trying to do. But France also went through industrialisation 150 years ago and so it does not equate economic growth and social mobility with more convenient, scientifically produced food. Processed food was not around then, and that is why the nation is not fat now. It never got the chance. Brazil, India, China and Mexico had the misfortune to modernise when they could equate the two.

THE CURE

In spite of a seemingly obvious correlation between growing economic prosperity and obesity, scientific causality between food manipulation and a fatter population has eluded the medical profession. Why? The reason has little to do with science and more to do with the fact that the same scientists conducting research into the food industry's role in creating obesity are also funded by the food industry.

With so little money set aside for independent research, and what little there is being cut, the food industry has become a vital source of income. This means not only are they slow to establish causality, the very same science going into combating obesity is being used to hone the products that are making us obese. Many of the scientists I spoke to are wary about going on the record, because they fear their funding by the food industry will be taken away if they speak out.

So how did the two become so inextricably intertwined?

Let me sketch two alternative scenarios. This is the first: in the late 1970s, food companies made tasty new food. People started to get fat. By the 1990s, the medical costs related to obesity were ballooning. Government, health experts and, surprisingly, the food industry were brought in to consult on what was to be done. They agreed that the blame lay not with them but us, the consumer. We needed to take responsibility, go on a diet and exercise. But the plan did not work. In the twenty-first century, people are getting fatter than ever.

OK, here is scenario two. Food companies made tasty new food. People started to get fat. By the 1990s, food companies and, more to the point, the pharmaceutical industry looked at the escalating obesity crisis and realised there was a huge amount of money to be made. A multibillion-pound cash cow encompassing not only low-fat foods, but diet drugs, home fitness, fad diets, crash diets, diet and recipe apps, with newly thin celebs promising an 'all new you' in just three weeks.

Seen purely in terms of profit, the biggest market was not the clinically obese (those people with a BMI of 30-plus). It was the billions of ordinary people worldwide who are a little overweight, and do not consider their weight to be a significant health problem. To make money from them, these millions of people needed to start seeing their weight as a problem.

To make it happen, the science needed to say they were at risk. And it all hinged on one deal on one day. On 3 June 1997, the World Health Organization (WHO) convened an expert consultation in Geneva, which formed the basis for a report that defined obesity not merely as a coming social catastrophe, but an 'epidemic'.

The word 'epidemic' is crucial when it comes to making money out of obesity, because once it is an epidemic, it is a medical catastrophe. And if it is medical, someone can supply a 'cure'.

The author of the report was one of the world's leading obesity experts, Professor Philip James,[6] who as a doctor in the 1980s had been one of the first in the world to spot obesity on the rise. In 1995, James set up a body called the International Obesity Task Force (IOTF), which reported on rising obesity levels across the globe and on health policy proposals for how the problem could be addressed.

It is widely accepted that James first put obesity on the radar, and thus it was appropriate that the IOTF should draft the WHO report of the late 1990s that would define global obesity. The report painted an apocalyptic picture of obesity going off the scale around the world.

The devil was in the detail – and the detail lay in where you drew the line between 'normal' and 'overweight'. Several colleagues questioned the group's decision to lower the cut-off point for being 'overweight' – from a BMI of 27 to 25. Overnight, millions of people across the planet would shift from the 'normal' to the 'overweight' category. Just as they had done when Louis Dublin first lowered the cut-off point in the 1940s.

Professor Judith Stern, vice president of the American Obesity Association, was critical and suspicious. 'There are certain risks associated with being obese. But in the twenty-five to twenty-seven area, it's low-risk. When you get over twenty-seven, the risk becomes higher. So why would you take a whole category and make this category related to risk, when it isn't?'

Why indeed. Why were millions of people previously considered 'normal' now overweight? And why were they considered in as much danger as those who are genuinely obese?

At his London apartment, I asked Dr James where the science for moving the cut-off to BMI 25 had come from. 'The death rates went up in America at twenty-five and they went up in Britain at twenty-five and it all fits the idea that BMI twenty-five is the reasonable pragmatic cut-off point across the world. So, we changed global policy on obesity.'

James had once again redefined who was fat and who was not. A decision that would affect the health outcomes of billions of people. It was a decision that directly influenced our global understanding of obesity and what could be done about it. And it was all based, as James told me, on 'prewar data provided by Metropolitan Life', the very data Louis Dublin had concocted in the 1940s.

Who stood to gain from the WHO report? I asked James where the funding for his report came from. 'Oh, that's very important. The people who funded the IOTF were drugs companies.' And how much were you paid? 'They used to give me cheques for about two hundred thousand a time. And I think I had a million or more.' And did they ever ask him to push any specific agenda? 'Not at all.'

James says he was not influenced by the drugs companies that funded his work, but there is no doubt that, overnight, his report reclassified millions of people as overweight and massively expanded the customer base for the pharmaceutical industry, looking to exploit the weight-loss market. The people who 'used to give me cheques'.

Back in the 1940s, Louis Dublin had created an obesity epidemic on paper when there wasn't one, and fifty years on Philip James had used the same data to expand the parameters of a real obesity epidemic.

His critics called it alarmist in order to benefit drugs companies, but James rightly points out that he needed the muscle of drugs companies to press home the urgency of the unfolding obesity crisis. But clearly these companies were not in it for altruism. If the WHO classified obesity as an 'epidemic', the drugs industry were in a position to supply the 'cure'. It needed to be globally critical to justify their involvement.

SPEAK TO THE MEDIA AGAIN AND SOME VERY BAD THINGS WILL START HAPPENING

The problem was that the cure was not easily at hand. Since the 1950s, the drugs industry's answer to weight loss had been amphetamines, prescribed to millions of housewives who wanted to lose pounds. In the 1970s, they were banned for being highly addictive and for contributing to heart attacks and strokes.

But now drugs were once more on the agenda as a 'cure' and the potential cash-in was huge. The drugs industry focused on one specific area: appetite suppressants called fenfluramines. After trials in Europe, the US drugs giant Wyeth developed Redux, which was approved by the Food and Drug Administration (FDA) in spite of evidence of women developing pulmonary hypertension while taking it.

Dr Frank Rich, a cardiologist in Chicago, began seeing patients who had taken Redux and started to develop what he felt were alarming symptoms. When a woman in Oklahoma City collapsed and died, Rich decided to go public, contacting the US news show *Today*.

We meet in Rich's Chicago home and he tells me what happened next. 'That was filmed in the morning and when I went to my office, within an hour I got a phone call from someone claiming to be a senior executive at Wyeth who saw the *Today* piece and was very upset. He warned me against ever speaking to the media again about his drug, and said if I did, some very bad things would start happening, and hung up the phone.'

The Wyeth executive concerned has denied Rich's version of events. But once legal liability cases began, evidence emerged from internal documents that Wyeth knew of far more cases of pulmonary hypertension than had been declared either to the FDA or to patients. Redux was taken off the market and Wyeth set aside $21.1 billion for compensation. The company has always denied responsibility.

But with Wyeth out of the game, obesity was now an open door for other drugs companies. 'Oh, let us be very clear,' Rich says. 'If you have a drug that drops your weight and doesn't do you any other harm in terms of side effects, that is a multibillion megabuck drug.'

IT'S A WAR, AND WE NEED TO WIN IT

I am standing on the floor of the planet Krypton with a marble atrium stretching high up into the heavens and glass shards hanging futuristically down to reception. A receptionist with a headset nods curtly and tells me Gustav is ready to see me. Gustav Ando is a director at IHS Healthcare Group, and one of the pharmaceutical industry's leading experts on drugs and obesity. His offices in central London are pretty damn impressive but – as Ando tells me – little of the money that went into creating this billion-pound empire came from obesity.

I want to know if the drugs industry's funding of the people who defined obesity as an epidemic had been worth it. How important was the WHO decision in making the industry money?

'It really turned a lot of heads. Defining it as an epidemic has been hugely important in changing the market perception.' Because the drugs companies could now provide 'the magic bullet'.

The race was on to manufacture this magic bullet. British giant GlaxoSmithKline (GSK) found its antidepressant Wellbutrin had a handy side effect – it made people lose weight. Blair Hamrick was a sales rep for the company in the US tasked with getting doctors to prescribe the drug for weight loss as well as depression, a move that would considerably widen its market and profitability. In the trade, this is called 'off-labelling'.

'If a doctor writes a prescription, that's his prerogative, but for me to go in and sell it off-label, for weight loss, is inappropriate,' says Hamrick. 'It's more than inappropriate – it's illegal; people's lives are at stake.'

GSK spent millions persuading doctors to prescribe Wellbutrin as a diet drug, but when Hamrick and others blew the whistle on conduct relating to Wellbutrin and two other drugs, the company was prosecuted in the US and agreed to a fine of $3 billion, the largest healthcare fraud settlement in US history.

Drugs companies have attempted to make a magic bullet and capitalise on obesity, but have failed spectacularly. Ando says 'the magic bullet' would be great if it existed. 'I haven't seen one yet.'

A cure would also mean no more customers. Simply medicating and managing the obesity crisis is far more lucrative than fixing it. Type 2 diabetes is a by-product of obesity and also one of the pharmaceutical industry's golden geese, continuing to lay for as long as there is an obesity epidemic.

And the drugs industry is not the only one benefiting from managing the health crisis. By creating diet lines for the huge grey zone of the concerned and slightly overweight, not just the clinically obese, the food industry, too, has an ever-refilling pot of gold.

There now exist two clear and separate markets. Those who go on endless diets, losing and then regaining the weight, and providing a constant revenue stream for the food, pharmaceutical and diet industries throughout their adult lives. And the genuinely obese, who are being cut adrift from society, having been failed by health initiative after health initiative by government.

As Dr Kelly Brownell points out, the analogy with smoking and lung cancer also goes deeper than you think.

'There's a very clear tobacco industry playbook, and if you put it next to what the food companies are doing now, it looks pretty similar. Distort the science, say that your products aren't causing harm when you know they are.'

But the solution to obesity could follow the cigarette trajectory, too. It was, Brownell says, only after a combination of heavy taxation on price, heavy legislation (banning smoking in public places), and a long propaganda campaign (warnings on packets; an effective, sustained anti-smoking advertising campaign; and most crucially, education in schools) was brought to bear on a resistant tobacco industry, that smoking became a pariah.

There was a generational shift in attitude and, Brownell says, it is only this kind of seismic shift that will do the same with obesity. The great unmentionable with health experts across the globe is that, as with lung cancer, a generation was cut adrift and allowed to die before this shift took place. In public, governments pledge health drive after drive to combat obesity, but in reality, they know it is futile.

It is ironic, that analogy with smoking. Because deep in the archive at San Francisco University is a confidential memo written by an executive at the tobacco giant Philip Morris in the late 1990s, just as the WHO was defining obesity as a coming epidemic, advising one of the food giants on strategies to employ when it started being criticised for creating obesity.

Titled 'Lessons Learnt from the Tobacco Wars', it makes fascinating reading. The memo explained that in the same way as consumers now blamed cigarette companies for lung cancer, so they would end up blaming food companies for obesity, unless a panoply of defensive strategies were put into action. The plan was to follow the same playbook: deny the science, discredit the critics, go on the offensive, do not give an inch. If the plan was followed, valuable time could be bought.

It's a war, the memo said, and we need to win it. There was a good reason why the food industry bought into dieting – it was nothing personal, it was simply business.

A POSSIBLE WAY FORWARD: SWITCHING THE CONTROL SWITCH

It is naïve to imagine there is a magic bullet. But there is one area of research that has recently proved promising. Developments in Cognitive Behavioural Therapy (CBT) suggest a possible long-term solution could come by reprogramming the brain to think about the routine of eating in a different way, and it is all to do with control.

Anorexics and binge eaters share an extraordinary ability to exert control over their intake of calories that is detrimental to their health. Contrary to the common belief that the obese lack control, binge eating – like self-starvation by anorexics – is a well-maintained routine, just one that's damaging, and potentially life-threatening.

But if this dysfunctional routine can be switched to a functional routine of healthy eating and exercise, then the obese could be given a routine that works for them, and a potential way out. A 2017 paper for the US National Institute for Health by psychologists Gianluca Castelnuovo, Giada Pietrabissa and Enrico Molinari, 'Cognitive Behavioural Therapy to Aid Weight Loss in Obese Patients: Current Perspectives', examined CBT's effectiveness. 'The literature on the psychosocial aspects of obesity has a long history,' they said. 'G. Stanley Hall, the first person to earn a PhD in psychology in the US, started studying eating behaviours and obesity in the nineteenth century (and) CBT is traditionally recognised as the best established treatment for Binge Eating Disorder (BED) and the most preferred intervention for obesity.' However, the report cautioned against seeing CBT as a new magic bullet for obesity. 'Although the comprehensiveness and the practical nature of the CBT approach are positive, this psychotherapy does not necessarily produce a successful weight loss.'

The authors evaluated numerous examples of CBTs available to obese patients as well as their long-term efficacy, noting several promising evolutions of the psychotherapeutic approach that may appear to offer more sustained success.

HAPIFED (the Healthy Approach to Weight Management and Food in Eating Disorders) was developed in 2015 by Professors Palavras, Hay and Touyz, offering 'therapeutic education' and CBT with emphasis on accompanying the patient through their weight-loss journey, plus strong emotional support (interestingly, one of the key planks of the Weight Watchers approach).

Castelnuovo, Pietrabissa and Molinari also identify 'third-wave CBT protocols such as acceptance and commitment therapy' as gaining traction with patients and support from clinicians. These include mindfulness and even the 'sequential binge approach' (making food unappetising and monotonous). Their conclusion is not so very different from the spokespeople for the diet industry: it works, but only for some, and not forever. Many factors are at play with obesity and the solution is not readily to hand, raising an obvious if pertinent question: when someone does manage to lose weight and keep it off, is this because they have been given the right treatment, or because they were going to succeed regardless of outside factors? If it is the latter, how can therapy tap into the inner strength and motivation of the few and pass it on to everyone else?

In the meantime, the baton for helping everyone else now appears to be handed to MedTech, where the use of health apps and even Virtual Reality may attempt to unlock the door to a solution that has eluded the diet industry for over half a century.

CHAPTER SIX
DRUGS: THE MEDICATION OF MODERN LIFE

The Deal: Henry Gadsden, CEO of Merck, proposes a plan for the pharmaceutical industry to deal with the potential crisis posed by the expiration of patents on its blockbuster drugs
Aim: To expand the number of illnesses for which prescription drugs can be prescribed
Where: Interview with *Fortune* magazine, New York
When: 1980

At 10.15 a.m. on 14 October 2008, I was in a meeting in London when something very odd began to happen. The floor began heaving beneath me. The walls started approaching me, then receding. I felt as if I were on a ship in a storm.

I went to the bathroom and splashed my face with water. The droplets in my hands wobbled. My reflection in the mirror was warping. Then my fingers began to tingle. The tingling moved through my hand, up my arm and into my shoulder. By the time I was on my way to hospital, I felt as if a giant hand had come down from the sky and was crushing my body into a tiny corner of the ambulance.

I was having a stroke, but I was lucky. I could speak and I knew who I was. In the hospital beds around mine were seemingly fit and healthy men aged between twenty-five and forty. A refuse collector, who did the equivalent of a mini-marathon every day; a City trader, who went to the gym three times a week; a barman, who did salsa in his spare time; a criminal informer, visited by two policemen who brought grapes; and me.

We had all suffered strokes, years before any of us imagined you should decently have one. Why? Stress? Everyone has stress, but not everyone has a stroke. I had lost some feeling, but it returned in minutes. I was not blind or struggling to stand, as some of the other patients were. 'When we had strokes,' the guy in the bed next to me said, 'we were hit by a hammer, but you ducked.'

I left hospital with a carrier bag of drugs.

I went home and looked at the drugs. There were bottles and bottles of them. They were a chalky terracotta colour and all had one word on them: Simvastatin. I popped one in my mouth.

THE GREY ZONE

The United States has 320 million people. According to the US government's National Center for Health Statistics, roughly half of all adults go to their bathroom cupboard every morning and take a drug like the ones I had just been given.[1] This is a way of life and our dependency on this way of life is escalating fast. In 2000, only eight per cent of adults took five or more prescription drugs, but in less than twenty years, that has more than doubled.

We are the most medicated society in history and on current trends by 2050, every American adult could be swallowing a prescription drug. To avoid one will seem freakish, even irresponsible.

We do not magically have more illnesses than we did fifty years ago. Since 2000, we have become older and fatter as a society, but increased use of prescription drugs vastly outstrips these needs. Pills are taken by all socio-economic groups: wealthier, non-Hispanic white Americans take roughly twice as many prescription drugs as poorer Mexican Americans, even though – if need was dictated primarily by wealth – the opposite should be true. Epidemiologists call it the 'Hispanic Paradox'.[2]

The drugs industry's backbone is built on the so-called 'Big 3 Ds': depression, diabetes and dementia. But the fastest-growing drug on earth is statins, used to lower cholesterol. The drug I was given when I left hospital.

Statins are the key to understanding how we all became hooked on medication. When I had my stroke, I entered the grey zone between the sunny uplands of health and the deep valley of the unwell. This grey zone is where the pharmaceutical industry's business lies.

In widening this grey zone to its fullest extent, the pharmaceutical industry maximised the potential of illness and stumbled upon a revelation. Instead of treating existing illness, they would medicate modern life itself. They would reinvent illness by labelling the nebulous anxieties and neuroses of modern life as medical syndromes. And so – in fact – we do magically have more illnesses than we had fifty years ago.

By having a stroke, I put myself in the lower foothills of the grey zone in which drugs are taken as a 'sensible preventative measure'. But millions of people across the globe who take Simvastatin have not even had a stroke. So why are they being prescribed statins?

A few days after being discharged, I asked the consultant who had been looking after me that question. 'Do you want the official line or what I think?' Both. 'OK. The official line is that even if your chance of another stroke is around 0.05 per cent, you should take statins for the rest of your life.'

So what about everyone else?

'About a decade ago, drugs companies came along and were given *carte blanche* to hand out statins to doctors not only for strokes, but for everything. So, we now prescribe them like sweets to anyone over forty as a preventative measure. It is sold to the patient like putting de-icer in your car or de-furring your kettle.

'But we don't know who they work on,' he continued. 'It could be less than five per cent with ninety-five per cent popping them pointlessly. But there's one thing for sure. There's a winner here and that's the drugs industry.'

I am not an anti-pharma person. Quite the opposite. I get angry with people who take a knee-jerk view that everything the pharmaceutical industry does is bad. Prescription drugs kept my grandparents alive. Drugs have kept my dad's high blood pressure at bay for forty years. The pharmaceutical business has prolonged life and alleviated pain on a daily basis for billions of people.

But here I was doubting that I needed to take a pill that I was assured would keep me alive. What was my problem? My problem was that I wasn't the only one in the new grey zone between health and illness. Everyone is.

A STICK OF WRIGLEY'S GUM

How was the grey zone created? The answer lies with the decision of one man. The vision of a beleaguered CEO of a multinational drugs company, who – in trying to save his business from collapse – quite simply changed the definition of illness, from something you get to who you are. He was to shift illness from an aberration to a state of normality and his aim was simple: to make patients of everyone.

In 1980, Henry Gadsden, the CEO of Merck Pharmaceuticals, was interviewed by *Fortune* magazine.[3] The six pharma-giants were in trouble for the first time in their 150-year history. The post-war boom in prescription drugs, reaching its apex in the 1960s with Valium, was now under threat. The patents they had relied upon to turn them from nineteenth-century corner shops into twentieth-century multinational conglomerates were about to go generic. And these patents were hitting the wall at the same time.

Henry Gadsden's solution was bold, transforming the lives of millions of men, women and children across the planet. 'The problem we have had is limiting the potential of drugs to sick people,' he told *Fortune* magazine. 'We could be more like Wrigley's Gum . . . it has long been my dream to make drugs for healthy people. To sell to everyone.'[4]

Gadsden's solution was genius. He wanted to turn preventative drugs into a stick of gum. Popped in the mouth every morning without thinking about it. Gadsden wanted the healthy to begin taking drugs and keep taking them for the rest of their lives as a preventative measure. It was a breathtaking vision for expanding the client base: from fifteen per cent of the population who are actually ill to one hundred per cent of the population who might one day get ill. It did not matter how small the risk was, it could be medicated. And for everyone else, a raft of new or obscure syndromes or illnesses could be diagnosed. Gadsden's plan was to make patients of us all.

In order to make his dream come true, drugs companies needed to strike out boldly from their comfort zone by inventing or rediscovering an entirely new slate of illnesses. Drugs companies would no longer be in the game of merely curing illness, but conjuring it.

MODERN LIFE MAKES YOU ILL

Fast-forward forty years and here's an example of what Gadsen was so scared of – the patent cliff – and the solutions the pharmaceutical industry employs when it chooses to view this patent cliff not as a disaster but a colossal opportunity. In March 2016, two investors called John Beighton and Guy Clark made a presentation in a wood-panelled boardroom at the Waldorf Hotel, London, to fellow investors. Their company, Actavis UK, was successfully selling a hydrocortisone tablet to the NHS, but it was about to lose its patent and go 'off-brand'; no longer subject to price regulation and producible by any drugs company as a 'generic'.

The basis of Beighton and Clark's ingenious solution lay in exploiting the very fact the drug was no longer subject to price control. Some drugs that go generic can be easily reproduced by competitors, but they had a different idea: if we develop a niche medicine with complex processing, we limit this post-patent competition and can maximise the true profit potential of the drug. We replace the patent with an exclusive licence, and the buyer (the NHS) has virtually no way of finding a cheaper alternative.

With the end of price regulation, the end of the patent became an opportunity to ramp the price to an astronomical level. Beighton and Clark proposed a deal between Actavis and the NHS on hydrocortisone, raising the price of a 10-milligram pack of tablets from 70p to £88. A 20-milligram pack was ramped up in price by 9,500 per cent.[5]

Because the drug was being used by patients with life-threatening conditions like Addison's Disease, this was a deal the NHS could not bargain over. Actavis could hold the pricing-gun to doctors' heads and effectively charge what they wanted. There was no alternative but to pay up.

In November 2017, the Competition and Markets Authority (CMA) ruled that Canadian drug company Concordia had overcharged the NHS by more than £100 million over the last decade, hiking the price of liothyronine, a life-saving treatment for patients with an under-active thyroid, by nearly 6,000% between 2007 and 2017. They had, according to the CMA, 'abused their dominant position to overcharge the NHS'.

This is how price fixing works when it is used to take advantage of patent expiry, but in 1980, Henry Gadsen had an even more radical and far-reaching solution: to invent new illnesses.

He had a surprising fellow traveller. In 1960, psychiatrist R.D. Laing published *The Divided Self: An Existential Study in Sanity and Madness*.[6] The book became a counter-cultural bible. It was

carried by hippies, beatnik poets and anti-war protestors mobilising on university campuses in America and Europe, quoting
Laing's dictum that insanity is a 'perfectly rational response to an
insane world'.

Laing's fame spread quickly. He became the figurehead of the
'anti-psychiatry' movement, advocating the end of mental-health
labelling. Laing viewed madness as a construct. In a society, he
said, that promotes war in Vietnam and the shooting of college
students on campus, the mentally ill can hardly be considered
any more mentally disturbed than society itself. In fact, labelling
dissenting voices as 'mad' was a way of silencing them.

Post-Vietnam and Watergate, the Shakespearean idea of the
mad as the only people who see the truth became a key tenet of
the anti-authoritarian left, articulated by dystopian sci-fi writer
Philip K. Dick, who summed up insanity as 'an appropriate
response to reality'.[7]

But R.D. Laing took this idea further by giving it medical
credence. Laing said that imprisoning the mentally ill in psychiatric institutions and force-feeding them pacifying drugs was
political oppression. The inmates were political prisoners. By
contrast, taking mind-expanding drugs like LSD could help the
public see through the charade of modern life.

Laing was taken very seriously. He appeared on earnest TV
discussion programmes and was hailed a genius at universities
across America. Laing argued that our entire understanding of
illness in modern society was flawed. It was not you who were ill,
capitalist society had made the public ill, forcing us to conform
to degrading rituals such as consumerism and office work. If you
sought to break out, you were labelled mad. But it was not you
who were insane, it was the system.

Laing's 'LSD Marxism' was everywhere, but with Vietnam
ending, Watergate receding in the memory, and the collapse of
counter-culture and the rise of New Right ideas in the mid-
1970s, he was suddenly out of fashion. His ideas disappeared as
quickly as they had appeared.

But then something extraordinary happened. In 1980, Gadsden did his interview with *Fortune*. America was now in thrall to yuppies, Wall Street and power lunches. But the drugs industry looked at Laing's discredited theories and saw something no one else had picked up on before.

If, as Laing said, it was not you who were ill but capitalism that had made you ill, this was useful to them. Illness could be created by your job, your home, your friends and your children. By your anxieties around cleanliness, or your neighbourhood. By sex, eating, your pets, crowds, shopping, big spaces, small spaces, quiet places, loud places, your partner, your car, sunlight, too much dark, or your phobia of everything from grass lawns to clowns at children's parties. And these illnesses could take the form of sweats, palpitations, irrational fear, dizziness, nausea, compulsive behaviour, even the simple fact that your leg was restless when you watched television. All of this could be redefined as 'illness'.

R.D. Laing, the high priest of anti-capitalism, had inadvertently come to the rescue of the drugs industry. Modern life could be shown to make you ill, but unlike Laing, the drugs industry had prescription drugs to fix it. And the key to getting these drugs to market was to get them passed by the US government's highest regulatory body, the FDA.

This however required evidence that a new drug was needed, and for this evidence help appeared from an unexpected quarter. In 1980, universities were given the means with which to potentially patent their own drugs and get them to market: the result of the passing of the Bayh-Dole Act. The stated intention was to allow any university, nonprofit organisation, or even small business with federal funding for a specific innovation or invention, to be able to patent and then commercially exploit that patent. In theory, this meant universities could compete with drug companies by producing their own drugs, but the reality was very different.

Senator Bob Dole was a friend of President Reagan and one of the most powerful men in Washington; he went on to become

the Republican nominee for president in 1996. But in 1980, he
was on the board of Verner, Liipfert, Bernhard, a law firm on a
retainer to drug company Pfizer. He wasn't simply looking out
for the interests of the universities, he had a commercial relationship with a drug company.[8]

Researcher Catherine Kirby carried out a report on the impact
of Bayh-Dole on universities for the McNair Center in 2016 and
discovered that universities were already exploring patenting for
their innovations prior to the passing of Bayh-Dole in order to
fill funding gaps and monetise their discoveries, and the act itself
made little difference to this trend. One very clear consequence
of the act, however, she says, was to cement the financial relationship between universities and the pharmaceutical industry. It
allowed universities to begin getting funding from drug companies in order to supply these companies with research to bolster
their claims for a new drug seeking approval from the FDA.

But to get this FDA approval for entirely new or previously
undiagnosed syndromes, the pharmaceutical industry needed
these departments to provide mountains of credible academic
research. They needed a plan.

The Food and Drug Administration had first been created in
1883 by chemist Harvey Washington Wiley and was known originally as the Division of Chemistry within the US government's
Department of Agriculture. As food and drug companies began
to build familiar brands at the end of the nineteenth century –
from soaps to cereals and painkillers – so-called muckraking
journalists like Upton Sinclair, who later went on to win the
Pulitzer Prize, began investigating what went into these products
and highlighting to the public the dangers of those that were
unregulated. Sinclair and his fellow muckrakers published their
findings and accusations in magazines like *McClure's*, which
began to lobby in its pages for greater federal regulation on pharmaceuticals and food stuffs.

In 1902, the death of thirteen children in St Louis, Missouri,
following their vaccination from a contaminated serum derived

from a diphtheria antitoxin, prompted the passing of the Biologics Control Act. Four years later, President Theodore Roosevelt enacted the Pure Food and Drug Act, making the interstate transportation and adulteration of food and drugs illegal. The drive for greater regulation in the 1910s and 1920s dovetailed neatly with the aims of the food and pharmaceutical giants, who themselves saw the need for greater regulation and standardisation in order to build reputable, trusted brands.

In 1930, the Division of Chemistry was renamed the Food and Drug Administration – the FDA – and eight years later the Food, Drug and Cosmetic Act gave the FDA the legal teeth it needed. It was no longer up to the FDA to prove a drug or foodstuff was unfit for consumption, but the responsibility of the manufacturer or drug company to prove it was safe. The FDA began to build a reputation as the toughest regulator on earth. When thalidomide was administered in Europe in the late 1950s as an anti-nausea drug to pregnant women, a drug that went on to cause terrible birth defects in newborn babies, Dr Frances Oldham Kelsey of the FDA had already refused to authorise its licence in the United States. An amendment to the 1938 act in 1962, the Kefauver Harris Amendment, further strengthened the FDA's regulatory power in light of the thalidomide tragedy, now requiring 'substantial evidence' of a drug's efficacy and how it would add medical value.

While this was hugely beneficial to many consumers, it was an issue for the pharmaceutical industry. The lengthy process of getting a drug authorised by the FDA had created what pharma executives referred to as a 'drug lag'. As doctor and pharma industry expert John LaMattina explained to *Forbes* in 2013, 'In the late eighties, drugs were being approved at a much slower rate in the US than in Europe. More than half of all drugs approved in the US had been approved in Europe more than a year earlier. As a result, patients, physicians, advocacy groups, and pharmaceutical companies were all concerned that access to important new medicines were being denied to Americans.'

This was the background to the crisis for the drugs industry Henry Gadsden described to *Fortune* in 1980. Pharma needed more drugs to be approved, faster, and to make this happen, new illnesses had to be concocted. Not only did these new mysterious illnesses need to be diagnosed and made bona fide, but the drugs for them needed to be approved in a far more streamlined way. The FDA was now the problem.

Peter Rost, a former drug-marketing executive at Pharmacia, says that the safeguards against untested drugs being blocked by the FDA were circumvented at a stroke by the passing of the Bayh-Dole Act and a new 'partnership' of drugs companies and university departments. A ping-pong game was created: a drug would be passed to the university, who would cook selective research, then test it on behalf of the drugs company with their 'independent' hat on, and give a heads-up on any possible FDA problems.[9]

Though the act was sold as giving greater choice of drugs to the consumer, not everyone bought it. When drafting had begun, a race had been on to sign up academics to give the bill some heavy-hitting credence. Professor John Abramson at Harvard, one of the world's leading experts on primary care, was approached and refused. 'The American public will look back upon this moment in fifty years' time as the moment government abandoned them to the pharmaceutical industry,' he said.[10]

It is now fifty years on. The bill was passed after Abramson, who initially opposed it, was told he would find it very difficult to get funding if he stood in the bill's way.[11] The act was passed in 1980, and the world was about to become ill from all sorts of disorders it had never heard of before.

The holy grail for the drug industry was to create a brand-new condition that the public did not even know it had. Vince Parry was an executive at Roche and described the process of discovering these new ailments as a careful process of cherry-picking.[12]

Parry's job was something wondrous to behold: 'to foster the creation of medical disorders, little-known conditions created afresh, and forgotten disorders reheated.' Parry called this process 'the branding of a condition'.

We meet in his New York offices where Vince now runs his own branding firm, utilising his years of experience in the pharmaceutical industry. Parry explains to me how branding a condition works, using the example of how, whilst working for advertising agency Saatchi, he transformed the fortunes of Zantac, a heartburn drug, by helping rebrand heartburn as the far more serious-sounding GERD (Gastroesophageal Reflux Disease).

'Instead of people going into the drugstore and asking for Rolaids, you want them going into a doctor's office and getting a prescription for a chronic condition. That's a vastly different behavioural change you're asking for.' So how did Parry achieve this for Zantac's manufacturer, Glaxo? 'We have to put a name around that (condition) and we have to put a serious rationale around that to justify the complexity of that transaction. In other words, we're going to go out there and make a big deal about this therapy, but no one yet knows they need it.' The key, Parry says, to turning heartburn into the more serious Gerd, and thus turning a prescription-only treatment (Zantac) into a mass market phenomenon, was tapping into the customer's deep-seated desire for normality.

'People fear not being normal,' Parry says. 'Being sub-standard. When people hear they can go to a doctor and get a name for that condition, that takes the terror of not being normal away.' The rebranding of heartburn as GERD was a runaway success. By the time Glaxo's patent on Zantac expired in 1997, 240 million people worldwide had prescriptions to treat Gerd with Zantac.

Gerd was not the only condition to appear from seemingly nowhere to afflict the public. A raft of new syndromes were created, popularised and broadened in their definition to cover huge swathes of everyday life: ADD (attention deficit disorder), ME, bipolar affective disorder, OCD, HRD, PTSD, IBS, metabolic syndrome, PMDD (premenstrual dysphoric disorder), SAD (social anxiety disorder and seasonal affective disorder). On top of dozens of new acronyms were a host of oblique phobias and addictions ranging from fear of shiny surfaces to the anxiety created by missing out on a bargain at sales.

The important thing for the drugs industry was that any hazy or nebulous feeling or anxiety could now become a cast-iron medical condition authenticated by university research. The task was not to create something entirely spurious. Many conditions had been around for decades and had genuine sufferers, for whom a diagnosis and medication could be valuable. But the business opportunity was in popularising and broadening the diagnosis to millions of other people for whom it had been hard to make a cast-iron diagnosis, but was no longer. They were now patients. The millions of people in the grey zone.

There was an upside. For core sufferers of irritable bowel or an obsessive-compulsive disorder, a genuine problem was recognised and believed. They were no longer isolated, they could form support groups and gain confidence from other sufferers. This diagnosis turned people's lives around. But it was not these genuine sufferers that were the huge exploitable market – it was the millions of people on the edge of a diagnosis who could now have a drug prescribed that roped them definitively into being labelled with something. It was the grey hinterland where the money lay.

A mechanism was magicked to make these millions of new patients aware of illnesses they never knew they had: DTC (direct-to-consumer advertising) which cut out doctors and targeted patients directly. In 1981, President Reagan appointed a new head of the FDA, Dr Arthur Hull Hayes Jr. Drug advertising to the public had hitherto been framed by a 1969 act that kept the control of pharmaceutical ads under the strict policing of the FDA. Under the old act, advertising was primarily aimed at doctors, who could theoretically read between the lines of the sales spiel and then recommend what was best for a patient.

But with the rise of patient rights advocacy groups in the 1970s, the public began to see themselves as informed consumers with a right to decide for themselves what was best for their own health. Hayes saw an opportunity the pharmaceutical industry had been waiting for.

In the early 1980s, Pfizer launched a public relations campaign called 'Partners in Health Care', publicising underdiagnosed critical conditions such as diabetes, angina, arthritis and hypertension. Pfizer believed that patient rights groups would lobby their doctors to prescribe new drugs. Pfizer's visibility in the Partners in Health Care initiative also appeared to put them above the parapet and on the 'side' of the patient and against the medical 'establishment' of experts and doctors.

In 1982, with the deregulation-minded Arthur Hull Hayes as head of the FDA, Merck and Dohme got in on direct-to-consumer drug advertising with Pneumovax, a pneumonia vaccine targeted at those over sixty-five. Eli Lilly launched Oraflex, an anti-arthritic in the same year. But they overdid it. The ads for Oraflex made claims beyond the approved product label and the drug was pulled by Eli Lilly only five months after it was launched.

Nevertheless, DTC became huge: the battering ram for getting the message of a new drug for a new illness beamed directly into millions of homes in the United States. And as the power of the drug industry grew in the 1990s and 2000s, the FDA – the governmental body tasked with protecting the public – began to face a funding crisis of its own, and became beholden to the drugs industry for help.

In a paper for the *Journal of Law, Medicine & Ethics* in 2013 entitled 'Risky Drugs: Why the FDA Cannot Be Trusted', Donald Light of the Perelman School of Medicine at the University of Pennsylvania argues that the FDA routinely approved drugs with threadbare 'proven' efficacy. He estimates that as much as ninety per cent of FDA-approved drugs since Bayh-Dole are no more effective than existing drugs. Moreover, Light says, 'since [the pharmaceutical industry] started making large "contributions" to the FDA for reviewing its drugs, as it [also] makes large contributions to Congressmen who have promoted this substitution for publicly funded regulations, the FDA has sped up [this] review process.'

Not only, Light argues, does the FDA approve 'drugs [that are] significantly more likely to cause serious harm, hospitalisations and deaths,' it simultaneously puts the approval of drugs for experimental treatments of aggressive conditions such as multiple sclerosis and cancer in the go-slow approval lane.

In August 2013, pharma industry analyst John LaMattina responded to Light's accusations of pharma-FDA complicity, in *Forbes* magazine: 'Unfortunately, as an academic whose work is supported by the Safra Center for Ethics [at Harvard], Light's word carries a disproportionate amount of influence,' he wrote. 'These comments perpetrate the view that there is an unholy alliance between the FDA and the pharmaceutical industry, an alliance that threatens the health of patients. This might make for a Hollywood movie plot. Truth be told, such a conspiracy doesn't exist.'

These are the specifics on the financial relationship between big pharma and the FDA. In 1992, Congress passed the Prescription Drug User Fee Act (the PDUFA). PDUFA provided a mechanism for pharma companies to be charged a tax for each new drug application filed. As LaMattina explains, 'the revenues from these "user fees" were used to hire 600 new drug reviewers and support staff. These new medical officers, chemists, pharmacologists, and other experts were tasked with clearing the backlog of NDAs [new drug applications] awaiting approval. Consequently, the FDA was able to reduce review times of NDAs to 12 months for standard NDAs and to 6 months for priority applications that involved significant advances over existing treatment.'

Those within the pharma industry laugh when it is suggested they have it easy with the FDA. In the year that Donald Light accused the FDA of being beholden to big pharma, Merck had an insomnia pill rejected; Allergan had a migraine treatment refused; and Aveo had a potential cancer drug thrown out. All were potential blockbusters worth billions.

But the economics do point to the FDA relying heavily on PDUFA funding. The fifth iteration of the act was passed in 2012, nine years after the first act. In 1995, the 'user fee' charged was $208,000 per drug. In 2014, it was ten times higher: $2,169,000. With approximately fifty NDAs submitted to the FDA per year, Congress is subsidising the FDA to the tune of $100 million: money directly supplied by big pharma.

Jessica Wapner of PLOS calculated in 2016, reporting to *Business Insider*, that the drug industry has contributed $7.67 billion to the FDA since the passing of the PDUFA. User fees now account for sixty-eight per cent of the FDA's review budget for pharmaceutical drugs and fifty-eight per cent of generics. Whether one views this degree of dependence on pharma funding as compromising the health of millions of people, or simply the economics of a hugely costly process of drug licensing, depends simply on which side of the garden fence you are standing.

NOOTROPICS AND THE
TECHNOSAPIEN: LIVING TO 150

The grey zone – millions of people diagnosed with anxieties, phobias, syndromes and obscure conditions – is where adult Britain and America now sits. The sweet spot for not only pharmaceutical companies, but a new industry created by Henry Gadsden's stick of gum: 'wellness'. A trillion-dollar behemoth incorporating everything from preventive medication to fitness and vitamin supplements. From wearable tracking technology to clean eating, superfoods, and the panoply of alternative therapies and diets we use to armour ourselves against modern life and the potential illnesses it brings. And that is just the beginning. Coming online are bespoke genetic editing programmes that won't just 'edit out' hereditary disease, but could edit in desirable attributes, like high cheekbones or intelligence.

The wellness industry is predicated on prevention not cure, and prevention is an amazing product to sell because it is impossible to test its efficacy. Who knows if it works or it doesn't? If nothing happens to you, then it worked. If you get ill, then something else is to blame. What matters is that you sign up to the ideology of wellness in the first place.

So, who benefits from you looking after your health? You do, when it works. But the underlying truth of wellness is that those who want to look after their health, will; and those who ought to, do not. As a health strategy for everyone, 'wellness' does not work, because it simply preaches to the converted.

In May 2014, Gallup published a RAND Corporation study on wellness programmes offered in US workplaces. More than eighty-five per cent of US companies employing more than one thousand people offer some form of wellness programme, but only sixty per cent of staff are even aware the programme exists. And of that, just forty per cent use it. Only twenty-four per cent of employees participated,[13] corresponding roughly with about twenty per cent of the US population who exercise to a recommended weekly minimum, but do it off their own back.[14]

The unpalatable truth for governments and companies running health programmes for their employees (not least because they improve the bottom line of attendance and productivity) is that most of us are immune to calls to exercise more, even if help is handed on a plate.

The hope that wellness will create a 'contagion effect' – spreading among employees as they crunch and plank their way to health – is less likely than a 'preach effect', people resisting wellness because they feel they are being told what to do.

A gulf is emerging between the well and unwell, with the twenty per cent who practise wellness pulling away from the eighty per cent who do not. In Britain and America, a growing 'quantified self' (QS) or 'life-logging' movement is gaining momentum. People who record and 'quantify' every activity and input in their life. This is not simply about 'wellness', but creating the ultimate 'optimised' you.[15]

They meticulously count every single calorie they consume and burn. Record the amount of caffeine in their body, the level of toxins in their food, stress levels, how much they work, sleep, the quality of the air they breathe, even how often they have sex and for how long, the chemical make-up of their urine and faeces. The goal of the quantified individual is to create a machine of their body – an 'optimal self' – functioning at maximum efficiency at all times.

Aligned to QS is the nootropic or smart drug movement – people taking drugs to enhance their cognitive ability and productivity.[16] This is not drug-taking to get high, but to focus. Students have long used amphetamines to work round the clock, but nootropics hone this to targeting areas of the brain for specific tasks: Adderall to improve working memory, methylphenidate to improve mental performance, or eugeroics like modafinil to short-circuit sleep deprivation. Nootropics are taken up most enthusiastically by millenials as a tool to get an edge at work. It has been estimated that as many as one in four students at British universities use smart drugs.

I am on a roof in San Francisco, overlooking the city. A man with a headband connecting his brainwaves to the internet is meditating. 'Alexa!' he commands. 'Play soothing rain!' If Eric Matzner meditates competitively enough, birdsong will spontaneously burst forth from Alexa and he will move on to his next task.

Downstairs, in his extraordinary steam-punk, techno-Victorian house, Eric does a three-minute workout in his state-of-the-art, chrome-and-leather gym. He then jumps up and speeds over to a deck of screens and begins typing furiously at the keypad while standing on a rubber platform. I ask Eric what he is doing. 'I'm racing other cars by seeing how many words a minute I can type.' Eric's fingers are a blur. His accuracy is pretty extraordinary, too. He can type about eight times faster than normal human beings. It is like watching a person on fast-forward. Eric is an evangelist for nootropics and two in particular: Noopept, a memory aid developed in the 1960s in Russia, and phenylpiracetam, which cosmonauts used to boost stamina.

Eric takes between seventy and eighty supplements every morning, grabbing them in handfuls and gulping them with water ('water is good'). He has them arrayed in glass jars and they range from the shell-casing of silk worms to deep-sea algae, dried and reconstituted as a bright-green gunk. Eric takes a potion out of a silver sachet and asks me to sniff it. It is one of the foulest things I have ever smelt. He drinks it in one gulp. Nootropics were inspired by Romanian scientist Corneliu Giurgea. Like Giurgea, he sees no reason why he should not live to 150 and use nootropics to do it. He plans to have communication with 'once-dead' scientific geniuses when they are cryogenically resurrected.

Eric is deadly serious. 'If somebody invented a drug that improved the brains of the world's ten million scientists by one per cent, it would be like creating ten thousand new scientists.' Eric is fantastically engaging company, though his nootropic habit has the unfortunate side effect of making him talk faster than any other human being I have ever met. For long periods of time, he is talking so fast, I have absolutely no idea what he's saying.

Eric sells his cognitive enhancers as Nootroo – a silver pill and a gold one, like the pills in *The Matrix*. His main competitor is Nootrobox, who have backing from Silicon Valley. Their founders tell me digital was the old frontier and 'the body is the new platform'. Twenty years ago, tech was an end in itself, but now the optimised self is the huge, untapped market; technology and data simply the tools for making the post-human technosapien happen.

These movements are the extreme version of what we all do now: monitoring our 10,000 steps a day, fat burning rate, or data on the quality of our sleep. We ostensibly use wearable technology like Fitbit to improve our body's performance. But for those who are already healthy, this is simply data confirmation of what they already know: they are OK and exercise and sleep enough.

For those who are unfit, it masks another agenda: policing of the body not for health purposes, but to label the unwell as a prelude to withdrawing health support. The same data you record and amass through wearable technology can be used by insurance companies or the NHS to deny or cancel a healthcare plan or benefit claim. Data supposedly collected on your behalf then becomes a weapon used against you.

If your phone says you have not climbed enough stairs today, or your watch says that you did not work hard enough in the gym, this data turns into irrefutable fact. In 2013, Boots introduced breathalysing for smokers and rewarding the clean with nicotine patches. The NHS plan to do the same with the obese, using data tracking on diet and exercise to offer or withdraw healthcare.

But is telling someone who is fat and does not exercise that – *drum roll* – the data confirms they are fat and do not exercise, benefiting them? Once someone has been definitively labelled as failing, more data only reinforces that label.

In 2016, Admiral Insurance began scrolling through the Facebook posts of first-time drivers to assess the risk they posed to other drivers.[17] This was based not on their driving, but how many pictures they posted of themselves drunk at parties. Facebook subsequently blocked Admiral from using their information to price car insurance. But if companies are making policy decisions culled from some blurry photos that magically become 'data', what will health companies do with 'data' mined from how many times you ate at McDonald's last month?

Data drives far more than individual health, it underpins the 'MedTech' revolution and the idea that responsibility for health in a post-NHS future will lie firmly with the individual. This is fine for those on the sunny uplands of good health who also happen to practise wellness. But for the chronically unwell, who also chronically fail to practise wellness, failure to hit your health targets will be a self-fulfilling prophecy. When the NHS door closes, the only option left will be a private healthcare provider likely to charge a far higher premium.

More than twenty-eight million Americans have no medical insurance,[18] creating a cost per capita of $6,223. The sixty-four million British citizens currently covered by the NHS have a per capita cost of £2,008. Half that of the US. But this could be about to change radically. The lesson of the demise of Obamacare and Trump's difficulty in finding its replacement was the crushing confluence of extreme need and inability to pay. The very people who need healthcare most cannot afford it at all, and will not take out insurance for that reason. Outside the system and defined in black and white as beyond help.

In Britain, the NHS still operates as a comprehensive health provider, but is moving rapidly to a new model in which access could depend primarily on your data. Doctors' surgeries heave with patients allocated ten-minute slots and allowed to discuss only one health problem per visit. In a system stretched to its limits, data steps into the breach to make a decision for you. Beneath the glowing surface of the prevention industry lies the hard reality of ending comprehensive healthcare and where this will really take us next.

I CAN'T PRESCRIBE A BETTER HUSBAND

Dr Marie Williams is a GP in Blackpool, Britain's most medicated city for depression. 'I can't prescribe a drug for a better job or a better husband or better housing. There is a direct correlation between poverty and bad health and yet dealing with the underlying causes is not my job. It's beyond my remit.' Does Dr Williams believe she is enabling poverty rather than treating depression when she prescribes pills? 'Wow, that's an immensely complex question. But short answer, yes.'

I spend a couple of days meeting some of the people whom Dr Williams sees. John (not his real name) is twenty-four and has tried to commit suicide a number of times. He never goes through with it, because he can always envision himself alive at the end and 'I don't want to feel the rope cutting into my neck.' When he is in an 'episode', he needs antidepressants to help him out of the hole. But sometimes they take weeks to kick in and in the meantime, he is dependent on talking therapy.

I meet a number of people like John in Blackpool with clinical depression and suicidal tendencies. They all say the same thing: talking therapy – maintaining an ongoing connection with an empathetic individual – is what keeps them going, not anti-depressants. Talking therapy costs the NHS a fraction of the ever-escalating cost of antidepressants and, according to Steve – a psychiatric counsellor I meet who works in the North West – is the only long-term solution for the patients that will bring them back into the functioning world. Certainly not anti-depressants.

John agrees and says that antidepressants are viewed in Blackpool like illegal drugs, 'but just don't make you feel as good.' They're traded with street drugs and simply provide another option for getting out of it, often in combination with temazepam or heroin.

Part of the self-fulfilling prophecy of an over-medicated society is that once it has been created, we demand the medication. Dr Williams says she has patients who come in because their pet has died, and they demand antidepressants. They are sad, she says, not depressed, and feeling sad is part of being human. But because unhappiness is not part of the brochure for modern life, we demand medication to obliterate it. 'People have an expectation that happiness should be a perpetual state of normality. It isn't, but we've created an unrealistic expectation that it should be,' and so drugs are there to make it happen.

Vince Parry worked for Eli Lilly in the United States, where the antidepressant Prozac was originally developed as a slimming drug. Then the company realised Prozac also had antidepressant qualities. Prozac could be remarketed far more lucratively as an antidepressant than as a slimming aid.[19] But Prozac wasn't merely going to treat depression, it was about to boot up the happiness industry.

For Prozac to stand out, it needed a unique selling point. Parry and Eli Lilly came up with one: Prozac would take the shame and stigma out of depression and make taking a drug to deal with depression a positive lifestyle choice. It would make saying you were on Prozac almost aspirational.

The problem with depression, psychiatrist Loren Mosher once said, is that it's depressing. If Eli Lilly could get users to brag about using Prozac, spreading its virtues by word of mouth, then it would have a major hit. Prozac was to become the first antidepressant drug you became happy to say you were on.

Prozac, a trade name for fluoxetine, was first developed as an antihistamine by two scientists, Bryan Molloy and Robert Rathbun, in 1971. It was known then by its compound name LY-110141, but was soon given an actual name: fluoxetine. This extraordinary compound exhibited numerous commercial possibilities. It could potentially treat eating disorders, be used as a slimming drug, reduce blood pressure and significantly reduce panic disorder and OCD, to name but a few applications. There were any number of ways the drug could be used, and at the time, depression did not appear to be a particularly lucrative one.

This was because in the mid-1970s antidepressants were largely restricted to use in psychiatry units. 'Anxiety' and nervous conditions rather than depression were more commonly diagnosed in the public outside these psychiatric units, and Valium was the go-to drug for these disorders.

However, at the very beginning of Eli Lilly's trials on fluoxetine, researchers had already identified its nascent antidepressant properties, specifically its ability to concentrate serotonin levels to boost the depletion of neurotransmitters in the central nervous system, a key chemical cause of depression.

Prozac is marketed as an SSRI, or 'selective serotonin reuptake inhibitor', and it was the potency of the drug in increasing concentrations of serotonin that first alerted Eli Lilly to its dramatic antidepressant potential. In 1974, scientist David T. Wong published a paper on fluoxetine's SSRI characteristics. But the market for antidepressant drugs beyond Valium wasn't there, so Eli Lilly bided its time. In 1974, fluoxetine was still ahead of the curve: a treatment the world was not yet ready for.

In 1975, Eli Lilly gave fluoxetine the trade name Prozac. The company filed an NDA (new drug application) for Prozac in 1977, but it took a full decade to get FDA approval, finally launching publicly in the United States in December 1987. Prozac's rapid success after launch has been credited to Eli Lilly's handing the drug's marketing to a company called Interbrand, responsible for the rebranding of some of the world's biggest multinationals, including Sony, Microsoft, Nikon and Nintendo.

Interbrand's strategy focused on the aspirational and easy-to-use aspects of the drug. The name was cool. As Anna Moore in the *Guardian* wrote at the time: 'Prozac hit a society that was [now] in the mood for it.' Depression was no longer a fringe medical condition, but was on the lips of middle-class couples at dinner parties, who by the mid-1980s had therapists and discussed therapy as openly as they discussed changing the colour of their Laura Ashley curtains. The culture was ready for Prozac. 'National campaigns supported by Eli Lilly,' Moore says, 'alerted GPs and the public to the dangers of depression. Eli Lilly funded a brochure entitled "Depression: What You Need to Know" and distributed 200,000 posters raising awareness. Previous anti-depressants were highly toxic, lethal if overdosed . . . Prozac was pushed as entirely safe, to be doled out by anyone. It was the wonder drug, the neurological Eldorado. When launch day dawned, patients were already asking for it by name.'

Within a year, US sales reached $350 million. Prozac dwarfed its antidepressant competitors and was soon to become as big as Valium had been in the 1960s, with global revenue of $2.6 billion.

Happiness is a universal human desire, but the expectation that we need to be perpetually cheerful has, Dr Williams says, made us more depressed and increased a sense in patients that they do not measure up. The bar has been raised and anything under it cannot be tolerated when we have unrealistic expectations to feel flat-line happiness at all times, and demand medication to maintain it.

And for subtle or nuanced mood swings that do not fit this Soma state of emoji bliss, we have definitive syndromes and drugs to put you on the cloud. Prescription drugs become a normalising sedative for any state: manic euphoria, restlessness, boredom, depression, overachievement and burnout, the maintenance of unendurable poverty and anything in-between. Drugs for coping with modern life, as Henry Gadsen had dreamt of, and a pill to flatten and numb any sensation. And nowhere is this labelling and numbing with medication more widespread than with 'difficult' children, millions of whom are scooped into being diagnosed with ADHD.

DSM III, IV AND V: THE JOURNEY TO ADHD AND THE MEDICATED CHILD

More than six million American children, eleven per cent aged four to seventeen, have been diagnosed with ADHD (attention deficit hyperactive disorder). The figure has doubled in a decade, and increases incrementally year on year.[21] And look at that age range again: four to seventeen. Four-year-olds are not the youngest children diagnosed. Two- and three-year-olds are regularly prescribed Adderall and Vyvanse for ADHD, and there is no lower limit to when a child can be diagnosed as a problem, placed on drugs, and normalised for the purposes of fitting in at school and at home.

Just as antidepressants enable the underlying economic structure of poverty to be maintained, so Ritalin and Adderall medicate 'problem' children, sustaining the architecture of the modern atomised family.

By parking drugged-out five-year-olds in front of an iPad or Xbox, parents stretched by long hours with multiple jobs, low income, and the stressful demands of home life have this pressurised structure enabled by drugs – both for themselves and their children.

In San Bernardino, I sit in on a therapy session between a psychiatrist and a nine-year-old diagnosed with ADHD. He was first diagnosed when he was five, though the therapist sees kids as young as three. The boy fidgets nervously throughout. When asked why he is here, he mumbles that he doesn't know. Asked how he feels, he wrings his hands furiously. I ask his parents why he is like this. 'He's medicated.' And do you think that benefits him? 'Definitely, he's far more focused at school.' How did he come to be diagnosed? 'We didn't think there was a problem, but when he started at school, the teacher said she thought he was ADHD, so he was diagnosed.' You didn't think there was a problem before? 'No.' How many kids in his class are like him? 'About thirty per cent are ADHD.'

Are the economic pressures on a modern family any greater than a hundred years ago? No. But the expectations are. Medication for ADHD kids provides a chemical childminder, a tool for keeping a class quiet, or enabling the overstretched family unit to cope at home. In the wider context, drugs are an enabler for stress and low pay to continue to bear down on millions of families and be normalised. Treating illness or promoting wellness does not come into it.

Parents often wonder if they are doing the right thing by giving their kids drugs, but they are given the drugs by doctors anyway. As one parent on an ADHD support chatroom said: 'Perhaps my child is just being a child.' The medical basis for ADHD is often questioned by the very people responsible for diagnosing it, and the journey this syndrome has taken from non-existence to cast-iron, bona fide condition illustrates the journey all syndromes take from invisibility to enabling modern life. A solution to a problem we never knew was a problem, till we were offered the solution.

The journey towards the medication of modern life took a decisive turn in the early 1970s. The psychiatric profession faced a reputational low. In the Soviet Union, psychiatry had been used to silence political dissidents by labelling them schizophrenic. Psychiatrists in the West began to examine the reliability of their profession's own diagnostic practices. What they were to discover and subsequently propose would change the way we define normality.

David Rosenhan, a social psychologist at Stanford, wanted to put psychiatry's diagnostic acumen to the test. While a student, Rosenhan had attended R.D. Laing's lectures at Stanford. It was at these lectures that Laing argued schizophrenia was 'theory not fact' and began to formulate his argument against the 'medical model of mental illness'. Laing was like a cult leader pronouncing before a rapt audience of devotees, and Rosenhan was as enthralled as anyone else.

In 1973, to test the medical basis for a diagnosis of schizophrenia, Rosenhan recruited a number of pseudo-patients, screened to exclude anyone with a prior history of psychiatric disorder. Rosenhan instructed them to show up at a local mental-health facility and complain that they were hearing voices in their heads saying things like 'empty' and 'thud'. Otherwise, they were to behave normally.[22]

What happened amazed Rosenhan. All the pseudo-patients were immediately admitted as inpatients and diagnosed as psychotic. Their psychosis was labelled schizophrenia: a diagnosis based solely on the patients hearing the word 'thud'. Even other patients spotted the fact that they were fake pseudo-patients, but the doctors did not. When eventually sent home, having ceased to exhibit further signs of psychosis, many were discharged with the label 'schizophrenia in remission'. One was refused discharge, however, and had to be rescued by Rosenhan after several weeks in confinement.

Two years after Rosenhan's experiment, Ken Kesey's book *One Flew Over the Cuckoo's Nest* was released as a movie starring Jack Nicholson as a pseudo-patient refused discharge from a mental institution. The 'anti-psychiatry' of R.D. Laing and Rosenhan was now box office: the anti-establishment message of anti-psychiatry meshing with America's widespread distrust of authority in the wake of Watergate. Politicians and psychiatrists were on a par in the minds of the public – equally distrusted and seen as part of an institutional culture of lies.

Melvin Sabshin, medical director of the American Psychiatric Association, believed psychiatry needed to fight back. In 1977, he said that 'a vigorous effort to re-medicalise psychiatry should be strongly supported.' Sabshin declared a public relations war on psychiatry's critics.

To re-establish its reputation, the psychiatric profession was to co-opt Columbia University's Robert Spitzer to come up with a plan to devise 'reliable' scientific criteria for all psychological conditions. A rock-solid, diagnostic bible that would leave no psychological condition unmapped or undefined.[23] If someone came in off the street hearing a word 'thud' in their head, they would be able to put an exact label on that thud immediately. Spitzer was to set America down the road of labelling everyone as a sufferer of something.

In less than three years, mental illness shifted from a broad series of symptoms subjectively read, to a categorical disease. A psychiatric bible was produced called the *DSM*, or *Diagnostic and Statistical Manual of Mental Disorders*.

To create a definitive clinical diagnosis, the *DSM-III* task force led by Robert Spitzer adopted a 'tick the boxes' approach to assigning symptoms and mental-condition labels. Find any six symptoms from a list of ten and *voilà*, you have before you a schizophrenic. Why six? As Spitzer later explained, six symptoms 'felt about right'.

This emphasis on symptoms benefited a number of interests. It helped silence the critics of psychiatry, who claimed that mental illnesses could not be defined in an objective way. It allowed clinicians to obtain reimbursement from insurers, and most crucially, it gave pharmaceutical companies specific mental illnesses for which they could now supply drugs.

Two more *DSM* bibles have been published since 1980, and each new edition comes with a raft of new mental conditions. The *DSM* tops the bestseller list and each edition is thicker than the last. Even its authors now argue that *DSM* has led to the widespread misdiagnosis of mental illness. Dr Allen Frances, who led the *DSM-IV* task force in 1994, later issued a *mea culpa*. He now confesses that the epidemic of new diagnoses of autism, ADHD and depression that followed the issuance of *DSM-IV* was largely 'iatrogenic' – the product of a series of well-intentioned mistakes on his part.[24]

We met in San Diego, where Frances now lives. He is a formidable character and shockingly forthright. 'There were reasons this all happened, you know.' Was it wrong? 'Of course it was wrong. We were wrong. Everyone involved has regrets. You can't go through life not talking about things you did that you regret – that's why you're here talking to me. Can we put it right now? I don't know. We have medicated billions of people we shouldn't have, based on the flimsiest evidence.'

Allen believes many of the doctors involved in the pushing of *DSM* over-diagnosis and over-medication have the same regrets.

In 2013, *DSM-V* was published. 'Most of the changes made to the *DSM-V*,' Frances says, 'are based on limited data, the evidence is remarkably weak for changing anything. *DSM-V* opens up the possibility that millions and millions of people currently considered normal will be diagnosed as having a mental disorder and will receive medication and stigma that they don't need.'

DSM-III created clear, standardised, psychopathological categories. This provided the drugs companies with an incentive to launch randomised controlled trials to test newly developed drugs for the treatment of specific new *DSM-III* disorders.

DSM-III was great news for the pharmaceutical companies. For any medication to be approved by the FDA, a drug needs to be proven effective in the treatment of a specific disease. If a number of drugs already do the job, approval is less likely, so it is far more likely a drug will be approved for a newly diagnosed condition than enter a crowded market for an existing one. And thanks to the connections FDA panellists have with pharma companies, it can be.

DSM-III created a massive new market. In the years following the publication of the *DSM-III*, billions of dollars were allocated by government and pharmaceutical companies for psychopharmacalogical research. Throughout the 1980s, the federal research budget allocated to the US National Institute of Mental Health increased by eighty-four per cent to $484 million annually.[25]

The ever-widening definition of mental illness, and its enshrining as medical fact in each new edition of the *DSM*, meant that millions more Americans each year found themselves on drugs. But it was when the *DSM* extended its reach over children, via ADD and ADHD, that a bridge was crossed and a taboo broken. By ceasing to see children as children but instead as patients, and expressions of childhood not as part of being a child but symptoms of an illness, a paradigm shift occurred.

Drugs companies and psychiatrists did not do this in isolation. Whether modern life became more stressful or not, adults began to perceive their lives as more stressful, and this willingness to accept a diagnosis of psychiatric illness in children was because this diagnosis then formed a justification for tranquillising them.

We would not have to deal with the problems a child displayed at home or in school, especially if we conflated the problem with the child. By popping pills before work, we could survive the day, and in the evening, domestic life. By giving pills to kids, they were no longer a 'problem'.

The medicalisation of modern life enabled modern life to function, and this was the brilliance of Gadsden's insight in 1980, when he first saw the future in a stick of gum.

AN ILLNESS NO ONE IS IMMUNE FROM

By 1987, seven years after Gadsden's interview in *Fortune*, his dream had not yet been realised. *DSM* was well on its way to hoovering up half the American population as mentally ill, but the drugs industry had yet to find one big blockbuster illness that no one was immune from. That was all about to change, and this is where my stroke drugs make a grand entrance. A disease was discovered that was bigger than cancer, bigger than heart disease, and everyone would get. It was called 'risk'.

When the medical profession treats people who are actually ill, they are treating a tiny percentage of the population. By treating people at risk, the number of patients given drugs grows exponentially. If you can define risk at its widest possible parameter, the entire game is changed. We are all patients.

Risk worked wonders reinventing Wall Street, but applied to illness, it could reap rewards that even those who pioneered its adoption in medicine could scarcely believe were possible. Risk has become the key medical concept of the last twenty years. It does in many ways the exact opposite of what Spitzer and the *DSM* sought to do with mental illness, to make diagnosis cast-iron.

With risk, the opposite needs to happen. A clear, diagnosable illness needs to become a fuzzily defined risk of potential illness that you might get in the future. 'You have cancer, here are the drugs to deal with cancer,' becomes, 'Here are the twenty risks associated with cancer, and here are the twenty drugs that can be taken to deal with that risk.' Risk is the clincher in creating the medicated society. Because we are all untimately at risk of getting something, and no one dares take the risk of not following the prognosis.

In 1987, risk found its vehicle. Merck launched Mevacor, a statin for cholesterol. Cholesterol had always been considered a factor in heart disease, but now it was to be made the main factor in heart disease and it was up to Merck – and Pfizer, with Lipitor – to make cholesterol the only game in town.

Here is how the magic happened. In 1995, thirteen million people in the US (five million in the UK) were said to be 'at risk' from high cholesterol. These figures were determined by the National Institutes of Health, the leading independent health body in the US. Figures based on the level at which a cholesterol reading is considered high.

How did it happen? Raymond Moynihan and colleagues at *PLOS Medicine* undertook a cross-sectional study of widening risk and the ties between experts and drugs companies between 2000 and 2013. Of sixteen publications on fourteen common conditions, ten proposed changes widening definitions, and only one narrowing them. Among fourteen panels with disclosures, the average number of ties with the pharmaceutical industry was seventy-five per cent.[26]

We might imagine a panel like the NIH, or indeed the FDA, to be independent bodies. They are not. It is normal practice for a large number of panel members on an 'independent' panel to have direct ties to one or other of the six pharmaceutical giants. It is naïve to think this does not happen; at one level it could even be considered necessary. The pharma giants are developing drugs that need constant testing and re-evaluation; they are inevitably and appropriately in consultation with the people deciding whether this drug gets a licence. The question is whether this closeness means they cross a line.

Panel members are under immense pressure, and when they get together and make a decision that will prevent a multibillion-dollar drug from gaining a licence, they are suddenly a problem. It is in the drugs industry's interest for that problem to not arise.

Following the decision of the NIH in 2001, the number of Americans defined as being 'at risk' from high cholesterol trebled overnight from thirteen million to thirty-six million. In 2004, it went up again to forty million. In Britain, there was a correspondingly miraculous leap from fourteen million to twenty-seven million. This was not an incremental increase, this was an unprecedented leap. In the same period, those diagnosed with Attention Deficit Disorder went up by eight hundred per cent.

This was a staggering jump in numbers, but could the cholesterol spike be explained by something else, such as the explosion in obesity over the same period? Not really. The obese have high cholesterol to begin with. They are already factored into the original numbers.

The explanation is simple: millions of people previously on the safe side of the line were suddenly swept up and dumped in the red zone marked 'at risk'. This is known as 'net widening'. Roping patients with relatively minor symptoms into a far more serious condition. In this way, osteoporosis becomes an umbrella term for anyone with some kind of rheumatoid ache.

Another way of net widening is diagnosing someone as 'on the spectrum'. Depression can be widened to include anyone feeling a bit down – the sad patients that Dr Williams sees in Blackpool – who demand medication. 'Spectrum autism' encompasses anyone from the socially awkward, right through to those genuinely severely autistic. There is another term for 'spectrum autism'. It is called being male. In 2014, the *British Medical Journal* estimated that forty per cent of men are on the autism spectrum. That is widening the net in spectacular fashion to forty per cent of fifty-two per cent of the population.

Net widening is sold as progress; greater complexity of diagnosis must mean a better understanding of a condition. But it could equally be the exact opposite: a fuzzing of previously distinct medical terms to net more potential patients, meaning more people taking drugs.

Once these potential customers have become alarmed by being told they are at risk from a disease, they can be further alarmed by the helpful information available about where those risks could lead. Peter Rost's job at Pfizer was to identify illnesses that could be 'astro-turfed': creating a fake grass-roots campaign, or groundswell of public opinion, quietly funded by a drugs company.

The Boomer Coalition emerged from nowhere in 2004, a patient advocacy group highlighting the healthcare needs of fifty-something baby boomers. Henry 'The Fonz' Winkler and 'Wonder Woman' Lynda Carter fronted the campaign. But buried in their seemingly innocuous drive to get middle-aged people to do more star jumps to stay fit was a call to 'know your numbers' on cholesterol.

The Boomer campaign got worldwide coverage, thanks to a video of Henry Winkler doing press-ups in his leather jacket going viral. But in the small print of their 'Boomer Manifesto' was a demand for statins to be prescribed to everyone over forty. It turned out that the marketing company working for Pfizer, the owners of cholesterol statin Lipitor, were behind the entire grass-roots campaign.[27]

Joe Dumit, associate professor of anthropology and science technology at MIT, has made a study of net-widening practices which, he says, work in two ways: genuine well-established conditions like high cholesterol, or osteoporosis, are used to scoop up millions of people with far milder versions under a single banner.

But 'I wouldn't draw such a clean line between manufactured and real diseases.' And the ambiguity is what makes it work for business. In the 1990s, Gulf War veterans seeking a meeting in Washington to discuss the appalling cluster of symptoms they were experiencing on their return from battle (nausea, depression, violent and suicidal thoughts) met a wall of silence. Gulf

War Syndrome was something both the Army and the White House hoped would go away.

But when they got the backing of drugs companies, the character of the debate changed. Gulf War Syndrome became conflated with the controversial socio-medical condition of 'post-traumatic stress disorder', or PTSD, a condition for which experts were still debating the medical basis. 'When Zoloft was approved in 1999 for PTSD, almost every article that came out about PTSD now more or less no longer questioned the existence of the disease, but instead talked about the treatment.'[28]

By attaching Gulf War Syndrome to post-traumatic stress disorder, Bayer could wheel out Zoloft as the solution. PTSD was now accepted as a condition and not simply for ex-soldiers waking in the middle of the night shaking with fear, but for a child who had fallen off a slide, or an old lady bitten by a dog. PTSD had been net-widened to include anyone, and trauma could be widened infinitely to mean anything nasty that might have happened to you.

FALLING DOWN THE K HOLE

Big pharma did sterling work in turning the once unpromising arena of mental health into a huge cash cow. But the problem Gadsen first identified in 1980 – the patent cliff – never went away, and has proved disastrous for psychiatric drugs, too. Zoloft, Prozac, Celexa and Lexapro have all taken a major hit from generic competition and the result has been for the drug industry to reluctantly turn its back on finding the next big blockbuster. Between 2006 and 2016, drug company research programmes into new psychopharmacological drugs shrunk by seventy per cent.

Why carry out years of costly research, they argue, only to have your drug go generic at the end of it? Even when an SSRI is profitable, many doctors, psychiatrists and patients continue to question their effectiveness, arguing that SSRIs are at best a placebo, at worst a chemical intervention that takes too long to work and can end up making you feel worse.

But they have not given up, and turned to an unlikely candidate as the next big anti-depressant: a horse tranquilliser taken by ravers. Richard Friedman, Professor of Clinical Psychiatry at Weill Cornell Medical School in New York, says, 'Ketamine is interesting because it is the first drug that shows acute anti-depressant effects that occur within hours, when currently available anti-depressants typically take two to four weeks to work.'

It seems that John in Blackpool, taking prescription drugs in combination with street drugs, was not so far off cutting-edge medical thinking on treating depression. '(Ketamine) targets the glutamate system, which is a fast-acting system no other anti-depressant targets,' Friedman says. A clutch of big pharma multinationals including Johnson & Johnson are reportedly in late-stage trials for ketamine-based anti-depressants.

I WILL SURVIVE AND IF I DON'T IT IS MY FAULT

We now medicalise every aspect of our lives, every last crevice. Each neurosis, anxiety, twitch or strange uncomfortable feeling we get while walking round a shopping centre or stuck in traffic, washing the dishes or telling off our children. All can be given a label, smoothed out and dulled, allowing us to float serenely through the day on a cloud of medication. Gadsden was more visionary than even he realised.

When he was interviewed by *Fortune* in 1980, you would have been hard pushed in New York to find more than a sprinkling of cranky health-food shops run by sallow people in home-knit jumpers, selling some dusty bottles of vitamins.

Today, the 'wellness' industry is worth $300 billion. Supplements, vitamins, superfoods, yoga, cranial realignment, mindfulness, serotonin therapy, colonic irrigation, detox your gut, liver, intestine, or simply retreat and reboot your entire being (for $500 a time) in a bleached-granite health spa with a single, strategic orchid on a huge, marble reception altar. Greeted by someone dressed in a lab coat, as if boarding your own private medical jet.

Gadsden made wellness not solely insulation from future illness, but an elitist identity. Wellness is really code for successful and wealthy. A marker of how seriously we take competing in the world. The fact that we have monetised our bodies and treat them as a commodity with a market value to be measured against other buff bodies, is a measure of how far the neo-liberal notion of the market has spread into everyday life. Gym clothes are now worn tight rather than baggy, as they were twenty years ago – as a display of your physical stock value, with its transferable value at work: proof you work hard in the gym becoming implied proof you will work tirelessly in the office. Gym clothes are even worn to the supermarket: an ostentatious display of physical prime.

Wellness is an identity for the successful and illness has become an identity for the poor. Just as the late 1960s and early 1970s saw an explosion in identity politics for the politically marginalised and disenfranchised – the Gay Liberation Front, the Black Panthers, feminist movements across the world, separatist nationalist groups from the Basques to the Palestinians – so identity politics became co-opted by those with medical conditions.

Just as the drugs industry piggy-backed on R.D. Laing's 'anti-psychiatry', now it piggy-backed on far-left politics, specifically the 'identity politics' of the disempowered. One of the key selling points of syndromes is to give the sufferer a label. As the disempowered gained empowerment by labelling themselves as 'gay', 'black' or 'feminist', so those suffering from a medical condition could now label themselves as 'bi-polar', 'clinically depressed' or 'cancer survivor'.

Positive thinking is deemed essential to surviving a disease such as cancer. But the subtext of empowerment is that it shifts responsibility subtly away from the healthcare provider to the patient. The onus is on you: if you survive cancer, then you did it yourself through courage and force of will. If you fail, you did not try hard enough.

'Positive thinking' is the mantra of our times. By dramatising disease as a battle between the hero (the patient) and the invader (the illness), we have turned health into the ultimate platform of hyper-individualistic self-determination. A battle with ourselves: our strong self-willed half versus the weak disease-ridden half. A fight for our own bodies. The real message of positive thinking is that only the most determined and focused survive, as in business. But this is medically false. You survived cancer because you did, and the drugs played a major role. But 'positive thinking' suggests that self-agency is the key, and everything else is background. A moral subtext described by writer and breast-cancer survivor Barbara Ehrenreich as 'smile or die'.[29]

Applied to the NHS, positive thinking and the self-policed body will ultimately be the battering ram for dismantlement. You do not need care if you work hard, and if you did not work hard, you don't deserve care. By obsessively monitoring cholesterol, calorie intake, steps taken, visits to the gym, the drive of the new self-help philosophy is to create a steel trap of irrefutable data that will decide precisely what you get when that need for help arises.

For those that failed to work hard enough, there will always be drugs. But there is a sting in the tail. Take statins. Statins make the pharmaceutical industry $35 billion. Dr Navid Malik, a pharmaceutical analyst at Matrix Partners, has analysed their effectiveness, just as my consultant did when I had a stroke: 'Statins are very high margin, so if a statin generates around twenty per cent of a company's sales, it's likely to contribute thirty per cent of its profits.'

But do they work?

'Statins have been the fairytale story in the industry,' says

Malik. 'But heart disease is still the number-one killer in the Western world, so one could argue how much value for money have we really got out of their use?' The miracle catch-all drug, the fastest-growing prescribed drug on earth, does not even touch the number-one killer.

TWO SPECIES

Professor Julian Savulescu looks out of the window across the immaculately manicured lawn of the Oxford college where he lectures, smoothing his pink shirt.

'I've been accused of being a Nazi.' (He's not a Nazi, he is a quietly spoken Antipodean academic.) 'Some of my colleagues are more out there.' (One – a Swedish geneticist called Anders Sandberg – believes human beings will be able to develop wings as a cosmetic genetic addendum, should they wish to do so.)

Savulescu is one of the world's evangelists for 'gene editing' – a bespoke advance on genetic engineering that allows certain genes, such as those for inherited disease, to be isolated and edited out at the embryo stage. It is made possible by an extremely precise technique developed in 2012 called CRISPR-Cas9, allowing the genome to be sliced and the offending gene removed. More controversial still, certain attributes (better cheekbones, intelligence, physical strength) could be 'edited in'. It is a chance, Savulescu says, to perfect humanity.

In April 2015, Francis Collins, director of the US National Institutes of Health, said that CRISPR-Cas9 is a profound danger to humanity. It is, he says, quite simply 'a line that should not be crossed.'

'There is already proof that you can gene edit monkeys to be more hard-working,' says Savulescu. 'Do we want this in humans? Do we want to be able to isolate Down's syndrome or autism and edit them out? These are questions for society, but the technology is there.'

But isn't that eugenics? 'It is eugenics, but so was what went before. The human animal is not some finely balanced master-piece of divine creation. It is the result of natural selection under particular environmental pressures. Humans exhibit some two hundred and fifty genetic disorders, only twenty to twenty-five per cent of embryos are fit enough to develop into a baby, and six per cent of newborns exhibit a major birth defect. DNA manipulation allows us to correct genetic aberrations ... it allows us to liberate ourselves from the biological constraints of evolution and move toward a state of self-designed evolution.'

To deny the power humans now have to supersede nature, with all nature's inherent cruelties and aberrations, would be, Savulescu says, a perverse error. Nazism, Savulescu has said, gave eugenics a bad name. Gene editing makes it possible for human beings to perfect themselves by eradicating everything unwanted: from serious hereditary disease such as Huntington's, to small cosmetic tweaks for characteristics we dislike.

Blonde blue-eyed babies? Why not? Savulescu says the deci-sion of whether to perfect your child will be yours – it will not be Nazism, but consumer choice. These moral decisions will to some degree be no different from today: if you wish to go ahead with or terminate a foetus with probable Down's Syndrome, that choice is given to you now with the CVS test.

According to Savulescu, the brave new world of gene editing is already here. It is an arms race and the West is losing it. China is experimenting on an 'industrial scale' with embryos, because it does not have its hands tied by the ethical constraints of the 'Judeo-Christian tradition'. What does losing this genetic arms race mean? 'Will China be able to make themselves a physically superior master race? Not just yet, but why ultimately not? They see no qualms about winning and how they win.'

THE WOMAN WHO STOPPED AGEING

Elizabeth Parrish is genetically modified. The world's first GM person. With injections, she has lengthened her telomeres, the ends of her DNA strands. Telomeres protect the genetic material held in DNA from damage caused by ageing. By changing her telomeres, Parrish has effectively stopped ageing.

We meet in London and I spent an overly long amount of time staring rudely at Liz's face. Parrish only had this gene editing done a couple of years ago so it's hard to see physical evidence of it working yet. Liz is running constant tests and thinks her genetic age could be ten years younger than her actual age, putting her biologically in her mid-forties, but genetically at thirty-five. 'But that isn't the goal, the goal is to reverse ageing till it stops at the peak age, which is around twenty-five.' It won't be like Benjamin Button. She won't end up a baby.

How much does this cost? 'It's prohibitively expensive at the moment.' Over a million pounds. So the rich, if they choose to do what Liz has done, will be perma-young while everyone else ages as they always have. Isn't it wrong to use technology in this way? 'The goal is not beauty treatment for the rich but to eradicate diseases associated with ageing.' Liz isn't doing this for fun, she's CEO of BioViva, a Seattle-based biotech company and the plan is to use herself as a human guinea pig to show the world what can be achieved. At a price.

'You know,' she says, 'it's pretty silly to see human beings as the polar opposite of technology. Human DNA is just a code sequence that runs as a program throughout your life. You are a machine running to the program and nature too is technology. So why can't we utilise that technology to enhance ourselves if we can? I see a squid swimming in the sea and I think there's a beautiful piece of technology. Some people might want to have the technology available to animals. Amazing eyesight like a bird has or to glow like a jellyfish, and soon we will be able to.'

THE GAME WE'RE ALL PLAYING

In East London, I'm at a five-a-side football match with a fantastically intense man called Eddie Perello, who is one of the few people in this brave new world talking any sense. Perello is founder of DeskGen, who don't just analyse the direction gene editing is taking humanity, but seek to establish some ground rules. Eddie has asked to meet at a football match, because he wants to explain where CRISPR gene editing could go.

'If you look at these players,' he says, the rain pelting down, 'what do you see?' 'Ten men playing football?' 'Right, with comparable DNA. Imagine if one wanted to be a better footballer than the rest and could use gene editing, would he do it?' 'For sure.' 'And the rest, once they found out why he was a better footballer?' 'They'd follow suit.'

An arms race would ensue. A different arms race from the one between nations. An arms race between people and one without end. Because the players would all be genetically enhanced, they'd effectively be back to square one on a level playing field.

Gene editing could lead not just to an arms race to get ever stronger and fitter, but to all manner of unexpected genetic side effects: some beneficial, some not. 'That same edit to improve football skill could thirty years down the line in old age strengthen bones, which would slow osteoporosis, so it would have an unintended knock-on effect.' Intervention to improve athletic performance would over time become a medical intervention.

To tinker with your genetic code is to throw a huge rock in a delicate genetic pool and create myriad unexpected ripple effects. Gene editing is precise, Perello says, but not so precise as not to potentially interfere and produce random ripples that amplify over time.

'Compare what happened with global warming. Humanity came to the table too late and even then, cannot agree on what to do. Gene editing has the potential to be every bit as far-reaching for the fate of humankind and what's needed is to get to the table now and agree an international code of conduct that we all sign up to.'

Intervening at DNA level with serious medical conditions such as cancer, MS, heart disease or Huntington's, isolating and snipping the gene is not the issue. It is lengthening lifespan and genetic enhancement – the arms race – that needs the code of conduct.

But if we were to look at global warming as a prelude to gene editing, then the future for a coordinated governmental strategy does not look encouraging. 'Governments,' Perello says, 'are so, so far behind the curve. How can they even begin to conceive what's being done in laboratories, be up with the latest developments in a field that's constantly moving?' They haven't a clue, nor a way of getting up to speed, let alone staying there.

The consequence of gene editing will be two separate species. Those practising gene editing will be able to take themselves to the next level of perfection – to a genetic state of superiority: stronger, fitter, better-looking and even glowing in the dark at cocktail parties.

The poor will continue as humans: subsisting as mere mortals with the same illnesses, facial features and tendencies to grow fat, old and as frail as their ancestors. There will be two teams playing football, but one team will be the Human A Team and the other the Human B Team. Twentieth-century economic inequality will have become twenty-first-century biological inequality: the wealthy will just have a different genetic make-up from everyone else. A better species of human, and it all began with a stick of gum.

CHAPTER SEVEN
WORK: FROM WHAT WE DO TO WHO WE ARE

The Deal: McKinsey and the 7S Framework deal with Siemens and PepsiCo

Aim: The creation of an entirely new system of organising companies and incentivising employees, devised by McKinsey analysts Tom Peters and Robert Waterman

Where: Siemens Headquarters, Munich, and PepsiCo Global Headquarters, Purchase, New York

When: November 1979

This is what twelve per cent of the population are going to do tonight: wake up and check their email. In the morning, fifty-one per cent of us are going to spend more time checking email than eating breakfast. Seventy per cent will check email on an hourly basis throughout the day, ten per cent every ten minutes.[1]

The line between work and personal time has gone, and the way we work has become a way of life. Eighty-one per cent of us check work email at weekends, fifty-nine per cent on holiday. One in ten parents at sports day are checking work email as their kid runs a race. People at funerals are tap-tap-tapping into their phone as the coffin passes. Work has taken over our lives, but those checking email at a funeral are not a freakish, work-obsessed few. Given a chance to work – anywhere, any time – we will.

At night, the technology we use to monitor work really comes into its own. The blue glow that phones emit wreaks havoc with melatonin, the sleep hormone, tricking our brains into thinking it is day. Consistent lack of sleep leads to higher blood pressure, increased risk of heart disease and diabetes, anxiety, depression, even a drop in fertility.[2]

The average person now spends more time on their phone and laptop than asleep: 8 hours 21 minutes versus 8 hours 41 minutes on media devices. Eighty per cent of thirteen-to-fifteen-year-olds use screens in bed and this generational normalisation of glowing screens on our pillow is changing the nature of rest.[3]

Scrolling through a phone and checking mail in bed creates 'active' shallow sleep by reactivating the working memory. Technology puts the brain in a state of borderline anxiety, prepped to wake at any moment. This means we never truly switch off when asleep. Three-quarters of all adults are now failing to get adequate rest at night, so we are exhausted when we wake.

Putting work first is sacrosanct, yet we hate ourselves for it. In the movie *Elf*, James Caan plays a workaholic father on Christmas Eve given the choice between looking for his missing son and staying late at work to go through a PowerPoint presentation. 'If you walk out that door,' his boss shouts, 'you're finished.' James Caan chooses to look for his son and leaves. It is an empowerment fantasy everyone wants to believe – choosing life over work – but the truth is that no one contradicts the boss for fear they will be finished.

In times of extreme stress, work provides an all-consuming diversion from emotional trauma. We turn to what we know, which now increasingly means burying ourselves in work rather than the emotional support of our families. How did this come to be? How did work embed itself so completely in our lives, and where is it taking us as a species?

THE INVENTION OF EFFICIENCY

In 1888, a jeweller in Auburn, New York, called Willard Le Grand Bundy invented a clock. The Bundy Clock did not simply tell the time, it allowed employees to punch in the exact time they 'clocked' in and out.

Unlike previous versions of punch cards and time clocks, the Bundy Clock had individual keys for each employee, so no one could cheat the system by getting one person to mass-punch a bunch of cards. For the first time, a fail-safe machine for policing the hours of the workforce had been created and its introduction was thanks to one man: Frederick Winslow Taylor, the man you can thank for waking yourself up at 3 a.m. to check your email.

In 1878, a decade before the invention of the Bundy punch-in clock, Fred Winslow Taylor, a Harvard law student with failing eyesight and from a wealthy family, ditched the law and became a machinist at the Midvale Steelworks, New England. Thanks to his eagerness for promotion (and his family connections to the owners), Taylor rose quickly from machinist to middle manager. Then, one day, Taylor approached his bosses with a plan.[4]

I've noticed, he told them, that my colleagues are not working as hard as they might. In order to maximise efficiency, Taylor suggested a 'scientific evaluation' of their work rates with a view to identifying the slackers. They did a deal.

Over the next six months, Taylor was a blur of activity, racing around the plant with a clipboard, frantically making notes and using a stopwatch to measure the productivity of the workers. The Midvale management were impressed with Taylor's findings: he supplied 'time studies' (later to become 'time and motion studies'), optimal lifting and resting periods calculated for the shifting of pig iron, and a 'science of shoveling'. Taylor had a forensically detailed breakdown of every task of the labour force; even an optimal time for toilet breaks. There was only one problem.

He had made the whole lot up. Taylor had worked late into the night falsifying charts and inventing data to give 'scientific' credence to his findings. Findings he knew in advance he was going to make.[5]

Taylor is now widely credited with inventing 'scientific

management'. But at the Midvale Steelworks, he had already applied the first rule of management consultancy: tell the client what they want to hear. Midvale had previously identified a number of inefficiencies. After months of 'scientific' evaluation, Taylor miraculously came to the same conclusion.

Taylor's real talent lay in using 'science' to justify a plan already being implemented. But this was crucially important: by claiming the conclusions reached were scientific, the management had 'evidence' that could not be argued with by disgruntled workers. Management could blame the expert, who could in turn point to the science. In this way, decisions appeared to cease being made by humans at all, and were instead made by an objective, God-like arbiter called data.

Following his triumph at the Midvale Steelworks, Taylor was hailed a genius and became the world's first management guru, thanks largely to his cultivation in circles of power by Boston lawyer Louis Brandeis. Taylor wrote a book, *The Principles of Scientific Management*,[6] which became a bestseller. In 1911, Taylor toured America to packed houses explaining his science of efficiency and how it would change the world.

The public lapped it up eagerly, because science appeared to be able to solve anything. In 1886, Charles Darwin used science to explain evolution. Freud had used science as a way of deciphering the subconscious mind. Management guru Peter Drucker said Taylor was a titan in the same league. 'The first man in history who did not take work for granted, but looked at it and studied it.' Drucker saw Freud, Darwin and Taylor as the foundation of the modern world: decoders of the scientific formula for all human behaviour.[7] American industry was soon queuing at Taylor's door: coal, banking and the railroads all sought his expertise. Taylor became a multimillionaire and one of America's richest men (a billionaire in today's terms).

Not once did anyone think to check that anything he said was true, and so in 1913, he was invited to brief government on how to implement his ideas for the benefit of America. When President

Theodore Roosevelt said in his address to the first Conference of Governors at the White House that 'the conservation of our natural resources is only preliminary to the larger question of national efficiency', he was channelling pure Taylor.[8]

A consultancy deal with government would have cemented his place at the heart of power and pocketed Taylor a fortune. But in 1915, Taylor died suddenly in the middle of the night. He never got to see his grand 'science of management' take over the world. But that is what it did: lighting a touch paper that has you burnt out after a long day at the office, still checking your email at 3 a.m.

THE ABERRATION OF A JOB FOR LIFE

We give our all to work, day and night, but we baulk at the idea that we are merely cogs in a super-efficient machine, as Taylor wanted. We crave freedom and autonomy, a sense of self-worth, not to be moving human parts of a production line.

In actual fact, Taylor did not want workers to feel worthless. He believed efficiency would lead to a greater sense of content-ment. By working to the best of our abilities, we would be valued by our boss. This value would bring job stability. Efficiency would become a virtuous circle.

In the 1880s, employment was as precarious as it is today. Taylor believed greater productivity by the workforce would create equilibrium for company and employee alike. Efficiency would buy security.

But viewing this quid-pro-quo trade-off in the first half of the twenty-first century, it is tempting to ask what went wrong. We have never worked harder and with less security. We are as vulnerable to laying off as the Midvale steel workers, threatened not only by cheaper labour, but the automation revolution. Taylor made us work harder, but we were cheated. The security he promised never happened.

Not quite. For a while, it did. For a thirty-year period between 1950 and 1980 there was an aberration called a job for life. So how did this historical anomaly of workplace stability come into being and who took it away again, bringing us back full circle to an age of uncertainty?

Take three generations of my family. My grandfather was a Corsican immigrant, who came to London in the 1930s looking for casual work. He played the cello and so began performing in café orchestras. Employed by a different café every night, my grandfather was paid cash in hand, but did not know from one night to the next if he had a job the following day. His life, and thus the life of his family, was balanced on a knife edge.

In the 1950s, everything changed. My dad, who had grown up with perpetual financial uncertainty, got a full-time job. He had the same state employer, the Greater London Council, for thirty years. Unlike his father, my dad got a guaranteed pay cheque at the end of the month. He did not need to go out and hawk for coins with a cello. He got up every day, shaved and went to work. A career structure was mapped out before him, with even a pension at the end of it.

But this security was a management construct, as the scientific efficiency of Taylor had been. In the 1950s, Peter Drucker, an Austrian sociologist (the one who had seen Winslow Taylor as an intellectual titan on a par with Freud and Darwin), moved to the US and reinvented himself as a management consultant.

Drucker wanted to change the mentality of the huge corporation. He believed a new kind of boss was needed. In the nineteenth century, sociologist Max Weber had modelled a vision of the corporation on the Prussian army: disciplined and hierarchical, with a CEO behaving like a general.[9]

After the Second World War, Drucker believed productivity would be better harnessed by a kinder, paternalistic boss. A father figure who would be looking after your long-term career interests and with whom you would play golf on Saturdays to gain advantage over your colleagues.

This was the world of work into which my dad stepped in the late 1950s. But this 'caring company' masked an equally tough drive for targets. Drucker advocated a new 'science' of the workplace – one in which the manager was still God, but psychological coercion rather than the stick of efficiency was used to get results.

Using Drucker's theories on psychological coercion, corporations like IBM would write to the wives of male employees, saying that Stanley would not be getting his bonus this year because Stanley had not worked hard enough: no bonus, no new fur coat for you – this was the pre-feminist world of *I Love Lucy*, satirised most acutely in the late-1960s comedy *Bewitched*, in which Samantha and her neurotic husband's entire lives revolved around what the boss thought of their new curtains. In this suffocating, controlled environment, Drucker wanted wives to become agents of the company. Drucker reasoned that the husband was far more likely to do what his wife said than what his boss demanded.

This paternalistic company was not so nurturing after all. It was a total system: an all-seeing eye, determining not only what happened at work, but using the family to push work, too. The company had seeped its way into the fabric of domestic life, keeping up the pressure when Stanley's wife poured him a drink at the end of the day and questioned why she had got that critical letter from his boss.

But then something happened that blew the world of Drucker away and brought efficiency into sharp focus. In 1973, the OPEC oil crisis plunged the world into global recession and suddenly companies were seeking profit not from finding new business, but by making internal cuts. The postwar boom, which had delivered an historical blip of stability and prosperity for millions, was over. The world of precariousness that my grandad had lived in was about to make a dramatic return, swallowing up my dad's job and defining the working world into which I would step.

The catalyst was swift. One morning in 1979, my dad arrived at work. A group of men he had never seen before, wearing what he described as 'Willoughby suits', had taken over a floor and were walking around each department with notepads, asking people what they did. Three months later, the redundancies began.

These Willoughby-suited men were 'management consultants' and were about to streamline the working world with a new 'science' of efficiency, every bit as persuasive as Winslow Taylor's. Their gurus were two men, Tom Peters and Robert Waterman, two rising stars at the world's most elusive and powerful agency: McKinsey.

In 1979, the day my dad went into the office and saw these men with notepads, what he did not know was that they were following a brand-new business model developed by Peters and Waterman.

It was called the 7S Framework, and it was a remarkable piece of work. Peters and Waterman said the successful business of the future would not be a rigid, hierarchical management pyramid, but resemble a complex molecule.[10]

The molecular business would have 'seven interlocking elements, all of which need to be in perfect alignment', like stars on a horoscope. These key elements all began with an S: 'strategy, skills, structure, systems, style, staff, and the nucleus, superordinate goals (or shared values)'. The boss would 'walk around' – micro-managing and generally nosing about. In fact, this would be called MBWA ('management by walking around').[11]

This soft-carpeted panopticon was nothing new – Drucker's corporation micro-monitored the employee – but Peters and Waterman's approach was about changing the employee's mindset. The new world, they said, was turbulent and either you were super-productive or you were out (McKinsey's dictum to its own employees is 'up or out'). Nothing short of total obedience to the company was required if you were to survive, but this obedience must be self-willed. Work would become your cult, and the staff would be devotees worshipping the company like a religion.

THE CULT

For inspiration, McKinsey looked to Japan, where employees knelt on the floor of the canteen each morning and prayed that Hyundai or Toshiba be more profitable. The Japanese cult of work was extreme: employees regularly died at their desk through exhaustion. It was so commonplace, the Japanese even have a word for it: *karoshi*. Outside Tokyo is a 'suicide forest', where stressed workers go to hang themselves. There are helpful instructions left at the foot of trees by previous visitors to the forest.

In the late 1970s, Japan was an economic miracle and the world was keen to learn its lessons. Peters and Waterman were as in awe as everyone else, and keen to apply its formula for success. They knew the Japanese work cult would not translate to the West, but wondered how you could create a self-willed version of devotion to the company.

The problem was that employees in the West had an entirely different mindset to the Japanese. The Western sense of self-worth had been shaped not by subsuming one's identity into the company or the nation, but by Locke, Descartes and the Enlightenment. Individualism is as deeply embedded in the Western psyche, as dutiful collectivism is in Japan. Jeffersonian freedoms are written into the US constitution. In short, Western workers would not buy a cult.

But Peters and Waterman had a plan. Instead of selling a cult, they would sell devotion to work as freedom. As 'creative' and 'fulfilling'. If the employee felt fulfilled by their job, they would be more likely to sign up to the company as a devoted follower of the company ethos. The cult would happen without anyone trying.

The first thing to do was get rid of the idea of work as a nine-to-five drudge. Work needed to become 'rewarding'. The goal of work would cease to be waiting for five o'clock to come around so you could go home, and would instead be the completion of the task, and that happened when it happened. Stay all night, but get it done.

People in the office needed to stop seeing themselves as wage slaves and start acting as autonomous, self-motivated mini-bosses. They needed to become freelance in their heads. The people around them would not simply be colleagues, they would have a schizophrenic new identity: friend and rival. A friend in the canteen, but a rival for promotion. Work should become an all-consuming concern, and you should be on your game at all times. Confide in colleagues as you would family (but not too much), and by putting emotional investment in work, you will work harder.

Here is an extract from an anonymous employment website written by a recruitment coordinator, who worked for Airbnb in Dublin:[12] 'The hours we had to work were beyond ridiculous and excessive. Having any kind of family or personal life is very difficult outside of work. A lot of the time it feels like a lot of very young people just running around not knowing what they are doing, pretending to be important with their meetings and high-fives. This company also wastes an enormous amount of money on . . . excessive alcohol for employee happy hours, sweets, cakes. You'd rather have (all) that going into your paycheck. There are people who have very weird job titles, and it is not really clear what they do . . . Their recruitment process is so intense . . . one of the things they interview you on is "core values", which have to match that of the company. Be warm and welcoming and a team player . . . selling hospitality. Well, most of the people I worked with were the exact opposite of this! I felt like I was working in the movie *Mean Girls* every day.'

In the mid-1970s, people stopped referring to each other in the office by their formal last name and began using first names.

'Good morning, Mr Johnson' became 'Hi, Pete'. The aim of this new management approach was to create a 'fun' faux-home environment. It began with coffee machines, then moved on to in-house leisure facilities such as gyms; organising team-building away-days; and mass nights out with colleagues to cinemas and restaurants. Tear down walls and make it open-plan, and create comfy, communal seating areas instead of hard, regimented rows of desks. By blurring the boundary between home and work, making the environment pleasurable, you would want to stay longer and give your all to work.

Today, most successful big brands have a cult of loyalty. I am at 'Fruit Towers', the headquarters of Europe's largest smoothie producer, Innocent. They have fake grass instead of a carpet and rows of park benches where desks would normally be. Every Monday morning, they hold a giant motivational meeting where the employee of the month is awarded the 'Lord or Lady of the Sash': a ribbon is worn and they stand before their colleagues, who bow down in mock obeisance. An idea the founders got from *Bill and Ted's Excellent Adventure*. In the courtyard, delivery vans covered in fake grass drive out with the first smoothies of the week. The staff gather and blow bubbles and cheer as each van leaves. It feels more like a movie premiere than Monday morning in an office.

I speak to the founder of the company, Douglas, and Dan who's been working at Innocent for eighteen years. It is laudable that they make work fun and energising, but haven't they merely taken the cult and put ironic comedy quotations round it? 'If people enjoy themselves at work, that's not a crime. It means they're more productive, so of course we get something out of it,' Douglas says.

Dan thinks the ceremonies such as bowing, a 'banana phone' the public can ring, Lego walls, table football, bunting hanging from the ceiling and a red phone box – the 'we're all having great fun!' and incessant 'everything is awesomeness' of the place might not suit everyone, but it masks the serious intent of the

198 The Deals That Made The World

business. They also have a giant switch on the wall which tells you to go home if it's late, and a sign reminding you which direction home is. 'We don't want people checking their email at 3 a.m. That's not cool and means they've lost sight of the work–life balance. Keeping that in equilibrium is key for us.'

Peters and Waterman realised that turning work into a loyalty cult was alien to the Western workplace, but it need not be. People needed to lose their inhibitions, they said. Give themselves totally to their work, and work would repay them by fulfilling deep emotional needs. Innocent have been shrewd in taking elements of the cult of work, but not others. For other companies, devotion is total and work has replaced family.

At the Barbican complex in London, I was waiting to go into the cinema recently when I heard screams and shouts of exaltation coming from one of the large conference halls adjacent, rented out for corporate events. I sneaked a peep round the door. A major high-street coffee brand was hosting its annual employee-of-the-year event. Baristas from across Britain had come to London to 'share' for one day what it means to them to be making soya cinnamon pumpkin lattes for £7.50 an hour.

I watched in awe as men and women in the same identical purple uniform bounded up to the stage and took to the mike stand. 'Hi, I'm Mario from Italy.' (Applause.) 'I just wanted to say I have been working with my team for two years now, and you guys are my life!' (Whoops and hollers.) 'Hi, I'm Veronica!' ('Hi, Veronica!') 'Give yourselves a round of applause, because I love you guys!' (More cheers and applause. Veronica leaves the stage, emotional.)

The deity they all worshipped hung above them: a giant coffee-cup logo, brimming with exultant froth. Their meeting was like a devotional church gathering complete with clapping, singing and a cup where a cross might be.

It is thanks to Peters and Waterman that people like this give themselves mind, body and soul to their employer. And the bigger the brand, the bigger the cult of loyalty, and secrecy. A food industry analyst I spoke to said that whenever he attends industry conventions, one group stand aloof from everyone else – 'the McDonald's guys' – as if they know something no one else does.

In San Francisco, locals often see the 'Google Bus' on a night out. Google employees from the 'campus' at Mountain View, Palo Alto, are driven into the city and eat at restaurants or go to the cinema *en masse* (agreed days before in a round of emails). Google employees believe in Google not as just any other company, but as the only company that matters, and you cannot fake that belief. There's a difference between wearing a sash on a Monday morning at Innocent and fostering a sense of world historic cult destiny as Google does.

Ask anyone with a serious stake in rising up the corporate ladder at any of these companies how critical they are of the company, and they will wince. Disdain and non-conformity are *verboten*. Criticism can be a useful tool of self-promotion, however – companies with a cult identity 'welcome' criticism from followers, because constant 're-evaluation of goals and aims' is part of today's corporate lingua franca. Just make sure the criticism is 'constructive'.

THE IMMIGRANT FLIP-FLOP

Peters and Waterman remade work as a cult and a family with a pay cheque at the end of the month. Big companies like Google, who now rival small nation states in power, gain unwavering loyalty from their 'citizens'. The vast majority of the coffee recruits I chanced upon at the quasi-religious rally were from South America and Eastern Europe. Thousands of miles from home, often with no support structure in a big city like London, work is genuinely a new family. They do not see themselves in a dead-end job, but lucky to be part of their coffee-chain family, and the family ties them in.

In 2016, Costa Coffee twice gave a pay rise to their workers above the national living wage of £7.20 an hour. Costa, like their high-street rivals Pret A Manger and Caffè Nero, use a high percentage of foreign workers, many of whom cannot afford the exorbitant rental costs. As a result, they have introduced loan schemes to help shore up housing rent for their staff. The company becomes a benefactor, one you cannot afford to turn your back on and for whom you are eternally grateful. In many ways, this directly replicates the Victorian philanthropy of employers like Lever Brothers, who built villages for their employees such as Port Sunlight (named after the cleaning brand they made).

Google are now building a twenty-first-century version of Port Sunlight outside Toronto. Quayside is an entire town built, they say, 'from the internet up' and including flexible housing units that can be taken down at speed to reshape neighbour-hoods, like giant Lego, as well as a hi-tech 'weather mitigating' system. Whatever that may be.

Every corporation or big brand now finds itself somewhere along the sliding scale of paternalism. From Pret A Manger offering free food at work and fifty-per-cent discount on eating there when you don't (Pret, in their recruitment literature say, 'you'll be joining the Pret family where we have fun and look after each other'), right through to the all-encompassing cocoon-ing Google plan for Quayside.

All these companies are service companies built on a strong promotional image of commitment to a diverse workforce (sorry, 'family') and inclusiveness. The British service industry boom of the 2000s of which Pret was a part was powered by immigrant labour, primarily from the new EU members of Eastern Europe: Poland, Romania and the Czech Republic. The story of how this boom happened is an intriguing addendum to the Brexit vote of 2016, and the road that led to it.

In 2003, as Europe waited to see what the effect of EU enlarge-ment would be, an economist called Christian Dustmann at

UCL was phoned up by the Home Office. Would he write a report predicting the likely immigration figures to Britain?[13] Dustmann pulled together a crack team of economists, including a researcher who would go on to become Chancellor Merkel's chief economic advisor.

Their prediction was cautious. They believed that in all likelihood the net numbers (once emigration and immigration had been set against each other) would be a couple of hundred thousand.

As Dustmann explains to me: You have to remember that in 2003, the British economy was booming. You couldn't get a plumber or electrician, and here were skilled people from Poland or Romania coming in with skills.' These workers were not seen by politicians or the public as a problem, but an asset. As the Blair government nailed its colours to the service economy, immigration from the EU was seen as necessary to power this service boom.

The underlying assumption in many of these new, fast-growing high-profile service brands delivering coffee, sushi and sandwiches with speed and efficiency was that British workers did not have the right attitude. They were diffident, did not work hard nor smile enough. Immigrants would do jobs no one else wanted to do, were prepared to smile twenty times a minute and would sign up to the cult of the surrogate family at work, because they were hundreds or thousands of miles from home.

In the late 1960s, with full employment and a fast-growing economy under a modernising Labour government, immigration from the West Indies and the Indian subcontinent powered a similar service boom – on public transport and in the retail sector – and so it happened again forty years later under Blair, in coffee shops, food chains, on building sites and in pre-school nurseries and cleaning companies, with workers from the new EU countries.

But there was a problem, Dustmann says. The plan was predicated on Germany and the other EU states taking the same kind of numbers as Britain. Dustmann and his colleagues had a get-out clause covering this eventuality: a small section of page fifty-seven of their report. It was the report's 'get out of jail' card.

Did anyone in government read your report when it came out? 'I don't know.' But what happened next? 'I wasn't prepared for what happened next.'

The numbers coming in far exceeded the report's predictions. Dustmann and his colleagues were attacked in the media and by MPs in Parliament. One called their report the most inaccurate economic forecast in history, out by thirty thousand per cent.

Germany had reneged on its part of the deal, just as page fifty-seven predicted. Did Dustmann know that the Home Secretary, David Blunkett, and the government already suspected Germany was not going to open up its borders in the same way, but carried on with an open-door policy for Britain anyway? 'I didn't know that. But why wouldn't they? Net immigration benefits the economy as a whole, those are the facts.'

I asked David Blunkett, with the grand backdrop of the House of Lords, if he knew Germany would not open its doors. Blunkett is remarkably candid about what happened. It was not only Dustmann who got it wrong. The government did, too. Blunkett had long warned of the dangers of 'opening up', but it was an unpopular and politically incorrect position; the political climate was boom and expansion, not recession and anti-immigration.

And as the economy flipped from boom to bust after 2008, Eastern European immigrants stopped looking like a good idea but a problem to the poorest paid, the very poorest of whom – Dustmann says – were adversely affected by immigration from the EU. The immutable fact of immigration benefiting the economy as a whole stopped mattering, when placed against the specific fact of the lowest ten per cent losing out. Britain was on a course for Brexit.

Britain was now taking itself out of Europe. Anti-immigration powered Brexit as immigration had once fuelled the service revolution: an economic positive had become a political negative.

Now every job in Britain is a service job in the wake of that 1990s service boom. The police have rebranded themselves from a 'force' to a 'service' and are sent on courses to learn how to arrest people politely. Debt collectors have stopped being enforcers and become a 'service' for people whose doors they are about to kick in. They even host annual 'debt collector of the year' awards.

Both the police and debt collectors have been at the sharp end of austerity in Britain since 2008 and it is no surprise they have become adjuncts of service culture. In order to do their jobs, they have had to turn into social workers by another name, dealing with the most vulnerable and needy in a moment of crisis. The police bear the brunt of cuts to social services and are now making decisions about extreme situations of need that once fell outside their remit.

And as one debt collector in Newcastle told me, 'If I'm not sympathetic to someone's situation, we can't make an agreement, and no one gets what they want.' Service is really just the most efficient way of doing business when times get tough.

HUMANYZE

I am in Boston outside an office building waiting to be buzzed in. In the lobby, I meet Gregg and Toni. I already notice something strange about them: they are both wearing small white boxes dangling from their necks emitting an intermittent flashing light.

What is that? 'Oh, that's my socio-metric badge,' Gregg says brightly. Every employee in the company wears one from the moment they arrive at work till the moment they go home.

These are the offices of Humanyze, with the most advanced form of workplace surveillance anywhere on the planet. Humanyze are taking micro-tracking of the employee to the next level by amassing and then analysing every single second of their day. It is Winslow Taylor's dream of total monitored efficiency of the worker come true more than a century after he proposed it.

The small white boxes around Gregg and Toni's necks collect data on everything: who they talk to and for how long, whether these meetings are formal or informal 'collisions'. How long they spend walking as opposed to sitting, on the phone or online, collaborating with colleagues in meetings, or in isolation in a glass box. Going to the toilet is a 'privacy issue', so the 'socio-metric badge' cannot monitor the data on what they do in there.

The badge can also detect subtle dynamics between colleagues. It registers speech patterns and assesses how dominant or passive you are. Who in a group is controlling the agenda. In short, it creates a total digital data map of your workplace character and every second of your productivity, or lack of it, throughout the working day.

Humanyze is reported to have contracts with Deloitte and Barclays, and is in dialogue with the NHS. Gregg and Toni show me what happens once they have collected all this data on their employees. I sit in a glass room with a huge screen. On the screen, various molecular structures appear and begin morphing into each other.

What's going on? 'These are algorithms that have crunched down on the group dynamic of the team. So, what you are seeing is the group interactions and channels of communication, and how well they work.' In March, the team were stoked because their San Francisco colleagues were in town, so there was a great deal of high energy 'symbiosis' between the two offices of Humanyze. But then something goes wrong in April. The molecular structures suddenly drag apart – they are no longer fizzing excitedly.

Gregg and Toni frown. There is a single orange blob connecting two rather forlorn-looking groups of molecules. What has happened? What is the orange blob? 'That's a bottleneck,' Greg says. 'We know who it is,' Toni adds.

The data is farmed anonymously. The management cannot know to whom specific data from the socio-metric boxes connects, but by looking at the patterns, they can work it out. They do not need to know who it is, because it is obvious.

Who is the orange blob, Gregg? 'We know.' So who is it? 'It's someone in management.' Management? 'Yes. Bottlenecks are often someone in management.' Someone who thinks they are doing a good job by rushing around and controlling everything. But they are not. They're doing the opposite.

The data, Gregg says, throws up unexpected patterns in productivity: who is and isn't pulling their weight, or doing their job properly. But this is not, he hastens to add, 'Big Brother surveillance of the office.' The aim is to create 'personal dashboards'.

Employees themselves access their 'personal dashboard' data to see how they can improve. This makes Humanyze the realisation, not of the crude work panopticon, but the Peters and Waterman managerial dream of the self-motivated worker, self-policing their own productivity through a personal data 'dashboard' and driving on to be ever better. The voice in the head to work harder that became a box round your neck.

In November 1979, as management consultants were making an audit of my dad's workplace, Peters and Waterman were preparing a presentation of their 7S molecular system with a series of seven hundred slides to the German technology company Siemens, in Munich.

Word of Peters and Waterman's new theory of work spread fast. Pepsi's chief, Andy Pearson, and his co-executives at Pepsi Global HQ, Purchase, New York, asked to meet Peters and Waterman, to see how 7S could transform their empire.

The distilled seven-point version of the Siemens and Pepsi presentation became a book called *In Search of Excellence: Lessons from America's Best Run Companies*. Far from being a calamity, global recession was an opportunity to reprogram the workforce. The postwar boom had created complacent employees with an overinflated sense of their own value. That value was now gone.

By pitting them against one another for their own jobs in an 'internal market', employees would learn to become competitive. It was corporate Darwinism. No one would work for anyone but themselves anymore. We would all henceforth be freelance.

The Japanese, who had inspired Peters and Waterman, had been working as hard as humanly possible for decades, yet that did not stop their economy going deep into recession, just as Peters and Waterman were extolling Japan as an economic model to follow. The book was a publishing sensation and the biggest-selling business title ever written.

In 1988, a film brought their philosophy to the big screen. In *Working Girl,* Melanie Griffith played Tess McGill, a receptionist whose brilliant business ideas got stolen by her conniving boss Katharine Parker, played by Sigourney Weaver. On Tess's first day in the office, she took her most prized belongings out of a box and placed them on her desk. At the top was a copy of *In Search of Excellence.* It was her bible for survival, and all the audience needed to know: nothing would stop this character. She was a winner.

When, thirty years on, anyone gets sacked on *The Apprentice* and utters the words 'Thank you for the opportunity, Lord Sugar,' they have Peters and Waterman to thank for instilling them with unshakable positivity.

I meet Tom Peters in a plush Boston hotel that used to be a nineteenth-century prison. It's a fitting place to discuss modern work culture: a plush, darkly lit restaurant with crisp napkins in the shape of swans and coffee costing $20 that masks the brutal panopticon it once was.

Tom bounds in like an excitable dog, raring to go. He asks dozens of questions in quick-fire succession ('Question: who do you think was the greatest consultant of all time? General Ulysses Grant, who rode down the line of the army he had just defeated doffing his hat. Now that is good management!').

Tom is dramatically engaged with ideas, throwing his arms up in the air in frustration or stamping his foot in delight, depending on whether he agrees or disagrees with what I say. He is, as an ex-colleague at McKinsey told me, 'quite a guy'.

The 7Ss emerged, Tom says, as a catchy way of encapsulating 'the core requirements of any successful business, but the 7Ss were not a plan as such.' Tom Peters was very clear this was an analysis of the overall culture of a company, and indeed, its advocates have said the brilliance of this analysis was to combine hard and soft managerial insight into an all-encompassing overview.

'A company could do these Ss well or do them badly, but no organisation could ignore them,' Tom says. Yet the message the world took away from the book was different. It was 'excellence' that mattered, not a series of words beginning with the letter 'S'. 'Excellence' was the brand that turned the 7Ss into the most successful business book ever written. And excellence – as interpreted in the context of a ruthless new business culture emerging in the early 1980s – was about individual drive and killing the competition.

Peters and Waterman were West Coast outsider intellectuals, the closest management consultants will ever get to being anarchists, who despised the management consultancy establishment. Management consultants obsessed about 'systems'. Tom Peters wanted to break this narrow-minded management thinking of the past – epitomised by Frederick Winslow Taylor and Peter Drucker – by tearing up convention and teaching managers to think 'outside boxes' or systems.

But the book was not taken this way; it was seen as a guide to creating a ruthless machine for productivity. 'I cannot legislate for the way big companies chose to treat their employees,' Peters says, in discussing how businesses have interpreted *In Search of Excellence*. 'Companies were going to rationalise workforces and drive for greater efficiencies with or without the book.' But the book gave them a bible. Then, in 2002, on the twentieth anniversary of its publication, Tom Peters gave a characteristically frank interview to *Fast Company*, admitting that, 'Okay, I confess. We faked the data . . .':[14]

In Search of Excellence was an afterthought . . . I had no idea what I was doing . . . there was no carefully designed work plan. There was no theory that I was out to prove. I went out and talked to genuinely smart people. I had an infinite travel budget that allowed me to fly first class and stay at top-notch hotels, and a licence from McKinsey to talk to as many cool people as I could all around the United States and the world.

So what? *In Search of Excellence* . . . said that from this point forward, the world changes . . . it's never going to be the way it was – and if you want to be a part of the way it's going to be, you have to read this book.

Was our process fundamentally sound? Absolutely! Start by using common sense, by trusting your instincts, and by soliciting the views of 'strange' (that is, nonconventional) people. You can always worry about proving the facts later. But that's not the confession. The confession is that I didn't go far enough.

Why did Peters tell the world that the 7S system – the greatest reform of the working environment in the last forty years – was fiction? 'Everything needs great packaging, right? That's what the 7S was: great packaging. People want to be told that other people know what they're doing. But the underlying principle was right: individuals need to take control of their own destiny. Read between the lines and that's what the book was saying.'

Tom feels he was misrepresented by the *Fast Company* article. And it's easy, having met him, to see how it happened. Tom is a born contrarian, and falls over himself to blow away the orthodoxies that stand in his way. In making his 'confession', he was also making a profound point about the bogus 'science' used to shore up management ideas. His point was: don't get taken in.

In the 1970s, he needed to use the language of scientific management to get his radical ideas through the gates of big business. So that is exactly what he did. And twenty years later, he had the guts to admit it was simply a necessary strategy. Like all visionaries, Peters marshalled his own facts to his greater truth.

I have one final question for him.

What do you have to say to all those people who put their trust in the corporate work environment and then found themselves shafted. People who are not able to determine their destiny? Tom fixes me with one of his steely stares.

'*Bonne chance*. Because you'll need it.'

THE VALLEY OF DEATH

Like all revolutionaries, Tom Peters and Robert Waterman believed in themselves. They did not make history, they read its runes and simply worked out that 'if you want to be a part of the way it's going to be, read this book.' They were a living embodiment of how to act if you were going to make it in the new world.

In a post-OPEC 1970s world of profound uncertainty, in which the old rules no longer appeared to apply to anything, consultants stepped into the breach because, as Tom told me, people want to be told that other people know what they are doing. Government and economists no longer seemed to have the confidence in their own expertise to govern or determine the direction of the economy, and in the vacuum created, a huge business opportunity emerged. For people who talked the talk and appeared to know.

John Bennett was a management consultant in the 2010s for one of the so-called 'Big Four': Deloitte, KPMG, PwC, and McKinsey. His specialism was advising on healthcare decisions that would affect millions of people.

'Every time you go into a client, you are looking to find new problems to expand the job. It's like being a car mechanic who looks under the bonnet of your car, sucks in their teeth and says it is much worse than you think. We call this strategy "land and expand".'

Bennett says that key to this management strategy is the initial rolling out of a piece of diagnostic work: a 'template'. This template is a 'foot in the door', often given away for free. The money comes in 'landing and expanding' the job once you are in.[15]

David Craig is an intense man with horn-rimmed spectacles and a stick, which he uses to point at huge words in capitals during his PowerPoint presentation. He meets me in a huge, darkened boardroom near Whitehall, where the only light comes from the overhead projector. The first words that appear on the whiteboard say VALLEY OF DEATH.

David worked for thirty years as a consultant selling millions of pounds of contracts to the private and public sectors. He explains to me how he landed and expanded business. 'You need to give the client a big shock. Something along the lines of: "It's worse, far worse than you imagined." You are sending them into what we call the Valley of Death. "Only by correcting this immediately is there any hope of turning this around."'

What happens after the Valley of Death? 'Then you provide the sunny uplands of salvation in the shape of an IT project worth fifty million.' Like the pharmaceutical industry, the serious money is not in a cure, but in medicating an ongoing critical condition. Bennett calls it the 'fostering of a partnership'. 'You are looking to create a long-term dependency culture on your firm.' Creating a permanent crisis situation in which government or the business cannot do without them.

In Wales, PricewaterhouseCoopers came up with an ingenious new kind of 'partnership' called a 'risk and reward contract' designed to make money from austerity cuts. This is how it works. Instead of doing a deal that is potentially embarrassing politically by paying consultants up front to make cuts, you hide the pay cheque. Consultants receive a percentage on all cuts made that they have suggested. In other words, the more cuts made to public services, the more they stand to earn.

Post-2008, when unprecedented austerity cuts were made to

the public sector, the use of outside management consultants, stepping in to save central and local government from the Valley of Death, doubled – not only at the front line, but in administering the cuts. They became indispensable to the life support which, as David Craig points out, is exactly where they want to be.

THE SLAVE ARMY OF BOSSES

We are all our own boss now. And in this new globalised, de-unionised world, whether you are a boss picking bananas on a plantation in Kenya, a boss driving a cab in Oslo, a boss delivering a pizza in Newham or a boss writing a book in Hackney, we are all part of a giant amorphous freelance class known as the precariat.

We are as precarious as my grandad was, but our mindset is different. My grandad always imagined that one day he would get to play full-time in an orchestra. We know this will never happen, so instead we live a paradox: boss of our own destiny, living hand to mouth. We are the boss and a slave simultaneously.

In 2016, Dr Rachael Orr at Oxfam carried out a study into the work attitudes of fourteen-to-eighteen-year-olds and noticed a consistent lowering of expectations for the future.[16] This plummeting of expectation has accelerated year on year in the 2010s, to the point where they now expect nothing from the future and are grateful for anything.

Dr Orr honed in on those at the very lowest rung of the zero-hours ladder in the US poultry industry. In Texas, poultry workers on eight-hour shifts wear adult diapers because they are not allowed to go to the toilet. Dr Orr interviewed one worker, who was told by his supervisor that safety was not an issue in the factory, because 'your life is less valuable than the chickens.' It was not only the conditions, but the fact that workers raised little issue with them, that exemplified the powerlessness of the globalised low-paid.

These workers are powerless and have no leverage. This is no surprise. What about the middle class? Do they still have bargaining power? The middle class, Dr Orr noted, have swapped real-term wage increases for 'fulfilment'. The pay-off for low pay and precarious work is to imagine our work makes us whole as a person. Economic think-tank the Resolution Foundation estimate that we are all no better off in real terms than we were twenty years ago, but middle-class professionals console themselves that what they do is self-determined. They have control, which is exactly what the poultry worker does not have.

The middle-class professional has dignity at work. But as wages go down, so too does that sense of self-worth. And as this army of slave bosses grows into an ocean of cheap available labour, so comes the biggest opportunity to transform work since Peters and Waterman invented the new cult of self-determination forty years ago. Now, for the first time, is the chance to create a planet of slave bosses.

THE CHAMPS-ÉLYSÉES EPIPHANY

It was a freezing night in January 2008, and two Americans were standing on the Champs-Élysées in Paris trying to hail a cab. Snow was falling thick and fast, and the traffic was rapidly grinding to a halt. They had less than an hour to make their flight to New York. As the Champs-Élysées gridlocked, horns beeping, a single, distant, yellow light flickered – the one free cab on the whole of the Champs-Élysées, trapped in traffic more than five hundred yards away. They were never going to make it.

Then one of them, a thirty-four-year-old UCLA dropout called Travis Kalanick, had a eureka moment. 'Imagine,' he said to his colleague Garrett Camp, 'if every car you see became a cab?' Not one flickering light, but hundreds of flickering yellow lights, all offering a ride to the airport. What if every single person you saw in front of you became a cab driver?

Kalanick had invented Uber. He had not merely created a new cab service. He had transformed work by reconceptualising the slave boss. In 2008, the world was crashing and rising simultaneously, like two tectonic plates in a disaster movie. The subprime crash had plunged the world economy into unprecedented debt, at the same time as the iPhone and mobile devices were 'freeing' the world to work in a brand-new way. One plate rose up, as the other sank into magma.

With wages and growth gridlocked like the traffic on the Champs-Élysées, Uber did not merely 'disrupt' the economy, it reinvented the future. We were now all our own bosses with a mobile device, all striving to be corporations of one.

At the same moment Kalanick was inventing Uber, two roommates in San Francisco called Brian Chesky and Joe Gebbia were struggling to pay the rent on their loft apartment. They had only two bedrooms, which they slept in, so renting out another room was not an option. Then Chesky had an idea. 'Why don't we turn the living room into a bed and breakfast?' They advertised their 'Airbed & Breakfast' on a website for an upcoming design conference in the city, and had three takers instantly. Airbnb was born.

Like Uber, Airbnb was a conceptual shift in what constitutes value. Uber redefined labour value, Airbnb told you to reassess the space you stand in, asking a profound question: what is the true value of any physical space and how can that true value be extracted? Why can't a home be a hotel and vice versa? Everything in the new world could be fluid, endlessly redefining its role and extractable worth.

In 2016, less than eight years after Chesky and Gebbia pumped up an airbed in their living room and invented Airbnb, it was worth $30 billion. Uber was worth $70 billion. But the potential value of both far exceeds that.

Uber's seed-funding allowed it to launch in San Francisco, but within a year, they had signed deals with Google Ventures, Toyota and China's largest search engine, Baidu. Airbnb had an equally meteoric rise, buying out foreign competitors such as German rival Accoleo, and opening offices from Moscow to São Paolo within twenty-four months.

Airbnb's spectacular growth has also created new moral dilemmas about how it benefits and distorts the housing market. Airbnb has driven down accommodation prices for consumers in cities across the world and altered the economics of those cities in the process. It is now possible to travel across the globe, as Airbnb says in its ads, ignoring the old monopoly of homogenised, overpriced hotels and instead immersing oneself in the genuine lived city: staying with local people and experiencing what it is to be a local inhabitant.

Up to a point. In Ibiza, Spain, Airbnb has prized an existing affordable housing crisis wide open. Residents have been priced out by tourists, and so too have the seasonal workers, flown in to service the very tourist industry dedicated to the people renting the Airbnb properties.

In Santa Monica, California, Scott Shatford became the first person to be convicted of snapping up leases on apartments in desirable areas to rent them on Airbnb. By the time he had seven properties intended for long-term leases under his control, and had ignored cease-and-desist letters from the city of Santa Monica, the city itself signed up to one of his flats for four nights in order to collect the evidence to convict him. Shatford has brilliantly turned his insights into a data analytics company called Airdna, crunching Airbnb data to give investors who are seeking advantage in the short-term housing market.

So Airbnb has both empowered consumers and exposed affordable-rental crises in dozens of cities across the globe. It has also become a lightning rod for protests. In Barcelona in summer 2017, tourists were smoke-bombed as they sat at outside café tables enjoying cocktails by local activists in balaclavas blaming them for the housing crisis. Tourism is an essential part of the economic model of Barcelona, and one the city has cultivated since 1992, when it hosted the Olympics. Yet now residents say they are paying the price, and Airbnb is to blame.

But cash-strapped residents are also using this very same mechanism to survive. In Los Angeles, where the median annual wage is $28,000 and the median rent for a one-bedroom apartment $2,000 a month, a growing number of people use Airbnb on a near-permanent basis to subsidise their own housing by giving over their sleeping space to strangers. For them, Airbnb is a lifeline to keep renting, not a tool to prevent them from doing so.

City authorities do not tend to see it that way. In 2016, Berlin banned the letting of whole properties via Airbnb's app. London, San Francisco and Barcelona have all sought to create caps on how many properties can be used for short-term rentals, and for how long, in order to help local residents gain a foothold once more.

Do Uber and Airbnb face legal challenges because they are genuine disrupters challenging vested interests, or because they threaten to make an existing problem worse – precarious employment in Uber's case, unaffordable housing in Airbnb's? Both.

In London in 2015–16, the number of properties being advertised on Airbnb soared by 126 per cent, and the story is the same in any big city where the basic laws of supply and demand apply. It is hard to restrict something when people see an opportunity to make money, and consumers see a cheaper service. When the Mayor of London temporarily withheld Uber's licence in 2017, more than half a million people signed Uber's petition in protest.

This was not just the wealthy elite of urban professionals: the petition was signed by a huge cross-section of London's estimated 3.5 million Uber users, from students and single women concerned about losing a safer form of transport to hospital patients, using Uber to get home conveniently from appointments. The petition was organised by Change.org, who called it the fastest growing online campaign they had seen. The ban split

London. For everyone who saw an Uber driver exploited, there were a dozen people who saw a service they relied upon being jeopardised. Uber and Airbnb have transformed not only the definition of value, but the easy off-the-peg moral positions taken.

Airbnb did with four walls what Uber did with four wheels, but they are now asking a bigger question of human beings: where is the extractable value in everything you do? Where is the slack in your life that can be monetised? Both business models dare us to find anything that cannot be turned into a commodity for sale.

A tsunami-wave of work apps already do the same – not with your car or your flat, but your time. Take the spare fifteen minutes you have at lunch. TaskRabbit matches free labour with local demand for dog walkers, pizza delivery, or someone to stand in a queue for the new iPhone. You can be back at your desk by two, before your boss even realises. But you are the boss, so what does it matter?

Who is anyone's boss? Your boss in the office is only your boss from nine to five. Say you need someone to pick up your dry-cleaning tonight. You sign in to a people-per-hour website and your boss, trying to earn some extra money on the side, picks it up. Then you are his or her boss for an hour. There is no boss anymore – merely the army of slave bosses and segments of time in which all our job titles change constantly. Only one thing is certain in this new world – you are the boss of you, because we are all corporations of one.

THE LIMB (B) WORKER

The last two paragraphs are, of course, a promotional lie. 'Micro-jobbing' and the 'gig economy' are Silicon Valley-sounding buzzwords that mask a very different truth. Making everyone an infinitely 'flexible' boss slave means making everyone infinitely exploitable. For some, freedom means freedom, for others it means a prison.

We are entering a new age that is redefining every worker, every job, and what a union is, too. And the people fighting the new battle to claw back rights and dignity for the lowest paid could well be looked back upon in fifty years' time as significant for twenty-first-century employment rights as Annie Besant and the striking 'match girls' were in 1888 to the Industrial Revolution.

Women at the Bryant and May factory in Bow, East London, who refused to put up with appalling working conditions, igniting trade unionism for the invisible low-paid strata subsisting below the unionised working class. Women who were not just invisible to their bosses, but to the so-called 'trade union aristocracy'.

Megan does two four-hour shifts a day for Deliveroo. She has no idea if she will be hired, she gets £7.50 an hour when she is, but burns so much energy cycling frantically across London to deliver food to people, she spends practically half her salary on chocolate and energy bars to simply keep her working. That means that after eight hours – having done the equivalent of a marathon each day – she is lucky to have £50.

'In the winter, it's so cold you can't feel your feet. Last year I tried to take some days off because I was so knackered and was tagged by Deliveroo as 'inactive', meaning I was not going to be offered work. It means you can't take a day off. There's no one to talk to, no human at the other end to treat you like a human being. My life is at their mercy and I am a slave to algorithms.'

Last year, Megan got to meet the boss of Deliveroo. Did you tell him how bad it was? 'Are you joking? And lose my job? You can't complain and I don't think they want to hear it. He genuinely believes the people who work for him love it.'

Meg believes the system is very clever. It depends on young temporary workers who will move on, so no one hangs around long enough to complain or cause trouble. There is never going to be an employee problem, as there's always someone new to do the job.

But now the low-paid workers are fighting back. In 2016, Maggie Dewhurst, a courier cyclist for CitySprint, another gig economy firm, won her case against the company at an employment tribunal. It ruled that she could justifiably be called a worker, not a self-employed contractor, and therefore eligible to rights and protection such as holiday and minimum wage. In the same year, two drivers for Uber won a similar case, the tribunal ruling that the company exerted too much control over them to call them legitimately self-employed.

In defining the 'gig economy', the tribunal had stressed its exploitative downside to workers rather than the entrepreneurial 'freedom' or 'flexibility' it gave. Megan tells me that there is now a twilight-zone legal term to define her and the millions of people who will soon be working in the grey netherworld between employee and self-employed: a 'Limb (B) worker'.

Under section 230(3)(b) of the Employment Rights Act 1996 and section 83(2)(a) of the Equality Act of 2010, a Limb (B) worker is defined as 'someone who undertakes to do or perform personally any work or services for another party to the contract whose status is not by virtue of the contract that of a client or customer of any profession or business undertaking carried on by the individual.'

You are not an employee or self-employed, you're Limb (B): a limbo worker floating between rights and no rights. But rights like sick pay – as one Uber driver tells me, 'you pay for yourself anyway'. So what is the company surrendering?

'It's really a genius idea,' an Uber driver tells me on a ride. 'They own nothing except the app – nothing. I buy the car, pay for everything: if I don't work, I lose money. And they take twenty per cent on everything I earn. Who's the fool?'

In 2017, Uber's founder Travis Kalanick took another Uber ride. Not on the Champs-Élysées, but wedged on the back seat in San Francisco between two women, playing distractedly with his phone and shoulder-shimmying to Daft Punk on the car radio. As the ride came to an end, the driver suddenly confronted

Kalanick.[17] 'I'm bankrupt because of you,' Fawzi Kamel said. 'Bullshit,' Kalanick replied. 'You're raising the standards and you're dropping the prices,' Kamel continued. 'People are not trusting you anymore. I lost $97,000 because of you. You keep changing everything.'

Kamel's problem lay with the fact that drivers for UberBLACK are required to drive recent models of select premium cars, earning a higher rate, but competing with Uber's cheaper UberX rides. Kamel would have bought or leased a car on the basis of projected income to cover it, only to have Uber slash fares and increase commission.

Kalanick fiddled with his phone as Kamel explained his situation and then Kalanick delivered the killer punchline: 'Some people don't like to take responsibility for their own shit. They blame everything in their life on somebody else.' Then he got out and wished Kamel 'good luck'.

Within a year, Kalanick had left the company; his exchange with Kamel, one of a string of misdemeanours and allegations of misconduct laid at him. But the two-minute argument with one of his own drivers also neatly encapsulated two competing visions of new capitalism that are relevant to all of us: whether to be a boss who is actually a boss, or your own boss, who is really a slave.

The 'sharing' or gig economy – a planet of slave bosses – is potentially the biggest transformation in our working lives since the first industrial revolution, in which trade unionism was forged. In 1998, a decade before Travis Kalanick stood on the Champs-Élysées trying to hail a cab, he dropped out of UCLA to create a peer-to-peer file-sharing service like MP3 music site Napster.

It was called Scour and like Napster, Scour was destroyed by the music industry. Metallica and Dr. Dre sued Napster's Shawn Fanning for infringing copyright, forcing it out of business. Kalanick found himself facing a lawsuit from the American motion picture industry, the Recording Industry

Association of America, and the Music Publishers Association. Scour was toast.

The idea of peer-to-peer seemed killed forever. Napster and Scour had tried to pickpocket the most powerful entertainment companies on earth. But they had created the germ of a new idea – one that Kalanick would resurrect a decade later when he found himself standing on a Paris pavement in the snow. Peer-to-peer with a difference. Instead of sharing music, share employees.

With peer-to-peer, peers are both suppliers and consumers at the same time. There is no one-way client-server. It is a collaborative system with peers contributing by dropping in and out. In the utopian sales bumph of the sharing economy, none of us has one job anymore, because we all do thirty jobs or three hundred jobs, whenever we feel like it. The only constant is that we are our own boss.

Optimists for the sharing economy refer to this free-market equality as 'dotcommunism'. In theory, dotcommunism undermines anyone setting themselves up as an authoritarian boss, because it empowers the individual to choose where and how to work. Infinite demands for different services mean work will become infinitely diverse and varied. We can stick it to any one evil employer, because they have no monopoly on employment. It destroys hierarchical structures by replicating the egalitarianism of social networking. Trade unions may no longer be able to protect our rights in the old-fashioned sense, but a new multiplicity of income streams will mean we will have some structural protection built into the system.

Here is the less optimistic view. Take Fawzi Kamel in his Uber cab. In theory, he has the opportunity to go and work for anyone, as Kalanick implies. But in reality, he is tied in to Uber, because Uber have a virtual monopoly on cabs in San Francisco. He could always make himself slave boss of another low-paid job, but he has invested in the cab and needs to pay it back. He is trapped.

Freelance or hyper-flexible, so-called 'contingent' work is

growing at an exponential rate – from thirty-four per cent of the US workforce in 2017 to over fifty per cent by 2020. That is a sixteen-per-cent increase in people becoming their own slave boss in only three years. When people migrated in the Industrial Revolution from countryside to city, it took twenty years. This is potentially more far-reaching and it is happening five times faster.

The word 'contingent' is interesting: it means that you are employed 'contingent' on there being anything for you to do. The new 'sharing economy' may offer new 'opportunities', but the number of people offering their services massively outstrips the demand. And with technology threatening to make billions of people redundant globally, we will all be slave bosses at the exact moment we have nothing to do.

PayPal founder and tech billionaire Elon Musk has suggested a solution – a 'universal basic wage'. We could essentially be paid to do nothing if automation delivers economic prosperity. Robots could be taxed on their labour and pay income tax, as humans currently do. The resulting revenue would then be used to pay us, and we could be paid to shop, as consumerism will continue to be the primary engine of growth. Shopping will be our paid job, and an important one: essential to the economy. Plus robots have not learnt how to shop, yet.

Robots would need to be taxed at a level humans never were. The average hourly wage has pretty much the same purchasing power it had in 1979. The $4.03 an hour rate of January 1973 has the same purchasing power as $22.41 today. And for this stagnation, we live a life where we never stop working, and never stop worrying that we are not working hard enough. But this is not accidental. It was a plan, and the irony is that it was sold to us as freedom to be our own boss.

In ten years' time, a staff job like my father's will be rare and highly prized. Everyone else will be CEO of their own business enterprise, whether they are Warren Buffett or the person cleaning out the bins under his desk.

THE CHEAP GOODS EQUATION

The global equation of low wages and zero growth depends on a third factor for its equilibrium: cheap goods. If things stay cheap, you do not have to be paid more wages. Take the package I have on my desk. It is a pen with cartridges bought online for £2. Less than the price of a coffee from Starbucks. It has been transported from India to London and cost more to process the transaction – £5.50 – than the object is worth.

This new age of flexible next-to-no-pay working is built on two founding stones: cheap goods made for next to nothing in the global sweatshop of slave bosses, where someone somewhere is being paid even less than you. To maintain full employment on low wages here, goods from elsewhere need to stay cheap, and get cheaper, to plummet in tandem with falling wages. Soon a child in a sweatshop in Singapore will have to pay me to take their T-shirt.

Glancing up from my computer, I see a package that arrived this morning from China. It contains a single item – a phone cable – that cost 99p. My books sit on a shelf that cost £24 from IKEA. There are books on that shelf that cost twice the price of the whole shelf. I am wearing a T-shirt that cost, shockingly, £2. The coffee mug I drink from cost £4. The beans that made the coffee cost more than the mug.

We are so accustomed to buying things cheaply that we cannot imagine it any other way, but we should. Because the price rise is coming, and we will not be able to afford it.

Cheap imports began with the entrepreneurial vision of one man looking for an opportunity from the Vietnam War. In 1967, shipping tycoon Malcolm McLean, the CEO of US container company Sea-Land Service Inc., did a deal with the US army, desperate to get supplies quickly over to Indochina. Sea-Land began transporting millions of tonnes of food, cigarettes and medical supplies in huge, oblong metal boxes over thousands of miles of sea. At a stroke, McLean had invented modern containerisation and by 1971, McLean's deal with the US army was worth $100 million a year.

There was only one problem: McLean's giant container ships were only earning money on their outward journey to Vietnam, returning empty to the East Coast of America. So McLean had a brilliant idea. Why not cut another deal, this time with Japan, the fastest-growing economy on earth.

Between 1960 and 1973, Japanese industrial output quadrupled. American consumers hankered for one product above all that remained prohibitively expensive, but one the Japanese could now supply cheaply: home technology.

Thanks to containerisation, the US was flooded overnight with hi-fis, radios and TVs. Once the preserve of the wealthy, technology was now 'Made in Japan' or 'Made in China' at a fraction of the price. These hi-tech luxuries were now affordable to anyone.

Cheap goods were a boon to consumers, but a disaster for Western industry. Imports coincided neatly with the collapse of manufacturing. Containerisation was the killer blow. Marc Levinson has calculated that 300 million containers are now crossing the world's oceans each year, twenty-six per cent of them coming from China alone.[18]

The downward price drive has continued relentlessly and we the consumer now expect it. TVs today cost three per cent of what they cost in 1980. Cameras are seventy-five per cent cheaper than they were in 2000, thanks to cameras on phones. Phones themselves are half the price they were in 2005. The first commercial mobile phone, the Motorola DynaTAC 8000X launched in 1983 cost $4,000. Technology, once the domain of the rich, is now owned by all of us as material recompense for stagnating wages.

But as wages are driven ever lower, can cheap goods keep getting cheaper with them? Not with the world's resources running out. Steve Howard, IKEA's global head of sustainability, says there is a problem. The coming global price hike.[19]

In the 1990s, before the internet took off, IKEA was offering a cunning template for how the internet would look if it was laid out like a store. Anyone who walks round IKEA knows how the layout ensnares: you follow a winding path that dictates your route but allows you to think you are diverting off to look at a bed, a toast rack, or some shelving. The layout of the store provides a hidden guiding hand, making you believe you have some choice in what you are looking at. It gives the illusion of freedom, just like Peters and Waterman's 7S work model.

Every item at IKEA is designed backwards, beginning with the space it will fill when flat on a shelf in the warehouse. It is also reverse engineered from the price backwards. The coffee mug has a fixed sale price of say £2, so all design decisions flow from there.

Eighty per cent of people who go to IKEA have in mind a single big purchase they are either buying that day or scoping out. But they get home with a sponge shaped like a strawberry, a rubber-duck wine stopper, scented candles and some Swedish biscuits.

What did all the things we did buy have in common? They were cheap. 'How long can we expect to push the margin, as the consumer demands cheaper and cheaper?' Steve Howard says. Price inflation will make an economic model built on low wages and stagnant growth simply unsustainable.

'At some point, prices will have to rise as resources get more expensive. This is the coming global price hike, and who's going to pay if it's not passed on to the shopper?' Steve says companies cannot pass it on because that will hit their customer base, so we have created an impossible conundrum.

At the moment, there is someone else picking up the tab: the person making the object at the other end. A woman in a Philippines sweatshop knocking out 100 jackets a day or the 200 million Chinese workers making smartphones using benzene, or using carcinogenic chemicals to extract gold, platinum or palladium from old laptops and phones.

Doubling the salary of a sweatshop worker would add less than two per cent to the retail price, but the companies that refuse to do this claim the consumer would not stand for it. Yet consumers are regularly polled on price and are willing to pay fifteen per cent more to know something has not been produced by someone on sweatshop wages.

At the moment, we think we have nothing in common with the people on the other side of the world making cheap goods for us, but very soon we will. We will all be the boss and with a small voice in our head – our inner boss – telling us to work harder. Or else.

CHAPTER EIGHT
UPGRADE: ENGINEERING DISSATISFACTION

The Deal: General Electric, Phillips, Osram and the Phoebus cartel of lightbulb manufacturers meet to limit the lifespan of an average lightbulb
Aim: To systematise planned obsolescence and invent the upgrade
Where: Lake Geneva, Switzerland
When: 1932

Forty miles outside San Francisco is the town of Livermore. Halfway down the main street lined with cafés and antique shops is a fire station, and high up on the back wall, away from the gleaming vintage fire truck, polished daily by retired volunteers with bushy white moustaches, is the one thing of which the residents of Livermore are proudest. Making a low hum, flickering an eerie yellow glow, is a light bulb. But unlike any other light bulb on earth, this one has not stopped working for 116 years.[1]

The Shelby Electric Company made the Centennial Bulb in 1901. A hand-blown carbon filament emitting thirty watts, it now gives four watts like a child's night light, but here is the remarkable thing: it still works. Why? It is a mystery, and begs the question: why, if Livermore Fire Station has a light bulb still burning after well over a century, does the rest of the world have ones that break after six months?

In that dusty Shelby bulb is the secret of consumerism. It is the first step on the journey to how planned obsolescence was first concocted and the continuous upgrade created.[2] Today the upgrade is a way of life. We change our phones every eleven months; twenty-eight per cent of us change our sofa every three years;[3] our partner on average every two years nine months (for the twenty-eight per cent, a sofa lasts longer than a relationship).[4]

We belong to the global cult of what product designers call 'infinite new-ism' – a distrust of anything not just 'old', but 'old' meaning we upgraded it only a couple of weeks ago.

The upgrade has even transferred from objects to us. Perpetual self-improvement is an obsession in every sphere of life: perfecting the body in the gym, becoming ever more productive at work, a better colleague, partner, cook, lover, parent, carer, human. This relentless and all-encompassing self-improvement drive is upgrade culture. It did not magic from nowhere, it was engineered, and the Shelby light bulb is the first clue as to how it happened.

The second is 5,600 miles away. In 1989, as communism collapsed and crowds clambered over the Berlin Wall, a historian called Helmut Herger walked unnoticed into a building in East Berlin: the headquarters of the Osram Electrical Company.

Inside, Herger found overturned filing cabinets and papers strewn across the floor. Herger began sifting through the administrative detritus and then something caught his eye. Confidential minutes from a meeting in Geneva in 1932 between two of the most senior members of the Osram executive board and the five biggest electrical companies on earth. When two decades on, I met Helmut in a Berlin café and I asked him what was so special about these papers, Helmut opened his briefcase.

The biggest light bulb manufacturers on earth were meeting in Geneva to make a policy decision that would change the course of history. They were to create a secret cartel, known as Phoebus, and with one aim: to put anyone out of business who created a light bulb that lasted more than six months.[5]

The papers prove something we all vaguely believe exists

when our kettle mysteriously stops working six months after we buy it, but it turns out actually does exist: planned obsolescence.

The Phoebus cartel was founded by William Meinhardt of Osram and Anton Philips, the founder of Dutch electrical giant Philips Electrical. They wanted to systematise obsolescence, imposing a global policy on the lifespan of a light bulb and breaking any company that strayed from the cartel's dictum.

Herger showed me the signatories of Phoebus's inaugural meeting. They included America's biggest electrical company, General Electric, AE from Britain, Compagnie Des Lampes from France, GE Sociedad Anonyma of Brazil, China's biggest producer of electrical goods, General Edison, Lamparas Electricas from Mexico, and Tokyo Electric.

The minutes mapped out their plan in precise terms: shorten the life of every light bulb to six months. Should anyone not stick to the plan, a sliding scale of fines would be imposed, all paid in Swiss francs or German marks.

These companies did not simply produce light bulbs. They provided the basic infrastructure of modern life: street lighting; copper wiring for phone lines; cabling for ships, bridges, train and tram lines. They made consumer durables such as refrigerators and ovens; provided the electrics for cars, homes and offices. And from 1932 onwards, it was all to be made to break.

Two thousand years of human ingenuity in manufacturing goods to last as long as possible was to stop. Henceforth, mass production would mean counter-intuitively reverse engineering an object from the moment it should break, backwards. Each object would have a different lifespan drawn up on a spreadsheet. Helmut Herger showed me the categories meticulously calibrated on a sliding scale of obsolescence, scrawled in boxes in spidery handwriting, each box stipulating lifespan. Crucially, the consumer was not to know a thing about it. The light bulb at Livermore Fire Station was the one that got away.

Was Phoebus doing anything wrong? In 1932, the free world

balanced on a knife edge between economic depression and recovery. Hitler was poised to take power in Germany. The Phoebus plan to systematise planned obsolescence did not simply sell more light bulbs, but saved capitalism and therefore democracy when it was most perilously threatened. It kept people buying.

THE NEWEST NEW THING

Outside the Apple Store on Regent Street, London, there are two thousand people queueing for the new iPhone. They stand patiently, scrolling through the last iteration of the iPhone (in ten minutes' time, obsolete). The police overseeing the queue scroll through their phones, too. The line snakes around the building, down the next street and into an adjacent park.

Those nearest the front have been waiting nearly forty-eight hours. The man at the very front sits on a fishing chair with a roll-up mattress and plastic tarpaulin to keep off the rain. He has a small gas cooker with which he heats up soup. He began queueing on Saturday afternoon. It is now Monday morning.

'Do you mind telling me,' I ask him, 'what the new iPhone will do that your old phone doesn't?' He frowns, annoyed at the stupidity of the question. 'What do you mean?' 'Well, you've been queueing nearly forty-eight hours in the cold, so I'm just wondering what's so special about the new phone?'[6]

He sighs and leans forward. 'It's new.' And that is the point. It is four minutes to nine, and when the doors open and the whooping Apple employees in their blue T-shirts try to hold back the rushing human tide, my new friend will be the first person to own the very newest iPhone it is possible to own anywhere in the world, for a very short period of time. In two minutes, the first buyers will put it on eBay and then it will be old.

Obsolescence is built into newness – it is the flaw at the heart of everything we buy. Not far from the Livermore Fire Station and the oldest bulb in the world is a warehouse filled with brand-new tech-goods that have never even been used: phones, tablets, laptops, printers, microwave ovens, satnavs, headphones, drones, wearable technology to help you stave off your own obsolescence by becoming the optimum you. It is all still in its boxes, unopened, donated to a charity by companies that bought the products in bulk but then upgraded to another product before even opening them.

'Where's all this stuff bound for?' I ask the manager of the warehouse. To Baltimore, Bangladesh, anywhere that people want it. The trouble is, he admits, they don't want it, because out-of-date technology is as unappealing to the poorest half of the world as it is to the richest.[7]

In 2008 I visited Malawi, one of the poorest countries on earth. Remote villages without clean water or electricity still had villagers with an iPhone, because they already recognised the smartphone as an essential tool for modernisation. As William Wallis of the *Financial Times* put it in 2016, 'the mobile phone is to sub-Saharan Africa what the steam train was to nineteenth-century Europe: the mechanical workhorse driving social and economic transformation.'

Mark Essien, a Nigerian hotel entrepreneur, says the very lack of infrastructure in Africa works to its advantage as Africa upgrades itself wholesale as a continent. 'The future of technology for Africa is not in playing catch-up. But in looking at the things we lack and using those gaps as an opportunity to invent something we can use to leapfrog the rest of the world.'[8]

McKinsey estimate that half of sub-Sahara's billion people will have internet access by 2025: that is 360 million smart-phones. There are already apps for herding cattle (iCow in Kenya); private security in Ghana (Hei Julor!); and an Uber-style service in Uganda connecting mobile washerwomen to people with dirty laundry (Yoza).[9] No one in Africa or Asia wants a ten-year-old Dell printer, and upgrade culture is grasped more voraciously in Africa and Asia than in the old developed world, because to upgrade is to be ahead of the game in two of the fastest-moving markets on the planet.

Tech companies are happy to oblige. Software updates like iOS render your phone or laptop redundant if you do not upgrade in step with the rest of the upgrading world. It is a train none of us can get off.

The Phoebus Cartel invented planned obsolescence and the rules companies would follow: the parameters for the upgrade diktat whether it be a light bulb or iOS software. But to become enthralled to the upgrade – to feel a psychological need to always want the newest new thing – required the failure of planned obsolescence, and a new idea to replace it. Obsolescence itself needed an upgrade.

ENGINEERING DISSATISFACTION

We think patronisingly of the 1950s as a naïve time when the public could still have the wool pulled over their eyes, but nothing was further from the truth. War had politicised and educated the public. As a result of working in factories and on production lines, people knew both how things were made and what they were worth. This meant they were now wise to being conned.

The 1951 Ealing Studios comedy *The Man in the White Suit* starred Alec Guinness as a scientist who accidentally invented a miraculous new material that would never wear out or go dirty. But instead of being hailed a genius, union leaders and industrialists ganged up to destroy his formula.

The Man in the White Suit was a satire about planned obsolescence and the complicity of industry and unions in perpetuating a con on the public. Its success revealed the depth of anger the public felt and the cynicism they showed towards those carrying out what appeared to be shady deals behind closed boardroom doors. Guinness's anti-hero wears a symbolic white suit standing for public integrity and honesty in a world of murky collusion.

But Roger MacDougall, John Dighton and Alexander Mackendrick's script is far from anti-capitalist. It pours scorn on both workers and bosses. This was a new kind of public disillusion: the disillusion of the consumer. Potentially far more dangerous than distrust of politicians, whom no one ever trusts. Disillusionment with consumerism threatened the growth of the economy at a critical moment, when Western governments needed the public to buy.

The year *The Man in the White Suit* was released, the Labour government was seeking re-election. They had delivered a welfare state in their first term, but failed to deliver a consumer boom. Winston Churchill sensed an opportunity to get back into office. 'What we need,' the Conservative manifesto stated, 'is abundance. The production of new wealth . . . far more beneficial than class.'

Churchill was making a stab for a new demographic: 'consumers'. And consumers had a very political role to play in the resurrection of Britain. In 1951, the Korean War broke out. The world faced a seemingly stark choice between two competing brands: 'communism' and 'capitalism'.

For capitalism to win, Churchill and President Truman needed the consumer to do their duty and begin shopping for big-ticket purchases in Britain and America, powering a consumer boom and thus economic recovery. Consumerism was not merely shopping, it was an ideological weapon for fighting the Cold War.

Both communism and capitalism offered alternative nirvanas built on competing ideas of freedom: communism had tanks and the West had shoppers. Communism promised freedom from class and capitalism promised freedom to shop, but the difference was that capitalism could offer nirvana today, not the classless tomorrow in a never-never future.

This was a distinct advantage when it came to the battle for hearts and minds. Capitalism had tangible proof to workers that it worked: the things you had bought in your house. Communism had only a belief in tomorrow. In the struggle with communism, goods were evidence today and the act of buying them was your duty as a citizen.

But there was a problem. The duty of buying had something rotten at its core, and consumers had rumbled it. Planned obsolescence made a mockery of the ideology of consumerism and the duty of the consumer. Why should we do our duty if the whole thing was a con? If manufacturers wanted to reboot the credibility of consumerism in the minds of the consumer, they needed a new conjuring trick.

Alfred. P. Sloan Jr was CEO of General Motors and had steered the company sensibly for thirty years. Though a proficient boss of GM, Sloan had for decades operated in the shadow of a colossus of the car industry: Henry Ford of Ford Motor Company.

Ford's genius had hinged on one simple breakthrough. In the 1880s and 1890s, he had become fascinated by meat packers in Chicago. They had figured out how to pull animal carcasses apart efficiently, piece by piece along a conveyor belt. In effect, they had created the first modern production line. What, Ford thought, if you reversed the process? Instead of using a production line to deconstruct a cow, what if one used it to construct a car?

Henry Ford pioneered mass production with the assembly line that built the Model T Ford in 1908. Now, in 1956, nine years after Ford's death, Sloan had his own idea to revolutionise the car industry, reinventing planned obsolescence by creating the upgrade.

At a 1954 advertising conference, Milwaukee industrial designer Brooks Stevens had addressed delegates with what he believed was the greatest challenge facing post-war industry: 'instilling in the buyer the desire to own something a little newer, a little better, a little sooner than necessary.'[10] Sloan saw how to make this happen. To resurrect the discredited doctrine of planned obsolescence, he would engineer a new mindset for the consumer, one in which we ourselves would choose to make a product obsolete. GM would not need to mechanically engineer a vehicle to break, but could rely on the customer to become unhappy with it. Sloan described the whole process in two brilliantly chilling words: 'engineered dissatisfaction'.

In Sloan's autobiography, *My Years with General Motors*, he outlined the theory in more detail: 'The changes in the new model (of car) should be so novel and attractive as to create demand ... and a certain amount of dissatisfaction with past models as compared to the new one.'[11] Sloan was going to manufacture dissatisfaction in the consumer by inventing the rolling upgrade.

In San Francisco, I meet the man who was at the heart of Sloan's project, Tom Matano, who grew up in late 1940s Tokyo marvelling at American design such as the Parker pen, the Coke bottle and the GE refrigerator. The first chance he got, Matano headed to the States to become an apprentice designer at General Motors.[12]

One of Tom's first assignments was to work on the first car designed to 'engineer dissatisfaction': the 1956 Chevrolet Bel Air. It is a beautiful spring day and Tom is driving me across the Golden Gate Bridge in an original model. 'You see the shine on the dashboard?' Tom points to the brilliant blue sheen reflecting the sky. 'That colour was derived from nail varnish. The car was to be an accessory, matching your new coat or handbag.'

The car came with a catalogue, too, showing you what the upgrade model would look like, available in just six months' time. The catalogue is key to understanding Sloan's thinking. At the very moment that you bought the Chevrolet, you were made instantly aware there was a better one coming, and so your new car was already obsolete. It was newly old and you felt automatic disappointment because you now wanted the new one.

How did Tom feel about working in this way? 'We were fashion designers, not car designers. The vehicle under the bonnet, no change. But we had to work on improving the add-ons:

upholstery, tail-fins, bright new colours. These were the things that drove the sale.'

Alfred P. Sloan had upended everything. Reliability and performance were now irrelevant to selling a car, what 'mattered were cosmetic changes. But there was a sour taste to this sweet new purchase: it was already out of date, and you would need to upgrade soon. You had done your duty by buying the latest model, but it wasn't right. Your dissatisfaction had been successfully engineered.

Tom's apprenticeship at GM stood him in good stead. He went on to become head of design at Toyota. But as an apprentice coming into the car business, did he think he was duping the customer with the Chevrolet? 'Not really. It was a genius idea of Sloan's, to keep the car under the bonnet virtually the same and sell it as a new car. That is brilliant.'

What Sloan did was reboot obsolescence by turning it into a nagging kernel of doubt that the new thing we have just bought has the clock already ticking on it and is inherently faulty.

Yet there is a brief moment of pleasure to be had: the moment you hold a brand-new purchase in your hand and these doubts are banished. It is the moment my friend at the front of the Apple queue was hoping to feel briefly with his new iPhone. The newest new thing, with no taint of impending obsolescence.

THE DRUG AND THE LOOP: DECISION, REWARD, ENDORPHIN RUSH

Gabe Zichermann lives a stone's throw from the Golden Gate Bridge. A bear of a man, with a Zen-like bald head and talking at lightning speed, he seems too big for his tiny ultra-minimal, Asian fusion house, complete with contemplation zone and bamboo garden.

Zichermann is one of the chief prophets of the neuroscience of selling, studying exactly what ignites in our brains the very moment we buy something.[13]

He talks with an intense energy about what happens: 'Once upon a time, we had brand loyalty over a lifetime to a cigarette brand or a washing powder, but now that loyalty is through the upgrade. It is what keeps us with the same brand of car or phone, because we now tell ourselves that we believe it is always improving.'

And this upgrade does not stop with the product. We think our lives should be pushing ever-forward, with a better job, house or partner. Upgrading in everything we do: a better holiday, body at the gym, dating on dating apps, clean eating our way to an upgraded health regime. Products fit this ever-improving narrative by upgrading as we do, and we in turn become an ever-upgradable product, on sale to other people. The human on a shelf, to be bought or left there.

Upgradable objects mark out the forward march of our lives. By surrounding ourselves with the latest and the newest, we tell ourselves we must be progressing with them. A kind of osmosis takes place between upgraded technology and our own sense of self-worth. We become as one.

Yet it is what happens at the very nanosecond of purchase that fascinates Zichermann, and has made him the go-to guy for big companies seeking to get truly inside our heads. 'When we buy something new, our brain treats this decision as a reward. And a small endorphin rush is created, which we enjoy, because it's a high. A drug. So a loop is created between decision, reward, endorphin rush. And this loop becomes addictive.'

A report by *Psychology Today* discovered that even the anticipation of shopping brings a release of dopamine into the brain, and this increases with online shopping. Of 1,680 shoppers polled by the journal, seventy-six per cent of shoppers say they get more excited when a product arrives in the mail than when it is bought in store, and the anticipation of the package is the height of the rush. Once it has been opened, they wish to repeat the dopamine rush, so another purchase is made.

We glibly use the phrases 'retail therapy' and 'shopping

addiction' as if we know what they mean, but these are crude terms for a complex neurological process that is real. It is not the object that we crave, but the endorphin rush that comes with purchasing something new. A rush that dissipates so quickly, it is gone before we have even received the confirmation email of purchase or left the shop. In order to get another hit, we buy again and the faster the better.

Sloan may have been rolling a new Chevrolet upgrade off the production line every six months, but today rolling obsolescence is a perpetual and unstoppable reality. A never-ending upgrade mindset. A non-stop nervy jangling in our heads that we cannot keep up. And with no purchase is this intense relationship of endorphin rush and the upgrade culture stronger than with the Apple iPhone.

ARE YOU GETTING IT?

It was 2007 and a tall man in a black turtleneck walked out into a lecture theatre to complete silence. A giant silver Apple glowed in the darkness behind him. The man stopped and faced the audience. 'This is a day,' he said, 'I have been looking forward to. Every once in a while, a revolutionary product comes along that changes everything. One is very fortunate if you get to work on one of these in your career.'

There was not a sound in the auditorium. The man paused, looked around and continued.

'In 1984, Apple introduced the Macintosh. It didn't just change Apple, it changed the whole computer industry. In 2001, we introduced the first iPod. It didn't just change the way we listen to music, it changed the entire music industry.' The audience started clapping quietly.

'Well, today, we're introducing three revolutionary products.' He turned to the huge screen behind him and an icon appeared. 'The first is a widescreen iPod with touch controls.' The applause began to intensify.

'The second is a revolutionary mobile phone.' A white telephone appeared magically in a green square. The crowd began to whoop and some of the audience got to their feet. 'And the third is a breakthrough internet communications device.' The place erupted.

'Three things. An iPod, a phone, and an internet communicator.' He repeated the words slowly and deliberately, over and over like a mantra. 'An iPod, a phone, and an internet communicator.' The icons began to spin around and around faster and faster, becoming one. 'Are you getting it? Are you getting it? These are not three separate devices. This is one device, and we are calling it iPhone.'[14]

Steve Jobs turned on his heel and the world was a different place. At the time, Jobs's hailing of the iPhone as 'revolutionary' may have seemed a bit of marketing hyperbole, but he had actually undersold his achievement. The iPhone was not to be part of the future, it was going to make it. The original iPhone had more computing power than Apollo 11, but its real power lay in what no one – not even Steve Jobs – could predict.

The iPhone was not going to become simply a digital tool for interacting with the physical world; it would remake the physical world to its own digital design. And all this from an object the size of the compass that Christopher Columbus used to reach America 515 years before. Like Columbus, Jobs had dared to be first to a new world of which he could scarcely imagine its true scale.

THE FIVE-SIDED CIRCLE SQUARED

One of the designers Steve Jobs brought in to develop the iPhone was Dan Crow. We meet in his London offices at 'Silicon Roundabout' in Shoreditch. The iPhone was an extraordinary invention, but I wondered how indebted its upgrade iterations (the 5, 6, 7, 8 Plus, etc.) had been to Alfred Sloan's theory of 'engineered dissatisfaction'. How conscious were they of a debt to perpetual upgrade when developing it?

Dan sips his water and replies. 'Apple had got better and better at iterating over many years, starting in the 1970s. Now partly that is driven by upgrade, right? And that is interesting. But the problem is that it's all driven by technology, and inevitably innovation with technology slows.'

Steve Jobs had spotted a problem with engineering dissatisfaction. At some point, even though you keep releasing iPhones with a 6, 7, 8, 9 in front, the public are going to see through it.

'You can put in a sensor or better camera or make the phone gold or whatever, but you are inevitably going to see a natural plateauing of the product. There's a point where it gets about as good as it's ever going to get.'

This inevitable slowing of innovation requires quitting ahead of the curve and inventing something new, which is why Apple did not stop with the Macintosh in the 1970s, they kept going. Jobs's genius was to create a giraffe, then throw the drawings away and create a rhino, then a lion and then a shark. He knew the public were never going to keep buying the giraffe, no matter how many times you resprayed it a different colour.

And colour, Dan Crow says, is the giveaway that something is over. When you get down to the colour changing on a product, you are scraping the upgrade barrel. Bright new colours are an unintended signal to the public that a product has done genuinely improving. It happened for the Chevrolet Bel Air and it hangs over the iPhone, which is why Apple are moving on, trying to invent the next elephant.

Steve Jobs learnt from Sloan and General Motors that you can only get away with the upgrade for so long. Ultimately you need the new species. The reason GM died was they never learnt that lesson and Jobs was determined that would never happen to Apple. That is what Jobs truly learnt from Alfred Sloan.

But before the iPhone, it seems Apple were not averse to some good, old-fashioned planned obsolescence, just like everyone else.

In 2004, a student in New York called Casey Neistat called the Apple helpline with a problem. The jewel in Apple's crown at that time was the iPod, and Casey Neistat's iPod had mysteriously stopped working.

Casey phoned Apple Support, wanting to know how to change the battery. 'That iPod had cost 400 dollars. So when the battery died, I wanted to fix it. The Apple guy told me that it would cost 250 dollars plus postage to get a new one. Then he said, "At that price, you may as well go and get a new one."'

Casey was perplexed. 'How old is your iPod?' the Apple Support guy asked. 'Eighteen months,' Casey replied. 'Ah. OK. It's past its year.'

It seemed Apple's sales policy was to get Casey – and all iPod owners – to buy another iPod, for another $400. And so, to spend potentially $400 on a new iPod every year.

The reason for this was that Apple faced a dilemma. Apple are more like Land Rover than Ford – they are a market leader and quite happy to keep a cap on market share if they can maintain their position as the number-one tech innovator. This matters more than sales, because without design excellence, there are no sales.

To make the iPod slim enough to work on your belt or in your pocket, the battery life had to be compromised. If the consumer wanted a longer-lasting iPod, that would mean a bulkier product. Design would be hamstrung by practicality and in Apple's world, that would mean the tail wagging the dog. Steve Jobs would not do it, which is why Casey's iPod died.

He was furious and began stencilling 'Apple's Dirty Secret: iPod's Unreplaceable Battery Lasts Only 18 Months' on the iPod ads of dancing silhouettes wearing headphones that adorned the streets of New York.

The accompanying video he made went viral on YouTube and was picked up by the *Washington Post*, *Rolling Stone*, Fox News and the BBC. In drawing attention to the iPod's battery life, Neistat kicked off a new grassroots anti-upgrade movement – 'iFixit' or 'downgrade' culture. Groups of tech volunteers, who tear apart new technology the moment it comes out in order to understand how it works, and do something most of us have long given up trying to do: fix it.

Shane Williams works in a small tech start-up in Silicon Valley, but instead of a uniform of chinos and button-down shirt, he and his colleagues at iFixit wear a proper uniform; the kind you would see in a car garage or depot: brown overalls with an iFixit logo on everyone's lapel. Williams and his co-workers are pulling apart every new upgraded piece of technology they can get their hands on to create something that most of us have not had with a fridge or TV for decades: an instruction manual.

He has written over two hundred such manuals and put them up for free online, along with a YouTube video, so that people can work out how to fix things manufacturers believe we cannot be bothered to fix ourselves. If we can't be bothered, Shane says, how come people are flocking to his videos and manuals?

In dismantling the iPhone, Shane found something strange. A unique five-sided pentalobe screw for which there was no screwdriver.

In his workshop, I asked Shane why he thought they had done this. 'To keep the customer out. If you manage to get inside the phone, Apple use standard Phillips screws, so clearly there's no aesthetic or practical reason for the five-sided screw on the outside, it's simply a kind of barbed wire to protect the phone from anyone trying to get in.' So Shane decided to make the only screwdriver in the world that can unscrew this five-sided screw, and now gives them away.

I wondered what the five-sided screw was all about and asked Apple for an interview. A smartly dressed man with glasses agreed to meet me in a giant glass office in central London. His name was Benedict Evans, a tech analyst and articulator of Apple's thinking.

'Do you think phones are really improving or are Apple just engineering dissatisfaction through upgrade?'

'We still see specific dramatic improvements. The products are built to last and Apple take great care to keep the customer happy.'

'But when I asked the man at the front of the queue for the latest iPhone what those improvements were, he couldn't even tell me.'

'It's not the consumer's job to know something is better, or have an opinion on something they've haven't seen.'

People like the iFixit guys are a tiny percentage of the consumers who use Apple products. These products have to work for everyone, Benedict argued, and most people just want their phone to function. If something goes wrong, they generally take it to Apple rather than try to fix it themselves.

As for upgrade, he says, what is really so terrible about that?

'The argument [against upgrade] says we were a lot better off when we had much slower consumption and much slower lives. When eighty to ninety per cent of the population were peasants. The story of humanity's move away from peasantry is in part the story of consumption.'

Apple have changed the lives of billions of people with the iPhone and if the unintended consequence has been an obsession with upgrade as a society, that is not necessarily Apple's fault.

Throwing virtually new goods away is a consumer choice created by upgrade. We chase something better, yet are never able to attain it. This ever-receding shore is the perfect product. Apple merely invented a platform for this perfect product to be chased, we do the rest.

Benedict asks me if I have ever seen the Bill Murray plane sketch from *Saturday Night Live*. Bill Murray plays a grumpy businessman on a plane, angrily complaining to the air stewardess that the ice in his whisky is not cold enough.

Eventually the stewardess has had enough. 'What you should

be doing, sir,' the stewardess says, 'is marvelling at the fact you are travelling at one thousand, two hundred miles per hour, thirty thousand feet above the ground. Not worrying about the temperature of your ice.'

The iPhone is the plane and I am Bill Murray complaining about the ice. Upgrade culture is bigger than the iPhone or criticisms of it. Upgrade culture subsumes everything and yet we know this mindset is a diminishing return. New products never really make us happy, and yet we don't care. We upgrade anyway. Why?

The upgrade is impervious to criticism because we were long ago conditioned to believe upgrade equalled technological progress, the most credible and unchallengeable kind of progress. It was a reprogrammed state of mind first conjured by the genius of Alfred. P. Sloan. And this state of mind comes from somewhere far deeper than wanting something new, or even the endorphin hit from possessing the newest new thing. It comes from wanting to become a better person.

THE BIOLOGICAL UPGRADE: HUMAN 2.0

We are now for the first time in history able to upgrade ourselves. The Shanghai super-rich have begun to breathe different air from people on the street below. In Beijing, penthouse apartments overlooking the city are supplied pure mountain oxygen pumped from the Canadian Rocky Mountains by companies like Alberta-based Vitality Air, who sell canisters of 'the cleanest air on earth' for between $20 and $32 a canister. Each one lasts between 150 and 200 breaths. 'Our Chinese website keeps crashing,' Vitality Air's Chinese rep Harrison Wang says. 'When the air (outside) is bad, we see spikes in sales. The smog is definitely our best advertising.'[15]

According to its website, another pure-air supplier, Aethaer, is 'filtered organically by nature as it flows between the leaves of woodland trees, absorbs pristine water as it passes over babbling brooks and forest streams.' It is sold in a glass jar for £80 a jar and founder Leo De Watts says it needs to be savoured when inhaled, like a fine wine.[16]

If you step outside and need to breathe polluted air, you can use a smart air-quality monitor called a 'laser egg' for $79. 'People want to have an objective way of seeing air quality, and technology can help us control our environment,' according to Origins founder Jess Lam, who sell the laser egg.[17]

Shanghai is upgrading its air. It is simultaneously one of the most polluted cities and home to some of the richest people on earth. In London, another polluted hub for the global super-rich, every stop on the Jubilee Line travelling east from Westminster sees life expectancy drop by a year. Those living in Canning Town, eight stops away from Westminster, live six years less. Seventy-two versus seventy-eight.

In the nineteenth century, the rich lived longer than the poor because they had a better diet and social conditions, but now the gap is widening still further as a result of the biological upgrade opportunities coming the rich's way.

BCIs or 'Brain-Computer Interfaces' are implantable devices intended originally to help the disabled move lifeless limbs, but they could now be used to create robotic prosthetics for a more powerful you: a 'self-optimised' human, neither machine nor flesh, but a seamless amalgam of the two and perpetually upgradable. Limbs as the plastic surgery of the twenty-first century.

To bolster this self-optimised you, uploading memory and linking the brain directly to the internet will create infinite memory storage, and mean the rich never forget, as well as think faster. Human cyborgs versus plain old humans. 2.0 *vs* 1.0.

I am at a discreet white door in Harley Street, London. It is an exclusive health clinic called Viavi ('Health Managed – Life Optimised'). I am ushered into a white room with a white bed and white curtains. The only bright colours in the room are the blueberries and strawberries in a pristine porcelain bowl, brought to me on a tray.

I am here to meet Dr Sabine Donnai, one of the world's leading authorities on the potential of the human upgrade. Before setting up her own exclusive Harley Street business, she was the medical director at Nuffield and clinical director at BUPA, so I wondered why someone at such a senior position at BUPA, the biggest private healthcare company in the UK, would suddenly strike out alone. The reason was simple: she saw the future, and went for it.

'We are now, thanks to bio-tech advances, at a point where we can collect an infinite amount of data on you: what you eat and when, how it affects your body, your stress levels, your glucose levels, blood-pressure levels, your sleep patterns, how your body is coping every second of the day. But we can drill into these numbers in a micro-way never possible before – each set of data can itself further be broken down with a level of precision no one would have dreamt possible even five years ago. The point is not the amassing of this data, but what you do with it.'

To show me what Viavi do with it – a bespoke biometric mapping service costing £13,000 a year used by everyone from film stars to CEOs, politicians and Premiership footballers – I had a go myself. Wearing an injected glucose monitor in my arm and uploading the data every five hours, a heart monitor blinking away measuring stress and heart rate for three days; spitting five times a day into different coloured serums to be analysed in a laboratory, urinating 'best morning urine' into test tubes and defecating into a space-age silver 'sleeve'.

The aim is to create the ultimate body MOT and use this data to become the 'optimum you'. Dr Donnai does not believe the super-rich clients she has actually seek to perfect themselves, but want to have a medical licence to live the way they want to live. With the data, they can find the 'weak links in the DNA chain, further weakened by lifestyle choices.' Their solution is a targeted strike on these weak links.

But the real opportunity lies not with the thousands of rich clients she has, but the potential millions she will have when she launches a cheaper high-street model of this service, rolling it out across Britain and Europe. Viavi will become the first high-street player to use state-of-the-art DNA editing called CRISPR. Boots meets *Blade Runner*. CRISPR has already identified the specific gene that causes cataracts and cystic fibrosis. It is being used to edit out potential hereditary disease and to perfect plants and animals for human consumption. Beijing-based BGI-Shenzhen, a Viavi of China, say they will be able to sequence your DNA for less than the price of an iPhone. Google's DeepMind is racing to be first to unlock the genetic basis for intelligence.

George Church, a geneticist at Harvard, is working on developing tools that scramble the genetic code allowing us to engineer bacterium resistant to viral infection. He does not dismiss the possibility of changing human DNA to create a new kind of human that does not need to rely on powerful, enhanced robolimbs, because it is biologically superior. A human 2.0.

I ask Dr Donnai if we should be scared by CRISPR and the future world dawning now, and fast. 'Not really. Twenty years ago, we were terrified by the thought of IVF babies. The scare stories were of genetic selection and super-babies, but the reality was millions of couples miraculously being able to simply have children they never thought they could have.'

Will the upgraded human be an upgrade for all as Donnai predicts, or the beginning of the creation of two species: Human 1.0 and its upgraded, faster, cleverer, stronger and richer relative?

Historian Yuval Noah Harari thinks the latter. We meet in London and he is tremendously upbeat and high-octane as he tells me that the human as we know it will be over in a hundred years. Harari sees upgrade inextricably bound to inequality, with the rich being able to take advantage of the confluence of gene editing and body upgrades made possible by the data and bio-tech revolutions to become a genetically superior species: one that will rule the planet.

'Only the upgraded,' Yuval says simply, 'will matter.' It will in essence be inequality made flesh. Oxford bio-technician Anders Sandberg refers to this bifurcation of the human race into the upgraded and unupgradable underclass as 'speciation'.[18] And what will begin as a medical divide created by income and access to DNA editing will after one generation become biological, irreversible and ordained. The upgrade will be passed on, just as genes are now.

When the Phoebus Cartel created planned obsolescence eighty years ago, the men sitting round that table in Geneva could not have imagined that the one thing ultimately made obsolete by the upgrade would be humanity itself.

CHAPTER NINE
POWER: THE FIRM WHO KNOW EVERYTHING

The Deal: Marvin Bower, director of the world's most powerful consultancy, McKinsey & Co. sells his shares back to the company at the exact value he bought them for years earlier

Aim: To show the world McKinsey, known as 'The Firm', was too important to be sold, cementing its position as the most powerful company no one knows anything about, or could take over – McKinsey 'advise' ninety of the top 100 Fortune companies and dozens of governments across the globe

Where: McKinsey Headquarters, Manhattan, New York

When: 1 August 1963

In 2014, I was in the Dorchester Hotel in London interviewing China's richest man, Wang Jianlin, chairman of the Dalian Wanda construction empire. Wang is worth $32 billion and was in London because he had $7 billion in loose change and was looking to spend it on something 'big'.

A parade of eager British business interests lined up to pitch Wang their 'unmissable' opportunity. Men and women in very expensive suits stood in the corridor with portfolios waiting to be summoned, including a film studio, a plan to build the world's tallest building in London, and a top Premiership football club.

How likely any of these deals were to happen depended entirely on how Wang was feeling today, such is the Caligulan

whim of those that sit on the very, very top cloud of the super-
rich stratosphere, unimaginably wealthier than the mere billionaires who sit on the lower clouds. His thumb might go up or
down. Wang is one of the 0.000001 per cent richest people on
earth. He is on the top cloud.

Wang remained unseen, like the Spectre boss in the Bond
movie. He sat in a private darkened room with eight of his business associates and a translator (Wang told me later that he
understood English perfectly well, but that it was useful sometimes to pretend not to). People had been ushered in discreetly
all day for their thirty-second pitch.

Minutes before I was summoned, two unassuming characters
had been rumoured to be skulking in the corridor, pacing nervously. They were called David and Boris – one, it turned out, was
the then prime minister of Great Britain and the other was the
mayor of London (latterly the foreign secretary).

What struck me was not that they were supposedly meeting
Wang, but they were waiting in line with everyone else. Once
Wang would have gone to Downing Street, lucky to be granted
an audience. Now they were lucky to see him, and had an allot-
ted window like the rest of us.

Business, not government, now calls the shots. And business
no longer has to even influence government, business *is* government. China claims on the tin to be communist, but it runs like
the largest company on earth, while a businessman is the president of the most powerful country on earth.

The job of government now is not to serve the people, no
matter what politicians say, but to manage the economy as best it
can on behalf of business. This is not a judgment, but a fact.
Socialists rail against 'corporate capture', but the truth is that
business believes politicians have done such a bad job managing
the economy, they have had to step in. They don't even want to
– it is just the deal.

The power relationship has been inverted. Seeing politicians
meeting successful business people like Wang is like watching a

simpering teenager meet a rock star. The politicians do not know what to do with themselves. It is embarrassing.

The corporations these business people run have become like elephants on the African plains, roaming imperiously across the globe in search of the best tax breaks and offshoring deals. These corporations operate above and beyond governments, who are too timid to challenge them, and have no tools at their disposal even if they wanted to do so.

Yet these companies also have more wealth to invest in a country than the GDP of some of the nations in which they have a stake. Billionaires like Wang have the means to transform the lives of millions of people with a swish of his wand. Wang was being wooed in London with an 'opportunity' to plough his billions into affordable housing. What was in it for him? The chance to build the world's tallest building, outdoing the Burj Khalifa in Dubai. I still have not seen Wang's tower on the London skyline, so clearly the deal did not happen.

How and why did business people like Wang become more powerful than government? Who made the decisions that enabled it, and if business now writes the rules, could it actually do a better job of running the state? To answer these questions, you need to understand how and why government was first subsumed by business.

THE PRESIDENT WHO WARNED THE PEOPLE

On 17 January 1961, President Dwight Eisenhower made his farewell address to the American nation. Eisenhower was a military man to his core. A five-star general and supreme commander of the Allied Forces during the Second World War. In 1944, Eisenhower oversaw the planning for the Normandy landings. He went on to become the first supreme commander of NATO and then president of the United States. He was the most powerful man on earth, which is why his parting words to the American public on leaving office in 1961 were so extraordinary.

Instead of uttering banalities about leaving America a better place, Eisenhower chose to use his address to make a stark warning. Democracy, he said, was at risk from an insidious new force operating in the corridors of power. A threat he believed the public needed to know about.

'Three days from now,' he declaimed, 'after half a century in the service of our country, I shall lay down the responsibilities of office. This evening I come to you with a message of leave taking.'[1]

Eisenhower began by outlining the known threat: communism. But this danger, he said, had given rise to another one hidden from view: the muscle wielded in the corridors of Washington by the arms industry.

'In the councils of government,' warned Ike, 'we must guard against the acquisition of unwarranted influence, whether sought or unsought, by the military-industrial complex. We must never let the weight of this combination endanger our liberties or democratic processes. We should take nothing for granted. Only an alert and knowledgeable citizenry can compel the proper meshing of the huge industrial and military machinery with our peaceful methods and goals.'

It is still pretty much the most extraordinary revelation an American president has ever made to the public (Donald Trump's twitter revelations don't come close). A clear-eyed warning from a man at the centre of power: eye to eye from president to electorate. Subsequent interpretations of the speech have rightly pointed out that Eisenhower faced a particular set of circumstances when he made the 'military-industrial complex' speech. The Cold War was escalating. Fifty per cent of government spending and ten per cent of GDP was going on military expenditure each year, and the figure was rising.[2] The potential threat to democracy of military might looked real.

Ike was a staunch anti-communist, yet the idea of the

'military-industrial complex' taking over government was co-opted in the 1960s and 1970s by radical left-wing thinkers like Noam Chomsky as an explanation for the conspiratorial workings of capitalism.

Ike had given the American public a glimpse behind the curtain of power and told them the deal. And this reality check was very much at odds with the public's belief in democracy as transparent. It was the day the American public began to believe dark forces were at work behind the scenes. Their slide into mistrust of politicians began, and a politician had taken them there.

Before Eisenhower made his speech, the public believed the arms industry was defending democracy, not endangering it by using its power as leverage to extract greater profit and influence. Eisenhower inferred that these unseen forces were lobbying to control the levers of power. So, who were the lobbyists and where did lobbying come from?

THE WILLARD HOTEL

In the 1870s, a gruff, portly man with a beard could be seen sitting in the lobby of the Willard Hotel, Washington, smoking cigars and drinking brandy. At sixteen, this middle-aged man had been nominated for the prestigious military academy at West Point. He had gone on to become a skilled horseman and deco-rated captain serving in the Mexican Civil War and at Fort Humboldt, eventually rising to commanding general of the US army.[3] But now he had a new job, which partly explained why he was sitting in the lobby of the Willard Hotel.

Ulysses S. Grant was the eighteenth president of the United States and in the afternoons he would go to the lobby of the Willard to get away from the politicians and bureaucrats on Capitol Hill. But there was no escape. They would sniff him out and confront him in the lobby to petition him and attempt to persuade him to support one piece of legislation or another. Grant had spent a lifetime in the brutal business of war, but did not take kindly to their tactics. He referred to them as 'those damned lobbyists' and the name stuck.

Is that true? The term 'lobbying' was already being used in 1850 to describe petitioners waiting to speak to legislators in the lobby of the New York State Capitol in Albany. Across the Atlantic in London, the same term described commoners waiting in the lobbies of the Palace of Westminster to speak to their member of Parliament.

Ever since the 1640s, following the English Civil War, this 'lobby' had been the accepted place to carry out confidential business with newly persuadable representatives of the people.[4]

For three hundred years, 'lobbying' worked to the mutual benefit of politicians and business. You scratch my back and I'll scratch yours. But in the 1960s, something changed. The power shifted and the lobbyists changed. Full employment, coupled with the rise of civil rights, brought two new powerful interest groups into the lobby – minority groups and organised labour. Consumer rights groups, environmentalists, gay rights, feminists, black rights, and the myriad new brokers of pressure-group politics came into the equation and were not simply an annoyance to the old brokers, they had muscle.

Politicians had a democratic duty to address (or be seen to be addressing) these groups. The lobby had been disrupted and these new players threatened to take the politician's ear away from business. Corporate interests felt muscled out of the corridors of power. Subversives and radicals were influencing the heart of government, pushing a reform agenda of special pleading. Voices in business began to become concerned. These new interest groups were not about getting a business deal through, or a piece of legislation amended, they wanted to change the nature of civil society. Something had to be done.

THE POWELL MEMORANDUM

On 23 August 1971, one of America's most respected and prominent lawyers, Lewis Franklin Powell, sat down to write a memo to his friend Eugene B. Sydnor. 'The Powell Memorandum' was to become a pivotal moment in the fightback, a *cri de coeur* for the business establishment in retreat.[5]

'Business,' Powell said, 'has been the favourite whipping boy of politicians for many years. But the measure of how far this has gone is found in the anti-business views now being expressed by several candidates for President of the United States.[6]

'It is Marxist doctrine,' he continued, 'that the "capitalist" countries are controlled by big business. This doctrine, consistently a part of leftist propaganda all over the world, has a wide public following among Americans.

'Yet, as every business executive knows, few elements of American society today have as little influence in government as the American businessman, the corporation, or even the millions of corporate stockholders. If one doubts this, let him undertake the role of "lobbyist" for the business point of view before Congressional committees ... one does not exaggerate to say that, in terms of political influence with respect to the course of legislation and government action, the American business executive is truly the "forgotten man".'

Business, Powell said, had been forced into retreat and persecuted by an array of liberal and outright Marxist enemies, who now had the ear of government. Powell outlined these enemies in more detail: 'television' and 'journalism'; the minority-interest groups of feminism, black and gay civil rights, who now constituted the lobby, and weak-minded judges in the Supreme Court, who had allowed these groups to contort the constitution to their own ends.

Then there were Marxist academics and student unions in universities, spreading an anti-American and anti-business agenda; union officials bent on thwarting productivity, who also had politicians in their pocket. Even the Chamber of Commerce, the business lobby in Washington, had proved 'impotent' in the face of this deluge of socialism.

'Current examples of the impotency of business, and the near contempt with which businessmen's views are held, are the stampedes by politicians to support almost any legislation related to "consumerism" (rights) or the "environment",' Powell said.

'Business must learn the lesson, long ago learned by labour and other self-interest groups. Political power is necessary, such power must be assiduously cultivated, and when necessary, it must be used aggressively and with determination.' He concluded, 'Business has shunned confrontation,' but there should now be 'no hesitation to attack.'

The fightback was about to begin and it needed to be dirty to take back control of government. Powell saw this as nothing short of a turning point in history: the 'fight for freedom'.

Lee Drutman, author of *The Business of America is Lobbying* sees the Powell Memorandum as the touchpaper that lit a new political ideology: neo-liberalism.[7] In the 1960s, there had been 'a regulatory binge spurred on by a new wave of public interest groups. Large corporations had largely sat by idly, unsure of what to do.' This is what Franklin Powell meant by 'socialism': the invisible Lilliputian knots and threads of a thousand pieces of legislation designed to tie business down.

The Powell Memorandum was pinned up to a wall by a clutch of pro-business pressure groups that sprang up in small offices across Washington: the Heritage Foundation (funded by Coors beer), the American Legislative Exchange Council (ALEC), the Manhattan Institute and the Cato Institute. The Carthage Foundation was founded in 1964 by tycoon Richard Mellon Scaife explicitly to fund and make possible Powell's vision of pro-business anti-socialist government. The foundation sought to roll back Keynesian interventionism and statist paternalism, which had begun with Roosevelt's New Deal, returning America to its rightful custodians: the industrialists.[8]

In Britain, the New Right think-tank the Centre for Policy Studies (CPS) was created. A rising star of British politics called Margaret Thatcher was its president. The CPS worked in tandem with the Institute of Economic Affairs (IEA), created by chicken-farming mogul Antony Fisher in the 1950s. Fisher had picked up a copy of the *Reader's Digest* by chance one day and read an extract of Friedrich Hayek's *The Road to Serfdom*.[9] He was now a convert to neo-liberalism and wanted to make these ideas happen, just as the Carthage Foundation did in the States.

The Road to Serfdom became their bible and Fisher had a Road to Damascus experience reading it, deciding he would use his business fortune to fund a think-tank dedicated to rolling back the socialist state that Hayek believed would enslave us all.

In the 1970s, these groups dovetailed with the rise of the supply-side economic revolution of Milton Friedman and the Chicago School. Together, they would become the foundation for an ideological revolution that would change the shape of the last third of the twentieth century, and mould the destiny of the twenty-first.

In his ten-part PBS series *Free to Choose* in 1980, Friedman outlined his grand vision: breaking the tyranny of government and freeing humankind through the sovereignty of markets. Friedman was indebted to the eighteenth-century Scots economist Adam Smith.

'Adam Smith's flash of genius,' Friedman said, 'was to see how prices that emerged in the market – the prices of goods, the wages of labour, the cost of transport – could coordinate the behavior of millions of independent people, strangers to each other, without anybody telling them what to do. (Smith's) key idea was that self-interest could produce an orderly society benefitting everybody.'

An 'invisible hand' was at work. In *The Wealth of Nations*, Smith talked about 'the way in which individuals who intended only to produce their own interests would promote public welfare by an invisible hand that was no part of their intention.'[10]

It was a key flip from socialism and the state, which were synonymous in his mind. According to Friedman, socialism made people selfish in forcing them towards a collective good. But by simply allowing people to follow their own selfish interests, they would inadvertently create a collective good.

It is impossible to overstate the significance of the deal that was struck between business and ideology. Fisher (businessman) plus Hayek (intellectual) equalled a revolution postponed. But when Friedman (economist) plus Thatcher and Reagan (politicians) came together in 1980, history was jolted off one axis and onto the axis we are on today.

The last eighty years divide into two neat spaces: before and after this moment. Between 1945 and 1979, government was the primary mover of history, with business attempting to influence them; and from 1979 onwards, it was the other way around.

In Klimov's cinematic masterpiece *Come and See*, about the German invasion of Belorussia, the last five minutes of the film involve twenty catastrophic years of history rewinding at speed before the viewer's eyes.[11] If history rewound at speed through Silicon Valley, the banking crash, deregulation, the fall of the Berlin Wall, and Milton Friedman first meeting President Reagan and Prime Minister Thatcher, it would suddenly freeze-frame in 1971, when Lewis Powell sat down at his heavy, leather-topped desk and began to pen a memo that kick-started the future.

Weeks after penning his memo, Powell became President Nixon's nomination for the Supreme Court. Eugene Sydnor, the head of the Chamber of Commerce to whom he had written the memo, began overhauling the Chamber from a relic of the past to an aggressive driving force for the business fightback.

Behind closed doors, a new secret lobbying organisation was formed, the Business Roundtable, with the leading CEOs of America's biggest firms. Their aim was to re-cultivate political influence in Washington and roll back the negative view of business on the campuses and workplaces of America. 'I think we all recognise,' Alcoa CEO John Harper told his fellow CEOs, 'that the time has come when we must stop talking about it . . . and do something.'

GET RID OF THE CIVIL SERVANTS

Their weapon was the lobbyist. And lobbying was to stop being a polite, discreet word in the ear and go industrial. Professional lobbyists were hired in their thousands and took over one street in Washington – K Street – a stone's throw from 'The Hill'.

Lobbyists badgered, cajoled, log-rolled, threatened and horse-traded their way round government. In London, they lined up down Victoria Street in glass office blocks and in anonymous Georgian-fronted houses in St James's Square. Lobbyists did not skulk around hotel lobbies anymore. They were an industry in their own right.

The major K Street firms became feared and respected. They got labour law repealed, taxes lowered and most importantly, prepped the ground for public distrust of 'big government'. In less than a decade, lobbying went from a forgotten art to the way business was done.

By the early 1980s, Lee Drutman says, their success put them at a crossroads. 'Corporations could have declared victory and gone home. Instead they stuck around and kept at it. Many deepened their commitments to politics. After all, they now had lobbyists to help them see all that was at stake in Washington, and all the ways in which staying politically active could help their businesses.'[12]

Lobbying was about to make its greatest leap: from a reactive to a pro-active machine. Up until now, the lobbyist's job had been to stop government from meddling in business, and they had succeeded. Now lobbyists were to step over the threshold into government, pushing for legislative change, drafting legislation and pushing back the 'socialist' state. Business was about to become government.

Just one thing stood in the way: civil servants. For over a thousand years, civil servants had quietly burrowed away at the heart of government. Civil servants first rose to prominence in Imperial China. The idea of a civil service based on merit, not inherited entitlement, was revolutionary, with far-reaching effects on Chinese society. At a stroke, the Xiaolian system destroyed the idea of jobs passed down as heirlooms. Instead, candidates sat a fiercely competitive exam. Those who passed got the job.

In 2009, tiny 'cheat sheets' were discovered in Qingdao, Eastern China, and on the southern island of Hainan, dating back to the 1750s. These tiny booklets, printed on silk, were under two inches long and could fit inside a matchbox, but contained 140,000 characters to help cheat in the exams.[13] The cheat sheets are testament to the importance that was placed on passing these civil service exams, a gateway to social improvement.

In 1847, the British consul to China, Thomas Taylor Meadows, wrote a letter praising the meritocracy of the Chinese civil service exam: 'The long duration of the Chinese empire is solely and altogether owing to the good government which consists in the advancement of men of talent and merit only.'

The result of Meadows's letter was to open up the British civil service in the same way. Under the Northcote-Trevelyan reforms of 1854, exams were introduced. Meritocracy became the bedrock of the British and Indian civil service, the Prussian bureaucratic system and the modern US civil service, laid down by the Pendleton Reform Act.

Meritocracy became the driving force for a new middle class. In China, it drove urbanisation and the spread of education. Applied to Britain and Central Europe a thousand years later, it drove the growth of a middle class and undermined the political authority of an aristocracy already teetering on the edge of collapse. Meritocracy was a mechanism for change without revolution and a hand-picked civil service would deliver it.

However, by the 1960s and 1970s, the civil service was perceived as having become a force of inertia. A self-serving bureaucracy, as complacent as the aristocracy had once been. Civil servants became a caricature of dull, grey men in grey suits, pushing paper round a desk, hindering change by smothering it in administration.

In the 1970s, professional lobbyists had got business through the door in Washington and Whitehall, but now it was time to change the civil servants in the room. It was time for that consultancy buzzword – 'transformation' – and first up for transformation was the civil service.

THE FIRM

One company would make it happen: McKinsey, the world's most influential consultancy firm. McKinsey 'advise' ninety of the one hundred biggest companies on the *Fortune* list, and dozens of governments across the globe. New recruits are selected from Rhodes and Baker scholars at Oxford and Harvard, just as MI5 and the CIA once recruited spies.

When you start at McKinsey, you are given two analogies to make you understand better the kind of place you are working in. The first is the Jesuits. A specially chosen holy order closed off to outsiders, with a life-long loyalty to the order. Other management consultants do not even refer to McKinsey by name, they call it simply 'The Firm'. The second analogy is the bespoke Savile Row tailor; anonymous people working discreetly in the background of government about whom you know nothing, but who know everything about you.[14]

In 1933, the man who would make McKinsey what it is today was hired to oversee its New York office. Marvin Bower was a super-smart lawyer from provincial Ohio, who had recently graduated from Harvard. At the time Bower joined McKinsey, it was little more than an engineering and accounting company. But when the founder who'd given the company its name, James O. McKinsey, died in 1937, Bower took over.

Today, Bower is widely regarded as the father of modern consulting: the man who laid the ground rules and placed consulting at the heart of corporate and governmental power. Bower had three unwritten principles: the client is everything; think the unthinkable; and it's not about money, but influence and reputation. He applied these principles on a daily basis at McKinsey. Bower hated the idea of McKinsey as a 'company'. He insisted on calling it a firm, like a lawyer's practice, with a discreet sense of purpose and integrity, rather than showy offices and fatuous mission statements. Employees were told to wear bowler hats, until one day Bower turned up without one on, and said without explanation that the bowler hat rule had gone. He had changed his mind.

Bower, though trained as a lawyer, did not have a lawyer's caution. He was a disrupter, decades before the term became fashionable and overused in business. Bower created the McKinsey mantra of 'up or out' – if you are not climbing up the company but coasting, you'll be fired. He once even told an amazed client: 'You, Mr Little, are the problem with the company!' Bower routinely told clients unpalatable truths, or rejected highly paid work that he felt would not benefit McKinsey, no matter how lucrative it might be.

By the mid-1960s, the founders of other successful management consultancies were cashing in their chips and either selling their companies or merging to form super-firms. This was when Bower made his most important contribution to the Firm, selling his shares back to McKinsey at the price they had been worth thirty years earlier. It was a signal to everyone who worked at McKinsey and more importantly, to their powerful list of clients and potential clients.

Whilst other companies may sell out or merge for money, Bower was saying, becoming indistinguishable management mush, the Firm will hold firm. The client comes first, not the money. The closed-off culture and aura of omnipotence that McKinsey now has in consultancy was forged in this moment.

Bower's symbolic act in giving back his shares was an anti-deal designed to cement McKinsey as the world's most powerful company, and it worked.

Today, McKinsey is a 'consultancy' firm in the way Google is a search engine. Its true remit is power, just as Google's actual remit is the control and real-world application of all data. McKinsey ranks only seventh in size beside global competitors such as Boston Consulting Group, Bain, PricewaterhouseCoopers, and Deloitte. However, as Marvin Bower made plain, McKinsey is not about turnover, but power. It is more important than all the others put together: the indispensable secret cog in the machine of government that no one outside the corridors of Washington and Whitehall has even heard of.

In the late 1960s, politicians fired up by the desire for change saw obstructive civil servants as a problem, and McKinsey was there to help. The technocratic revolution – the 'white heat of technology' – had delivered confident, new, smooth-talking experts, who looked far more dynamic than the old-fashioned civil servants.

They did not go to the Garrick Club for a long lunch, they talked the breathless modern management-speak of flip charts and graphs. They were efficient and they were outsiders. Tony Benn, energy minister under Harold Wilson, distrusted the civil service to implement the kind of radical modernising reforms he sought, and began to bring in these new outside 'experts'.

In the 1970s, politicians began to use consultants more widely, and primarily McKinsey, which offered 'independent' strategy advice. 'Policy not politics' was the new mantra, and the civil service were seen as mired in the latter. McKinsey's sharp-suited soldiers on the ground, by contrast, had the aura of clever people in a rush to the next meeting, too busy for politics. Politicians were in awe of this confidence and McKinsey were to become the new quiet word in a politician's ear. They appeared to know something no one else did.

The Firm were instrumental in restructuring the entire staffing and running of the White House.[15] In Westminster, they were at the heart of the mammoth privatisation programme of the Conservatives in the 1980s. When the Conservatives shipped out and Tony Blair arrived in office, McKinsey stayed. Under New Labour in the late 1990s and early 2000s, McKinsey were integral to Blair's 'modernisation' of Britain, 'transforming the thinking' on health, education and in the key areas of government where they were now deemed to be indispensable. They asked politicians to think the unthinkable – there was nothing that could not be radically reformed. Nothing was sacred.

In 1997, McKinsey crystallised their revolution in just four words: 'The War for Talent'. Twenty years earlier, McKinsey had reconfigured the workplace with the '7S System' developed by McKinsey strategists Tom Peters and Robert Waterman. The 'War for Talent' was the next stage of evolving the human in the workplace.

McKinsey's Ed Michaels, Helen Handfield-Jones and Beth Axelrod looked at seventy-seven flourishing US companies over a broad spread of industries, and made a surprising discovery.

'Talent' is in short supply. Only twenty-three per cent of the executives McKinsey polled believed that their companies attracted the best employees. Yet revenue for these firms had grown at twice the rate of GDP in the previous five years.

The fact that these companies were growing so fast in spite of employing the least talented people was seen by the McKinsey consultants as proof of their theory, rather than its contradiction. If they ran dry on their most precious commodity – good people – they were over, they said.[16]

The subtext of McKinsey's declaration of a 'War for Talent' was a restatement of the need for employing McKinsey. In a booming economy, they said, do not be fooled by the numbers. Things will turn bad and when they do, you need the best people around you, not dead wood. You need us.

THE EMPEROR'S NEW SUIT

The immediate impact of the War for Talent was to justify an explosion in CEO pay, which jumped exponentially from double-digit multiples of the lowest employees' wage to seven hundred or eight hundred times that wage. I met Martin Sorrell, the founder of the world's biggest advertising agency, WPP, and worth an estimated £250 million. 'Do you know how much you're worth, Martin?' 'I couldn't really say.' 'Or how much you pay yourself?' 'I'm paid what the market decides I'm worth. That's the value we all have, Jacques.'[17]

The War for Talent was in reality merely a reheating of the 1950s McKinsey executive Arch Patton's tireless drive to promote higher corporate pay. At one point, Patton's own wages accounted for a tenth of the company's entire billings.

Talent was now king. It meant you could pay yourself whatever you wanted, because McKinsey had decreed that talent was the kryptonite of business. The 'talented' were immune from scrutiny and they ceased even pretending to play by the same rules as everyone else, because . . . they were talented.

In 2000, Houston-based oil company Enron was a success story like no other: the model for aggressive, expansionist, go-getting business with a reputation in the energy industry for doing whatever it takes to get their own way. It was also the poster child for McKinsey's 'War for Talent'.

Enron's extraordinary growth in the energy-trading business had been built by one man, Jeff Skilling, who had previously been a McKinsey consultant for twenty-one years. And Enron, with Skilling at the helm, were now paying McKinsey $10 million a year for their 'advice'. This advice included over twenty reports by McKinsey, as well as McKinsey endorsing the accounting methods of Enron. The relationship was symbiotic. Richard Foster, a McKinsey partner, repaid the compliment by interviewing a senior Enron executive in his book, *Creative Destruction*.

'We hire very smart people,' the executive said proudly, 'and we pay them more than they think they're worth.' Pure 'War for Talent' thinking.

In October 2001, the fruits of the War for Talent were reaped. Enron collapsed in spectacular fashion: the most dramatic implosion of a single corporation in US business history.[19]

Enron had really taken McKinsey's War for Talent to heart: they had allowed flashy fast-talking executives with little or no expertise to rise quickly through the company, making decisions of huge import because they seemed like they knew what they were doing. Other executives pursued multimillion-dollar initiatives on a whim. No one knew what anyone else was doing. The place was utter chaos masquerading as a responsible business. But at the heart of this chaos was the principle that talent should be given its head. McKinsey's Richard Foster called it 'creative destruction'. In slavishly chasing the 'creative', Enron had brought about its own 'destruction'.

At the same time as McKinsey was devising the Enron strategy, it was also advising Wall Street banks, promoting the securitisation of mortgage assets, and encouraging them to fund their balance sheets with debt. As financial journalist Ben Chu reported, 'driving down their equity safety buffers in order to juice profits (with) a practice that poisoned the global financial system and precipitated the 2008 credit meltdown.'[20]

The McKinsey boss himself was not immune from putting his hand in the pot. In 2012, company chief Raj Gupta was convicted for insider trading, passing on confidential information on corporations to a billionaire hedge-fund friend. Another McKinsey partner was also involved in the insider dealing ring.

Enron stung McKinsey. When Malcolm Gladwell wrote a piece in 2002 for the *New Yorker* – 'The Talent Myth' – unpicking the connections between McKinsey and Enron, McKinsey broke their code of silence and issued a rebuke. Something they never do.

In New York, I meet with Beth Axelrod, one of the McKinsey executives responsible for 'The War for Talent'. 'That article really hurt McKinsey,' she says. What about the collapse of Enron, did that not hurt McKinsey rather more? Arthur Andersen, the accountancy firm involved, went under in the aftermath, but McKinsey went from strength to strength. 'Some outrageous bad practice was going on at Enron, but that wasn't McKinsey's doing.' Would you not see your report, 'The War for Talent', as directly responsible for that same outrageous bad practice? Beth winces. 'No, I don't think you can connect them in the way you seem to be implying.'

McKinsey was bulletproof, and kept bouncing back. In 2012, Republican candidate Mitt Romney said that when he became president, McKinsey would be called in to 'fix' government. One of Mark Carney's first decisions on becoming governor of the Bank of England in 2013 was to call in McKinsey to review the central bank's operations.

In spite of McKinsey's spiritual father, Marvin Bower, stressing the importance of influence over making money during his tenure as boss, there is disagreement on whether McKinsey even do anything. Duff McDonald, author of *The Firm: The Story of McKinsey and its Secret Influence on American Business*, says they have undoubtedly streamlined government in some way, simply by virtue of having stuck around at the centre of power for so long, but Chu says there is not a 'single major technological or commercial development that McKinsey can claim even some passing credit for bringing into the world.'

If this was the case, it would be no mean feat for a company. To have remained at the heart of government since the 1920s and done precisely nothing. But perhaps they have simply followed the rule for success that Bob Hope followed when he was asked for his secret to show business: 'keep turning up'.

PFI AND THE PUBLIC SECTOR
MEAT IN THE ROOM

So Enron collapsed, McKinsey's boss was found guilty of insider trading, and the seeds were sown for the financial crash, but McKinsey continued to move closer to the heart of government.

Britain and America's power-broking landscape was transformed unrecognisably by the War for Talent and key to this was allowing business to gain the whip hand in its relationship with government. Put simply: they had the talent for dynamic change, politicians did not and knew they were useless, because they had been told so by consultants.

Three small letters came to symbolise this shift in power: PFI. The 'private finance initiative' behind every major infrastructure project.

PFI put business in the driving seat when it came to making long-term investment decisions worth billions, sometimes trillions. In opposition, Labour had opposed PFI, but two months after taking office in 1997, health secretary Alan Milburn said, 'It is PFI or bust.'[21] George Monbiot in the *Guardian* made the observation that 'the free market has become a corporate welfare scheme.'[22]

Just as civil servants had been taught to lose confidence in their own ability to do their job, so now politicians underwent an existential crisis of self-doubt. And as the public purse tightened, business could step in to save the day with PFI.[23] Allyson Pollock has studied the use of PFI in the NHS as funding became an issue under Labour, and has found that although funding might seem an obvious rationale for explaining PFI, the one used by politicians was poor management by the public sector – by themselves.

The Chancellor of the Exchequer, Gordon Brown, 'declared repeatedly that the public sector is bad at management, and that only the private sector is efficient and can manage services well.'[24] Funding was an issue, but the real issue was that business would do a better job. A message broadcast by politicians with McKinsey in the shadows.

The reason was simple. By repeating the narrative that business would do a better job with government money, that narrative became fact in the minds of everyone: the voter, business and most importantly, government itself. The only people sceptical were the professionals in health, education or social services, who actually did the job on the ground. From that point on, PFI, outsourcing, and its endless upgraded permutations were simply logical outcomes. And McKinsey was always there in the background, whispering this narrative in the politician's ear. The new civil service.

As the old civil service became hollowed out through rounds of redundancies, McKinsey and other consultants watched them depart Whitehall carrying thirty years of work in cardboard boxes.

Consultants were now the trusted ones and their role as the new civil service was real, because they had become the only continuity. They had outlasted the civil servants, and now they would outlast the here-today, gone-tomorrow politicians. They had made themselves indispensable to the working of government simply by turning up each day, like Bob Hope. But unlike the civil service, or Bob Hope, they had an agenda.

THE COMPANY WITHIN A COMPANY

McKinsey are not the independent experts they appear. They wear two hats, advising government and simultaneously looking out for the business interests of their private clients, many of whom specialise in areas of government that McKinsey also happen to advise on.

In 2010, as the UK government embarked on the biggest healthcare reforms in the history of the NHS, McKinsey were at the heart of the drafting.[25] The plan was to have a collaborative open process involving doctors and health professionals as well as ministers, and of course, McKinsey.

Meetings took place not in Whitehall, but in McKinsey offices.[26] Dr Laurence Buckman represented doctors at the negotiations. I met him at his busy North London surgery between appointments. Dr Buckman said he could not believe what happened when the talks began. 'Every time you went to a meeting, someone had written a report that appeared to be a *fait accompli*. Those of us who thought we were actually going to have a say in how this happened were continuously sidelined or told, "This is how it's going to be." '[27]

Buckman soon came to realise that there was nothing open or transparent about the process, or what he believed would ultimately happen to the NHS. He says McKinsey were calling all the shots, and being paid millions to advise on cutting services. But that was not where the real money lay.

In 2016, the *Financial Times* investigated McKinsey and discovered that the company's partners run a private hedge fund for themselves. A company within a company, called MIO Partners. When advising on NHS reforms, McKinsey are in a position to suggest private outsourcing companies, often private med-tech companies that McKinsey have a direct stake in via MIO.[28]

Buckman is in no doubt that the long-term objective of the NHS reforms is full privatisation, and that is not down to ideological belief, but the intersection of a crisis of funding and the continuous lobby from the sidelines to privatise and ease the crisis. It is attrition, but we're getting there, said Buckman. McKinsey could benefit directly through connections with private healthcare companies with which they have a relationship. But because MIO is a private company, the public have no way of finding out. The links cannot be made, because MIO is not transparent.

MIO Partners, the secret company within a company, allows

McKinsey to be at the heart of the most lucrative and far-reaching reforms planned by the governments they 'advise' across the globe. But MIO and its role within McKinsey remains a mystery to anyone outside the inner sanctum of top partners. Even McKinsey employees do not know about its detailed workings.[29]

MIO Partners say they are fully regulated, delegate investment decisions to the division's management, and have a 'rigorous policy to avoid conflicts of interest'.

Alan Leaman speaks for the whole consultancy industry. I met him in his giant glass box in London to find out what kind of controls are imposed on McKinsey by the industry when it comes to such a potential conflict of interest.

'Unfortunately,' Leaman tells me, 'you'd have to take that directly up with McKinsey. They aren't signed up to our code of conduct.' 'They don't follow your code of conduct? But you are the industry's watchdog. If you can't police them who does?' McKinsey are a law unto themselves.[30]

The key to McKinsey's hold over governments across the globe is their alumni, and the Jesuitical code of loyalty that comes from having worked for the Firm. Sheryl Sandberg, COO of Facebook, is ex-McKinsey; so too are Tidjane Thiam, chief executive of Credit Suisse; Charlotte Hogg, the former COO at the Bank of England; and James Gorman, CEO of Morgan Stanley.

But it is with government appointments that the tie is strongest. Barack Obama's OMB director designate, Peter Orszag, was ex-McKinsey; the foreign secretary under the Cameron coalition, William Hague, worked for McKinsey. Their alumni mop up the post of finance minister across the world: Corrado Passera in Italy, Lazar Krstic´ in Serbia, Eric Wiebes in Holland, Jayant Sinha in India and Toshimitsu Motegi in Japan.

McKinsey have even fostered a deep relationship with the Communist leadership of China. Walter Kiechel, author of *The Lords of Strategy*, has made an in-depth study of McKinsey working practices in emerging markets and says, 'The Firm's ability to insinuate itself into local elites drives its competitors slightly berserk with envy.'[31]

Shortly after the 1994 US presidential election, Republican whip Tom DeLay called prominent Washington lobbyists into his office. He had pulled the public records of the political contributions to the two main parties. He reminded them that the Republicans were now in charge and the lobbyists' donations had better start addressing the new reality 'or else'. According to Craig McDonald's anti-corruption group Texans for Public Justice, the 'or else' was a threat to cut off access to the White House.[32]

Compare McKinsey's soft-power approach with this crass attempt to bully government. In 2007, the Honest Leadership and Open Government Act was enacted by Congress to put a stop to the 'K Street Project', an explicit attempt by the GOP to pressure Washington lobbying firms to hire Republicans and to reward loyal GOP lobbyists with access to influential officials and committees.

Blatant cronyism is very much not the style of McKinsey, who have successfully made themselves part of the DNA of government. McKinsey operate rather like a consulting version of the Cayman Islands – a subtle and discreet mechanism by which corporations can call the shots without ever seeming to 'do' anything.

How did this discreet approach of McKinsey fare under Trump? When he won the presidential election in 2016, it was McKinsey's rival, Rich Lesser, CEO of Boston Consulting Group, who was invited by Trump to the White House to be part of his Strategic and Policy Forum. Disney, JPMorgan, IBM and General Motors were also asked to join Trump's Forum. But not McKinsey.

It suddenly seemed that the Firm, who had built their relationship with the White House over nearly a century, were out in the cold.

One perhaps apocryphal, perhaps not so apocryphal story of

the culture clash between McKinsey and Trump came from a graduate applicant to McKinsey posted on the anonymous employment website Glassdoor, who claimed that he had been rejected flat-out by McKinsey at interview stage, because he told them he had proudly voted for Trump in the 2016 election.

It was certainly implicit that McKinsey's way of doing business was very different from Trump's. The Governor of Delaware, Jack Markell, wrote in *Forbes* in July 2016 that as 'an ex-McKinsey consultant', he believed Trump's values and instincts were entirely antithetical to 'forward-thinking business'. McKinsey reports – on healthcare and the future of robotics – continued to be quoted occasionally by Trump's administration, but it was unclear if the Firm anymore wielded the direct influence on the President that they had over the previous forty years.

McKinsey did break surface when Ivanka Trump met the German chancellor Angela Merkel in 2017. Merkel had cunningly identified the president's daughter as a potential back channel to Trump. Merkel ingratiated herself further by inviting Ivanka to speak at the W20 Women in the Workplace summit in Berlin. Ivanka was reported to have prepped for her big speech by immersing herself in hundreds of pages of McKinsey reports on gender inequality.

As with so much in Trump's White House, it was difficult to read this as evidence of a demotion for McKinsey, or the opposite. Ivanka was not a traditional political player – she was not a middle-aged male congressman – but she could hardly be said to have been outside the circle of power.

Traditionally, there has been no gap between McKinsey and the governments they 'engage' with. Whether they were ever out in the cold under Trump or simply chose to be, as Marvin Bower might have chosen to be ('You, Mr President,' he might well have said, 'are the problem with this country.'), it is impossible to ascertain. One thing is for sure: McKinsey have no need to persuade anyone of anything. They are McKinsey, and whatever they say is a given.

CHAPTER TEN
BUSINESS: WHY
CORPORATIONS
TOOK OVER

The Deal: The World Bank vote to create a closed-off international court, the ISDS, allowing global corporations to sue nation states
Aim: To woo foreign investment to poorer countries in exchange for allowing business legal sovereignty over the elected government of those countries
Where: The 19th Annual World Bank Meeting, Hotel Okura, Tokyo
When: September 1964

HITLER'S BANK MANAGER

In the 1930s, Hermann Abs was a partner at private German bank Delbruck Schickler & Co. Delbruck Schickler managed a very special account, one that the bank took great pride in having secured and looked after so well: the bank account of the Nazi Party.

Hermann Abs was Hitler's bank manager, responsible for paying the Reich chancellor's salary each month. As he wrote in his memoir: 'The Reich Chancellery in Berlin was (the) largest account, and it was through this account that Adolf Hitler received his salary as Chancellor of the Reich.'[1]

Abs had a personal connection to the Nazi Party, too. Abs was a friend of Martin Bormann, head of the Chancellery. In 1943, with the creation of the Nazi banking committee, Abs was able to assist Bormann in transferring capital, gold and stocks to Switzerland.[2]

But Abs was no card-carrying Nazi. He was above all a banker, maintaining an arm's length from Hitler while simultaneously doing everything – including assisting in the 'Aryanisation' of Jewish businesses – to protect himself should any criticism of disloyalty ever come his way. He was, according to Abs's biographer, Princeton historian Harold James, elusive. An enigma swathed in cigar smoke that no one, not even the Nazis, could read.

After the war, unlike the Nazi collaborators imprisoned or executed, Abs became chairman of Germany's largest bank, Deutsche Bank. Abs oversaw the loans that rebuilt West Germany under President Adenauer. Like Wernher von Braun, the rocket scientist who invented the V2 bomb that obliterated large parts of London and was given safe passage to the US to work with NASA on the space programme in the 1960s, Abs was both too 'talented' and too clever to be connected to anything in the war that would mean he would be punished.

In 1958, as a powerful and respected business figure, now head of Germany's biggest bank, Abs stepped into history to make a bold proposal. The post-war world has been framed, he said, by a discussion of rights. There has even been the creation of a declaration of human rights, not least to prevent a repeat of the atrocities carried out by the Nazis. But what about, Abs said, the rights of business?[3]

Abs believed business had been marginalised after the war, coming second to the needs of the burgeoning government machine. But business, not government, should be ultimately sovereign over its own destiny. Abs proposed an international 'Magna Carta' for private investors, enshrining their sovereign rights over government.[4] In other words, corporations and banks should have the legal machinery to sue governments if they felt their inalienable right to make a profit was compromised.[5]

If a 'Magna Carta' for private investors was to be made real, it needed special international courts that could protect capital from the meddling of these politicians. Investment decisions were too big and too important to come under the legal jurisdiction of the country in which a company had invested. Governments, Abs inferred, should not be able to stop corporations going where they liked or doing what they wanted.

Abs had been key to the smooth running of the Nazi machine, and in the smooth tarmacking of a new democratic Germany, was now instrumental in erasing any trace of this past. But his real legacy was in proposing a fundamental realignment of power in post-war Western democracies – away from government and into the hands of the emerging global corporations, which could now make government their servant.

'ISDS' – ONE WORLD UNDER A GAVEL

This court was to be called the Investor-State Dispute Settlement (ISDS) court and was set up by the World Bank in 1958. Abs's dream come true.

It was created to adjudicate over disputes between nation states and multinationals in a 'corporate court': one in London, another in Paris, two more in Hong Kong and The Hague. But the most important court was at the International Centre for Settlement of Investment Disputes (ICSID) in the World Bank's J Building in Pennsylvania Avenue, Washington DC.

Forty years before terrorist suspects were interrogated on 'black sites' – physical spaces that do not exist on a map where the CIA decide the rules for torture – corporate black sites already existed for lawyers to interrogate governments.

In October 2014, *The Economist* explained how these corporate courts work: 'Foreign firms (have) a special right to apply to a secretive tribunal of highly paid corporate lawyers for compensation whenever a government passes a law to, say, discourage smoking, protect the environment or prevent a nuclear catastrophe ... through a process known as "investor-state dispute settlement" or ISDS.'[6]

As Claire Provost and Matt Kennard, research fellows at the Investigative Fund at The Nation Institute, discovered in their comprehensive 2015 analysis of the ISDS system, the courts were initially sold as a way of helping the developing world grow:[7] 'In the 1960s, the idea was taken up by the World Bank, which said that such a system could help the world's poorest countries attract foreign capital. "I am convinced," the World Bank president George Woods said at the time, "that those who adopt as national policy a welcome (environment) for international investment – and that means, to mince no words about it, giving foreign investors a fair opportunity to make attractive profits – will achieve their development objectives more rapidly than those who do not."'[8] In short, suck it up.

The deal came in Tokyo in September 1964 at the World Bank's 19th annual meeting. Twenty-one countries – every Latin American nation plus Iraq and the Philippines – strongly opposed the motion. The twenty-one voted on block against ISDS and their vote became known as the 'Tokyo No'. It was a clear display of unity and one of the biggest shows of opposition against a World Bank initiative ever recorded.

Chile's representative Felix Ruiz put their position succinctly to the two thousand delegates from 103 countries. 'The new system ... would give the foreign investor, by virtue of the fact he is a foreigner, the right to sue a sovereign state outside its national territory, dispensing with the courts of law. This provision ... would confer a privilege on the foreign investor, placing the nationals concerned in a position of inferiority.'

But he, and the twenty-one countries, were ignored.

American legal academic Andreas Lowenfeld observed the vote unfolding and later said, 'I believe this (is) the first time that a major resolution of the World Bank had been pressed forward with so much opposition.'

The twenty-one countries who opposed ISDS were sold the resolution as an opportunity for them to receive huge injections of foreign cash. But they did not see it that way. To the twenty-one nations, the word 'development' meant 'exploitation' and in spite of a desperate need for investment, these countries made it clear they were not prepared to put the rights of their citizens second to foreign business.

If ISDS happened, they argued, these companies would be able to build what they wanted, pay as little as they chose in wages and pollute at will. But the twenty-one developing nations that stood against ISDS were overruled by the richer nations – Britain, the US, Japan and The European members – who passed the mechanism in a simple thirty-second vote.

Then, nothing happened. The first ISDS case was not filed until 1972. The wave of corporate actions against governments simply did not materialise. There were only twenty-four between 1972 and 1988.

But in the mid-1980s, something suddenly changed. According to Robin Broad, Professor of International Development at the American University, ISDS was slipped into the small print of every business deal being cut between a country and a corporation. 'ISDS moved centrer-stage,' she says, 'thanks to ISDS clauses (being) inserted into bilateral, multilateral and investment agreements . . . in 2012 alone, forty-eight new cases were added to the ICSID (International Centre for Settlement of Investment Disputes) docket. All the forty-eight new cases were filed against governments of developing countries, more than one-third (seventeen or over thirty-five per cent) relating to extractive industries.'

Investment has now become contingent on a country accepting ISDS (ICSID) as part of a trade deal they are cutting. It is woven into the very fabric of business. This in effect puts all the cards in the hands of corporations, who can strong-arm the court when a dispute emerges, and have the lawyers to do it. Developing countries cannot muster the same legal firepower and are powerless to put up a credible fight in court. Since 2000, hundreds of companies have sued more than half the world's governments behind the closed doors of these courts, and won.

Vodafone took India to court for trying to make them pay tax. Vodafone won. US agribusiness giant Cargill/ADM sued Mexico for introducing a sugar tax on soft drinks to fight childhood obesity. Cargill/ADM won. Mexico was sued for daring to put a cap on the price of water, access to which is a basic human right under the UN charter. The manufacturer won and as a result, Coca-Cola is now cheaper to drink than bottled water in Mexico.[9]

In 2006, Houston-based Occidental Petroleum sued Ecuador for hindering a huge mineral extraction programme, and won. Ecuador was forced to pay the equivalent of its entire health budget for one year.

It is not just the developing world that loses in the ISDS courts. Energy giant Vattenfall sued the German government for attempting to stop a coal-fired power station, widely opposed by the public. Vattenfall won.

Hermann Abs's 'Magna Carta' for business is now a reality. We live in a two-tier world: governments and corporations, the two tiers intersecting when they meet in an ISDS court or where there is a dispute over tax. When they cooperate on major investment and infrastructure projects, it is because the terms are to the corporation's liking, and ISDS is written into the deal as an insurance policy. Governments can also sue companies for their actions, but the odds are stacked against them winning.

Corporations now operate horizontally across the planet, free to move at will, and governments are bounded vertically within the physical and legal constraints of national borders.

The effect of these grinding one-sided victories for corporations in the ISDS courts is the 'stick-flinch' effect. If corporations sue an entire country successfully, it makes other countries think twice before introducing policies with social or environmental benefits that will bring them into conflict with a corporation. Governments flinch before the stick has even been raised.

In Guatemala, Canadian mining giant Goldcorp faced huge public outcry, as well as a recommendation from the Inter-American Commission on Human Rights that a gold mine be shut down. The public demonstrated, demanding closure. The government opposed the mine, too, but let Goldcorp carry on because they knew they would lose down the line in an ISDS court.

The reason why the 1964 Tokyo agreement passed, in spite of huge opposition from the poorer countries at the World Bank, was because the rich Western powers never thought it would happen to them. But it has.

Forty years on from the Tokyo deal, any government can be sued. People from the rust belt of America to the sweatshops of South-East Asia understand what globalisation has meant for them. One world under the gavel of the corporate court.

PRESIDENT TRUMP *VS* PRESIDENT ZUCKERBERG

ISDS was the mechanism that delivered the reality of globalisation and the capitulation of elected government. The business of politics now is between competing business leaders with two very different visions of the future: Globalisation Good *vs* Globalisation Bad.

On Thursday, 16 February 2017, a man posted a question on Facebook. 'Are we building the world we all want?' Facebook founder Mark Zuckerberg then outlined what he meant by globalisation. 'History is the story of how we've learned to come together. In times like these, the most important thing ... is develop the social infrastructure to give people the power to build a global community that works for all of us.'

His post was widely interpreted as an attack on President Trump.[10] Zuckerberg was quick to say he was not making a bid for the White House. Yet, 'I am reminded of President Lincoln's remarks during the American Civil War,' he concluded. '"We can succeed only by concert. It is not 'can any of us imagine better', but 'can we all do better?' The dogmas of the quiet past, are inadequate to the stormy present. The occasion is piled high with difficulty, and we must rise with the occasion. As our case is new, so we must think anew, act anew."'

Zuckerberg's State of the Union address on Facebook offered a utopian vision of an integrated global community meshed by shared progressive values, enabling change on a platform with global reach. It was called not democracy, but Facebook.

Here was the new political fault line. A straight-up face-off between President Trump, holding every political position from A to Z, and Team Silicon Valley, representing the relentless march of twenty-first-century globalisation. Building world democracy using one all-powerful company.

This stand-off was simply the age-old divide of America: the liberal California–New York axis against the rest of the country, represented by Trump. In this regard, to have seen Trump, or even Zuckerberg, as anything fundamentally new was to buy their packaging.

HOW BUSINESS CONTAINED THE CHILD PRESIDENT: FIRM PARENTING

When *Fire and Fury*, Michael Wolff's eye-witness account of a year spent sitting on a sofa in a corridor at the White House, watching the Trump administration lurch daily from catastrophe to catastrophe, was published in January 2018, the wider world became privy to what Capitol Hill insiders and Trump's own closest advisors had been saying privately throughout his first year in office: that Trump was a child with no plan and a needy desire for constant gratification.

But business had not been slow in recognising this from the start, and found a way of containing him: firm parenting. Initially, however, they didn't understand the nature of the beast, assuming not unreasonably that a Trump presidency might be like dealing with any other adult president.

There were high hopes of a close and grown-up relationship, when in 2016 Trump convened an Economic Forum of business leaders to advise him on strategy. They included IBM's CEO Ginni Rometty, Indra Nooyi of Pepsi, and Mary Barra of General Motors. But the Forum collapsed in acrimony in August 2017 following Trump's failure to criticise white supremacist violence in Charlottesville, Virginia. It was a final straw for many members.

One unnamed CEO at the Forum described their meeting with Trump following Charlottesville as a 'firestorm'. CEO of pharmaceutical giant Merck, Kenneth Frazier, walked out saying, 'As CEO of Merck and as a matter of personal conscience, I feel a responsibility to take a stand against extremism.'

Other Forum members were as concerned by Trump's policy schizophrenia. 'You don't know what's coming next,' one exasperated CEO commented. 'What he's going to say or do next.'

It was dawning fast on business that Trump was a giant and very dangerous child, who needed to be contained for the sake of their own commercial interests, if not the wider welfare of the United States. Perhaps the security of the planet.

But it wasn't quite that simple. Trump's pro-business policies – a huge cut in corporation tax, the repeal of the Dodd-Frank Act brought in by Obama to prevent another speculation-driven financial crash, and the dismantling of environmental laws curtailing mining and drilling – were all welcomed by Wall Street.

Markets were on a surge not seen since Reagan, unemployment was finally falling and wages beginning to rise. Whether this recovery started under Obama (as many analysts pointed out) was a moot point. By January 2018, when Wolff's book came out, a recovery was happening under Trump's watch.

Wolff's excoriating portrayal of a hapless, even mentally unstable president provided Trump's critics with the 'evidence' they craved. But to the rest of America – the millions who had voted for him in the first place and the waverers put off in 2016 by Trump's misogyny and seemingly bottomless list of failings, Trump appeared against the odds to be delivering the goods on the economy.

The charge sheet from Trump's critics included the criticism that he didn't 'expect to win the election' – but neither do most politicians. He didn't 'have a plan'. Most governments promise as little as possible, and achieve a fraction of what little they have promised.

Nevertheless in 2018, he began to feel the heat. Trump was scoring the lowest approval ratings ever recorded for an incumbent US president; the FBI seemed to be getting ever closer to uncovering a money trail to Russia; and business leaders were publicly turning against him (even the owners of his two previous closest allies, Breitbart and Fox News, distanced themselves).

The Economic Forum collapsed in 2017. Silicon Valley had by and large despised Trump from the start (a point Rupert Murdoch made to Trump in a phone call, allegedly adding that Obama had also allowed Silicon Valley to do pretty much what it wanted, and this had aided his presidency). But none of this mattered if Trump were to stage a battle to re-win hearts and minds, because these people – the liberal elite, including the tech industry – were always going to hate him.

At the start of 2018, Trump became convinced he needed to hunker down and shore up his business base. After all, feeding the base and doubling-down on his friends in the energy and extractive industries was what got him in the White House in the first place.

In January 2018, Trump quietly did something no president had ever done before, opening up all previously protected US coastal waters to unrestricted drilling for oil. If the world turned against him, Trump would keep the oil industry close, come hell or high water.

On the one hand, this oil free-for-all was the beneficent gesture of a dutiful son to his corporate father, ExxonMobil CEO Rex Tillerson, appointed Secretary of State in 2016.

On the other hand, and if one believed that Trump was as uninvolved in day-to-day policy-making as his critics alleged, then Trump had next to nothing to do with it. He was simply there to rubber-stamp drilling/mining/fracking/an end to carbon emission limits: the ostentatious flick of a fountain pen from a President Who Wasn't There.

Tillerson had been one of Trump's first appointments and unlike most of the others, had stayed in his post beyond three months. But Tillerson had rumbled long before anyone else in the administration that Trump was, in his own succinct phrase, a 'moron'. Tillerson saw an infant with huge egotistical needs before him, and to get Trump to function as a grown-up president, Tillerson began firm parenting.

He started by limiting Trump's number of hours watching Fox News. He then set strict time-outs on Trump's tweeting. Trump's closest aide, Hope Hicks (dubbed 'the real daughter' by Trump's inner circle) played a parenting role, too, soothing his ego and manoeuvering Trump away from petty internecine conflicts or potential flare-ups by distracting him with positive news, much as a parent distracts a hyperactive child with a sweet.

Trump felt maligned by this widespread representation of him as a child, but to be precise, Trump appeared a child stuck at a specific stage of the developmental process. In Swiss psychologist Jean Piaget's famous theory of cognitive development, in which a child must pass successfully through four stages of physical and emotional development to reach adulthood, Trump appeared to be stuck at stage three (the 'concrete operational stage' typically experienced between the ages of seven and eleven).

This meant that though he could understand concepts of right and wrong, and there being views other than his own, he did not have the psychological architecture to entertain or evaluate these views. Piaget says the child that fails to evolve beyond stage two becomes stuck in an emotional prison: he perpetually reads situations literally, sees everything as a fight rather than a negotiation. Even having to envision another view creates dissonance, threatens the fragile ego, and he becomes more rigid in his beliefs.

The seventy-year-old president with a cognitive age of seven was a fitting metaphor for the infantilising of elected office. When Eisenhower warned on leaving the Oval Office in 1961 of the dark influence of the 'industrial-military complex', of backroom deals and clandestine lobbying threatening the sovereignty of government and the integrity of democracy, he did not foresee this scenario: the CEO of the world's largest oil company setting time-outs for a president on watching TV and deciding at what time he must go to bed.

As this firm parenting of Trump was being attempted, business quietly and efficiently got on with doing business as usual. The tricks required to persuade the executive in Truman's day – bribes, coercion, the iron fist in a velvet glove – were no longer needed. In the White House at least, there was no one to convince or even take seriously as an obstacle. Business could do exactly what it wanted.

This created a problem for business. Because with power came responsibility. For all the pyrotechnics of the Trump presidency, below the surface, corporatised government appeared a completed project. And yet it was a measure of how far the agenda had shifted under Trump that business stopped looking like a threat to democracy, and began to look like a potential bulwark against a dangerous president.

In the meantime, the actual machinery of government around the president remained untouched, and as ready to be persuaded via lobbying as ever. Three branches: an Executive (the President), a Legislature (the Senate and House of Representatives) and a Supreme Court, all requiring immense effort and time to build a coalition of support for a new bill, the abolition of an old law, or even a simple amendment to an amendment of an amendment.

Neither big business nor Trump could necessarily strong-arm these people into anything fast. When Trump delivered his first budget in May 2017 before a Republican-controlled Congress, Texan Senator John Cornyn said blithely, 'Almost every president's budget proposal is basically dead on arrival.'

Obama's budgets had been ignored by Democrats for eight years and Trump's first budget was laughed out of Congress by Republicans. Why? Politicians have their own agenda: their own constituents, and their own calculations about appearing to support an unpopular president and how that will backfire on their own re-election. Neither will they automatically vote to cut welfare schemes they might profess to hate on ideological grounds at election time, but tacitly support for pragmatic reasons when the election's over. In short, they are playing the long game, and Trump was marginal to this Congressional politics of survival, unless he looked like he would screw it up for them. Then they'd become interested in what he had to say.

Trump may have redefined the Presidency in his own special way and provided ever more implausible drama to entertain and terrify. But away from the Oval Office, the separation of powers enshrined in the Constitution of 1787, first proposed by Montesquieu in *The Spirit of Laws*, remained implacably sovereign. The Separation of Powers had been an insurance policy for the American people against dictatorship for over two hundred years. But part of the price for this insurance was the swamp that came with it – a place where players outside the steel trap of the legislature could influence government by bending the rules to suit their agenda. In spite of, or perhaps because of Trump, the Swamp was wider, deeper and murkier than ever.

DRAINING AND REFILLING 'THE SWAMP'

The problem with draining swamps is that they have a nasty habit of refilling. During the UK general elections of 2010, 2015 and 2017, the number of management consultants employed by government fell suddenly before election day, only to increase again once a new government was in place and the spotlight moved on. After the 2010 election, the use of consultants in government more than doubled.[11]

As Tamasin Cave and Andy Rowell found in their investigation on the influence of lobbying in government, *A Quiet Word*:[12] 'The influence of lobbyists increases when it goes largely unnoticed by the public . . . they operate in the shadows deliberately.' Cave and Rowell identified ten strategies that lobbyists use to make it virtually impossible to drain the swamp of its dwellers.

First, they 'control the ground': dictate the parameters of the conversation on an issue they want to influence. Then they get the media and industry to sing from a 'common hymn sheet'. When accountancy giant KPMG's head of health Mark Britnell said in 2011 that the 'NHS will be shown no mercy and the best time to take advantage of this will be the next few years', lobby group NHS Partners Network moved quickly to get industry back on message with a 'common hymn sheet'.

Once this has been achieved, lobbyists 'engineer a following' – create a fake grass-roots movement; 'buy in credibility' – hire experts; or sponsor a think-tank – take an existing organisation and part-fund them, yet keep the relationship seemingly at arm's length. The neo-liberal Institute of Economic Affairs is part-funded by the tobacco industry, but remains an independent think-tank.

It is important for lobbyists, Cave and Rowell say, to 'consult with critics' when criticism arises, in order to appear to be listening. In this way, opposition can be 'neutralised'. When all of this groundwork has been done, the door is prised open to a politician's office, not forgetting that the door is revolving and the politician could be working for the same lobbyists in six months' time.[13] This 'log-rolling' means everyone involved has a vested interest in keeping the whole thing spinning.

When thousands of competing companies are all attempting

to influence government using these tactics, government becomes a miasma of complex, seemingly contradictory inter-connections. No one really knows who anyone else is working for, or what their real motives might be. To think the post-Trump world offered ideological complications and contradictions that did not exist before was simply to have not seen them before.

Trump hated the swamp largely because navigating its murky waters was anathema to his brutal style of hand-to-hand combat. He couldn't do it, so he wanted it gone. But it was a fantasy to imagine this complicated mire of deals done in dimly lit corridors, or over a phone call in the dead of night, could ever be eradicated.

To enter this murky world is to enter a soup of doublethink and triple bluff. Here is what happened when I tried. In 2012, researching the roots of the food industry's role in the global obesity epidemic, I was pointed by an esteemed academic, who advises government on health policy, to a secret deal being cut by a rival academic and a global food-industry giant. The gist of the accusation was that he had taken compromising funding in exchange for putting his name to a diet product the food company was developing.

'Why are you telling me this?' I asked the academic. 'I thought you ought to know,' she said. 'And who funds your research?' I asked. She named a rival food firm, developing a rival product.

Ten companies – Nestlé, PepsiCo, Coca-Cola, Unilever, Danone, General Mills, Kellogg's, Mars, Associated British Foods and Mondelez – control practically every large food and drinks brand on the planet.[14] In a moment, the academic had taken off her independent, advising-government hat and quietly slipped on her partisan, food-industry hat, in order to rubbish a rival. She had simply omitted to tell me she had changed hats in the middle of our conversation.

Because everyone in this world of hidden persuasion is a player with a concealed agenda, Donald Trump's description of government and the people who influence it as a 'swamp' was apt: knots and weeds tether those on the surface to something far bigger, lurking ominously at the bottom.

A decade before Trump stood for president promising to drain this swamp, I interviewed Sir Michael Wilshaw, then head of a hugely successful academy school in Hackney, but soon to be promoted to become head of Britain's school inspectorate, Ofsted. I asked him what was the greatest hindrance to reforming education.

The problem with reforming anything in government, he said, was that it was 'like throwing a hand grenade into fog. The fog clears dramatically for a second and everyone congratulates themselves, only for the fog to descend again.' In Britain, it is a fog. In the US, a swamp. Neither can be eliminated on a whim when government itself is the obfuscating ecosystem. A system that hides but also protects itself when it comes under predatory attack.

IN PRAISE OF ELITES

In *Jaws*, there is an early run-through of the Trump *vs* Zuckerberg showdown. The crew are about to assemble for the mission to kill the shark. The bad-tempered Quint, played by Robert Shaw, does not believe Chief Brody's shark-expert friend, the 'college-educated' Hooper, has what it takes to catch a great white. Quint tests Hooper's seamanship skills by asking him to tie a sheep-shank knot in front of him. Quint is unimpressed. 'You've got city hands, Mr Hooper,' Quint says, 'from counting money all your life.'

Trump painted himself as Quint, the outsider and champion of working-class America. But he was no more working class or outsider than Hooper.

Ironically, the West Coast tech billionaires Trump cast as an 'elite' were in fact largely self-made. Facebook's Sheryl Sandberg and Mark Zuckerberg, Apple's Tim Cook, and Jeff Bezos of

Amazon tapped softly away on keyboards and talked quietly about the positives of globalisation. Trump said in 2016 he did not trust them and neither, he surmised, would the US electorate.

It is not only these tech billionaires who are seen as untrustworthy, so too is their industry. They mine people, not coal. Trawling our confidential data and creating gossamer threads of networks, using algorithms to spy on us as we gaze impassively at glowing screens; an underpaid world in its downtime, scrolling Instagram and Facebook, mainlining Taylor Swift as we ourselves are milked for every last detail of our lives.

The battle for the moral supremacy of one of these business elites – Trump and the twentieth-century extractive industries of coal and oil versus twenty-first-century tech – is misleading. The common dirty word with both is 'elite': no one wants to be associated with an 'elite'. Mark Zuckerberg wore a grey T-shirt and jeans and cycled to work, so he didn't look like he was in an elite, and Trump spat the word out like an expletive.

Once upon a time, elites were revered. They were trusted to the same degree they are supposedly distrusted today. A select few scientists, engineers, mathematicians, philosophers, clergy and business people understood what was best for the masses, and we the masses understood that they knew the best for us.

The 'representative democracy' of Parliament is in itself a form of structural elitism: MPs make legislative decisions on behalf of those who elected them, rather than consulting this electorate on every decision as they would in a direct democracy. Capital punishment – a life for a life – has historically been a legislative decision the elite would never enact, but the public would. Because the elite governed on our behalf, it never happened. Brexit would not have happened if it had gone through the elite of Parliament first. But because the elite made its fatal 'mistake' of putting it to the people, it did.

Elites have been conjured in times of crisis to fix the problem. In 1917, President Woodrow Wilson created a close-knit group of academic advisors called 'The Inquiry' to prepare him for the Versailles peace negotiations following the First World War. In 1933, President Roosevelt used a 'Brain Trust' of ten experts, including Columbia law professors Rexford Tugwell, Adolf Berle and Raymond Moley, to formulate the first 'New Deal'. This team broke up due to differences over strategy and the second New Deal was shaped by Benjamin Cohen, Tom Corcoran and Felix Frankfurter – an elite triumvirate from Harvard Law School.

In *The Revolt Against the Masses*,[15] Fred Siegel, a senior fellow at the Manhattan Institute, tied the rise of this belief in a new sharp-suited, post-war elite to the burgeoning expansion of the state. He described this new technocratic elite as a 'clerisy', a modern-day version of the clergy.

Siegel's book updated and broadened the scope of John Carey's classic attack on elitism, *The Intellectuals and the Masses*.[16] Carey accused the literary and intellectual titans of the early twentieth century – D.H. Lawrence, Virginia Woolf, Ezra Pound, H.G. Wells – of being modernist elitists enthralled to a sense of narcissistic Nietzschean destiny, and having a deep disgust for 'the masses', for whom the elite believed eugenics or sterilisation was the only answer.

Siegel widened this attack on a ruling class of elitists to include the post-war expert, the manager, the technocrat, the academic and that self-appointed custodian of moral right, the media. *The Revolt Against the Masses* came out a year before Donald Trump announced his candidacy for president, but set the groundwork for his particular attack on elitism, and specifically the West Coast Silicon Valley technocratic elite and the East Coast media elite of CNN, the *New York Times* and the *Washington Post*. Old Pronouncement Media *vs* New Post-Fact Echo Chamber Social Media, known for short as 'Twitter'.

This clerisy, Siegel said, operates under two delusions: first, they believe themselves independent-minded and objective, but in truth their fate is tied directly to the continuing growth of the state. They do not join these dots. Second, they see themselves as liberal and democratic in outlook. In reality, Siegel says, they despise the masses and the 'middle class', just as Virginia Woolf and D.H. Lawrence did. They are as narrow-minded as the people they secretly despise. The clerisy's true belief system is a cultural and intellectual superiority complex over voters. A prejudice reinforced by voters continually wanting things the clerisy would never allow.

The prosaic truth is that the context determines how elites are judged at any moment in history. Sometimes we like and need them. Sometimes we don't. When things go economically well, we go along with elites, but when the wheels come off, we blame them. The surface noise becomes anti-elitism, but beneath the surface, the elites are regrouping, mouthing the language of anti-elitism to curry favour with the masses and mask their true elitist identity.

Team Trump and Team Zuckerberg – two elites that will continue to battle for power with new champions when Trump and Zuckerberg are long gone – both talked the language of anti-elitism. This Business *vs* Business struggle is really a battle between two victors. The Silicon Valley elite and the new Washington elite of self-styled 'Leninist' outsiders clustered round Trump, who were intent on burning down the old house.

Because both sides came from business, neither side saw why anything should stand in their way. It was a zero-sum game, with only one winner left standing. Unless, this being business, they did a deal.

THE NATION-SHAPED COMPANY

Like Trump, Silicon Valley saw itself as above and beyond government. In 2016, Apple refused to cooperate with the FBI when asked to unlock San Bernardino shooting suspect Syed

Farook's phone.[17] Apple CEO Tim Cook said it was a civil liberties issue and Apple, not the government or the FBI, would decide what was morally right. 'This case is about much more than a single phone or investigation, so when we received the government's order, we knew we had to speak out.'[18]

In the past, companies would at least pretend to acquiesce to the demands of government. Not anymore. They are above it. And in the past, presidents would at least pretend to acquiesce to the demands of business. Not when you are a chairman president: CEO of a nation-shaped company.

The irony was that Trump behaved more like a parody of a CEO than the real thing. His *modus operandi* as president owed more to his TV persona as a 'business leader' than the reality of being a business leader. But his administration was determined to use the tough rhetoric of the TV boardroom. When Trump's prospective ambassador to Europe, Ted Malloch, was asked what he thought of a bilateral agreement between Britain and the US post-Brexit, he said it was best to view it as a business merger: one very successful company (the US) taking over a smaller, failing one (the UK). It sounded no-nonsense, but the reality of Trump running America as a giant business was chaos taped together with bravado: a superannuated Enron. Trump changed policy on a whim, because he was not weighed down with the ideological baggage of conviction.

By 2017, Trump was not the only world leader acting as if he was the CEO of a country. The three most powerful economies on earth each offered an alternative model for how to run a country as a global corporation.

Trump was like a charismatic 1970s captain of industry, high-fiving his way across the USA with a corporate logo baseball cap plonked awkwardly on his head. Trump's nation-shaped company looked and smelt like Pan Am just before it went bust.

Vladimir Putin, by contrast, was CEO of Russia. A brand with renewed takeover ambitions. Putin was a company man who had worked his way up from the post room. Putin held every job in the corporation over twenty years and as a result, had a file on every employee and all his rivals, too. He achieved what only a few CEOs on the cover of *Fortune* ever accomplish: total omnipotence and oneness with the brand. Tsar of all he has surveillance on.

Xi Jinping, the quiet spreadsheet-loving CEO of the fastest-growing portfolio on the planet, China Unlimited, was the least readable of the three. Xi had the biggest job on earth. But was he a progressive running a dictatorship or an autocrat accruing more power to himself than any Chinese leader since Mao? Both. In 2017, Xi was formally given the role of supreme ruler over party, military and the people: 'Paramount or Core Leader'. What might be parodied as 'boss of all bosses: the boss to end them all'.

This job had impossible written into it. Xi had to reconcile a voracious demand for growth over the next decade, accelerating global warming by putting unprecedented strain on rapidly depleting resources, whilst simultaneously pledging to clean up the mess this will create. To achieve this, Xi had one very important thing on his side. He did not have to play politics, simply run China as the best-run company in history.

Business has not taken over government, it has erased government by becoming the only way to understand how government can be run successfully. Quasi-autocratic leaders of the three most powerful nations on earth are CEOs, not politicians, because of the way they need to think. They were neither ideological nor managerially minded, just ambitious for their brand and what it could achieve.

Democratic politicians in less powerful nations – small to medium-sized businesses like Germany, France or the UK – were by contrast hamstrung by the consequences of political gambles, whether it be Brexit or the far-right backlash in Germany. Any attempt to grapple with the fundamental challenges facing Western economies – growth, the robot revolution threatening work, the health crisis, the ageing crisis and its attendant care crisis, plus the housing crisis facing everyone – were all inevitably overshadowed by politics, deals, and negotiating their way out of political gambles that had gone wrong.

Politicians have thus stopped being able to offer any meaningful solutions to the fundamental challenges they should be addressing. How did run-of-the mill politicians rub themselves out? By eroding the confidence of the public through pulling the same old economic levers and nothing happening. Low interest rates simply meant we habituated to low interest rates, with the promise of lower, potentially negative interest rates down the line. Politicians now pinned their hopes not on a manufacturing recovery, but more consumer spending, which meant more consumer debt (even Russia and China face that same problem).

No matter what levers they pulled, growth stayed resolutely at zero. When a business flatlines it is bankrupt, but you cannot foreclose on a nation. In this context, handing it over to be run as a business is not corporate capture, but the logical next step.

A country run as a business does not have to concern itself with the tropes of post-war liberal inclusiveness (tolerance, open borders, a welfare state, even taxation) only with its shareholders: the voters. China has the edge over its nation-shaped business rivals, because it does not even have an electorate of shareholders to worry about. It is a private company run on behalf of shareholders who have no voting rights. The board run the show. When you run a country like a business, democracy simply gets in the way of efficient management. So it was no surprise 'the crisis of democracy' became a major preoccupation of business.

DAVOS: YOU'RE NEVER MORE THAN TEN FEET FROM A GIMP MASK

In May 1912, Thomas Mann visited his wife, Katia, at Dr Friedrich Jessen's *Waldsanatorium* in the mountain village of

Davos, Switzerland. Nobody knew what was wrong with Katia. It was initially believed she had tuberculosis, but X-rays failed to find anything physically wrong. She was sent to the Wald Sanatorium to recuperate.

After visiting Katia, Mann decided to make the sanatorium in Davos the inspiration for the Berghof sanatorium in *The Magic Mountain*.[19] In Mann's novel, the consumptive bourgeois of Europe flocked to Davos to inhale its fresh Alpine air and cleanse themselves of sickness, alleviating symptoms for illnesses nobody knew the cause of nor had the cure for. As the book progressed, it became apparent that the idea of illness was itself the illness – drawing everyone sane and well to the sanatorium and into its psychosomatic clutches.

The Magic Mountain is set on the eve of the First World War and represents an allegory for a sclerotic European elite on the edge of extinction. It is not difficult to make a parallel and thus a cheap joke at the expense of the world's leaders and business elite that gather for the Davos World Economic Forum in the same village a century on.

Davos is its own sealed-off sanatorium, where this new self-questioning elite gather to cleanse themselves of the ills of the world for which they feel responsible. They sit in claustrophobic rooms debating the crisis of democracy, global warming, global poverty and global inequality. Then they get back on Learjets and fly home feeling a lot better about themselves and the future of the globe.

Rob Hersov is a South African mining mogul and one of the continent's most important power brokers between government and business, brokering deals with foreign investors and heads of state. I met up with Rob in London and asked him what he made of Davos. He smiled. 'Well, the thing I've noticed about Switzerland. Do you want me to tell you?' Please. 'You're never more than ten feet from a gimp mask.'

Rob recognises a sexual undertow to Davos: the fetishisation of power. The leaders of the world's mightiest economies mingle

at warm coffee with the leaders of the world's most virile companies, surrounded by an army of advisors and consultants – the
groupies of power, the predatory big-hitters of the swamp –
aspiring to be close to this flame. It is a strange combination of
self-congratulatory, self-reflecting importance and buttoned-up
sexual tension.

Davos, like the Silicon Valley–Trump showdown, is really a
gathering of winners. They are at Davos because they have made
it, rule the planet, and this is the public display of that power.
World leaders and CEOs mingle as equals, but they all know the
real deal. Business is ascendant, CEOs are the alpha players and
have relegated governments to the position of consultants on
their business vision.

I asked Ken Rogoff, one of the world's leading economists,
why he goes to Davos, expecting him to say that it matters.

'Because if you don't, then you stop being invited.' The real
point of Davos is itself. To reflect its own reflection back upon
itself, like those tiled walls of the Berghof sanatorium. And to
have a space where business can debate with itself what it should
do with this new global omnipotence.

THE NEW CAPITALIST STRUGGLE: THE BOSS *VS* THE SHAREHOLDERS

This omnipotence poses a dilemma if you are a CEO. Do you
press home the advantage or use your new-found power for
global good like a Marvel Avenger? Global corporations face the
conundrum described by military strategist Sun Tzu in *The Art
of War* in 500 BC when faced with a drowning enemy: help him
out of the water or push him under till he is dead?

The most powerful business people on earth find themselves
now playing God with the same conundrum: maximise profit or
save the planet. Paul Polman is a quietly spoken Dutchman and
to hear him talk, you would think he was a member of Occupy,

not CEO of Unilever, one of the world's largest multinationals with annual global turnover of $50 billion.

'How long can we steal from the future?' he tells his audience. 'Our system is a great system, but it's not designed to function long-term. We could be the generation, in the next fifteen years, that solves the issue of poverty, that solves climate change.' Polman is a boss who even baulks at being called a boss. 'I always say I represent one of the biggest NGOs.'

Polman argues passionately that an obsession with profit is destroying sustainability and ultimately capitalism itself. Two seemingly contradictory impulses must coexist 'without compromise. Profit is not a purpose. It's an end product. I always want a deeper result. People assume that if you do something good, it must cost money. I don't know where they get that idea from.'[20]

Over at PepsiCo, another of the world's biggest corporations, accused of stoking obesity, CEO Indra Nooyi says, 'I believe we need to attack obesity. Let us be good industry that does one hundred per cent not grudgingly, but willingly.'

Polman and Nooyi are not bleeding-heart liberals from charity backgrounds parachuted in to greenwash their companies with some empty sound bites. For their entire working lives, they have climbed the corporate ladder. They are one-hundred-per-cent business people.

But they now see an unprecedented threat, not merely to the survival of the planet, but their bottom line. When Christine Lagarde of the International Monetary Fund talks about inequality, she says it is not simply iniquitous, it is the single greatest threat facing the long-term survival of capitalism.

Not so long ago, the capitalist struggle was simple: workers versus bosses. But with global labour value plummeting steadily since the 1970s, thanks to the end of the long post-war boom, billions of workers across the globe were no longer protected from the scrapheap.

Corporations could suddenly go where they liked on earth, employing workers wherever favourable employment laws would dictate the lowest wage. Skilled workers, who had once had lever-age thanks to their skills, were now expendable, too. The Marxist battle between capital and labour was over. The workers had lost.

But an unexpected new struggle in capitalism emerged. The battle within a company between the CEO and the investors and shareholders. On one side, progressive reformers like Polman and Nooyi and on the other, the people who put the money in, and want to see much more money coming out the other end.

When these two sides clash, it is not on a picket line with plac-ards and fires made from piles of tyres. It is in giant anonymous conference rooms hired for the week in Las Vegas or Hong Kong, where shareholders, investors, venture capitalists and hedge fund managers sit in silence sucking in their teeth as the CEO spouts on about 'social responsibility' and giving back to the planet.

To them, the progressive NGO-CEO is a profound threat to their return. They recognise the boss needs to make the right noises to the outside world, but not to endanger what Hermann Abs called the natural right of a business to make a profit.

Polman has stated his position. 'I don't think our duty is to put shareholders first. I say the opposite.' He showed his reformist cards from the beginning by championing 'slow money': long-term investment in small sustainable businesses, rather than relentlessly chasing short-term profit. He has declared that one of his biggest successes at Unilever was ridding the company of its reliance on hedge funds, cutting them by half during his tenure as CEO.

Polman is clear where he stands with the paradigm shift from government to business, too. With corporate power over the destiny of the planet comes responsibility and to shirk that responsibility is not merely bad for business, it is immoral.

At Pepsi, one of Indra Nooyi's first decisions on taking over was to declare that she wanted the company to fight obesity, becoming 'post-sugar', in the same way that BP aims to go 'post-petroleum'. Nooyi started by hiring the World Health Organisation's Derek Yach and diversifying Pepsi's portfolio into a host of healthy brands such as Quaker Oats. She faced huge internal opposition.

Dr Marion Nestle, one of the world's leading nutritionists, made a study of the boardroom struggle within Pepsi following Nooyi's attempted health reforms of the company and found that Nooyi was effectively marginalised within her own company.

'Investors got very upset. In 2012 (they) got mad at Indra Nooyi for focusing on getting revenue from healthy products.' It put a fault line through the company and Nooyi was the axe. An accommodation was required: a deal between investors and the boss.

'Pepsi (now) wants to have it both ways,' Nestle says. 'To appear to promote healthier beverages, while it fights public health measures to reduce soda intake.'[21] Nooyi was perceived by investors to be undermining the core brand: sugary drink, and now has to be mindful of seeming to protect it. It was a victory for the investors.

A struggle that once took place between workers and bosses now takes place between CEOs and investors in such hushed meetings. But it is a showdown every bit as fierce with far-reaching implications for all of us.

Who wins this internal battle – championing slow money versus chasing the fast buck – will determine the moral tenor of capitalism for years to come. In essence, it will determine whether business decides to save the earth, or squeeze every last dime of profit out of it before it dies in approximately sixty harvests' time.

The CEOs talk the talk of 'sustainability' – which will soon become the word 'survivability' – but there is a clock ticking, not only on the planet, but on how long they will be humoured by investors. While they feed the bottom line, progressive CEOs are safe. But when the economy constricts, the pressure on this bottom line becomes critical and the determination of the reforming CEO to maintain a defiant reforming course against investors is properly tested. How many of them are around after this is the real test.

In the early 1970s, parts of the US motor industry sought some tentative accommodation with the growing environmental movement, but found all momentum for change washed away by the global economic convulsion and downturn that followed the OPEC crisis. It was back to business and that meant making money first and worrying about the planet later.

Paul Polman strategically frames this dilemma not as a trade-off – an either/or – but as the most important deal Unilever will ever be part of. Get on board with sustainability and slow money now, rather than slavishly extracting profit every quarter, or the whole ship goes down with all hands, and that includes the shareholders and investors. For Polman, as for every progressive CEO, two letters stand in the way of the planet's route to survival: 'QR'.

THE NUMBER

QR is the central doctrine of post-1980s capitalism. If you are a shareholder, it is the only thing that matters. If you are a reforming CEO, it is the single greatest obstacle to meaningful reform. Both Nooyi and Polman have declared open war on QR, and seen a revolt from shareholders as a result.

Quarterly reporting began in the early 1980s, as Wall Street saw a way to speed up the cycle of profit. Instead of investors and shareholders getting an annual report on the company's profitability, it would now come every three months: every quarter.

This was not simply a change in accounting, the accelerator had been pressed down. As a result of QR, if a growing company failed to show the same rate of growth this quarter as in the previous quarter, then it was deemed to be slowing down. Thanks to QR, a successful company was now defined as failing.

On 17 August 1982, Henry Kaufman of Salomon Brothers wrote a note to clients. As you know, he said, five days ago the

Dow Jones Industrial dropped to its 1980–82 recession low of 776.92. Almost the exact figure at which the Index closed in January 1964. Double-digit inflation is over, interest rates are about to hit an all-time low, the White House is removing the last regulations holding business down and slashing tax. The time is now for an explosion of free enterprise.[22]

Kaufman was firing a flare into the sky above Wall Street and lighting up the coming bull market: the biggest the world would ever see. Shareholders and investors, Kaufman said, could now put their foot to the floor when it came to demanding something unprecedented: a quarterly increase in profit. Then demand more the next quarter, and more again the quarter after that.

It was time to drive hard. The pedal to the metal would become the new mantra of Wall Street, and there was no reason not to demand the impossible each quarter, because the underlying economics were all there to deliver it. The biggest, longest bull market in history was about to begin and Kaufman's message was crystal clear: ride it into the ground.

CEOs who could handle this breakneck ride would become legendary. The CEO was transformed overnight from a glorified 1950s bank manager to a 'captain of industry', lauded on the cover of *Time* and *Fortune*. They became alchemists who could conjure perpetual profit, and QR was their Excalibur.

In *The Number: How the Drive for Quarterly Earnings Corrupted Wall Street and Corporate America*, Alex Berenson charts how QR took over Wall Street in the 1980s and early 1990s.[23]

Berenson identifies QR as the key driver in changing the course of American capitalism: from long-term investment to short-term profit demanded by investors.

It was a simple but profound switch in priorities and the only way to maintain this relentless drive for greater profit was to cut the long-term plan. There was only one thing that mattered: the wall you were going to hit in three months' time. Everything else was irrelevant.

It was all dependent on timing. While the bull market built

momentum, QR was an achievable hurdle, but when it began to slow, that three-month hurdle began to look like an increasingly high bar. And as the bull market turned slowly but inexorably into a bear market, then the reality of QR started to become apparent.

QR was a running machine no one could get off, and it was increasing in speed. You think you cannot cope now? See how much faster it will be in three months' time, and three months after that.

To survive, a new kind of boss was required. One who aligned with investors, not his or her colleagues in management, and saw the inertia of the company – the inability to run ever faster or jump ever higher – as the enemy. For this kind of CEO, it was not investors or the market who were the problem, it was the culture of the very company of which they were boss.

In the comedy film *Ruthless People*, Danny DeVito played a caricature of this new hard-hearted 1980s boss. He slammed shareholders at the annual meeting for failing to understand the new dog-eat-dog world. Little old ladies and kind old colonels stared guiltily down at their shoes as DeVito laid down the law: kill the competition and extract the last drop of profit by any means necessary.

QR was the rationale for these new ruthless people, but the film itself was sentimental for a loyal kind of shareholder that had already disappeared. Hedge fund managers had bought out the little old lady investor and were switching portfolios as quickly as a card shark changes hands. Hedge fund managers were the human equivalent of QR – constantly moving on. No one had any loyalty to the company anymore, just loyalty to profit. Only the customer still bought the brand.

Huge established American household brands, which had traded successfully for decades, were now being run as vehicles for hedging and shorting on the projected profit of the company, not just in three months', but in three hours' time. The CEO and the board were now bystanders watching the price of their own company fluctuate on a flickering screen. QR was their *raison d'être*, everything else was background noise.

Two approaches to business began to calcify. CEOs like Unilever's Paul Polman who attacked QR, and companies who embraced it. Amazon, Twitter and Uber frequently fail to turn a profit, but keep investors fully informed of their long-term goals. For a company like Amazon that needs to innovate incessantly, QR is not about the relentless drive for a quarterly return, but what is happening next: total data regarding what the company is up to gleaned from the quarterly report; and if shareholders have that information, they are willing to take risks over the long term.

Amazon has invested in drone deliveries and stores staffed by robots, like their fully automated, human-free store in Seattle, because to them, disruption, risk and investment are the same thing. It is their business. For Unilever, built on huge, super-long future planning for a massive portfolio that takes in food, chemicals and household goods, QR makes no sense. For Amazon QR works, for Unilever it does not.

Quarterly reporting was fifty years in the making. In 1934, at the height of the Depression, companies were first required to file annual reports and disclose more information to investors. In 1955, this became semi-annual, and in the late 1970s and early 1980s, quarterly.

With QR, the game changed. It was all about the curve and the curve needed to keep going up. This perpetual drive was primarily psychological: it was deliberately unobtainable in order to maintain a pressure that would never go away and could never be satisfied. It would never stop and that made investors happy. It was an insurance policy against stagnation and complacency.

Pro- and anti-QR business now stands face to face, daggers drawn. In 2015, law firm Wachtell, Lipton, Rosen & Katz weighed into the battle, calling on the Exchange Commission to do away with QR. A joint report by City University, London and Duke University concluded that firms that increased QR necessarily reduced spending on long-term assets. It is a trade. One or the other. You cannot have both.

In 2016, on the election trail, Hillary Clinton said that 'the decline in investments for the most part reflects the effects of managerial myopia induced by increased reporting frequency.' She believed that slamming QR was a winner with both business and the electorate. 'CEOs and shareholders need to focus on the next decade, rather than just the next day.'

But she lost, and Donald Trump won.

IF CARLSBERG RAN A COUNTRY, IT WOULD PROBABLY BE THE BEST COUNTRY ON EARTH

In 1983, Orson Welles voiced the first of Carlsberg lager's 'Probably the Best' series of ads. 'In a brewery in Copenhagen, Carlsberg's finest brewers endeavour to improve the taste of their lager. But given that Carlsberg is probably already the finest lager in the world, they have little hope of success.'

The 'Carlsberg . . . Probably the Best' ad campaign was rolled out to include all kinds of dream scenarios: if Carlsberg ran a bank, it would give free money to all its customers whenever they needed it; if Carlsberg ran a taxi service, the taxi would be there when you clicked your fingers. Uber before its time.

The underlying message of the Carlsberg ads was radical: it does not have to be this way. A parallel universe exists in which everything could be better if it was run by Carlsberg. Twenty years before the internet, these dream scenarios seemed simply that, but now we have credit on tap and Uber to deliver a cab at the tap of your phone, the Carlsberg fantasy is a reality.

In government, a similar fantasy was entertained and this time the dream was not that Carlsberg ran things, but John Lewis. Under the Blair and then Cameron governments, the 'John Lewis Model' of an inclusive, reputable business structure with employees as 'stakeholders' was revisited repeatedly as a path the public sector could follow, too.

Now the business fantasy for government is Google. Why, the argument goes, try to get Google to pay their taxes (and fail) when you could get them to run entire government departments like the school system or the NHS? At a tax reform event in Geneva where I spoke in 2016, the discussion among the corporations present was not how we avoid tax by finding the best offshore arrangement, but what our duty as nation-shaped companies is: how do we save the bankrupt countries in which we do business?

Why give them our tax when they misspend it and we could do a better job? Our inalienable right to make a profit, first laid down by Hermann Abs, is already a done deal. The challenge now is what will actually be done in the name of the responsibility that has come with that power.

CHAPTER ELEVEN
NEWS: WHY THE FACTS DISAPPEARED

The Deal: Corporate raiders led by Laurence Tisch's
    Loews and Cap Cities, backed by Warren Buffet, buy
    the three big US TV networks – ABC, NBC and CBS –
    in a daring swoop
Aim: To scoop up undervalued media assets and turn
    them into huge entertainment platforms, part of
    which means bringing market forces to bear on news
    output
Where: Wall Street, Manhattan
When: 1986

SKIN CREAM AND GUN CONTROL

In April 2013, Professor Dan Kahan at Yale University decided to run an experiment. He asked a thousand people for their political views: were they Republican, Democrat or more extreme, and if so, how extreme? He then gave these same thousand people facts on two unrelated subjects: skin cream and gun control.

Kahan provided them with data on a new skin cream formulated to reduce skin irritation. Did the facts show the cream to work or not? He then asked the same people to go through the facts on gun control and tell him whether the data proved gun control would reduce crime.

Kahan was taken aback by what he discovered. When it came

to the skin cream, a subject that had no underlying bias to it, the thousand participants were able to analyse the facts accurately and dispassionately, coming to an easily arrived consensus: yes, on balance the skin cream would work on a rash.

But when it came to gun control, the story was very different. People ignored the facts. Democrats shown data that gun crime was not as prevalent as they thought, did everything to resist the evidence. And Republicans shown that gun control would significantly reduce crime, did everything they could to avoid coming to a conclusion at odds with their pre-set view.[1]

'People,' Kahan concluded, 'interrogate the evidence and waterboard it until it tells them what they want to hear.'[2] The evidence on whether gun control actually reduces crime is not clear cut. It is messy. But no one wanted to hear that. They wanted to believe there was one answer, and that answer needed to be what they already believed.

The 'post-truth' debate that emerged in the presidential campaign of 2016 did not factor in Dan Kahan's experiment and his discovery that people are not interested in the truth to begin with.

The emergence of the 'post-truth' phenomenon was itself premised on a falsehood: that once upon a time, people listened to the facts and then rationally made up their mind who to vote for. This was never true. The extraordinary thing about 'post-truth' was not the promotion of lies to truth, but that we ever thought people listened to truth in the first place.

THE FIRST FAKE NEWS

When a politician stands for election, they need to tell you a lie: 'I want change.' They don't. They want to confirm your prejudices, and the politician that gets closest to confirming those prejudices – or 'core values' – wins.

In 1979, Mrs Thatcher offered policies that were closer to the newly aligned values of Labour voters than the Labour party did. When Attlee won in 1945, Labour offered a position that was closer to the newly radical values of a post-war Britain demanding change.

Churchill had won the war, but his reward for losing touch was to be voted out of office. What we mistake for a radical government is actually a radical public that has realigned its values and a politician who merely sticks their finger in the air at the right moment and judges the new mood correctly.

When Karl Rove masterminded the surprise re-election of George W. Bush in 2004 – an administration mired by a war on the ground in Iraq and the looming threat of terrorism – no one believed he would be re-elected. So Rove went back to basics by 'feeding the base'.[3]

'Feeding the base' meant retrenching around the core fears of the Republican base, and it worked. In 2016, while Hillary Clinton sought to 'build bridges' and create rainbow coalitions, Trump was advised by Team Trump (Jared Kushner, Kellyanne Conway, Steve Bannon, and others) to 'feed the base', exactly as Rove had for George W. Bush. It worked for Bush, and it worked for Trump.[4]

Voters only entertain a 'vision' when it chimes with what they are already feeling. When JFK and Harold Wilson offered bright, new, shiny visions for America and Britain in the 1960s, it was because the economy was buoyant and this was what the voters wanted to hear. Fear was out and optimism was in. But generally, fear is in.

In 2001, years before fake news was diagnosed as a symptom of a 'post-truth' society, Professor Brendan Nyhan, of Dartmouth College, New Hampshire, decided to create fake news to see how easy it was to disseminate and affect public opinion with false information.[5]

Nyhan invented a story that Saddam Hussein was planning to seize weapons of mass destruction (WMDs) and give them to terrorists. He then published a retraction, making it clear there was no truth to his first article and no evidence of weapons of mass destruction in Iraq.

The results astonished Nyhan. People who wanted to believe there were WMDs not only resisted the truth that there weren't any, but became more convinced that there were WMDs when they heard that there weren't any. Nyhan called this 'the backfire effect'. Everything, he said, is processed through the prism of our existing prejudice. With new information, we are simply seeking to reinforce this existing prejudice and actively searching out information that does. Facts that run counter to this prejudice are 'waterboarded' until they fit.

Today, the 'echo chamber' of social media is a filtering system that simply makes this prejudice reinforcement a more instantaneous hit, but before Twitter and Facebook we had the echo chamber of newspapers; each with its own position, or ideological filter, to fit our existing prejudices.

Even when confronted with facts challenging our worldview, it is reinforced anyway. 'You'll be sitting thinking "no" and actually thinking of arguments why that is not the case,' Nyhan says.[6] 'In developing these counter-arguments, people become more entrenched in their false beliefs.' We believe what we want to believe and shut out cognitively dissonant information. But we can be convinced of something new: that we are threatened.

FREUD, MAD MEN AND FEAR SELLING

The most potent way to connect with your electoral base is to connect with their fears, and years before Hillary Clinton and Donald Trump stood at the 2016 election podium conjuring fears about the election of the other, fear had already been sharpened as a tool for selling.

On Madison Avenue in the late 1950s, a tight-knit group of advertising geniuses – Bill Bernbach, George Lois and Jerry Della Femina – were attempting to do something no one had done before: understand the primal, subconscious drives that can be used to persuade someone to buy something. They were in the business of bottling an intoxicating potion with which to beguile the public for the next century.

Consumer choice, like a political prejudice left, right or centre, is already set. All that is needed is to trigger the purchase. Bernbach, Lois and Della Femina – the original 'Mad Men' – did not have neuro-science to pull this subconscious trigger, they had Freud.

Freud argued that all our rational decisions are motivated by subconscious desires. We seek either to free these desires or suppress them, but because liberating these desires is too dangerous for a society predicated on rules of what is and is not 'normal', we suppress them.

In the 1920s, thirty years before the Mad Men of Madison Avenue, Freud's nephew Edward Bernays invented public relations by enlisting Freud's theories of mass manipulation and the desire of the crowd to be manipulated. Wall Street banker Paul Mazur suggested that Freud could be used to reboot economic growth: 'We must shift America,' he said, 'from a needs to a desires culture.' Ernest Dichter used Freud to sexualise every mundane consumer purchase from eating chocolate to puffing on cigarettes.

By applying Freud to advertising, our sublimated desires could be exploited to sell us products that contorted these desires into the shape of something we wanted to buy: a pair of shoes, a car, or a perfume bottle. Just as we 'waterboard' facts until they tell us what we want to believe, the subconscious was to be strait-jacketed into a thing that could be consumed.

Telling the consumer about the facts of a product – how fast a car goes, how many washes you will get from a detergent – is irrelevant. They don't want to know. They do not even know they don't want to know.

They seek a deeper release from buying, and no purchase is what it appears to be on the surface: a sports car is really a mid-life crisis; washing powder does not simply clean clothes, it scrubs away 'dirty' repressed desires behind the curtains of suburbia. Consumerism – these Mad Men said – was not merely shopping. It enabled sublimated fantasies to be satiated through a socially acceptable purchase.

But there was one advertising guru striking out on a very different path from the Mad Men. Rosser Reeves was one of Madison Avenue's most charismatic ad execs. A brilliant and original thinker, Reeves believed advertising should not make false claims for a product – the consumer would soon rumble this – but instead, hone in like a guided missile on its 'unique selling point' or USP, distilled into a single strapline such as M&M's 'melt in your mouth, not in your hand'.[7]

Reeves is famous for coining the term 'sex sells'. Except Reeves never said 'sex sells'. What he actually said was the complete opposite: 'Sex sells if you're selling sex.' The impulse that really drives a sale, Reeves said, is fear.

Reeves took the received wisdom on selling – that it fulfilled repressed desires – put it in a filing cabinet and pushed it off the top floor of Madison Avenue.

What consumers truly seek from their lives, he said, is happiness. And modern life, Reeves argued, had made us fearful. We fear failure, we fear rejection, our spouse leaving us, our boss demoting us. These fears are real, and in order to sell this fearful consumer a product, we must push these fear buttons to maximise anxiety and then – and this is the bit Reeves's business clients liked best – sell them the solution.

Reeves became the primary inspiration for Don Draper, the central character in the TV series *Mad Men*. In the first episode, he explains his philosophy to clients: 'Advertising is based on one thing: happiness. And you know what happiness is? Happiness is the smell of a new car. It's freedom from fear. It's a billboard on the side of the road that screams reassurance that whatever you're doing is OK. That you are OK.'[8]

Reeves did not care about the product – it was the

manufacturer's job to make that as good as possible – he cared about the mind. By offering freedom from the fears of modern life, Reeves was providing a solution that would never stop us buying, or the manufacturer selling.

Today, we consume thousands of everyday products offering freedom from fear. They cover the supermarket aisles: breath fresheners and deodorants that take away the social stigma of smelling; anti-wrinkle creams that offer temporary respite from fear of ageing; surface sprays and wipes that play on our OCD fear of teeming germs.

The big fears are catered for, too: a luxury holiday for your children because you fear being an inadequate parent; 'peace of mind' life insurance to maintain a roof over their heads when you drop dead working too hard to pay for their holiday.

Rosser Reeves summed it all up in two words: 'fear selling'. The geniuses of Madison Avenue had turned facts into something new. Facts were simply putty in their hands to be moulded into whatever alternative reality or 'story' they wanted to tell. Facts were to be marshalled to a greater cause: the sale.

When Donald Trump offered up fear of Mexicans and the solution of a 'great, great wall' in 2016, it was pure Rosser Reeves. Fear is now a finely calibrated weapon of mass persuasion and to find out how brilliantly it is now being used, I arranged to meet the man who dragged fear selling into the post-9/11 world, and laid the foundations for the end of facts.

THE MAN WHO USED 9/11 TO SELL CARS

It is 7 a.m. and I am driving down a tortuous winding lane in Normandy looking for a castle. As my hire car drops with the road, I am plunged into soupy fog. My phone informs me a seventeenth-century Gothic chateau lies just ahead. I drive up the huge gravel driveway, lined with trees, and spot my host.

I am greeted by one of the strangest men I have ever met. Dr

Clotaire Rapaille is in his seventies, with wild, backcombed white hair. He wears a red velvet suit with military medals on his lapel. A long, black silk scarf drapes dramatically behind him. White foundation is caked heavily on his face with a hint of lipstick and he is wearing sunglasses. Rapaille walks confidently out of the mist to shake my hand: a cross between Louis XIV and Michael Jackson.[9]

In the early 2000s, Rapaille took Rosser Reeves's idea of fear selling to a whole new scary level, paving the way for the 'post-truth' world. In his chateau, among suits of armour and huge family portraits of his ancestors, is a self-portrait: hands clamped on his head, crouched in a cave semi-naked, howling at the wind. It is hard to know what it means, but one thing's for sure: Rapaille knows fear and how to tap into it.

Rapaille's life divides into two halves. The first as a psychologist in hospitals across Northern France, diagnosing and working with autistic children. Rapaille was a successful and respected specialist in the field. Then, in 2000 as Dick Cheney and Tony Blair conjured the imagined 'fact' of weapons of mass destruction in Iraq, Rapaille glanced up at his TV one evening and saw a report on CNN that set fireworks off in his head.

Following the 9/11 attack on the Twin Towers, the report said, sales of Humvees were going through the roof with suburban car buyers. Ordinary Americans were buying a military vehicle designed to withstand a one-hundred-pound mortar-bomb attack in order to do their weekly shop at the supermarket.

What, Rapaille thought, would Freud have made of this? Humvee sales were exploding because the unconscious part of the American consumer's brain was responding to the primal fear of another terrorist attack. What Rapaille called the 'reptilian brain'.

Humvee had not marketed their vehicle at domestic consumers, people had just gone out there and started buying them. They had identified the irrational fear they had and bought themselves the solution.

The events on 9/11 had turned what Rapaille calls the 'thermostat of anxiety' up to 1,000. In that moment, his life changed and a new course was set: as the world's leading advertising guru of fear selling, and heir to Rosser Reeves.

Rapaille's genius would be to upscale freedom from fear. We were not simply fearful of bad breath or neighbours not approving of our new car. We were now terrified of the phantasms of terrorism, paedophiles, refugees and global warming. These were new, expanding fears to be exploited to sell products and provide the consumer not with happiness, but security.

His first deal was with Chrysler. Rapaille met with the company's execs. He told them that suburban cars needed to start looking like Humvees to cash in on the post-9/11 climate of fear. What Chrysler needed was a new 4x4 that sold the same illusion of security as a Humvee, but at a quarter of the price: a high-up tank with bull bars and a steroid-enhanced chassis offering the appearance of safety in an unsafe world.

Rapaille was very clear about the uncompromising message the car should send out to other road users: 'I'm a weapon. Don't mess with me. If you want to bump me, I'm going to crush you and kill you.'

The Chrysler PT Cruiser was the result and it was an instant success. Ironically, like all SUVs it was more likely than a regular car to roll over in high winds. The very things that gave it the illusion of security – the high-up 'turret position' for the driver – made it potentially lethal.[10] The facts did not matter. The PT Cruiser looked safe and that is what drove sales.

Rapaille believes the new climate of fear drove the rise of a brand-new genre of defensive car: sports utility vehicles or SUVs. In the early 2000s, the SUV went from zero to a fifth of all car sales in only three years. Every design detail reinforced the illusion of safety. Even the cup holders, Rapaille says, are not cup holders. 'They send a message of stability: put a cup here, I'm that stable.'

Rapaille was now an 'anthropologist of anxiety', selling his reptilian brain theory to the biggest companies on earth: everyone from tobacco giant Philip Morris to Kellogg's Corn Flakes. Fear selling was a blanket of safety that could be thrown over any product.

Nintendo carried out extensive research on the post-9/11 fears haunting the American family and spotted a huge gap in the games market.[11] Instead of designing a console for solitary teenagers to shoot up Iraqi insurgents in their bedroom, Nintendo set about designing a new console that would bring the family together around a cosy digital fireplace, playing bowling and *Mario Kart* together. They called it the Wii. The 'ii's nodded to the Asian market; the 'we' suggested togetherness.

Coca-Cola followed suit, introducing a 'whiteboard of anxiety' into their brainstorming meetings with executives. At these meetings, they would list the top anxieties they believed the public were currently experiencing and how Coke could be marketed to provide a dozen swigs of respite.[12]

Whether these fears had a basis in reality, was not the point. What mattered was not the facts, but the emotional undertow for the public. Companies exploited clouds of nebulous anxieties thrown up by incessant news coverage of a collapsing planet: global warming; the implosion of the Middle East and subsequent migrant crisis; terrorism; pandemic; even the 'toxic home'.

Fear was a phenomenal tool for selling. We had never in history been safer in our homes, or less in danger of being killed by war or disease, but the perception of escalating fear was being ramped to a new plane of hysteria. The fact that you are more likely to be killed by your toaster than a terrorist attack was a fact that did not come into the equation.

Some products threatened to jump the shark. The BrickHouse Child Locator was an electronic tag you attach to your child. It was launched off the back of a spate of news reports about child abduction.

'Every parent's worst nightmare,' begins the advert. A mum is darting frantically around the playground searching for her missing son. This was anxiety at a heart-palpitating level. 'We enjoy the experience of the rollercoaster ride,' according to Rapaille, but was child abduction a step too far? Today the BrickHouse GPS Child Locator retails at $27.99 and is a massive commercial success.

In 1997, bird flu spread fear of a pandemic that would sweep the planet's airports. Bird flu was followed by dengue fever, SARS and then in 2004, the re-emergence of the great white shark of pandemics, Ebola.

The fear was now visceral, and the soap industry was on hand to sell us the solution. We wanted something to annihilate germs and destroy the coming contagion: 'antibacterial' soap was invented to purge the fear. Soap went from a once-a-day luxury used in the bathroom soaking in a long bath, to a weapon used in a minute-by-minute battle with germs: in the kitchen with food; in the bathroom to protect children; and even with our pets.

The battle with germs was really a proxy battle with the contagions of the world we could not wipe clean with an antibacterial cloth – disease, pollution and the concocted phantasm of immigrants. All things beyond the control of the fearful consumer. But hygiene was a war we could win. Every domestic surface was identified in adverts as crawling with salmonella, *E. coli* and legions of microbes in need of manic spraying every fifteen seconds.

Antibacterial soap also tapped into a whole new market propelled into existence by pandemics: the OCD sufferer. Marketing that tapped into our worst fears about hygiene made antibacterial soap the obsessive-compulsive sufferer's new drug of choice.

Barry Shafe is a quiet man in a suit. In the early 2000s, he was head of product development at the world's largest soap manufacturer, Cussons, and the man behind Carex: the product that would launch antibacterial sprays on the world.

Exploiting the fears of the public, Barry says, was not even necessary. 'The background noise of pandemic fear was all that was needed to drive consumers to antibacterial soap.'[13] Why create scare stories in adverts when the news, filled with terrorist attacks and Ebola, does the advertising for you? Just like the Chrysler PT Cruiser, antibacterial sprays sold an illusion: security in a perilous world.

But this 'security' came at a real price. As we purged our domestic environment of germs, there was an accompanying rise in child asthma and eczema directly linked to this newly toxic home. The Environmental Protection Agency estimate that the average home is now two to five times more polluted than the air outside as a direct result of 'off-gassing' from household cleaners, air fresheners and strong antibacterial sprays.

In making our home germ-free, we had made it poisonous. But the facts of the toxic home created in decontaminating it were disregarded when placed beside the lurid fantasy of the 'dangers'. The fear was simply too intoxicating and trumped the facts. A frightening outside world filled with demons to be slain was a narrative we bought: no one wanted to hear the truth.

HOW NEWS KILLED THE FACTS

In 1986, three big networks owned American television: NBC, CBS and ABC. In a daring swoop, Wall Street corporate raiders bought the lot. NBC went to General Electric; CBS was bought by Laurence Tisch's investment company Loews; and Cap Cities, backed by Warren Buffett, bought ABC. The deals ranged from $2–3.5 billion, but the buyers saw it as a fire sale, scooping up hugely undervalued assets at a bargain price. It all happened within a matter of weeks.

Why? America had grown up with these networks. Each had an instantly recognisable logo, and news anchors such as Walter Cronkite whom the nation trusted. For this reason, they provided platforms from which to launch a revolution in commercial TV: new niche and satellite pay-for-view channels homing in on everything from movies and sports to kids and entertainment.

Goldman Sachs were asked by the Cap Cities–Warren Buffett consortium, who bought ABC, to carry out an in-depth analysis of the economics of the network (a study that became a template for the way all TV would be audited). Goldman quickly made a simple discovery: everything costs too much.

Goldman Sachs already identified that TV had what would later become known as 'the *Friends* problem'. Series one, Jennifer Aniston gets $10,000 a show, but by series three, it is a million with a huge cut of the back-end. What was needed, Goldman Sachs concluded, were repeatable formats; and news that runs as a continuous stream. And no Jennifer Aniston.

The year following the Goldman Sachs audit, *Survivor*, the first reality TV format, was launched. It was TV exactly as Goldman Sachs said it should be: mass-produced, high-volume content with no expensive returnable stars, just disposable ones who could be replaced each season. If news was going to pay its way, it also needed to provide more screen time for less buck; and that meant 'rolling news'.

The star was no longer to be Walter Cronkite, but a kid who walks into his high school and kills his classmates with a gun. To hold viewers, news had to up its game and get dramatic. It needed to become catastrophised if it was to stand out in a competitive marketplace.

The shift to catastrophised news was fast. In 1994, BBC satire *The Day Today* parodied this new bombastic way of presenting unfolding events with exploding graphics and breathless 'updates' of a story that had no urgent updates to report, but filled the need to put something on TV. Cataclysmic reporting built on half-truth or no truth at all.

The escalation of rolling news, building to a crescendo of hysteria, was inherent in the format. The truth became merely a servant of the incessant update that required an escalation every fifteen minutes: a 'development'. This meant turning everything, no matter how comically mundane, into 'news'. In Channel 4's

Brass Eye, Chris Morris played a stony-faced anchor delivering non-headlines as if reporting on the end of the world: 'Child's Face Used as Satellite Dish!' News was already a hyper-dramatic parody of itself.

BUDD DWYER - THE TEMPLATE FOR CATASTROPHISATION

In order to make this news loop of imminent invented catastrophe and shooting, robbery, assault, shooting, robbery, assault watchable, it needed to become dramatic.

We needed to know detail, and the detail needed to be gory. Just as reality TV heightened reality by faking and over-dramatising conflict between the contestants, so catastrophised news needed to go from reporting the facts in a balanced and measured way to hyping the story and becoming entertainment every bit as gripping as drama.

Yet there was an inevitable problem. More TV news needed more exciting things happening all the time to fill it. This created a moral dilemma for the people making it. How far can we push what we show? News got its first test on 22 January 1987.

The Republican treasurer of the Pennsylvania State Senate, Robert 'Budd' Dwyer, had just been convicted of receiving a bribe to secure a multi-million-dollar contract: an elaborate scam involving tax compensation for the wrongful penalisation of thousands of state employees.

Throughout the trial, Dwyer vigorously protested his innocence, even writing to Ronald Reagan pleading with him to intervene. But he was found guilty. Sentencing was scheduled for 23 January and Dwyer faced a potential fifty-five years behind bars.

The day before sentencing, Dwyer called a press conference. Five TV news outlets sent a crew. Dwyer handed out his resignation speech from a manila envelope. He thanked his constituents for their support and reiterated his innocence: 'Please tell my story on every radio and television station, and in every newspaper and magazine in the United States.'

He then took out another manila envelope from which he produced a loaded Smith & Wesson Model 27 revolver. The assembled press gasped. Dwyer continued talking calmly, 'Please leave if you have a weak stomach or mind, since I don't want to cause physical or mental distress.' Two ushers tried to grab him, but Dwyer stepped back to avoid them, waving the gun. 'Don't, don't. This will hurt someone,' he warned them. Dwyer then turned to the main news camera and looked directly down the lens – known in TV as 'looking down the barrel' – as if anchoring a news report about himself. 'Joanne, Rob, Dee Dee. I love you. Thank you for making my life so happy. Goodbye to you all. On the count of three . . .' But by the time he got to two, he had fired the gun into his mouth and blown away the top of his head.

Dwyer had timed his suicide to make the midday news. He knew what they wanted and did not disappoint. The channels were torn between the horrific graphic content and its dynamite potential to pull in viewers.

WPVI-TV in Philadelphia and WPXI-TV in Pittsburgh both showed the suicide. One channel chose to show Dwyer pulling the trigger, but cut before the blood. Local Pennsylvania networks WCAU, KYW and KDKA froze the footage at the moment of the trigger-pull, but continued playing the audio of the gunshot and the horrified screams that followed. *Action News* broadcast the suicide from beginning to end. The *New York Times* questioned the morality of showing Dwyer's suicide, but it was a ratings winner.[14]

Dwyer had a co-defendant at the trial, another Republican politician called William Smith. In 2010, twenty-three years after Dwyer killed himself, Smith admitted that he had lied under oath about Dwyer's involvement in the bribe in order to get a lighter sentence for himself.

Dwyer had been right all along about being framed. He was

innocent and had killed himself because no one had investigated his claim. Smith received a one-year jail sentence for lying under oath in order to frame Dwyer and returned after six months to politics.

The news networks did not investigate Dwyer's claim that he had been framed, because they were too busy rehashing his suicide and finding new ways to cover it. Doing some journalism and discovering the reason why he killed himself in the first place did not happen. The news cycle was turning too fast for that.[15]

Budd Dwyer's suicide was a test of the moral code of news in the new, highly competitive world. Dwyer had known what news wanted, what 'newsworthy' now meant, and used it to get coverage for his case.

Choosing between dignity for Dwyer and his family over graphic coverage of his suicide, the new channels went for the latter. Thanks to the sudden commercialisation of news, channels now demanded impact and the world obliged.

News will deliver the facts when we need them – during national disaster or crisis – but because of the underlying commercial imperative, the pressure to deliver a scoop, it can also turn into a machine of misinformation when we least need it to be histrionic. In 2013, following the Boston Marathon bombing, CNN's John King was quick to identify the suspect as a 'dark-skinned male'.[16] Fox News's Megyn Kelly upped the ante by falsely confirming a suspect had been arrested. The *New York Post* published a picture of two men with rucksacks in the crowd, declaring them the 'Bag Men: Feds seek these two pictured at Boston Marathon' (they didn't, and it was not them). There was a rush to find the culprit – a 'mobilisation of bias' – and the truth fell by the wayside.

News has not just been weighed down by commercial pressures, it has faced cuts. The result has been to slash investigative and new journalism, that seeks to look in unexpected places for a story, in favour of rehashing the familiar and becoming increasingly dependent on easy sources: press releases by pressure and consumer groups, the political circus of Westminster and Washington, the same talking heads talking about the same old tried and trusted 'issues', rather than ones deemed less palatable to the audience. News became an echo chamber long before the term was coined.

Budd Dwyer's suicide had pre-empted live 'as it happens' and on-the-spot reporting, but as news became rolling news, and the commercial imperative combined with cuts to dedicated long-form investigation weighed down on new or accurate reporting, 'fake news' became inevitable.

SCIENCE BECOMES SCIENCE FICTION

T.S. Eliot once said that 'humankind cannot bear very much reality' and this was the lesson TV news learnt from Budd Dwyer. If a car bomb decapitates a child, we see a news report of that event deemed acceptable to Western audiences. It is a finely calibrated halfway house between what really happened and the 'acceptable', sanitised version, shots chosen deliberately in order to convey symbols of horror (a bloody shoe, a crying parent) without showing the graphic detail of the explosion: this is the trick of news reporting and constitutes 'truth'. The reported fact on what happened.

But news is not alone in needing to create a hybrid truth in order to walk a moral line, simultaneously catastrophising news stories, yet policing this inflation of claims. Science, too, has had to up the ante and the reason is that research needs coverage on news in order to maintain funding. If it is going to get coverage, it needs to be extreme, emphatic and wrong.

In 2013, Professor John Ioannidis at the Seventh International Congress on Peer Review and Biomedical Publication in Chicago made a shocking revelation.[17] Most scientific studies are wildly inaccurate, and they are wrong because scientists are more interested in funding and furthering their career than scientific truth.[18]

Ioannidis illustrated his point with the *Boston Cooking-School Cookbook*. Of fifty randomly selected ingredients from recipes, forty had been linked with increasing or decreasing the risk of cancer. These cancer links had been reported and repeated in news and media reports thousands of times. Yet meta-analysis showed, Ioannidis said, that the scientific studies were 'correct' in almost no cases.[19]

Science by its nature needs to be measured and circumspect, yet this is the opposite of what news wants. If a news editor is given a choice of a story that blueberries have marginal health benefits versus 'blueberries cure cancer', or even better 'blueberries give you cancer', which will they run?

The public stopped believing claims for 'superfoods', and 'wonder drugs' or vitamins, when the claims changed every month, but what this process has done is to undermine confidence in science as a profession. It has turned science into fake science.

And when it comes to science around curing disease, it does not get any better. When genes were linked to specific diseases, Ioannidis said, analysis of hundreds of studies found a genuine provable link in only 1.1 per cent of cases.[20] When biomarkers of diseases were found in 127 prediction models, a high relative risk almost always turned out to have been exaggerated. Only a fifth of those 127 models even had further studies to validate them.

Ioannidis concluded that scientific bias is rampant, overinflated claims are rife and the reason is simple: people need funding and to get funding for their work, they need to get noticed. As scientific 'research' has become a useful resource for the media to report dramatic 'developments' in science, both escalating health dangers and unrealistic solutions are reported as fact. In reality, they have been catastrophised, just as news has been.

Each week, waves of danger are reported approaching society like a tsunami, then washing over us and leaving society unscathed. Yet each wave is deemed more dangerous than the last: super-bugs, super-rats, super-bots, super-malware, super-fraud; super-summer smog and winter smog, everything from an approaching meteor about to destroy earth to an indestructible Japanese knotweed that will strangle your garden. These 'epidemics' are actually a containable event catastrophised and upgraded into an imminent threat to humanity.

Science has become part of the fake news business, working with news to disregard the facts for the sake of a better story: 'killer coffee', 'killer tea', 'miracle coffee', 'miracle tea', 'harmful effects of cigarettes mitigated by drinking coffee and tea'.

But beneath these headlines is a power play. Behind every 'killer this' and 'miracle that' is scientific research funded by a specific commercial interest looking to lobby government, or shift a new product using the cloak of science. Research is covertly funded by either the food, health or drugs industry, each pushing a specific commercial product looking for a licence or to create a demand. Science does not work in a neutral zone of 'facts', any more than news does.

Sometimes this can be dangerous: in 1992, the contraceptive pill was suddenly declared to cause deep-vein thrombosis. The following year, abortion figures rose unexpectedly, yet fears about thrombosis mysteriously vanished as quickly as they had first been made. The NHS put out advice that there was no increased risk with the progestogen-only contraceptive pill and only a 'slightly increased risk' with the combined oestrogen and progestogen pill. The victim was not the drugs company, or the media who reported the exaggerated claim, but those women who believed they were at risk.

THE ABERRATION OF 'TRUTH'

News and science did what they did for a reason, but it had an effect: the public simply stopped believing in the 'facts'. The Pew Research Center is a non-partisan 'fact tank' based in Washington that has been monitoring levels of public trust in government and journalism for forty years.[21]

In 1958, during Truman's administration, seventy-three per cent of Americans said they could trust government 'just about always or most of the time'. They trusted journalists, too. Trust in both professions remained high throughout the 1960s, reaching a high-water mark under President Johnson – when people felt safest – but in the 1970s, thanks to Vietnam and Watergate, trust in government plummeted spectacularly: thirty-six per cent in 1974; only twenty-five per cent by 1979.

Yet at the very moment trust in government collapsed, journalism came into its own. As a force for 'truth'.

In 1970, Seymour Hersh broke the story of the My Lai massacre. In 1972, Bob Woodward and Carl Bernstein unearthed Watergate. The *Sunday Times* Insight team exposed scandal after scandal throughout the decade: from thalidomide to the secret manufacture of nuclear weapons by Israel.

With trust in politicians crumbling, there was one place where the public felt it could reliably turn to tell the truth and keep politicians in check: the media. Belief in the power of this fourth estate grew in inverse proportion to plummeting respect for politicians.

In the 1970s, the public viewed journalists as knights in shining armour, bringing truth to the people: Watergate's Woodward and Bernstein were played by Robert Redford and Dustin Hoffman in *All the President's Men*. Journalism was a full-beam force for truth, unsullied by the weakness and venality perceived to have corrupted government.

But then there was a power shift. Proprietors who had sided with the outsider voice of journalists suddenly began wanting a slice of real power once more, which meant siding with politicians. They wanted to be insiders again.

In 1903, Lord Northcliffe, the first press baron of the twentieth century, saw the potential for power that his newspapers gave him: 'Every extension of the (voting) franchise renders more powerful the newspaper and less powerful the politician.'[22]

By 1918, Northcliffe believed he had single-handedly won the First World War by using his power to remove Asquith and install Lloyd George as prime minister.[23]

In the 1930s and 1940s, Lords Rothermere and Beaverbrook used their power to interfere directly in affairs of state. Rothermere, owner of the *Daily Mail*, endorsed the British Union of Fascists and was openly sympathetic to Hitler, whom he saw – as a substantial section of the British public did – as a strong European leader surrounded by weak ones.[24]

Beaverbrook, who owned the *Daily Express*, the first newspaper to have a circulation of two million in the 1930s, joined forces with Rothermere to try and oust Prime Minister Stanley Baldwin. Effectively a *coup d'état*.

On 17 March 1931, at the Queen's Hall in London, Baldwin said, 'Their newspapers are not newspapers in the ordinary acceptance of the term, they are engines of propaganda for their constantly changing policies, desires, personal wishes, personal likes and dislikes of two men. What the proprietorship of these papers is aiming at is power, but power without responsibility, the prerogative of the harlot throughout the ages.'[25]

The press barons of the early twentieth century had affected seismic change in politics. They were not simply players at the same table as politicians, they wanted to decide who would sit there.

The 1970s changed that. Journalism has skewed the power play by creating an aberration called 'truth'. Facts were no longer to be marshalled to garner political power for proprietors, but a force for revealing the lies of politicians to the public: diamonds in a mine to be discovered by investigative journalists and brought out into the light.

The proprietors went along with this version of events so long as it was good for business, but when it ceased to be, the press baron – now reborn as the media mogul – was to go back to the default setting of a big-time power player, influencing who sat at the table of power. And one mogul led the way.

THE FOX

In 1985, an Australian newspaper tycoon with an American passport, who had owned a bust of Lenin while a student in Britain, bought a tiny US news channel called WTDG.

Frank O'Donnell was a producer: 'For the first three years, he left us alone, partly because we were so successful. But one day, we received an order that we should cut away from our newscast and start airing a fawning tribute to Ronald Reagan that was airing at the Republican convention. We were stunned, because up until this point, we were allowed to do legitimate news. Suddenly we were ordered from the top to carry propaganda.'[26]

The staff of WTDG saw Rupert Murdoch as something new, but he wasn't. He had inherited his media empire and then built shrewdly upon it, just as Northcliffe, Beaverbrook, Rothermere and Cecil King had before him.

But Murdoch was shrewder and more ambitious than all of them. He had been a Leninist at university and his desire for revolution continued long after he stopped toying with student socialism.

O'Donnell believes that what he was witnessing first-hand at WTDG with the top-down edict was the birth of 'post-truth', coming to fruition twenty years later. But this WTDG post-truth was merely a remarshalling of the facts as it had been under the old press barons: to influence and shape power.

In 1996, Fox News was launched with Roger Ailes at its head, an ex-strategist for Nixon, Reagan and Bush Senior. 'We expect to do fair and balanced journalism,' he said: the watchwords for the channel. Within hours, memos were being sent round the building instructing journalists what could and could not be talked about. Abortion was, said Ailes, 'a trademark issue': Fox policy was pro-life. Race was another: it was a left-wing issue. AIDS, too. When the 9/11 inquiry began, one memo warned staff not to 'turn this into another Watergate'.[27]

Dissenting voices were booked for studio discussions merely

to be shot down, or have their microphone cut in the middle of a discussion. This was not old-school 'balance', but balance was not the point. This was a full beam of polemic fired like a laser at Washington, and it worked. Fox host Bill O'Reilly (later sacked for gross sexual indiscretion) told over sixty separate interviewees to 'shut up' and cut them off mid-sentence. Journalists schooled on Woodward and Bernstein were shocked.

In 2016, Roger Ailes left Fox with a $40 million pay-out following a string of sexual harassment claims against him, swiftly moving on to work for Donald Trump's election team. Bill O'Reilly left Fox in 2017 following at least five settlements over sexual harassment claims. Fox had even renewed his contract, but advertisers abandoned his show in droves, making his position untenable.

Whilst Ailes and O'Reilly controlled the corridors at Fox, they were untouchable. Disgruntled staff said that apart from inappropriate behaviour, they were bullied into running stories that were either inaccurate or spun – like the Columbine shootings – to push the pro-gun lobby position. No one in control of Fox cared about these outdated criticisms. They were making the future of journalism, and soon everyone would understand.

Robert McChesney, professor of journalism at the University of Illinois, who made a study of Fox News, said the network was the catalyst for 'post-truth' by creating the 'total elimination of journalism',[28] but Fox was really the elimination of journalism as 'truth' in order to make it once more a tool for political power. Murdoch was not doing this to create a right-wing channel or erase the news. He was doing it to become a power broker.

Murdoch, like the new breed of proprietor in the late 1970s and early 1980s – James Goldsmith, Robert Maxwell and Tiny Rowland – wanted to influence government from within by replicating the conditions in which Rothermere and Beaverbrook had wielded empires, as sticks by which to cow politicians.

To become a player meant two things: taking an overt political stance and reining back on journalists digging into the misdemeanours of the people with whom you were seeking to get into bed, so undermining any bid to enter the inner sanctum. Or if you did find dirt, using it as leverage against them. It was a fork in the road: facts and journalism versus power. It was a choice, and the new proprietors chose power.

On 4 January 1981, the deal was done.

At a private lunch at her country residence of Chequers, Prime Minister Thatcher and Murdoch carved up the map of power as the lamb was carved before them. Thatcher needed a supportive press for her revolution, Murdoch wanted to buy the *Sunday Times*. They decided to do business.

The following day, the rules that applied to media monopolies suddenly changed. Murdoch was free to buy the *Sunday Times*, *The Times*, the *Sun* and the *News of the World*. He bought the satellite TV company BSB and renamed it Sky Television. In return, all were guaranteed to fire a concentrated beam of Thatcherism at every home in Britain.

In Wapping, Murdoch built a giant de-unionised fortress where he would roam the corridors like a ghost, saying little but watching everything. And adjusting any carpets he judged slightly askew.

The *Sunday Times* saw a power struggle with the champion of *Sunday Times* past, Harold Evans. Evans lost. In the US, where Murdoch's outsider credentials dovetailed with Reagan's, Murdoch bought Twentieth Century Fox, HarperCollins Publishers and the *Wall Street Journal*.

Murdoch was impossible to pin down – he was mercurial and all-powerful, his news and TV empire stretching over every continent. Over 100 TV channels, 175 newspapers, forty book imprints and one very big movie studio: Fox. Murdoch's combined media firepower reached a global audience of 4.7 billion people: three-quarters of the entire population of planet earth.

Politicians seeking power now sought his blessing. In 1995, Tony Blair flew to Hayman Island, off the coast of Australia, for a formal anointment. Murdoch did not want nor need to consult with Blair; he merely needed him to be on the end of a phone in ten minutes, should it be required. As Murdoch wryly said, 'I've never asked a politician to do anything in my life.' He did not need to.

In the early 2000s, Fox stepped up its game by promoting itself as the authentic voice of America against the new 'liberal elite' of Washington. Fox was no longer the outsider voice, but the mainstream voice. It was a genius sleight of hand: minorities and corporate interests, not the American people, had wheedled their way into the heart of government. Graphics wrapped the Fox logo in the American flag.

Blatant partisanship gave Fox an almost cool, outsider status in marked contrast to the staid news channels, regurgitating press releases and trotting along to Washington junkets. Their journalists were not fierce, right-wing firebrands like Fox's, but dull, bored men who talked to camera in a monotone drone, hamstrung by their version of balance and their version of the facts.

Fox was delivering news as edgy, echo-chambered entertainment and the reasons were nothing to do with Murdoch's real politics, which are those of any shrewd, opportunist businessman. Owning an opinionated right-wing channel was merely good for business, and right for the times.

Fox began to redefine what the American right were about, coalescing first around the Tea Party, then Steve Bannon, Breitbart News and the alt-right. And the alt-right cleverly defined themselves in terms of what they were not.

They were not for gay marriage or the special pleading of minorities, they were not for gun control or abortion or immigration. They were not for elites or Washington or Islam. A negatively defined platform for a new political movement, but its calling card – what Rosser Reeves would have called its USP – was a refusal to believe in 'facts' as defined by traditional media.

There was a justifiable neurosis on the part of this so-called liberal 'elite' that the absolutist hegemony it had enjoyed for thirty years was over. But it was. We were back to the power play and 'truth' was merely a weapon in the fight.

Murdoch had not invented post-truth or erased the facts, he had taken advantage of the vacuum created. A disillusionment created by the incremental erosion of the credibility of news through its catastrophisation, and the accompanying inflated and schizophrenic claims of science. If people wanted extreme, he would give them extreme. It was a strange kind of honesty. In 2016, Fox News topped the ratings as the most watched cable news channel in America.

THE MYTH OF FACTS

In 1855, at the height of the Crimean War, Roger Fenton's photograph, 'The Valley of the Shadow of Death', published in *The Times*, poignantly captured the aftermath of British retreat in the face of the Russian army with a single image of an empty battlefield. There was only one problem. Fenton had constructed the entire scene, moving cannon balls artfully until he had the perfect image.

In 1945, on the beach of Iwo Jima, legendary war photographer Joe Rosenthal captured the most famous image of battle ever taken: the raising of the Stars and Stripes as American soldiers took the summit from the Japanese. It won him the Pulitzer Prize.

Both are a lie. The actual capture of Iwo Jima took place two days before Rosenthal even arrived. The real moment of victory was marked by a pathetically small flag raised on a makeshift flagpole and a sergeant named Louis Lowery recording it for posterity on a cheap camera. But the historic moment needed a fittingly heroic composition, so the army restaged it.

These falsified images dramatised a fact. A thing that actually happened. And the public believed it happened. In the 2014 blockbuster movie *Interstellar*, Matthew McConaughey's character marches into his son's school outraged that his son is being taught that the moon landings were faked.

But this is now the received wisdom for the majority of the population. Seventy-three per cent of the American public believe the moon landings were faked, fifty-two per cent of British adults believe the same. The younger you are, the more sceptical you will be. Seventy-eight per cent of eighteen-to-thirty-year-olds think the landings that Walter Cronkite solemnly reported as 'the greatest achievement in the history of mankind' were simply a couple of actors in a studio hamming it up in spacesuits and a sandpit.

Yet the moon landings are believable in the eyes of the public when placed next to news: ninety-four per cent of the US population believe all news reported by mainstream media is distorted or plain made up.

It is not balanced reporting that gets people's attention, but the high beam of a polemic that Fox pioneered. 'Facts' are marshalled into a compelling single argument, driven home by their selective use, pummelled into the intended target like bullets. The 9/11 conspiracy documentary *Loose Change*, arguing that the Twin Towers was a covert operation by the US government, is one of the most viewed documentaries online.[29] The fact that it has been widely discredited and debunked did not dampen its impact.

'Fake news' has been at the heart of the news as long as there has been news. Following the Spanish Civil War of 1936, George Orwell wrote:

> Early in life I had noticed no event is ever correctly reported in a newspaper. But in Spain, for the first time, I saw reports which did not bear any relation to the facts, not even the relationship that is implied in an ordinary lie. I saw great battles reported where there had been no fighting, and complete

silence where hundreds of men had been killed. This kind of thing is frightening to me, because it often gives me the feeling that the very concept of objective truth is fading out of the world.

In April 2016, the world's mainstream media descended on the small Macedonian town of Veles. For some strange reason, Veles had been identified as the source of thousands of fake news stories on Facebook such as 'Michelle Obama is a Man' and 'Wikileaks Just Killed Hillary!'

Serious journalists from some of the world's best-respected broadsheet titles could not comprehend why such a thing could happen. They searched the town for meaning, interviewing sullen teenagers on street corners who might have been responsible. Even the Macedonian teenagers looked mildly embarrassed when asked by middle-aged reporters schooled on Watergate 'why they had done it?' Why do anything? they said. Boredom and money.

A twenty-two-year-old computer-science student from Veles tried to explain to the *Guardian*: 'I thought, what would interest Americans the most, and it was either this or American Football. Some of the news I write, and other parts I take from other web sites, I then translate them. I really don't know if what I translate is true or not, I am only doing this because of the Google ads.'

The Veles students were not trying to 'do' anything. They were not trying to help Trump to win. They were not alt-right or left, they were not satirists or YouTubers. They were merely entrepreneurial teenagers in a depressed Macedonian city who had done their research and identified a niche, and were now looking to do something wholly American: make money.

Fake news did not put Donald Trump in the White House, any more than Joe Rosenthal's faked capture of Iwo Jima changed the course of the Second World War. But the difference was that Trump's victory happened within a context in which very few people under twenty-five now believe the news is anything but propaganda, and President Trump tapped into that.

Orwell lamented the 'fading out' of 'objective truth' and the subordination of facts to those making a naked play for power, but to those in power, power is the only fact that matters.

CHAPTER TWELVE
ROBOTS: THE HUMAN MACHINES

The Deal: the Fokoku Mutual Life Insurance Company
  of Japan sign a deal with IBM to bring Artificial
  Intelligence software Watson into the first workplace
  on earth
Aim: To use AI to make healthcare decisions for millions
  of customers, speed up claims and in the process,
  make 127 employees at Fokoku redundant – the first
  people on the planet to lose their jobs to AI
Where: Tokyo, Japan
When: March 2017

THE IMITATION GAME

'I propose to consider the question: can machines think?'

So opens Alan Turing's most famous paper written in 1950.[1] Turing had been integral to winning the Second World War by deciphering the Enigma Code of German U-boats. After the war, Turing used what he had learnt from code-breaking to take on what he considered to be the biggest challenge facing humanity.

To break the Enigma Code, Turing had used unimaginably complex sequences. These, thought Turing, now offered a glimpse into the future consciousness of machines. Could a computer develop to such a point that it could successfully mimic a human? 'Are there imaginable digital computers,' he wondered, 'which would do well in "the imitation game"?'[2]

Turing created a test: a human talks to a number of other humans behind a screen. But one of the humans is not human at all – it is a computer pretending to be human. If the questioner cannot tell which one is the computer, then the computer has successfully passed itself off as human. It has won the 'imitation game'.

Artificial intelligence, Turing said, would cease to be artificial, but real. And more importantly, humanity would have crossed the Rubicon to a world in which humans would ultimately be governed by robots. Turing surmised that computers would pass his test in 'about fifty years'.

It took sixty-two. In 2012, Vladimir Veselov at the University of Reading created a software program that successfully mimicked a thirteen-year-old Ukrainian boy called 'Eugene Goostman'.[3] Veselov's reasons for this adopted persona were cunning. 'Our main idea was that Eugene can claim that he knows anything, but his age also makes it perfectly reasonable that he doesn't know everything.'

Computers trying to pass the Turing Test in the past had fallen at the first hurdle by failing to even understand the question asked by humans. But increasingly complex machines since 2010 have been able to adapt strategies to fool humans: they change the subject, ask questions of the judges and even simulate moods and typos in text exchanges: strategies to make themselves look more human. Their 'imitation' has become increasingly devious.

As a result, the bar for the Turing Test has been raised. For a computer to successfully pass today, it needs to fool at least one judge from a group of three human judges after a number of conversations lasting up to two hours.

This is a transcript of the conversation between Eugene and a human in 2012:

Judge: What music do you like?
Eugene: I like Eminem – because he doesn't have a thing to do with polite-correctness.
Judge: OMG I love Eminem, he's my favourite artist!

Eugene: I wonder what Eminem's nick mean. I associate it only with a word 'enema'. But he is a cool guy, I like his 'The Real Slim Shady'.

Judge: I know what his nick name means, his real name is Marshall Mathers. From the initials M&M phynetically (sic) sounding like Eminem.

Eugene: Eminem is a famous crapper. No, raper . . . ripper . . . Yeah, I like his 'Stan' and 'The Real Slim Shady'.

Judge: I like 'Hailies song'.

Eugene: Interesting tastes. I like science fiction books, by the way.

How anyone could seriously be fooled by Eugene is hard to imagine. But Eugene, in spite of 'his' idiosyncratic answers, successfully passed thirty-three per cent of such conversations.[4] And in 'passing' the Turing Test, it became apparent that the Turing Test might be missing the point about robots.

Robots are not about a bad simulation of humans; they are about something new entirely. In 2017, I visited Uber's headquarters in San Francisco to meet one of their head designers, Didier Hilhorst. On the face of it, Uber is a cab app. But it is not. For Uber, providing an app that can merely order a cab is only the beginning.

Uber has the potential, Didier says, to immerse itself fully in a digital representation of the city. It is a form of 'augmented reality' – a hybrid of real life and a parallel representation on screen in which the digital enmeshes itself in your day-to-day life, and so becomes your life.

At the moment, Uber only provide cabs and food, with a little car you can follow on screen *en route*. But the data Uber are amassing allows the algorithms to begin predicting your needs and suggesting them: would you like to go to a favourite restaurant, take your child to day care or to your girlfriend's place? How about somewhere or something you have never done before?

The next step is a sophisticated representation of you in a

virtual environment: a figure walking through the city. You in five minutes' time. Do you want a coffee? It is ordered and ready in the coffee shop as you approach. You see an avatar of yourself approaching the coffee shop and the barista making it.

'In five years' time, will we still be using phones and apps to do these things? It's doubtful we'll still be using anything so clunky as having to take a device out of your pocket and tediously press screens. We already have contact lenses developed with screens projecting directly onto the eye allowing instantaneous decision-making. The job is to make the Uber experience as seamless as breathing. The potential for augmenting reality and making that our version of singularity is very exciting.'

This 'total Uber experience' will mean the avatar of you will be three steps ahead of the real you: shopping, buying tickets for the cinema, or dealing with problems such as a traffic jam before you have to, and using voice recognition or retina technology to do it. Whatever you do now on your phone will have been 'gamified' into the 'total Uber experience': no longer on your phone, but projected on the retina of your eye.

This is not Us Versus Robots, but a future enmeshed together in which the boundaries of where they end and we begin are blurred. Didier sees this robot future not as a Jetsons world of tin-can machines doing things for us, but digital technology and human life as a seamless whole: a singularity.

This augmented reality in our eye will be supplemented by in-body technology – blood-cleaning nano-computers; thermostatic control of heart rate, blood pressure and stress levels. This is not a world of giant striding machines, but microscopic tech hacks of human life.

Uber watched in 2014 and 2015 as Alexa and Siri were promoted by Amazon and Apple to provide mass-market automated assistants. A soothing voice that will book you a restaurant, turn on your lights at home, coach you through your morning workout, or play your favourite playlist. Anthropomorphised ads were run on TV in December 2017, offering friendly machines as calm reliable servant/managers, who know us better than we know ourselves, and what is best for us, too.

But Didier and Uber are thinking beyond this to a world in which robot intelligence and human needs are utterly inseparable, and we ourselves have become the robot, with human parts.

So, what happens when there is no singularity? I asked Didier what was the main problem with driverless cars. Uber already have trials of driverless fleets with paying passengers in San Francisco, Pittsburgh and Tempe, Arizona.

New technology in itself was not the problem, Didier explained, but when human error and new technology collided. In other words, the old human infrastructure of a higgledy-piggledy city clashing with the new technology of driverless cars inevitably creates a period of transitional mess.

For the technology to truly revolutionise our lives, it requires an entire reboot of the infrastructure: a clean slate from which to start again. The kind of thing that only happens after natural disaster or a war.

PROJECT TITAN

In 2009, Apple filed for a patent for in-car camera technology, one that tech analysts predicted could be used to detect hand gestures and control a car or as part of an augmented-reality experience. In 2011, Apple filed for another patent: a small but crucial modification of the iPhone allowing the user to unlock and start their car using their phone.

Apple was not simply getting in on driverless technology, as Tesla, Google and Uber are all jockeying to be a part of, but something more spectacular. Apple CEO Tim Cook teased shareholders with a cryptic comment: 'Do you remember when you were a kid, and it was Christmas Eve, and it was so exciting? You weren't sure what was going to be downstairs.'

Cook promised that it won't be too long before we go downstairs and find out. Unlike Google and Tesla, who have been testing their driverless cars on public roads, Apple's engineers have been using a disused Second World War naval base outside San Francisco, as the *Guardian* revealed in May 2016. According to the base's owners, GoMentum, it is 'the largest secure test facility in the world.'

The *Wall Street Journal* investigated Apple's car ambitions and discovered that since February 2015, Apple has hired Doug Betts from Fiat and Paul Furgale, the Swiss researcher who led the V-Charge project to develop self-parking cars. It has also hired fifty top engineers previously at Tesla, and a clutch of battery-life tech experts from Samsung in South Korea and from electric car battery maker A123 Systems.

Apple's next big project is called Titan and is not the creation of a driverless car, but the entire transportation system on which all driverless cars operate. Titan is the infrastructure reboot Didier at Uber talked about, minus the need for a war to erase the outmoded infrastructure. Apple are doing nothing short of reimagining what the world looks like and how the interlocking pieces will work together seamlessly. In short, they are building *Tron* for real.

In August 2017, tech expert Steven Milunovich uncovered a secret Apple office in Berlin devoted, he said, to realising this new transportation system, using the car experts hired by Apple. 'Project Titan is likely to be a transportation platform – not a car,' Milunovich said, 'but the entire experience.'

In June 2017, Tim Cook confirmed the rumours by revealing to Bloomberg that Apple is focusing on 'autonomous systems . . . a core technology that we view as very important. We sort of see it as the mother of all AI projects.'

If cars drive themselves, coordinating the transportation system becomes the real AI challenge, not the car itself. Apple already has AI interests in health care and IT systems, but cracking a coordinated AI transportation system dwarfs these as a challenge.

It doesn't end there. Cook told *Good Morning America* in September 2017 that Apple was developing augmented-reality technology because 'it gives us the capability to sit and be very present, talking to each other, but also have other things – visually – for both of us to see.'

By applying augmented reality to driverless cars, the inside of a car becomes an AR entertainment pod moving within a transportation system powered by AI, and Apple will run both under the umbrella of Project Titan. Augmented reality alone is predicted to be worth $165 billion as a market by 2024, and the autonomous car is predicted to be on the market by 2021. If Apple pulls off a worldwide *Tron* transportation system, it will have taken a leap making the invention of the iPhone look modest.

I, FOR ONE, WELCOME OUR NEW COMPUTER OVERLORDS

Apple want to own the system, but building a robot that out-humans the humans remains as great and hotly contested a challenge. As the thirteen-year-old 'Eugene Goostman' was being built in Reading, another computer was being prepared for a very different test, one with far more serious consequences for the human race.

In January 2011, Ken Jennings and Brad Rutter, two former champions of the US TV quiz show *Jeopardy!*, sat down before a TV audience of twenty million to face their toughest opponent yet: IBM computer Watson.[5]

In 1998, an IBM supercomputer called Deep Blue had destroyed the world chess champion Garry Kasparov over six frantically fought matches. Deep Blue's emphatic victory was hailed as a kind of Turing Test being passed, but it was not. Chess is a game with distinct rules and finite (if multiple) options for any one move. It is merely a test of computing complexity, not AI.

In 2004, IBM executive Charles Lickel was in a steakhouse near Poughkeepsie eating dinner when he noticed something strange: the restaurant emptying. The diners were rushing out to the bar to watch the TV. On it was America's longest-running quiz show, *Jeopardy!* The diners were hooked on a phenomenon gripping America: the latest instalment of the amazing, seventy-four-game winning streak of Ken Jennings.[6]

In that moment, Lickel had an idea. Days later in a brainstorming session at IBM, in which executives were being asked to come up with IBM's next 'grand challenge', Lickel suggested they take on Ken Jennings in the ultimate *Jeopardy!* showdown. Man versus Robot.

That is the legend. In truth, a physicist at IBM called Dave Ferrucci, a fiercely smart New Jersey-born Italian-American with a brain the size of an IBM computer, had been badgering his bosses for over a year to create a more demanding challenge. I met Dave in New York, where he is now working with the world's largest hedge fund, Bridgewater, to use artificial intelligence to hire and fire the staff handling $160 billion worth of assets. I assume he needs to get his new job right, just as he did with Watson playing *Jeopardy!*

'In terms of complexity, *Jeopardy!* was a huge step up from playing the world chess champion,' Dave says, 'which was merely a test of computing power.'

The randomness of *Jeopardy!*'s questions – from obscure 1980s pop culture to seventeenth-century philosophy – and phrased in a quirky, counter-intuitive and problematically human way – made it a far more difficult challenge for a computer. Compared to *Jeopardy!*, a game of chess was child's play,[7] because *Jeopardy!* was outside the computer's comfort zone.

IBM had no idea what they were up against. To begin with, Watson was uploaded with a Wikipedia's worth of information. But searching through this database using algorithms for an answer took Watson hours, not seconds.

'We initially made progress very quickly, but then it slowed and that was frustrating. We played an early game and it was terrible. Watson was destroyed and we just thought this was impossible.'

In 2009, five years after starting, IBM finally began testing Watson against former contestants of *Jeopardy!* as a dry run for the Jennings showdown.

Watson still had glitches. Responses could be unpredictable and wildly inaccurate. Questioned about the main characters in Dickens's novel *Oliver Twist*, Watson said, 'The Pet Shop Boys.' Asked what 'no' is in German, Watson answered, 'What is fuck?' (The answer was 'What is nein?').[8]

Ferrucci realised that even when Watson could get the answer right, it would take hours to find it. Dave brought in an entirely new team of programmers simply to deal with the idea of what a question was to a computer, and another to deal with the speed at which this information could be processed.

'I was called in by the bosses at IBM and told, Get this right. This whole thing rests on – and they pointed their finger at me – you.'

Luckily for Dave and Watson's other programmers, the difference between machines and humans is that machines keep relentlessly improving. As humans learn more, the curve of improvement plateaus out. But with robots, it steepens dramatically: a lesson the contestants of *Jeopardy!* were about to learn the hard way.

In 2011, Watson was ready for its big day on TV. A large computer sat in the studio between two humans. Watson was 'about the size of a restaurant fridge'. But it was the most complex machine ever programmed.

A blue, convex robot eye stared out impassively and HAL-like from the middle of a blank screen as two humans fidgeted on their podiums. Watson was facing off with the all-time *Jeopardy!* champion, Ken Jennings, and another *Jeopardy!* super-brain, Brad Rutter.

Dave sat in the audience with the IBM bosses. He was so

nervous, his fingernails dug into his legs. 'I knew we were going to win, though.' How come? 'We had worked so hard, we knew it. Watson was ready. It was going to be a walk-over.'

But it wasn't. Initially, the contest appeared pretty even. But then Watson suddenly kicked in. Dave breathed a sigh of relief. It began beating Jennings and Rutter to every answer faster; the same solemn unblinking eye staring out over the audience as it delivered correct answer after correct answer.

The glitches had gone. Jennings and Rutter looked at each other in bewilderment. Watson's supremacy over its human rivals was breathtaking. 'There were still times it could have gone the humans' way,' Dave says, 'because with *Jeopardy!* there's always a chance you can come back. And that came into my head. But I was the human rooting for the computer, it was strange, and all I was doing was demonstrating my irrational human fears.'

By the final question, these were the positions: Brad Rutter had amassed $21,600; Ken Jennings, $24,000; Watson had $77,147, over three times as much.

When the very last answer was given, 'Bram Stoker', and all three correctly answered the question – 'Who wrote *Dracula*?' – it didn't matter. Watson had crushed its rivals.

Watson's victory was greeted with stilted applause from the audience. Humans were applauding their own defeat. Ken Jennings smiled wryly and wrote a message on his answer card, which he showed to the millions of people watching at home: 'I for one, welcome our new computer overlords.'

THEIR WEAK SPOT: MAKING A BED

On 5 April 2014, two of the world's foremost AI experts, Professors Erik Brynjolfsson and Andrew McAfee of MIT, held a meeting in New York with a hundred of the world's top programmers. The agenda: the implications of the Watson victory.[9]

Brynjolfsson and McAfee showed a graph with two lines of blue dots. One line marked the cognitive advancement of human *Jeopardy!* players; and the other showed the progress of Watson from the moment IBM began work in 2004 to the day Watson trounced Jennings and Rutter in 2011.

'Look at the dates,' Brynjolfsson said.

The human advance of dots went moderately upward. But Watson's advance of blue dots was astonishing: initially tentative; then moderate; then suddenly steep. But from 2008 on, the dots went up like a skyscraper. Watson had gone through the gears from terrible to genius, but its rate of learning in the last twelve months had accelerated at a speed never seen before.

What did this mean? It meant, Brynjolfsson and McAfee said, that once robots get to a baseline of learning, they can learn to do what we do very, very fast. They then move on, colonising what we cannot do fast as well.

In terms of the workplace, robots first conquer the manual stuff within their physical ambit, then they dry-run for them-selves managerial skills, which means they can oversee and manage what humans do. They become the boss, and do not need to be programmed to do this. They just do it.

'Think of the world of work,' Brynjolfsson said, 'as divided between "power systems" and "control systems".' The power systems are people, fork-lifts, planes and trucks. They move things. The control systems are plant managers, business plans and engineering diagrams: they decide where things move.

In the nineteenth century, the first industrial revolution auto-mated engines and factories and created a machine age that potentially threatened the entire usefulness of humans; our reason for existing. The power systems were disrupted and reshaped. But after a period of dislocation we adapted, taking over the control systems by becoming engineers and managers.

But this second machine age is very different. Now machines are not only reshaping the power systems, but taking over the control systems, too, and there is no possibility of humans fighting back.

In 2017, McKinsey estimated sixty per cent of all jobs will be thirty per cent computerised in less than a decade. But this presupposes jobs of the near future will be recognisably the same as they are now. An automated warehouse looks very different from one employing people. It can be packed to the ceiling with no floor space and moved around by overhead winches, not people on the ground. It doesn't need lights, because robots work in pitch black, too. The automated accountancy firm does not need an office at all, just software.

This is the start of a long and winding road for us, and as Elizabeth Kolbert succinctly put it: 'Ken Jennings (the human *Jeopardy!* opponent of Watson) might be described as the first person to be made redundant by Watson.'[10]

In March 2017, thirty-four employees at Fukoku Mutual Life Insurance in Tokyo became the next humans made redundant by Watson: the first employees anywhere in the world to be openly replaced by artificial intelligence.[11]

The Watson software had been bought by Fukoku to automate health insurance across the whole of Japan. The IBM computer that had won *Jeopardy!* would now be deciding who has an operation in a country of 127 million people.

Fukoku management calculate they will save 140 million yen (£1 million) a year in wages by cutting these thirty-four jobs. But by laying off 34,000 people in similarly well-paid, middle-management jobs, they could save billions of yen.

IBM say that Watson possesses 'cognitive technology that can think like a human enabling it to analyse and interpret all data, including unstructured text, images, audio and video.' Fukoku will use Watson to read tens of thousands of medical certificates, working out length of hospital stays and appropriate surgical procedures before calculating payouts. When humans did this job, they used their own judgment before making a decision. Fukoku say there is no need. The data will decide.

In south-western Japan, Henn-na Hotel is staffed entirely by robots. There is a multilingual dinosaur on reception and a hairless doll concierge with blinking geisha eyes that answers any queries about breakfast. A robot trolley takes your bags to the room: face recognition is used as your key. A drone delivers room service. There is only one permanent human member of staff: Hideo Sawada, the owner.

Japanese hotels are expensive, but the Henn-na costs only 9,000 yen ($80 a night). The hotel is covered with security cameras and these are watched by a human from a security centre 200 miles away.

Yet when it comes to making your bed, there is a chink of light for humanity. The robots can't do it. No matter how hard Hideo Sawada tried, he could not get robot maids to successfully fold down and tuck under a sheet, pulling it tight to the degree that humans desire.

Beds, it turns out, are surprisingly complex in AI terms. They vary in size and shape; they are positioned differently in hotels, with surrounding furniture making access difficult. They require moving and repositioning. Making a bed is a multidisciplined affair, it requires both delicate skills and spatial awareness as well as manual strength, and it stumps robots.

So the only other human staff at Henn-na Hotel, apart from Mister Sawada, are the maids with the requisite and exclusively human skills of turning down a bed: skills the robots cannot master. Yet.

As well as hotels, robots are used extensively in care homes across Japan. Twenty per cent of the Japanese population are sixty-five or older; in the US, it is thirteen per cent (set to double by 2050); in Britain, the projections are similar. Merrill Lynch has projected a shortfall of a million careworkers in Japan by 2025. This care crisis has already hit Britain. But in Japan, the solution is ASIMO: a 'carebot' built by Honda.

'Carebots' are a fraction of the cost of humans to employ and appear to offer a way out of the coming global care crisis, but carebots also raise unexpected legal questions.

Gurvinder Virk is a professor of robotics who has developed industry standards for human-robot interaction in the event of litigation due to an accident. If a robot drops or crushes a resident, who is responsible? It is not as straightforward as it seems.

Virk's robot litigation criteria is called ISO 13482 and it covers three types of robot: physical assistance robots, mobile servant robots and people carrier robots.[12]

These three models cover the basic needs of a care home resident: 'Resyone' is a robotic hybrid device that transforms from a bed to a wheelchair with no humanoid characteristics. This is because humans are used to being moved around by vehicles that do not look human.

'Robear' is more overtly humanoid in appearance and is a lifter. The developers believe a semi-human-looking lifting device is comforting and reassuring to clients, as it feels nurturing, like a giant mechanical hand.

The Riken robot lab are working on a fully human-looking nurse, capable of complex bedside care combined with factory robot strength, for moving 'multiple persons'. Riken's care-bot may well be able to make a bed, too.

Robots in Japan are already being used in every conceivable scenario: from care homes to hospitals, airports and hotels, to domestic kitchens and construction sites. Robot cats are used in care homes to keep the elderly company.

Robots are also being used to decommission the three reactors in Fukushima, which went into meltdown in 2011, the worst nuclear disaster since Chernobyl. Japan is fully embracing its robot destiny and this is because the Japanese government are spending nearly half their R&D budget on robots.

Companies across the world are also racing to produce the first fully functioning sex robot. The sex industry has always been quicker to take up new technology than other industries. Pornography pioneered the switch from film to video tape in the

1980s, and streaming on the internet in the 2000s. Now four companies – Realbotix and BodAi in the US, Z-Onedoll and Doll Sweet in China – are all looking to launch synthetic sex robots with AI that are 'fully responsive'.

By integrating the dolls with virtual reality and eventually adding warmth to the skin and genitalia through heat pads, these silicon companions could retail at close to $70–80,000.

But this karaoke version of a robot future – machines as dolls and servants, rather than our master – is based on a fast-evaporating assumption that humans will determine the relationship with robots and maintain the whip hand.

Alan Turing assumed that for a computer to pass the Turing Test, all it needed to do was to become more like a human. What he did not factor in was an alternative scenario: that we would become more like robots.

HOW WE BECAME THE ROBOTS

In 2013, the coalition government of David Cameron got an intimation of the next ten years. A research paper by Carl Frey and Michael Osborne at Oxford University gave a stark prediction of where Watson would shortly take the human race. By 2030, they said, half of all jobs could be automated.[13]

Pre-2013 crystal-ball gazing about automated work suddenly looked irrelevant. It was quickly becoming apparent that obsolescence meant anyone: doctors, lawyers, accountants, supermarket staff, cab drivers, care workers, journalists, even tech analysts assessing the future of robots. In May 2017, an AI algorithm developed by the Illinois Institute of Technology made high court judges obsolete, correctly predicting seventy-two per cent of high court verdicts (human judges could only predict sixty-six per cent).

Advocates of the robot revolution who saw such predictions as overly pessimistic pointed to the first industrial revolution and the so-called Luddite Fallacy: fear that automation would end human employment was cancelled out by the creation of millions more jobs. Most AI experts say this is different.

Brynjolfsson and McAfee, working with colleagues Daron Acemoglu and David Autor, put it like this: 'Imagine a matrix with two axes, manual versus cognitive and routine versus non-routine. Jobs can then be arranged into four boxes: manual routine, manual non-routine, and so on.[14] Jobs on an assembly line fall into the manual-routine box, jobs in home healthcare into the manual non-routine box. Keeping track of inventory is in the cognitive-routine box, dreaming up an ad campaign or writing a book is cognitive non-routine.'

The highest-paid jobs are clustered in the last box: managing a hedge fund, litigating a bankruptcy, creating a piece of art, are cognitive and non-routine. Manual, non-routine jobs tend to be the lowest paid: emptying bedpans, waiting on tables at a restaurant, cleaning hotel rooms. Factory floor and payroll or accounting jobs tend to fall in-between.

Of these four boxes – four boxes that categorise all human jobs – robots could potentially do three and a half.

Middle-class jobs are the easiest for robots to take over: clerical, administrative and any number-crunching such as accountancy. Robots struggle with making beds – as we know – and delivering a parcel in a city when no one is in, so these will remain human jobs a little bit longer.

But most jobs will be colonised, leaving only the odd doctor or supermarket supervisor to troubleshoot the occasional problem the robots cannot handle, as they already do in supermarkets when the checkout fails to scan a bunch of bananas and someone has to come over and punch in the code number.

AI expert Martin Ford says the big problem with this is not even the robots, but our complacency. We assume our job is safe because it is 'complex', when often it is not. We conflate the complexity of being human with the specificity of the job, which does not require human complexity.

As Ford puts it, 'A computer doesn't need to replicate the entire spectrum of your intellectual capability in order to displace you from your job: it only needs to do the specific things you are paid to do.'[15]

Governments quite simply freaked when they read the reports written by experts like Ford, Brynjolfsson and McAfee coming out of MIT and Oxford. President Obama was sufficiently panicked to commission a White House report: 'Artificial Intelligence, Automation and the Economy'.

'In recent years,' it concluded, 'machines have surpassed humans in the performance of certain tasks related to intelligence. It is expected that machines will continue (rapidly) to reach and exceed human performance on more and more tasks . . . aggressive policy action will be needed to help Americans who are disadvantaged by these changes.'[16]

Governments across the world began commissioning their own reports and all came to the same conclusion: we need to do something, but what? If machines make everyone redundant, how will we earn a living and what is everyone going to do all day? It was not just Turing who had prophesised this future. In the 1930s, Keynes painted the utopian and dystopian alternatives to automation – would we be enslaved, or lie in fields sunbathing all day long?

In 2016, the tech billionaires weighed in with their solutions. Elon Musk resurrected the idea of a 'universal living wage': an amount of money we are all paid to exist.

Bill Gates said we need to attack the wealth creation problem from the other end and tax robots on their labour. By charging companies on the savings made from cutting humans, a universal living wage could be funded and continue to pay for the state: roads, hospitals and armies.

Daron Acemoglu and Pascual Restrepo at MIT, two of the AI experts the US government had been reading assiduously, began to view this coexistence less as an inevitable, anxiety-inducing *fait accompli*, than an arms race to tool up and be smartest. A race humans need to win.[17]

THE ROBOT SWAP

At this fork in the road for humanity, a question arises: what is the best strategy for winning and what kind of human being do we create to win? Do we become human versions of robots or maximise our human traits?

Technology has already roboticised our lives: we work hard to targets, often set in jobs by algorithms, we monitor our productivity using health apps and wearable technology; chain ourselves to Instagram, Facebook and Twitter. We are incrementally replacing conversation with email, shutting down human interaction in public spaces by screen-blanking each other, and constantly seeking data-driven improvement: the creation of a machine-like optimal self. An automated self.

At the very moment robots are becoming more human, we are becoming more like robots. But in terms of survival in the workplace, is this good or bad? Should we continue automating our behaviour – out-roboting the robots – or punch out of the box and maximise our USP: our humanity?

In 2000, Tony Blair's government in the UK, already fearing children would become irrelevant in a brutal new workplace if they did not 'raise standards', embarked on 'academisation': the most radical reform of British schools since the war.

To its critics, academisation was the roboticisation of children. Education would no longer be open-ended learning and discovery, but passing tests relentlessly. Children's minds would be narrowed not opened; they would be ticking a box, instead of thinking outside it.

Tony Blair's chief educational advisor was Michael Barber. Under Barber's tutelage, Blair and then Gordon Brown embarked on the wholesale rebuilding of Britain's schools.

The programme was mammoth. Overnight, Victorian buildings and leaking 1960s comprehensives were ripped down, replaced by bright, shining, new, open-plan academies, created in 'partnership' with business: painted in primary Lego colours with giant IT rooms filled with computers donated by business and a central 'reception' staffed by someone wearing a headset.

Critics of academies called them soulless and a betrayal of education, selling off schools to business. Critics of the critics said this was middle-class elitism: what was wrong with children bettering their results and focusing on vocational training? What was so terrible about working-class kids getting a chance to go to university?

The very things that liberal parents and teacher unions hated about academies were the things their advocates loved. Academies prepared pupils for the workplace by building schools that looked like offices. Factories of productivity: good, said their supporters.

A decade into academies, the fear has shifted as the reality of automation begins to dawn. Have we done the wrong thing by turning children into robots at the very moment they need to optimise their human skills to survive?

Under the Blair government, Michael Barber was hailed a genius for his new vision for education. After leaving his government post, Barber went to work for management consultants McKinsey to advise them on what he had identified as the biggest, untapped cash cow of the digital revolution, worth $500 billion in the US alone, trillions globally: 'EdTech' or 'Educational Technology'.

THE MIRACLE OF THE HOLE IN THE WALL, NEW DELHI

EdTech is breathtaking in its scope. In a nutshell, it seeks to capture and monetise global education by turning every child on the planet from a school pupil into a personalised client of software.

Underpinning this momentous deal is an underlying proposition: teachers are over, and should be replaced by technology. Teaching, the argument goes, is an inherently unpredictable practice delivered by a human, with all the quirks and inconsistencies a human brings to the job.

Teachers do not promote a child's welfare, they hinder it by bringing their prejudices to bear – on a subject they like or dislike, and on an individual pupil they either favour or dislike. Computers are different: they do not have these prejudices. A child can excel by 'personalising' their own software teaching program to what they are interested in.

The inspiration for the EdTech revolution was an experiment carried out by educational guru and TED talker, Professor Sugata Mitra of Newcastle University. In 1999, a computer appeared overnight in an empty ATM hole in New Delhi. No one knew how it got there. Street kids began to gather round and after a few minutes, they had figured out how to turn it on.

Within a day, these same kids – some of whom did not go to school and did not know how to read or write – were solving complex mathematical problems by asking the internet, which they had worked out for themselves how to use.

They could solve questions of moral philosophy and quantum physics, and they had worked out these answers with ease, because they had not been discouraged by a teacher; no one had told them that the questions were hard to solve.[18]

What the kids did not know was that they were part of an experiment. Mitra wanted to test how technology would be used by children in the absence of teachers. The results, he said, were mind-blowing.

Mitra said the absence of a teacher had freed the kids to learn fast themselves. When all the world's knowledge is available at a swipe, teachers are not merely redundant, he argued, they actively hinder the child's learning.

Word of Mitra's experiment spread like wildfire through Silicon Valley. This was music to their ears. Mitra argued that teaching and schools were themselves a colonial Western construct. The Indian school system had cemented inequality, designed originally to provide an army of obedient workers to service the British colonial machine.

Technology, however, offered the keys to freedom for the poor of the world. But Mitra had his critics. He wove, according to educationalist Neil Selwyn, 'a seductive story that masked insidious hyper-individualistic Silicon Valley thinking, at complete odds with genuine learning. Global standardisation under the smokescreen of freeing the child.'

By selling a utopian vision of barefoot children, in awe at the wonderment of technology that they had discovered at a hole in the wall in New Delhi, Mitra – his critics argued – was cloaking the business interests of the tech giants, who wanted in on the EdTech cash cow.

The second sleight of hand was to sell the roboticisation of children as liberation from the shackles of teachers and schools. By getting rid of teachers, the tech giants could roll out software worth trillions and conquer the global education market.

Tony Blair's education guru, Michael Barber, had identified this key business target when he moved from government to working for McKinsey as their EdTech guru.

If children were to be turned into human robots, then the first thing you needed to do was claim they were being freed from teachers. To this end, Barber had been inspired not by Mitra, but two American academics from Stanford University, John Chubb and Terry Moe, authors of two books proposing a free-market revolution in education: *Politics, Markets and America's Schools*[19] and *Liberating Learning*.[20]

'The world,' Chubb and Moe said, 'is in the early stages of a historic transformation in how students learn, teachers teach, and schools and school systems are organised.'

Chubb and Moe said teachers are 'vested interests' that block change or progress by protecting their own jobs at the expense of the needs of children.

Moreover, the kind of person who goes into teaching often has an inherent bias against business and enterprise. They are invariably left-wing or openly socialist, they want to turn children against business, rather than admire financial success. Teachers bring these prejudices into the classroom and further disadvantage children by indoctrinating their pupils against success.

Schools need to be opened up to the market, and business should be brought into the heart of the curriculum, even finance the school system itself. An ideological transformation of the entire school culture is required.

Schools are not a 'job scheme for teachers', Chubb and Moe argued. They need to cut out the politicians and teachers who keep parents and business from running them properly together.

But it was how this revolution was to happen that was the most controversial part of Chubb and Moe's plan. Teachers should not be attacked through direct confrontation, but technology.

THE TECH TROJAN HORSE

I met Terry Moe at Stanford University in the huge, circular, wood-panelled room where presidents, philanthropists and now tech billionaires have come to address professors and alumni about their grand plans for the future for over two hundred years.

Terry was not what I expected: a wiry man with a sceptical twinkle in his eye. Terry told me excitedly how he was now working on a book about New Orleans after Hurricane Katrina.

Because the city's entire infrastructure was wiped out, the 'vested interests' of the teacher unions were washed away, too, allowing the education system to be built again from the ground up. The results, he said, had been 'remarkable'.

What was his problem with teachers?

'I'm painted as this neo-liberal market guy, I'm not. Teachers have a role to play, I'm not saying they don't, but the vested interest of teacher unions is not in the interest of children.'

Whether teachers like it or not, Terry said, the 'tech revolution is coming'. So what advice would he give to teachers facing redundancy? 'Understand what is happening. It's over. Accept that they need to work with the future happening now, rather than fight it.'

In *Liberating Learning*, Chubb and Moe had a cunning plan for how technology can be used to deal with teachers: it should 'seep' into the classroom, drip, drip – first through iPads, then rolling out personalised teaching to every single child, so gradually marginalising teachers in their own classroom. The more technology seeps in, the closer teachers come to obsolescence. Till one day, they are suddenly obsolete.

Chubb and Moe's *Liberating Learning* was described as 'an excellent book' by the then Minister of Education, Michael Gove.[21] Did Terry know he had been lauded by the British education secretary? 'No, I wasn't aware, but I am flattered.'

Their strategy for using technology as a Trojan Horse to break the unions could work not only in education, but across the public sector: in health, social care, in all forms of public service. The two authors were hailed on the New Right as neo-liberal prophets, although Moe is diffident about the association.

Chubb and Moe had created a template for a wholly privatised future through the Trojan Horse of technology. One that cleverly sidestepped difficult and unpopular political conflict with groups held in high esteem by the public: teachers, or doctors and nurses. Instead, by using technology, they could do the whole thing smoothly and silently.

I wanted to see what Terry Moe's school of the future might look like, so I visited the Flex Tech Lab in San Diego, one of the most advanced examples of so-called 'blended learning' using technology in the world.

The school was quite extraordinary. The principal, Sean, showed me round an open-plan class with about seventy pupils. They all work with laptops or desktop computers. There is only one teacher for the entire room, whom pupils merely consult if they have a problem.

Each pupil I met was pursuing their own interest, which had become their personalised learning plan: Stephanie, who was sixteen, wanted to be a marine biologist. Brendan was interested in astrophysics and was watching an advanced astronomy lecture online. He made notes on the side of the screen and stopped the lecture if he wanted to go back.

Sean, the executive principal, was evangelical about Flex Tech. But it was not the straightforward Terry Moe transplant. Sean said the school had undergone 'several iterations using technology. We began with a far more technology-based model and found it was too much, it didn't work. The teacher needed to come back in the classroom to guide learning and so now we have what we describe as "blended learning".'

I talked to the teacher, Steve. What is it like overseeing seventy pupils? 'Sometimes, it's a bit like being one of those checkout supervisors at a supermarket waiting for something to go wrong with a barcode. But for the children, it's a huge improvement. They are genuinely self-motivated and learn at their own speed, rather than having that dictated by a teacher at the front.'

How important is it that education is rooted in the job they will do when they leave? 'It's fundamental. It's everything. There is so much pressure and stress to do well at work. You don't have the luxury of screwing up at college and getting into student debt on the wrong course. You need to focus now. We have kids who stress and go too fast through the curriculum because they want to do well, and we actually have to slow them down. That's where the teacher comes in. It's not just about success, it's about being happy, too.'

Flex Tech has a waiting list of over a thousand pupils and is undoubtedly a very successful school. They are now talking to the designers of Google Maps to create a 'Google Maps for learning'.

But it is also in a prosperous part of San Diego – would it work in a deprived area of Detroit or Dagenham? Terry Moe says technology favours poorer pupils over wealthier ones, because they are less likely to be in a class setting dominated by more assertive, middle-class kids putting up their hand every five seconds.

Sean, the principal, also sees a paradox at the heart of their success at Flex Tech. 'We are using technology in a blended learning setting to create focus, where technology has defocused kids through phones and video games. We have never seen children more defocused and demotivated than now, and our job is to reverse that.' Technology to fight technology.

Sean thinks children are robots before, not after, they come into his classroom. They have already been trained up for repetitive work by the repetitive-task patterns of social media and gaming. He believes technology in the classroom can be used to deprogramme and focus kids: as a Trojan Horse for good, not bad.

THE MONEY

Whether EdTech will free children from becoming human robots, or turn every child from Riga to Rio into the perfect robot KFC employee, remains to be seen. What is not in question is the money to be made from this revolution.

In 2005, Michael Barber met New York mayor Michael Bloomberg and his education guru, Joel Klein. In effect, Klein was setting out to create a laboratory for educational experimentation using EdTech as the apparatus.

In the same year, Klein made the decisive move, putting out what researchers Tamasin Cave and Andy Rowell describe as a 'call to arms to corporate America. The business community needed to step up or America's position in the world was going to be significantly in peril.'

Klein's call was answered by a group of America's big-money philanthropists dubbed the Billionaire Boys' Club: Google's Eric Schmidt, Microsoft's Bill Gates, Facebook's Mark Zuckerberg, Apple's Steve Jobs, Eli Broad of Walmart and Michael Dell of Dell Computers.[22]

Klein's appeal to them was an appeal to the heart: school children are being failed by a crumbling school system, but technology can set children free. Education reform lobbyist Rick Berman said, 'We need to hit on fear and anger,' when talking to a gathering of wealthy philanthropists, 'and how you get the fear and anger is by reframing the problem.'

Berman was famous for his work attacking American unions and lobbying on behalf of the tobacco industry. Cave and Rowell have researched Berman's strategy. 'He told reformers that rather than intellectualise the education debate, they needed to trigger an emotional reaction in people.'

'Emotions will stay with people longer than concepts,' he said. So rather than a rational debate on the merits of their plans, reformers needed to motivate supporters by tapping into their fears for their children's future and provoking anger at those opposed to reform.'[23]

But Joel Klein and Michael Barber also appealed to something more fundamental to these billionaires: their wallets. EdTech will be worth $70 billion worldwide by 2020. The market for devices like tablets is set to be $32 billion. The online learning industry is looking to nearly double in size, worth $24 billion in the US alone.

And for governments, the appeal is a huge cut in the wage bill of teachers. If you have one teacher overseeing seventy to a hundred pupils, then you save billions overnight with a single swipe of the iPad.

This is not a gift horse, Klein told the tech billionaires, you want to be looking in the mouth. The global tech company that plants its flag in EdTech has the future of the human race in its hands; how it learns, can work more efficiently than a robot, and thus survive as a race.

Join the revolution, he said. But here is what's really in it for you. By 2020, EdTech will overtake MedTech as the biggest data gold rush on earth.

When Sugata Mitra first put his computer in a hole in the wall in New Delhi in 1998, he saw technology as a liberation from formal schooling. Schools had been used in India not to educate the poor, but to turn them into obedient workers for the Empire.

Yet EdTech had the potential to do exactly the same digitally: create the ultimate worker, tested and drilled on an iPad from four to sixteen years old, before going on to have the same at work with a day dictated by algorithms.

In 2015, Bill Gates's Microsoft bought LinkedIn for $26 billion. Many financial analysts were stumped by the deal. It appeared to make no business sense. But the LinkedIn deal is the key to EdTech.

LinkedIn has 433 million users: the biggest recruitment database on earth. Attaching this database to a child's pre-LinkedIn history means tracking from four to sixteen and beyond, determining employability from childhood to middle age.

By linking school 'career' and actual career and making them a continuum of monitoring, Microsoft have the potential to create the ultimate employment profile for a potential boss, tracking levels of conformity at any point in their lives.

At a job interview, the question becomes: 'Why did you go off the rails with your results when you were twelve, and again at work when you were thirty-six?' You create the most unquestioning employees on the planet: people who will work from day one of their school careers like robots.

The EdTech race is on. Microsoft have created the 'school in a box'. Google want to be first to plant their flag in EdTech, too. The sales pitch for Chromebook is that it is 'the foundation for a one-hundred-per-cent web classroom'.

THE CAR-WASH PARADOX

Teachers in academies have begun to notice an interesting shift. Children are able to pass tests and tick boxes spectacularly, but when it comes to interviews, they clam up. They are so used to conforming to rules, they do not know how to question them.

In this new world of robot children growing up to be robot employees, old-fashioned schools will still exist. Private ones will continue to teach Greek and Latin and play rugby on playing fields. These playing fields are symbolic. They send out a message: they broadcast ownership. We own education.

In these selective, 'elite' schools, future politicians, and CEOs who will employ the human robots in warehouses and fast-food chains, will continue to have their minds broadened and be taught to question the question, just as Aristotle defined education two thousand years ago.

However, as Mitra discovered with his hole-in-the-wall computer in New Delhi and Flex Tech are discovering in San Diego, technology can do miraculous things as well as further enslave. Children have the whole of human history and knowledge at their fingertips on a phone and are creating their own path to the future, regardless of what educationalists or tech entrepreneurs have planned for them. Technological advance and the speed at which work is revolutionised are the unstoppable givens. The response of the human gatekeepers is to prepare for the storm.

As Sean at Flex Tech told me, 'The children you see in front of you will have ten, twenty, maybe fifty jobs in their lifetime. Who knows? What we are teaching them is not a lump of knowledge, but how to adapt and pick up new skills continuously. That is the only way they will survive.'

But for those who are not able to take command of their destiny, algorithms will tell them what to do. Robots will not replace them, they will be the boss. In fact, they already are.

Take a delivery driver. He or she makes forty or fifty deliveries in a day. Algorithms decide where they go next and if that last delivery was late. The algorithm can question why you turned left at that last junction, instead of right. You would have saved two minutes thirty-seven seconds if you had turned right.

In the future, ten such small errors a day and you will be ten deliveries down on your target. You will have cost yourself £40. Four days a week like that and you will not be able to pay your mortgage.

The first industrial revolution, after its initial technological disruption, created hundreds of millions of jobs. It did not lead to the end of work, it led to its total reinvention. Workers could organise and campaign for better wages by forming trade unions. Employers had no choice but to form a social contract with unions because workers held the cards. Their labour value was high.

This second industrial revolution – the robot revolution – is the same as the first one in one key respect. It will transform employment, and not in an obvious way.

Instead of ending human jobs, it could lead to full employment with the creation of billions of low-paid, routine manual and non-routine manual jobs. The difference from the first industrial revolution is that this time, there is zero value to labour. Companies can pay what they want and we will be grateful for it.

This, in effect, is the robot swap. As robots become the boss, managing the logistics of our work, we become the robots working to their algorithmic program of efficiency.

We are seeing the beginning of this now, but have trouble computing this paradox of full employment on super-low income, because we still work with an economic paradigm of wage inflation and full-time employment created in the first half of the twentieth century. We cannot square the circle, but we will.

Seemingly contradictory economic trends happening in tandem will be the norm for the robot age: ever-rising employment with ever-lower wages. Precarious employment on casual terms for an amount we cannot live on, accurately reported as 'full employment'. This is the final irony of the robot age – it will deliver full human employment on ten per cent of the wages.

For this squared circle to function and not result in social unrest, it requires another piece of the equation to work: prices for basics like food and heating to stay at an historic low.

In February 2017, David Freeman, a senior statistician at the ONS, explained how the squaring of the circle is working: 'The unemployment rate is now at its lowest in over a decade, but wage growth remains subdued by historical standards.'[24]

In the meantime, the robots are coming to oversee cheap labour from a fully employed workforce. Paul Mason calls this paradox 'the economics of the car wash'.[25]

The machine car wash of the 1970s promised a sparkling robot clean for your Ford Capri. Big furry buds would roll all over your car, leaving it spotless and shining.

But since 2010, something unexpected has happened. Automated car washes have disappeared and been replaced by small gangs of humans frantically working over your car with sponges and cloths. Car washes are not showpiece machines working on ostentatious display as the centrepiece of a garage as they were in the 1970s. They now exist tucked away in cheap dead spaces: old disused car parks and derelict gas station forecourts. They pop up and disappear again in days.

The humans that replaced the machine can wash a car in half the time; they do a better job because they are terrified they will lose their job; and here is the key thing, they cost less.

The automated car wash broke down, needed servicing and constant human attention. It was not the shiny future it promised, it became a cumbersome headache and stopped paying its way. And so, the automated car wash has become a model for how all work could go: humans replacing machines you pay nothing, who look after themselves, and need only the stick of unemployment to make them work harder.

This is the future of work. Watson in the control centre, an unblinking blue eye monitoring how many cars you and I are able to wash in an hour.

THE HUMAN BUSINESS

Are we inevitably, structurally doomed? No. Only if we continue to see ourselves as passive employees of ghosts of companies, rather than boss of ourselves. One who need not be a slave of the business we choose to run.

The explosion of small businesses in unpromising nooks and crannies around the planet over the last decade is unprecedented – from the 'maker movement' using artisanal handcraft skills such as knife-making, bread baking, or micro-brewing, through to 'interstitial' data specialists scraping niche intel off tech giants like pilot fish on whales, offering numbers on everything from differentials on flat rentals to the comparative margins on life-saving drugs.

Across the world, and most markedly in Africa and India, mobile money has allowed small businesses like food wholesalers and electrical goods suppliers actually to run books as businesses without need of a bank or bank account. In towns and cities from São Paulo to Copenhagen, people sit on laptops in Starbucks conjuring up the next insane but highly investible Fintech innovation, whether it be a cryptocurrency of virtual bananas or a gamified trading app based on Crash Bandicoot.

Between 2010 and 2016, the number of such small businesses in Britain alone hit a record high of 5.5 million, increasing twenty-three per cent in just six years. But these are not entrepreneurs in the 1980s sense of the word. 'Social good' apps designed round community needs like 'Uber childcare' (pooled and flexible rather than overpriced and inflexible) or jogging and fitness apps that involve visiting someone elderly and isolated as part of your routine. All are ingenious life hacks built into a business idea and testament to a potential future built around people, not algorithms.

These are businesses built by exploiting the cracks opening in the new world and engaging with two seeming opposites: the data revolution and the widening holes in the fabric of society.

Social entrepreneurship was once a fad, but is now a given first line of a pitch for a start-up looking for investment from angel investors in the City. This is not altruism on the investors' part but good business. Offering tangible benefit to the vulnerable in society as a by-product of your product makes it a shrewd investment at a time when the state is retracting comprehensive care: unable and unwilling to pay for the sick, the old and the isolated. Social entrepreneurship is stepping in selectively where the state once operated as a comprehensive welfare blanket. Will it replace the state? No. Is it ethical? It's happening.

It is possible to see a way through the atomising society to a better future. The generation beginning businesses now see their business and the challenges facing society as fundamentally linked. What the world looks like when this particular kind of entrepreneur steps up to regain control over the robot future is anybody's guess, but it is the not inconsiderable task ahead.

CHAPTER THIRTEEN
TECHNOLOGY: FIVE COMPANIES TO RULE US ALL

The Deal: Demis Hassabis, Shane Legg and Mustafa
   Suleyman, founders of Artificial Intelligence start-up
   DeepMind, sell their company after just two years
   to Google – Larry Page says it's the most important
   acquisition Google has ever made
Aim: To put the brain inside the Google machine,
   utilising DeepMind's work on decoding the DNA of
   intelligence to change the world
Where: Googleplex, Mountain View, California
When: December 2014

Imagine you turned on your computer and Google had gone. Next you turned on your iPhone. Black screen. Facebook, Twitter, Amazon and Microsoft had been wiped out, too.

It could not happen. Except that in 2007, it did: with the banks.

Overnight, the world was engulfed by the biggest financial crisis since 1929. No one predicted it, bar some bank insiders not powerful enough to be listened to, and some maverick financiers who foresaw the whole thing and shorted on it.[1]

The banks that were allowed to go under were not too big to fail, but the 'Big Five' tech giants are. When Lehman Brothers went bust, the banking system did not collapse. But the Big Five are so deeply enmeshed in the functioning of Planet Earth, they cannot be allowed to go under. They are not an addendum to the system; they are the system.

The key difference between the banks and the tech giants is this: when you have a heart attack, the blood can still be pumped artificially to the brain. But if the brain stops, you are dead. The banks pump the blood, but the Big Five tech giants are the brain.

This is how the brain breaks down in numbers: in just one year, 2016, Apple had revenue of $233 billion with profit of $53 billion, assets of $239 billion, and market cap of $586 billion. Alphabet (Google) did comparable numbers. Microsoft, Amazon and Facebook took the other chairs at the Big Five table in diminishing order of size. But their size is not what matters. The banks could be bailed out by government, but the tech giants are bigger than any one government. They built the world we live in and they own the keys.

Government could bail out the banks, because banks do only one real job: provide liquidity. When banks judder to a halt, governments pump money back into the system. For all the deliberate impenetrability of banking argot, what they actually do is remarkably straightforward: lend you money they themselves have borrowed.

What is a bank? 'Bank' is purely another word for other people's money and specifically, other people's debts.[2]

Before 2007, banks, like economists, operated behind a façade of competence, using the impenetrability of financial language successfully as a protective wall to keep people from asking too many questions. Like the modern-day use of Latin, its true purpose was to exclude. On Wall Street, the only really important calculations before the crash were to work out how long the charade could be kept going.

Once the myth of the competence of banks was blown by the crash, banks had to operate behind a different façade: independence. Since the bailout, banks have been a nationalised industry held up by the grace of taxpayers' money, yet masquerading as independent. Banks are like petulant children in a playground. They think they are able to do everything themselves, but when something goes wrong, they call in the adults to sort it out.

The tech companies do not. They don't need anyone. This is because they do not simply operate above and beyond the scope of any one national government. They have manoeuvred themselves into a position where no one else can step in and do their job.

THE RHIZOME

The Big Five are not actually tech companies at all. Together, they form five interlocking parts of a hugely complex machine unlike any seen before.

No one controls this machine, because tech companies are the unwitting fulfilment of an idea formulated by the French philosophers Gilles Deleuze and Felix Guattari in their 1980 treatise, 'A Thousand Plateaus'.[3]

Deleuze and Guattari said the future destiny of capitalism lay not in its control by individuals with agency, but its mutation into a self-sustaining organism. In this new capitalism of a 'thousand plateaus', there was no hierarchical structure or bogeyman pulling the strings behind the scenes, only an impossibly complicated matrix of intersections; interwoven, overlapping and all-encompassing.

Deleuze and Guattari called this structure a 'rhizome': a term from botany to describe a vast root system growing fast and horizontally outwards in every direction.

Banks are not rhizomes, because they are finite entities with one overarching role, lending. But the Big Five tech companies have created the root system for trillions of transactions every millisecond of every day, between you, me and all the businesses on earth.

These transactions are not solely financial – we post and

search oceans of information: videos, pictures, shares, vines, memes, likes and dislikes, we rate everything and transact advice, comment and pass opinion on nothing and everything. This sub-universe of data transactions, a continuous, fizzing digital world, is perpetually auctioned by algorithms sifting the digital detritus for sellable data.

To be able to even conceptualise these digital auctions is like playing 3-D chess in space. As you stick a word in Google, an infinite hall of algorithmic mirrors opens up without beginning or end, reflecting forever to the data horizon.

For the moment, banks and tech companies have reached an accommodation on data and payment systems – they work together – since accommodation is easier than a fight. But this relationship is lopsided, because the rhizome of tech companies is ever expanding, and potentially limitless. Long-term, banks need tech companies, but tech companies do not need banks, whom they will ultimately subsume into the rhizome.

SHAVING A MILLIONTH OF A
SECOND = A BILLION DOLLARS

I am on the roof of a tower block in New Jersey looking back to Wall Street. A light flashes fifteen miles away through thunder-ous clouds, beaming from the top of One World Trade Center, the tallest building on Manhattan, built on the site of the Twin Towers.

You would think Wall Street was the nerve centre of global finance, but Wall Street cannot function without the infrastruc-ture of the tech companies.

In 2010, the fibre-optic company Spread Networks built a data centre in an anonymous suburban part of New Jersey. The location – 1600 MacArthur Boulevard, Mahwah – was deliber-ate. The Spread Networks data centre for the New York Stock Exchange is a huge foreboding structure without windows on anonymous scrubland, protected by thousands of security cameras and electric fencing.

The data centre cost $300 million to build and provided a fibre-optic tunnel to Wall Street, allowing transactions to take place 0.7 of a millisecond faster between New York and Chicago. This infinitesimal increase in speed translated to billions more dollars transacted every second.

But it was not fast enough. A couple of years later and only a few miles away from Mahwah, on the top of the desolate tower block I am standing on, a laser technology company rented space on the rubbish-strewn roof to shave a further 4 milliseconds off a transaction. Huge white machines bristling with wires and antennae hum quietly; machines facing One World Trade Center communicating at light speed in code with machines facing Asia.

The block itself is poor project housing: the flats are damp; shouts and screams fill the corridors intermingled with the heavy smell of weed. But just above the heads of these residents, billions of dollars are being beamed every millisecond from Wall Street to the rest of the world. It is perhaps the most extreme convergence of incalculable wealth and poverty within a few metres of each other anywhere on the planet.

THE SAGRADA FAMÍLIA

In 1882, Antoni Gaudí began work on La Sagrada Família cathedral in Barcelona. Forty years into construction, Gaudí was asked when he thought his extraordinary creation – spiralling up above the Barcelona skyline and without a single straight line – might finally be finished. Never, Gaudí replied. It is alive and the very process of living is itself completion.

Like the Sagrada Família, the Big Five tech giants are in a perpetual state of becoming. Constantly striking out laterally by strategically acquiring companies that speak to the bigger plan, but make no sense to anyone else.

Google, Microsoft and Amazon plough profit relentlessly back into R&D and new acquisitions, because their eyes are on a distant prize only those within the top echelon are privy to. Bill Gates put this limitless ambition and necessity to mutate the plan in a simple aphorism: 'We overestimate what we can do in two years, and underestimate what we can do in ten.'[4]

The Big Five are the central roots of the rhizome from which everything we do flows. These companies are not only too big to fail, they are too big to define, because they are perpetually mutating and expanding what they do. Not one of the Big Five is focused now on what it was doing six months ago.

This leads to fevered speculation about what they are really up to and the inevitable conspiracy theories this creates.

In his 2013 novel *The Circle*, Dave Eggers makes a thinly veiled attack on a cult-like tech company, with its utopian rhetoric, sealed-off tech 'campus' and smiling, evangelical employees hiding a sinister plan for world domination.

The title of the book refers to the long-term goal of this imaginary tech giant: completion of 'The Circle'. Absolute control over every moment of our lives, and all under the perpetual gaze of an unblinking eye that sees and knows everything about us.[5]

Conspiracy theories package messy truth into a childishly simple plan executed by a handful of fiendish individuals in a room. But with *The Circle*, Dave Eggers described an all-controlling version of a fictional company that was an amalgam of the Big Five: a version that the Big Five tech giants could well argue is not so much a searing critique but actually undersells their ambition.

In 2015, Google became the least interesting subsidiary of Alphabet, a new umbrella company headed by Google's founders, Sergey Brin and Larry Page, and with a mind-boggling collection of new acquisitions.

Alphabet's aim is simple: to seek to improve the very nature of what it is to be human. What humans do, what humans are made of and how our brains function. This is not hyperbole, it is simply what they are about.

Alphabet's interests and acquisitions range from bio-tech (Life Sciences) to cracking longevity and eternal life (Calico); space; driverless cars; flying cars; the internet of things (smart everything); next-stage drone-delivery systems; using technology to leapfrog infrastructure gaps in the developing world; EdTech; pollution and global-warming solutions; nano-technology: in-body tech hacks, such as injectable nano-robots and microscopic DNA devices that fight leukemia, or nano-gels that secrete insulin to tackle diabetes.

The founders believe that being seen as 'just' a company is wide of the mark.[6] Alphabet are like an independent state hacking their way into the future.

Alphabet's acquisition of DeepMind marked their intention to begin decoding the very essence of intelligence: what it is, how it works, and how humans and machines will interact and communicate when intelligence has been cracked. What singularity will actually look and feel like.

Alphabet have honed this ambition to a single word: knowledge. Decoding it, and owning it. Dave Eggers's *Circle* conspiracy for a fictional tech giant did not do justice to the scope of ambition of a real one.

On 10 August 2015, CEO Larry Page explained what Google's metamorphosis into Alphabet meant. 'As Sergey (Brin) and I wrote in the original founders' letter eleven years ago: "Google is not a conventional company. We do not intend to become one." We did a lot of things that seemed crazy at the time. Crazy things (that) now have a billion users like Google Maps, YouTube, Chrome and Android.[7]

'We've long believed that over time companies tend to get comfortable doing the same thing, just making incremental changes. But in the technology industry, where revolutionary ideas drive the next big growth areas, you need to be a bit uncomfortable.'

Much was made of Alphabet's decision to drop the Google promise of twenty years ago: 'to do no evil'. But Alphabet are not evil, nor intend to do evil. They have their eyes fixed on a distant point beyond. On a world entirely rebuilt from data insight. A world they will control.

THE FIRST GOOGLE

The grand tech ambitions of the Big Five began a long time ago. In 1997, I was in Seattle visiting the Microsoft campus. Microsoft had the same ambitions then that Google have today and were seeking to do something equally amazing: write a universal language for what we then called 'computers'.

In 1997, there was no iPhone. No Facebook, Amazon or Google. Apple, run by outsider genius Steve Jobs, was considered a failing company stuck in the 1970s, resigned to cult status making expensive computers. Microsoft, not Apple, was king. On their 'campus' deep in the forest, they were writing the code to make a new world. They called this new world the 'digital world'.

Their CEO, Bill Gates, lived in a $60 million mansion on Puget Sound accessible by boat. Over the bay were the palatial homes of other Seattle icons with growing brands such as Howard Shultz, the CEO of Starbucks. Gates was rarely there, but one detail about his house emerged that encapsulated the snobbery against him and the coming tech takeover of the world.

Gates's vast property – Xanadu 2.0, named in homage to *Citizen Kane* – with its sixty-foot swimming pool playing underwater music, 2,500 square-foot gym, artificial river stocked with salmon, and a beach with imported sand from Hawaii, also had state-of-the-art technology.[8]

Each bedroom and corridor was rumoured to be filled with 'plasma screens'. In 1997, this was an amazing and extravagant thing to own. They were said to line the long corridors like oil paintings.

Instead of having actual paintings, Gates would press a remote control and be able to access the world's greatest artworks via a blocky pixelated image on a screen. Gates could turn his house into the Louvre or MoMA in a moment, a blurry *Mona Lisa* staring out as he prepared his granola breakfast.

A famous English novelist who lived in Seattle at the time and despised Gates asked him at a private party why he did not buy the original paintings. He had enough money. Plasma screens were such bad taste and surely anyone would rather have the real thing if they could?

Why? Gates replied. Those paintings are owned by the public. They are not for sale, and everyone in the world should have access to them via a plasma screen.

A decade later, when Gates's friend and former colleague Steve Jobs transformed Apple with the iPhone, everyone was given the equivalent of a mobile plasma screen and could suddenly have access to the world's art galleries. Bill Gates was right and the novelist was wrong.

When I arrived at the Microsoft campus in 1997, land-scaped to be low and unobtrusive in the forest near Redmond, it looked more like a Buddhist retreat than a tech company. Inside was a different story. Twenty-something coders lived on campus in a perpetual state of intense, frenzied industry. They would code for ten- to eighteen-hour stretches, drinking endless Coke and coffee, then crashing out to wake with their face in a stale pizza. They were Jesuitical in their belief in Microsoft.

These coders lived in small cells customised to look like student dorms with posters of obscure grunge bands and the obligatory Einstein or Jim Morrison. There were piles of takeaway cartons and more pizza boxes, floppy discs for coding strewn across the floor, and somewhere beneath the detritus, their Microsoft pass on a chain.

Their boundless devotion and unstoppable obsession with coding the future, and doing it for the company, was clearly genuine. And naturally approved of and promoted by Microsoft, who created an entirely self-contained community on campus.

There was a supermarket, restaurants, gyms, a spiritual garden, date nights, Cuban-dancing Thursday, and a cinema club showing French New Wave films. Very similar in fact to the fictional tech campus described in *The Circle* by Dave Eggers twenty years later.

Coders earnestly rushing around campus had a quiet air of world-historic determination about them, like slacker versions of code breakers at Bletchley Park. They knew they were important, making the future by inventing a new language that would soon be spoken all over the world: 'Windows' – the operating system to be spoken by every machine on earth.

One morning, I stopped a young coder in the canteen and asked him whether he felt like a 'Microserf' – the term coined by author Douglas Coupland to describe a slave coder at Microsoft.[9] Wasn't he a bit of a shmuck for giving away his intellectual property (IP) in exchange for a wage, rather than shares in the company? He seemed genuinely amazed by the question. 'I'm not a slave,' he said. 'I'm privileged to be here.' I pointed out to him the strange rootless ambiance of the campus. Coding deep in a forest, you could be anywhere in the world: Kyoto, Adelaide or Finland. It does not even feel like America. 'That's true,' he said, musing, 'but I'm not an American. I'm a citizen of Microsoft.'

THE 'SOMEONE IN A GARAGE GUNNING FOR US' MYTH

Twenty years on, millenials see themselves as citizens of their belief system, rather than the nation they were born in. They have greater affinity with peers who share their moral outlook three continents away than with neighbours in close geographical proximity who hate immigrants or gays.

Microsoft understood back in the mid-1990s the importance of an employer tapping into this global belief system – this moral rather than geographical citizenship – and utilising this belief to make them believers in Microsoft. A complete alignment of employee and corporate morality which creates total devotion to the brand. This is why the 'citizens' of the Big Five tech giants, for whom Microsoft provided the template, are together creating an immense, aggressively expansionist eco-system. Because they have the hearts and minds of the foot soldiers to do it.

People who work for these companies, from the top to the bottom, believe one hundred per cent in the evangelical mission of their founders. Zen-like masters whose pronouncements are treated like pronouncements from Buddha. The employee's identity and self-esteem are umbilically tied to the success of the company and if they work for one and move on to another, they simply transfer their zeal: zealots trying a new religion.

Even we believe in the brands. They have so entrenched themselves in our lives, made themselves so indispensable, railing against them is like saying you are against sunlight or the ocean.

Tech analyst Farhad Manjoo believes that however powerful they are now, we have not seen anything yet. 'They have built several enormous technologies that are central to just about everything we do. In tech jargon, they own many of the world's most valuable platforms – the basic building blocks on which every other business depends. These platforms are inescapable; you may opt out of one or two of them, but together, they form a gilded mesh blanketing the entire economy.'[10]

In 2016, these five tech giants made up half of the world's top ten most valuable companies. Their wealth stems from their control of the inescapable digital infrastructure on which much of the rest of the economy depends – mobile phones, social networks, the web, the cloud, retail and logistics, and the data and computing power required for future breakthroughs.[11]

But this is where the tech ends and the rest of the world – the physical world – begins as an opportunity. Since 2012, they have begun to set their sights on the biggest industries outside tech: cars, healthcare, retail, transportation, film, music entertainment, and taking over from the banks.[12]

The great myth of Silicon Valley is what Alphabet's Eric Schmidt calls 'someone in a garage, gunning for us'. Someone, somewhere, inventing a new idea that challenges the hegemony of the Big Five.[13]

The truth is that it won't happen, and Schmidt knows it. These companies were pioneers on the digital frontier and they own it for good. But now they are expanding onto everyone else's land and they will own that, too.

THE WOLF THAT TURNED INTO A DOG

You can understand the level of their ambition when you see how they are redefining what they do. Alphabet seek to own the DNA of knowledge itself and then apply this knowledge of knowledge to everything we do.

Amazon seek to reshape our world by transforming the nature of delivery and service, becoming every shop and every service using robots. In 2016, Amazon's founder, Jeff Bezos, trialled their first physical store in Seattle without humans, only robots, and no money passing hands.

Amazon Go is a 1,800 square-foot supermarket selling everything from food, drinks and groceries to clothes and books. You go in, scan an app as you enter, pick up what you want and walk out. No money is paid. Sensors throughout the store identify the items and charge them to your account.

But that's not even the clever bit. Thousands of cameras track your movements and by looking at these movements in the store, tracking you and your phone as you browse, Amazon are able to collect data not only on what you bought, but did not buy: what you considered or put back. It is a treasure trove of data and these nudgeable 'live' decisions you will make next week, rather than 'dead' purchases you made today, are where data becomes gold.[14]

Beyond running robot supermarkets, Amazon seek to revolutionise all service delivery using drones: whether it be food, a book, or emergency triage at a traffic accident in India.

In this new world, Microsoft are the central operating cortex. They built the rails on which ever faster, smoother and 'frictionless' services run. Microsoft are no longer a tech company: they are a linguistics provider who invented the global language of Windows that machines speak.

Apple no longer seeks to merely produce phones, tablets and laptops, it seeks to be the platform for all commerce and the organising brain for a digital world: running the networks driverless cars move smoothly round, or the interface for humans and robots to converse with.

Facebook's ambitions are different. They seek to become the world's biggest vault of human data. As the largest data-bank on earth, holding intimate details on the lives of 1.8 billion people culled from photos, likes and dislikes, friend networks, and expressions of hopes, fears and expectations embedded in posts, Facebook will become the most powerful repository of human behaviour ever created.

Algorithms are the tool for making this happen and for the first time are ingratiating themselves properly with their quarry: human beings. How they do this is similar to how wolves became dogs.

Wolves were predatory animals that found it tough to get meat in winter, so ingratiated themselves and allowed themselves to be domesticated in order to guarantee food. We thought we were in charge, but the wolf was. Algorithms are the digital wolf.

We humans know this and resist the slide into algorithm dependency. In 2016, a paper called 'Algorithm Aversion' by University of Pennsylvania's Berkeley Dietvorst, Joseph Simmons and Cade Massey for the *Journal of Experimental Psychology* concluded that humans mistakenly continue to believe their judgment to be better than algorithms. We use this human bias to reinforce a fallacy of human superiority.

At this moment in history, the fallacy needs to be shored up for psychological reasons: humans are attempting to hold on to what makes them human at the very moment they see it slipping away forever.[15]

As an example of this human bias, the Penn University report cited the example of pilot error in plane crashes. The likelihood of a crash has been reduced dramatically by ground-proximity warning systems and autopilot. This is statistical proof that machines can outperform humans, but we humans do not want to know.

In everything from medical diagnosis to meteorology and finance, algorithms could at least match and usually surpass human analysis. Algorithms could more accurately predict the likelihood of a convict lapsing back into crime, or a start-up going bust.[16]

Yet in spite of this, humans are determined to think they are better. Google Maps only has to send you down a slower road once, or a playlist choose a depressing record when you are feeling OK, and we cite this anomaly as proof of the fallibility of algorithms.

The most glaring example is driverless cars. More than 30,000 people are killed each year in car crashes in the US. Ninety per cent are down to human error. The *Harvard Business Review* estimates that driverless cars could save up to 1.5 million lives in the US and up to 50 million globally over the next fifty years.

Yet in a March 2016 poll by the American Automobile Association, seventy-five per cent of American drivers said they don't care about the facts, they do not trust a driverless car.

In spite of this, we are slowly tipping from open distrust of algorithms to grudging trust and this is because algorithms are underscoring basic needs and tasks throughout the day: viewing suggestions, cheapest flights, most compatible dating partner. We are beginning to see the error of our ways and trusting the data. The wolf is turning itself into a dog.

ALL HAIL THE NEW GOD: 'DATA-ISM'

If we hand over life-changing decisions to algorithms, what will this mean? In 2013, Angelina Jolie took a genetic profiling test and discovered she carried a dangerous mutation of the BRCA1 gene. This gave her an eighty-seven per cent statistical likelihood of developing breast cancer. Though she was not ill, she made the rational decision to have a double mastectomy. This was preventive, data-driven decision-making. Any resistance to this would come from human bias, otherwise known as emotion.

In medicine, data can be used to determine a black-and-white decision. Emotion is extremely resistant to being overridden, but when overwhelming evidence that you might die is presented, it is. The trust we once put in doctors, we are now putting in numbers, and to such an unquestioning degree that historian Yuval Harari calls data a new secular religion: 'Data-ism'.

'Just as divine authority was legitimised by religious mythologies, and human authority was legitimised by humanist ideologies, so high-tech gurus and Silicon Valley prophets are creating a new universal narrative that legitimises the authority of algorithms and big data.

'This novel creed may be called Data-ism. In its extreme form, proponents of the Data-ist worldview perceive the entire universe as a flow of data, see organisms as little more than biochemical algorithms, and believe that humanity's cosmic vocation is to create an all-encompassing data-processing system, and then merge into it. We are already becoming tiny chips inside a giant system that nobody really understands.'[17]

Data-ism is a new God, because data understands us better than we understand ourselves. It does not get clouded by human bias. 'We are now,' Harari says, 'at the confluence of two scientific tidal waves. On the one hand biologists are deciphering the mysteries of the human body and, in particular, of the brain and human feelings. At the same time, computer scientists are giving us unprecedented data-processing power. When you put the two together, you get external systems that can monitor and understand feelings better than we can.'[18]

Robots already designed to read a human's feelings through facial recognition can give accurate and nuanced readings of shifts in emotion – data that humans might choose to ignore about ourselves, because it may create discomfort to register. Big Data systems already know us better than we know ourselves, but now we are on the cusp of believing and acquiescing to it. When this happens, authority – not simply number-crunching – will shift from humans to algorithms. Once it was the Catholic Church and the KGB who knew everything about us and this was unquestioningly accepted. Now, that theocratic mantle is to be handed to the tech giants.

To see the Big Five as humanity's enemy seems perverse. Are these companies really as Orwellian as they sound? Take a look at Sergey Brin, Tim Cook or Mark Zuckerberg. They do not look like bad guys. They wear T-shirts from Gap, drive electric cars (if they drive at all – Zuckerberg cycles to work) and give extraordinary amounts of money to charity. They do not appear to want to control every aspect of our lives and turn us into cyborgs.

Their stated mission is to do the opposite of control us. They want to set us free from poverty, inequality, global warming and disease. What they have is power and the potential to bring about colossal change. Like Robert Dall, the man who invented securitisation on Wall Street leading to subprime and the banking crash, and who compared himself to Robert Oppenheimer, they have done the tech equivalent of split the atom. How they choose to use that colossal power is what we are waiting to see.

IF A SUPER-INTELLIGENT MACHINE DECIDED TO GET RID OF US, I THINK IT WOULD DO SO PRETTY EFFICIENTLY

In December 2014, three young Londoners flew to Los Angeles to do a deal. Demis Hassabis, Shane Legg and Mustafa Suleyman were the founders of DeepMind Technologies, a small AI company in East London. They were on their way to cut a deal with Larry Page of Google.

No one on that flight knew it, but the three men sitting in row 43 were on their way to sign the most far-reaching deal in history.

DeepMind had come onto Google's radar within three years of starting. Unlike every other artificial intelligence start-up on earth, they did not concern themselves with the human/machine 'interface' – the functionality of machines and brains, and their interaction.

DeepMind was about something more fundamental. The root of intelligence. Not artificial or human intelligence. All intelligence. DeepMind had gone back to first principles: humans and robots are both merely outer shells driven by decodable intelligence. If you decode that intelligence, you understand how anything works, and you rule the world.

At Googleplex, Mountain View, California, the three young Londoners and Larry Page shook hands on the deal. Google paid $650 million for a company barely three years old. It was not only the most important deal in Google's history. It was the most important deal for humankind.

In creating the planet's most popular search engine, Google had built the most powerful machine on earth. But in buying DeepMind, Google has the potential to own intelligence. They could then put the brain inside the Google machine.

What does a brain inside the Google machine mean? The Google DeepMind deal opened the door to the creation of a new organism from what DeepMind call 'cognitive machine tissue'. Neither living nor dead, but cognisant. An entirely new species.

DeepMind's founder, Shane Legg, was remarkably upbeat and post-human about what this new species meant when interviewed in 2011.

'Eventually I think human extinction will probably occur, and technology will likely play a role in this.' Asked if he thought humans would suffer, he said, 'If by suffering you mean prolonged suffering, then I think this is quite unlikely. If a super-intelligent machine decided to get rid of us, I think it would do so pretty efficiently. I don't think we will deliberately design super-intelligent machines to maximise human suffering.'[19]

Elon Musk, a man not easily overawed by a dystopian future, was staggered. He called artificial intelligence 'more dangerous than nukes'. Stephen Hawking said it would 'end mankind'.

But Legg was simply being 'post-human' about the way events were going to pan out. Once intelligence is decoded and the brain is in the machine, why do humans have moral primacy over any other form: living or machine?

It was merely logical that once you connect cognitive machine tissue, an organism is created that can decide whether humans are needed or not.

For technology that would make us extinct, the Google DeepMind deal garnered remarkably little response from the rest of the human race. Stephen Hawking said an independent ethics committee was needed to scrutinise DeepMind's research, as it took us deeper into a brave new future. But it never happened.

The incredible thing is that no matter how terrifying the DeepMind deal appears, it does not stop there. A Pandora's box has been opened that neither Google nor DeepMind can shut, nor control. And they were about to get a glimpse of what that meant.

THE ROBOT LANGUAGE HUMANS CAN'T UNDERSTAND

In September 2016, Google Brain – the AI research department of which DeepMind was now a subsidiary – turned on something called the Google Neural Machine Translation (GNMT).

GNMT is a program that allows machines to translate entire languages in the blink of an eye. It is first given an example of translation. It then scans entire sentences in the foreign language, gives the translation of that sentence, then extrapolates the whole language from these individual sentences.

After a month or so, researcher Mike Schuster at Google Brain began to notice something strange. Machines were blindly translating entire languages without being given the translation first. Schuster saw translations between Korean and Japanese, when Korean-to-Japanese examples had not even been shown to the system.[20]

Then the machines started going one step further. The system began making 'reasonable' translations of languages it had not even been taught to translate. Google Brain's AI machine was taught Portuguese to English and English to Spanish. It then began to translate from Portuguese directly to Spanish. 'To our knowledge, this is the first demonstration of true multilingual, zero-shot translation.' Schuster said, as perplexed as he was astounded.[21]

However, it was what happened next that really concerned the programmers. The machine began creating its own entirely new language.

'Visual interpretation of the results shows that these models learn a form of interlingua representation for the multilingual model between all involved language pairs,' Schuster said.

An 'interlingua' is a type of artificial language which is used to fulfil a specific purpose. In this case, the interlingua was being used by the machine to explain how unseen material could be translated.

'Using a three-dimensional representation of internal network data, we were able to take a peek into the system as it translated a set of sentences between all possible pairs of the Japanese, Korean, and English languages,' the research team wrote in a blog spot.[22]

The neural network was 'encoding something' about the semantics of a sentence, rather than comparing phrase-to-phrase translations. No one could quite work out what this 'something' was.

The system was inventing a language. An entirely new encrypted language only other machines had the capacity to learn. Humans would be shut out, because they did not have the computing power to decode it.

'We interpret this as a sign of existence of an interlingua in the network,' the team said. The machines had invented a machine language by working out the rules of what a language was and then creating their own. But they had taken it upon themselves to make an encrypted language for other machines, keeping humans out. The wolves that became dogs were becoming wolves again.

When I asked IBM Watson programmer Dave Ferrucci what he made of this new machine language, he expressed no emotion.

'It's scary, Dave. Don't you think?' 'It's an interlingua. It's there to solve a problem.' But it's a new language. 'Sure, yes. It's a new language. But are the machines ahead of the race with humans? Not yet.' Not yet.

The lesson from the GNMT experiment is clear. We think we can control this, but we cannot. Humans may have set this journey off, but machines will decide where it leads.

Alphabet, the umbrella company for Google, may have dropped 'Do no evil' from their pledge, but humans will not be doing the evil, machines will. And it won't be evil, it will simply be the logical imperative of code.

THE TRADE-OFF

In 2016, DeepMind suddenly popped up back in London. The *New Scientist* revealed what Google were up to next. They were secretly negotiating a deal with the Royal Free NHS Trust operating Barnet, Chase Farm and Royal Free hospitals, and which holds the confidential data of 1.6 million patients.[23]

The deal would allow DeepMind to access millions of highly sensitive records without the consent of patients. Everything from data on acute care, accident and emergency to pathology, radiology, HIV and abortion stats.

Then in 2017, they showed their hand. Google announced the launch of Streams, an app that triggers mobile alerts when a patient's vital signs or blood results are flagged as abnormal.

'Ten thousand people a year are dying from acute kidney injury,' DeepMind's Mustafa Suleyman said. 'These are entirely preventable deaths. We can trigger an alert that allows nurses or doctors to take preventative action, like giving intravenous antibiotics when your kidneys are dehydrated, to prevent escalation to the ICU.'

Streams appears to be a remarkable piece of technology, but it is also a foot in the door. It will initially be used to spot people at risk of kidney problems, but is due to be expanded over the next five years. And the clue to understanding what it will do next comes in DeepMind's claims for it.

Suleyman sees Streams becoming key to the everyday running of the hospital. Not solely detecting acute conditions such as blood poisoning, but – and here's the key phrase – 'coordinating patient treatment'. Technology will sit at the beating heart of the hospital, algorithms not doctors potentially deciding what care you get, and Google holding the keys to the data.

Critics of the deal saw it as profoundly dangerous. Cambridge University's Julia Powles, and Hal Hodson called the deal with the NHS 'inexcusable' and DeepMind's claims for Streams 'specious'.[24]

Google hit back quickly. An article appeared in technology magazine *Wired* claiming that Streams was 'saving NHS nurses two hours a day.'[25] Suleyman then followed up by announcing DeepMind were developing a bitcoin-style racking of patient data using blockchain technology to protect it.[26]

Google was beginning the fight to win the hearts and minds of a sceptical public and healthcare professionals. Trust us, they were saying. And this is the trade-off.

Take 1.6 million patients data-mined (ten million if it is rolled out nationally) and what do you get in return? The cutting-edge technology you desperately need and the alleviation of pressure on the scarce time and meagre resources of frontline staff.

Technology enables a silent takeover of the health system, but DeepMind would say this is not a zero-sum game: you may all be patient zero, but you benefit. Using DeepMind, Google can steal a march on their Big Five competitors in the NHS and more lucratively, the biggest goldmine of the twenty-first century: global healthcare.

Hooking up with the World Health Organisation and the NGOs on the ground to roll out health systems across the developing world, the tech giants are the new shining knights in white convertible jeeps.

Once upon a time it was the Red Cross and Médecins Sans Frontières who did the triage in medical disasters, but with the funding crisis in British and American healthcare, the triage zone has widened exponentially and hence the potential market that can be captured when these health systems of the developed world collapse, too.

ONE RING TO RULE THEM ALL

In *Minority Report*, the 2002 movie adaptation of the Philip K. Dick novel, Tom Cruise plays a police officer in the LAPD 'Pre-Crime' unit. Using the premonitions of sentient mutants called 'pre-cogs', the police are able to predict when someone is going to commit a crime, swooping down from helicopters and arresting them on the street before they have committed the offence. Their 'crime' is that they merely thought about it.

Palantir, the CIA-backed start-up, is *Minority Report* come true.

Palantir are to data what McKinsey are to consultancy. All-powerful, yet no one knows they even exist. Palantir do not have an office, they have an SCIF on a back street in Palo Alto.

SCIF stands for 'sensitive compartmentalised information facility'. Palantir say their building 'must be built to be resistant to attempts to access the information within. The network must be "airgapped" from the public internet to prevent information leakage.'[27]

Palantir's defence systems include advanced biometrics, and walls impenetrable to radio waves, phone signal or internet. Their data storage is blockchained: it cannot be accessed by merely sophisticated hacking, it requires digital pass codes held by dozens of independent parties, whose identities are themselves protected by blockchain.[28]

What is Palantir protecting? A 'palantir' is a 'seeing stone' in J.R.R. Tolkien's *The Lord of the Rings*. A dark orb used by Saruman to be able to see in darkness or blinding light. Palantir means 'one that sees from afar'. A mythical instrument of omnipotence.

In 2004, Peter Thiel created Palantir with ex-PayPal engineer Nathan Gettings, and Joe Lonsdale, Stephen Cohen and Alex Karp from Stanford University. Their intention was to create a company that took Big Data somewhere no one else dared to go.

In 2013, Alex Karp, Palantir's chief executive officer, announced that the company would not be pursuing an IPO, as going public would make 'running a company like ours very difficult'. This is why.

Palantir watch everything you do and predict what you will do next in order to stop it. They have a secret arm called Palantir Gotham. Their clients include the CIA, the FBI, the NSA, the CDC, the Marine Corps, the Air Force, Special Operations Command, West Point and the IRS. Up to fifty per cent of their business is with the public sector. In-Q-Tel, the CIA's venture arm, was an early investor.[29]

Palantir track everyone from potential terrorist suspects to corporate fraudsters (Bernie Madoff was imprisoned with the help of Palantir), child traffickers and 'subversives'. But it is all done using prediction.

In Iraq, the Pentagon used Palantir software to track patterns in roadside bomb deployment and worked out that garage-door openers were being used as remote detonators by predicting it.[30]

Palantir allowed the Marines to upload DNA samples from remote locations and tap into information gathered from years of collecting fingerprints and DNA evidence: the results returned almost immediately.

Without Palantir, suspects would have already moved onto a different location by the time the field agents received the results. Using the most sophisticated data mining, Palantir can predict the future, seconds or years before it happens.

Samuel Reading, a former Marine who works in Afghanistan for NEK Advanced Securities Group, a US military contractor, says, 'It's the combination of every analytical tool you could ever dream of. You will know every single bad guy in your area.'[31]

Palantir are at the heart of the US government, but with their other arm, Palantir Metropolis, they provide the analytical tools for hedge funds, banks and financial services firms to outsmart each other.

Palantir do not just provide the Pentagon with a machine for global surveillance and the data-efficient fighting of war, they run Wall Street, too. Palantir is exactly what it says it is: a giant digital eye like Saruman's 'seeing stone' in *The Lord of the Rings*.

MINORITY REPORT FOR REAL

On the streets of Chicago and Los Angeles, Palantir are getting closest to Philip K. Dick's vision of the future, now. In the film, a premonition of an Orwellian thought-police state, crime rates drop to zero as the 'Pre-Crime' unit successfully imprisons thousands of individuals for merely thinking of committing a felony.

However, when Cruise's character begins to question the morality of what he is doing, his superiors detect a threat to the entire 'pre-crime' programme. In order to get rid of him, Cruise is framed for a murder by altering the data of his thought history. In the final showdown with his boss, it is explained to Cruise that sometimes the numbers need to lie for the greater good of society.

Minority Report is set in 2054, but Palantir are putting 'pre-crime' into operation now. The Los Angeles Police Department have used Palantir to predict who will commit a crime by swooping *Minority Report*-style on suspects. Palantir call their work with the LAPD 'improving situational awareness, and responding to crime in real time.'[32]

Military-grade surveillance technology has now migrated from Fallujah to the suburban neighbourhoods of LA, 'predictive policing' on illegal drivers and petty criminals through a redeployment of techniques and algorithms used by the US army dealing with insurgents in Iraq and with civilian casualty patterns.[33]

When America is described as a 'war zone' between police and young black males, it is rarely mentioned that tactics developed by the US military in a real war zone are actually being deployed. The use of Palantir predictive-policing software by the Chicago Police and LAPD has coincided with a sharp rise in fatal shootings of black male suspects. Is predictive policing as a counter-insurgency tactic a contributing factor in the epidemic of police shootings of unarmed black men in the last four years?

One could argue that sophisticated pre-crime algorithms are not necessary when being black and male is seen as reason enough for the police to swoop. What predictive policing has done is militarise American cities, creating a heightened culture of suspicion and fear in areas where tensions are highest and policing is already most difficult.

Professor Geoff Parker is an expert on data broking and says, 'The mere presence of police arriving in an area because of an algorithm creates tension.' Enough to ignite a powder keg and push a delicate policing situation over the edge.[34]

Ana Muniz is an activist and researcher who works with the Inglewood-based Youth Justice Coalition. 'Any time that a society's military and domestic police become more similar, the lines blur. The military is supposed to defend the territory from external enemies, that's not the mission of the police – they're not supposed to look at the population as an external enemy.'[35]

In 2010, the LAPD announced a partnership with Motorola Solutions to monitor the Jordan Downs public housing project with surveillance cameras. In 2013, they announced the deployment of live CCTV cameras with facial-recognition software in San Fernando Valley, reported to be programmed to ID suspects on a 'hot list'.[36]

Whitney Richards-Calathes, a doctoral student at the City University of New York who researches predictive policing, warns that 'we have to be really critical about built-in assumptions made when data bases are created for "public safety", yet kids as young as nine and ten are being put in these data bases and automatically labelled gang members.'[37]

Data merely becomes a new way of reinforcing old prejudices. Critics of these analytics argue that from the moment a police officer with the pre-crime mindset that you are a criminal steps out of their patrol car to confront you, your fate has been sealed.

In 2013, TechCrunch obtained a leaked report on the use of Palantir by the LA and Chicago police departments. Sergeant Peter Jackson of the LAPD was quoted as saying, 'Detectives love the type of information (Palantir) provide. They can now do things that we could not do before.'[38]

Palantir are immensely secretive. They wield as much real-world power as Google, Facebook, Amazon, Microsoft and Apple, but unlike them, Palantir operate so far under the radar, they are special ops.

BREAKING THE MONOPOLY

Together the Big Five (plus the invisible sixth ring, Palantir, the all-seeing eye) compose a new superclass of corporate might.

But post-Trump, Brexit and the resurgence of nationalist parties in Europe, they face a new threat: governments with a popular vote seeking to claw back national sovereignty from corporations.

The public mood on these companies is turning. They are no longer shiny new platforms delivering the future now, they are a twenty-year-old monopoly challenging the authority of government and even democracy.

On 21 January 2016, EU commissioner Margrethe Vestager opened the door of her office in Brussels to Tim Cook, CEO of Apple. Cook was there to talk about Apple's tax arrangements in Europe. Witnesses reported hearing shouting coming from the office as Vestager pushed back on Cook's version of what Apple should or should not be paying in corporate tax.

Seven months later, Cook got Vestager's verdict. 'Apple's tax benefits in Ireland are illegal,' she announced to a packed press conference. Apple owed £11 billion plus interest. When Cook heard, back at Apple HQ in Cupertino, he was reported to have called the judgment 'political crap'.

The tech giants have started to look like the American dream gone sour. Apple perceived as tax dodgers and Amazon, once edgy tech-disrupters, as slayers of small local businesses on the high street. Apple appeased the Chinese government's demands to close down apps giving Chinese people access to the outside world, while simultaneously refusing the US government access to a suspected terrorist's iPhone.

In May 2017, when the world faced a cyberattack from WannaCry malware, made possible by exploiting software allegedly stolen by a hacking group called Shadow Brokers from the NSA, Microsoft's president and chief legal officer Brad Smith blamed governments for stockpiling vulnerabilities and leaving the world open.

The tech giants are also battling among themselves. Uber's then boss Travis Kalanick was hauled before Apple CEO Tim Cook for secretly tagging iPhones even after Uber's app had been deleted and the devices erased. A fraud detection manoeuvre that violated Apple's privacy guidelines.[39]

Julius Genachowski is the former chairman of the Federal Communications Commission and says, 'During the periods where incumbents are battling disrupters, in general the US has done a good job of encouraging disrupters.' Under Obama, he says, the Big Five were not a threat to government, they were the future, and various parts of the United States regulatory and legal infrastructure sought to protect and nurture them.

During Mr Genachowski's term at the FCC (and then again during the term of his successor, Tom Wheeler) the commission passed rules favouring so-called 'network neutrality', meaning companies could not favour some kinds of content online over others. A policy favoured by tech companies.

But as the disrupters grow into monsters, the dynamic shifts.

'The next part of the arc,' Genachowski says, 'is that disrupters become very successful and in some ways turn into incumbents, and then you see two things: battles between incumbents and other incumbents, and a next generation of disrupters tackling incumbents.'

That is where we are now. The Big Five have become the incumbents and they are treated as such by governments, who look to both sides of the ledger – their benefits to society as well as their potential costs – when deciding how to police them.

But are the new players – Uber, Airbnb, Snapchat or their foreign competitors like Baidu – any real threat? The battles for dominance in cloud services, artificial intelligence and data mining, as well as real-world dominance of driverless cars, drone deliveries and robot jobs – that is all between the original Big Five.

When Uber's Kalanick faced off against Tim Cook at Apple Headquarters in 2015, because Uber had pulled a fast one by camouflaging their app from Apple's engineers, it was a microcosm of the incumbent-versus-new-disrupter battle and there was only going to be one winner: Apple.[40]

The history of capitalism has been a war waged for and against monopolies. In 1890, the Sherman Antitrust Act created the famous 'Sherman Hammer' allowing the White House to smash companies seeking to create monopolies.

Tobacco, oil, steel and the banks have all been subject to anti-trust legislation that tried to curtail monopolies working against the public interest. The Glass-Steagall Act held in place for nearly sixty years preventing banks from becoming overly powerful and creating another Wall Street crash.

This was only possible because a baton passed quietly from legislature to legislature for over a century. A determination to maintain the authority of democracy. This was not an election pledge from a smooth-tongued politician seeking office by attacking big business, it was done quietly behind closed doors for the benefit of the public.

Tolkien had one ring to rule them all and tech giants have an uncompleted circle, buffering as they race to be the first to download humanity. When the tech companies are able to complete the circle, singularity will be upon us.

But there is no talk of breaking up the Big Five monopoly. They challenged the authority of government, and government – unlike the governments of the last century – capitulated. The Big Five know they cannot be tamed. They are remaking what it is to be human, and whether humans are even part of that story.

CHAPTER FOURTEEN
GLOBALISATION: HOW ASIA REWROTE THE RULES

The Deal: Chinese President Xi Jinping signs the One Belt One Road (OBOR) agreement with sixty-eight countries, including the United States

Aim: To invest an estimated $1 trillion in giant infrastructure projects across the world, from the building of road systems and ports to power stations and new cities, creating a new Silk Road and making China the most powerful nation on earth

Where: Beijing

When: 13 May 2017

DENG

In 1992, three years after the Tiananmen Square massacre, Deng Xiaoping, China's all-powerful leader, stepped up to a challenge he had been waiting for his whole life. Changing the future course of China, and in so doing, the world.

Deng was quite simply the most brilliant leader of the twentieth century. But his brilliance stemmed not simply from his consummate ability to chart a course of reform for the most populous nation on earth, and to swim through the shark-infested waters of the upper echelons of the Communist Party with deft ease.

His true brilliance lay in setting a tripwire that would go off twenty years after his death. Because it is only now that Deng's plan is coming to fruition, reshaping the destiny of the twenty-first century by having reconfigured the paradigm of communism versus capitalism in the twentieth.

Deng wanted to win the globalisation game by shifting the axis of world power decisively back to the East once more. Without him, China would not be the pivotal nation state on earth. And two decades after his death, the ideas that made it happen are falling into place.

Deng came from a well-to-do, land-owning family in Guang'an, in the Sichuan province, but travelled as a young man to Moscow and Paris – half a century later he told the Queen he was disappointed he could not see England from the top of the Eiffel Tower: the kind of conversational trap that Deng set for Western leaders.

When Deng returned to China in the 1920s, astutely he dropped any air of well-travelled cosmopolitanism in toeing the austere Maoist party line. But Deng kept what he had seen in the West in his pocket. He knew what capitalism had to offer people and how this could threaten the long-term survival of the Communist Party.

Deng rose quickly within the party hierarchy, playing an instrumental role in the Long March of 1934, where he gained Mao's trust. Short and pugnacious, with a habit of spitting frequently, Deng played the party disciplinarian to a tee, giving nothing away about his prosperous upbringing.

In 1949, Deng made his mark in the Communist defeat of Chiang Kai-shek's Nationalist government. His future at the top of the party was assured and Deng's credentials as a loyal servant of the proletariat were now beyond question; something that would later prove very useful.

In 1956, everything changed. The new Soviet premier Nikita Khrushchev launched his famous attack on the Stalinist principles of Soviet communism. Khrushchev had effectively questioned God and it rocked the Soviet Communist Party to its foundations.

Mao Zedong feared an equivalent attack on the cult of Maoism in China. In the West, consumerism had begun to deliver on the promises of capitalism – freedom and fridges – and it was only a matter of time before this 'propaganda' polluted the Chinese proletariat. Mao believed communism needed to go back to first principles and crush reform.

It was in this moment that everything hinged: stick or twist for Deng, who saw a chink of light and an opportunity to open up. He made his move. Far from creating collective wealth, he said, the 'collectivisation' of farms – a central plank of both Stalinism and Maoism – had impoverished millions.[2]

Mao's 'Great Leap Forward' had industrialised China rapidly, but also created famine on an unprecedented scale. Deng took it upon himself to order the reversal of collectivisation and the return of farms to the ownership of smallholding peasants. To individuals. When Mao heard of Deng's plan, he quipped, 'Which emperor authorised that?'[3]

Like Khrushchev, Deng had questioned the principles upon which the system was built. It was a direct challenge to Mao's authority and Mao sensed a rival building a power base. Deng had committed heresy and at its heart was the elevation of the individual and markets.

IT DOESN'T MATTER IF A CAT IS BLACK OR WHITE, SO LONG AS IT CATCHES MICE

Deng had set himself on a collision course with Mao. In July 1962, Deng addressed the Communist Youth League and made a gnomic statement that would travel with him to his grave. Sixteen words that set out his theory of realpolitik and would determine the future course of Communist China.

'It doesn't matter,' he told the young Maoist zealots, 'if a cat is black or white, so long as it catches mice.'

It was classic Communist Party Confucianism pitched

perfectly at two audiences. What did it mean? To the Maoist faithful, it was interpreted as 'the ends justifying the means'. If the goal was communism, then we must achieve that goal by any means necessary.

However, to the reformers, it was an epiphany. Maoist dogma, he was saying, was a blind path. China must be open – as it was two thousand years ago – to learning from the West, even if that meant adopting elements of market economics. Communism must be able to mutate and evolve on its own terms. Above all, to be pragmatic.

Communist China, Deng said, could choose whether to disregard or subsume these new ideas, but the important thing was to be adaptable. The cat could be any colour, but it was the end goal that mattered, not dogma. Only by winning did the cat catch the mouse.

Deng could not have chosen a worse moment to renounce Maoism, which is why it was so important that it appeared to be not a disavowal of Maoism, but its endorsement.

In May 1966, Mao eviscerated any chance of Deng's market-reform plans by exploding the Cultural Revolution on the heads of 1.6 billion people; the most brutal obliteration of Western 'influence' on Chinese society in living memory. A total war, not only on Mao's political enemies, but on the very concept of ideas and anyone other than Mao daring to have them.

Red Guards armed with sticks rounded up teachers, academics, doctors and dentists, who were beaten or executed for harbouring 'bourgeois' Western values. Books were destroyed, as were reading glasses – another bourgeois implement for spreading the 'false consciousness' of education. Thousands were arrested and families torn apart as Maoist students denounced and informed on their 'counter-revolutionary' parents.

Meanwhile, counter-revolutionary students at universities in cities were forcibly removed to the country to work on the land in order to re-indoctrinate them with Maoist first principles.[4]

The Communist Party was purged of reformers, and this

meant Deng Xiaoping. By the early 1970s, the Cultural Revolution had done its work. The entire administrative and managerial architecture of China – the veins and arteries of the body politic – had been destroyed. There was simply no one left qualified to do a job beyond tilling a field. The country was in ruins.

THE FIRST TIANANMEN SQUARE

On 4 April 1976, thousands of protestors gathered in Tiananmen Square demanding a reversal of the disastrous consequences of the Cultural Revolution.

As Mao grew increasingly ill, the Maoist clique of the 'Gang of Four' took control. Hardliners Jiang Qing, Zhang Chunqiao, Yao Wenyuan and Wang Hongwen, sought collectively to prevent a return for Deng and the reformers.

Yet nearly two million protestors came to Tiananmen Square in support of Deng and his recently deceased reformist ally, Zhou Enlai. The Gang of Four called the campaign 'counter-revolutionary'.

Like the second Tiananmen Square protests of 1989, the demonstrators were ruthlessly crushed by force. But only months later, following Mao's death and the arrest of the Gang of Four, the reformer Deng began to outmanoeuvre Mao's weak, anointed successor Hua Guofeng in what became a classic boardroom coup, taking power for himself in 1978.

Deng was now the boss: the leader of the most powerful nation on earth in waiting. And the seeming contradiction of a communist leader in thrall to market economics was no contradiction at all.

Deng Xiaoping believed in the 'socialist market economy' – business and Marxism coexisting in one nation – as deeply as Mao believed in Maoism. The principle that outlined Hong Kong's independence from Britain in 1997 could have been written for Deng's China as a whole: 'one country, two systems'.

Thirteen years after the suppression of the first Tiananmen Square uprising, there was another. In 1989 Deng found himself again on an inspection visit to a rural region of the South, just as he had been in 1961. This time he had only two words to say: '*kai fang*'. It was time to 'open up'.

MADE IN CHINA

Playing with my Hot Wheels car set as a kid, I was struck by something odd. To a child growing up in the late 1970s and early 1980s, Hot Wheels was the epitome of cool American culture. The cars spoke of Evel Knievel jumping gorges on his stars-and-stripes rocket bike; the go-fast flames on the Mustangs and Dodge muscle cars were pure *Dukes of Hazzard*. Yet if you turned the car over, it was stamped not with 'Made in the USA' but 'Made in China'.

So how did China become the world's workshop?

The reason is simple, as Harvard economist Joseph Nye explains: 'If we looked at the world in 1800, you'd find that more than half of the world's people lived in Asia and they made more than half the world's product. Now fast forward to 1900: half the world's people – more than half – still live in Asia, but now they're making only a fifth of the world's product.

'What happened? The Industrial Revolution, which meant that all of a sudden, Europe and America became the dominant centre of the world. What we're going to see in the twenty-first century is Asia returning to being more than half the world's population and making more than half of the world's product.'[5]

Deng did something in the late 1970s that reverberated in the 2016 US election: he remade China from an inward-looking, rigidly socialist backwater into the workshop of the world, carving the heart out of the Western manufacturing base.

It was not only Hot Wheels that got made in China. The cheap consumer goods that fuelled the spending boom of the West had 'Made in China' – or Korea or Japan or Singapore – stamped on them, too.

Tiny metal toy cars became big real cars as Asia began to dominate the world's car market. Japanese tech innovation enabled a spectacular volte-face on electrical goods, turning a reputation for cheap, shoddy radios and TVs in the 1970s into reliable, affordable excellence a decade later.

Toyota, Nissan and Sony became General Motors and Chrysler. Asia drove hard at the West and planted a flag at the heart of manufacturing, turning the West's own Great Leap Forward – the Industrial Revolution – to rust.

Two centuries ago, Napoleon warned: 'Let China sleep, for when the dragon awakes, she will shake the world.' It was not simply China that reawakened to show the world what it could do, it was the whole of Asia.

China's economy is today bigger than India's, Russia's and Brazil's put together. Growing at six per cent a year (compared to India's seven per cent) China will still create the equivalent of two new Indias by 2020. China has a middle class of 100 million people and in spite of extraordinary pollution levels created by rapid industrialisation – as bad as the industrial heartland of nineteenth-century England – life expectancy is seventy-six, higher than the world average or in any developing country.[6]

Yet it is China's impact on the world economy that is truly breathtaking. Less than ten per cent of the world's population is fully industrialised. As China industrialises further, it could treble that global figure, sucking in and industrialising a further twenty per cent of the planet's population by igniting growth in Asia, Latin America, Africa and even reinvigorating the industrial West. Protectionist guru Peter Navarro's fear that the West will inevitably suffer 'death by China' could well turn out to be the opposite, 'rescue by China'.[7]

China's continuing growth will stimulate colossal demand for raw materials, energy, imports and capital flow. This reboots everyone else. Their win is not necessarily at everyone else's expense. But their economic implosion would be.[8]

China is the largest market for seventy countries and the largest trading partner for 120, more than half the population of the world.

China imports the equivalent of £1 trillion worth of goods and over the next five years will import $8 trillion of goods. It will be a bigger net importer than the European Union by 2020. As the former chair of Goldman Sachs, Jim O'Neill, puts it succinctly: 'China is the biggest example of growth and poverty reduction in history.'[9]

And as China and Asia begin to come into their own once more, if the West retreats to the comfort blanket of protectionism, it will be as effective as hiding under a desk before a nuclear war.

The only leverage the US now holds over China is how much money it owes China. Like a bigger Goldman Sachs or Citi, the US is now a superpower that is 'too big to fail'.

This astronomical US debt perversely gives the US a new form of power. In 2016, then-presidential-nominee Trump said: 'We owe them money ... this gives us tremendous power.' In February 2017, that debt to China was estimated at $1.059 trillion.

HOW CHINA CHANGED THE RULES BY STICKING TO THE OLD ONES

Why did China win? It quite simply had more: more people, more resources, and a phenomenally larger market. But it also had a game plan that involved taking advantage of the poor game plan of its opponents.

In 2016, Goodyear Tyres closed the gates of their UK factory in Bushbury Lane, Wolverhampton for the last time.[10] For eighty-nine years, workers had built tyres for the US rubber conglomerate founded in 1898. In 2008, Goodyear was ranked sixteenth in the *Forbes* annual listings of companies with the best reputation as an employer in the world.

Cyril Barrett, one of the union representatives at the Wolverhampton plant said, 'It's a really sad time as the workforce is really like a family. We've seen generations grow up with the company. It's a time of great emotion. In times gone by, Goodyear was a great company and that's what makes it even sadder.'[11]

The jobs were going to Mexico. On a noticeboard in the factory, employees were told that anyone interested in a job could move to Mexico, where Goodyear would be happy to re-employ them. The staff response was to wear Mexican hats on their last day.

This is globalisation. But globalisation as a simple zero-sum game does not really exist. What exists is the flat earth of markets, wages and the rules that apply to both being constantly renegotiated. Turkish economist Dani Rodrik at Harvard believes that China's victory in the globalisation game has simply been an ability to bend these rules to suit their game plan.

In the 1990s, Rodrik says, globalisation became 'hyperglobalisation' and this was 'not about creating healthy economies, but removing all barriers to trade, so we confused ends with means.'[12]

While the West played the game of hyperglobalisation one way, China played it another, cunningly embracing its freewheeling, brutal nature whilst simultaneously and fiercely protecting its own economy from the adverse effects of hyperglobalisation that everyone else experienced: offshored jobs, depressed wages, deskilling and a permanent state of precariousness. But forty years earlier, hyperglobalisation had itself replaced rules established in the aftermath of World War Two for the stable running of capitalism. Rules drawn up at Bretton Woods.

THE MYTH OF BRETTON WOODS

In leafy New Hampshire on 1 July 1944, a deal was struck by the most powerful post-war economies on earth – the forty-four allied nations – at the United Nations Monetary and Financial Conference at Mount Washington Hotel, overlooking the sleepy town of Bretton Woods.

The aim of the Bretton Woods Agreement was simple: creating a stable structure for post-war capitalism to flourish. National currencies would be tied to a fixed exchange, pegged to gold and the US dollar, and a bank of last resort called the IMF would provide nations with bridging loans on imbalances of payment.

The message of Bretton Woods was as important as the mechanisms: rules and institutions rather than the market would govern the flow of global finance. Free trade across the globe would be policed within firm parameters. Nations were locked into a system that both constricted their behaviour, but enabled them to trade equitably.

But did Bretton Woods really create stability?

Keynesians and those on the Democrat or Centre Left view the twenty-seven years it was in operation – between 1944 and 1971 – as a golden age of capitalist stability.

Because the dollar had been pegged to gold, it became the default world currency. This was both a blessing and a curse. The United States contributed the most cash to the IMF and the World Bank, originally set up 'to facilitate the investment of capital for productive purposes' to the defeated war nations (Germany, Japan and Italy), to its broken Western European allies (Britain, France), as well as the developing world (South America, Asia, Africa). This meant the US could run a trade deficit without having to devalue its currency.

For twenty-seven years, there was unprecedented stability and prosperity. Bretton Woods prevented the spread of communism in Western Europe by using dollars instead of tanks to contain its advance. In 2014, Paul Volker, Chairman of the Federal Reserve under Presidents Carter and Reagan and one of the world's most respected economists, made a speech on the twenty-first of May anniversary of the annual meeting of the Bretton Woods Committee at the World Bank HQ in Washington.

'What about a new Bretton Woods?' Volker asked. A return to a 'more orderly, rule-based world of financial stability . . . by now I think we can agree that the absence of an official, rules-based cooperatively managed monetary system has not been a great success.'

But many economists, predominantly on the neo-liberal Right and some on the far Left, say this stability was a mirage. What 'stability' capitalism experienced in the 1950s and 1960s was not, they argue, the result of Bretton Woods at all. Matt Johnston, formerly of the World Economic Forum, argued in *Forbes* in December 2015 that 'there were signs of instability throughout the era and perhaps not enough has been made of the relative difficulty in trying to maintain the system. Rather than seeing Bretton Woods as a period characterised by stability,' he concluded, 'it's more accurate to consider it being a transitional stage that ushered in a new monetary order.'

How did Bretton Woods really work and why did it collapse? The rebuilding of European and Asian economies in the aftermath of the Second World War with US dollars using the Marshall Plan and World Bank took its toll on the US economy. By 1958, thirteen years after the end of the war and fourteen after Bretton Woods was established, Germany, Japan, France and Britain were in turnaround. They were no longer weak post-war nations in need of help, but serious trade rivals. The US had printed money to rebuild these economies only to be repaid with competition and a balance of payments crisis.

By the 1960s, there was an insatiable demand for dollars, and because its value was pegged to gold, gold reserves held in vaults began to creak under the strain. There simply was not enough gold to underwrite the explosion in world trade being transacted in dollars. Solutions other than a dollar pegged to gold were frantically sought, including the creation of a so-called Gold Pool. In 1961, gold from apartheid South Africa and even the communist Soviet Union was chucked in to the gold reserve, but it wasn't enough. The entire Bretton Woods pyramid of world trade bore down with immense pressure on a single point – availability of gold. It could not hold.

Western capitalism was perilously threatened. A run on US gold reserves looked inevitable. By the late 1960s, US foreign liabilities were four times the amount of US monetary gold reserves. And whilst some bankers were beginning to grow very nervous, others sensed an arbitrage opportunity in the gold crisis. France leaked an intention to cash in its dollar assets for gold and Britain requested to exchange $750 million for gold in the summer of 1971. It was a sign that the gap between demand for dollars and gold to underpin that demand was becoming unbridgeable. Behind closed doors, capitalism was on the brink.

On 15 August 1971, President Nixon unilaterally terminated convertibility of the US dollar to gold. Bretton Woods had collapsed. The G10 countries met at the Smithsonian Institute in Washington in December 1971 to sign the Smithsonian Agreement to formally establish that exchange rates would henceforth float without the reserve backing of either gold or silver. Nixon called the Smithsonian Agreement 'the most significant monetary agreement in world history.'

It was, at a stroke, the end of governments determining currency price. From now on, they would be set by commercial trades on Forex, the largest and fastest moving currency trading market in the world. Open twenty-four hours a day, five days a week, Forex is not a physical space, but a global currency exchange through which New York, London, Tokyo, Zurich, Frankfurt, Singapore, Sydney and Paris all continuously trade currencies and perpetually recalibrate their value.

At the Smithsonian Agreement, capitalism changed to the system we have today. The keys were handed over from men with clipboards in Washington and Geneva, who had been prescribing what nations could and could not do for twenty-seven years, to traders across the world, scrutinising the markets twenty-four hours a day.

Regardless of your view on the true stability of Bretton Woods, or the wisdom of adopting the dollar as a fixed exchange pegged to gold in the first place, there is little doubt Bretton Woods was instrumental in rebuilding the post-war world. It allowed US trade surpluses to be recycled by countries with trade deficits, which enabled the United States to continue sending money to rebuild Germany, Japan and Korea.[13] By 1971, however, the world was rather different from the one in which Bretton Woods had been first devised.

Yanis Varoufakis, the former Greek minister of finance, believes Nixon's desire to come off the gold standard was not the primary reason for the collapse of Bretton Woods.

'Bretton Woods worked till the US stopped running trade surpluses,' he says. 'After 1971, the system simply couldn't continue because the US lost its surpluses. Then America started recycling everyone else's surpluses. It was operating like a vacuum cleaner, sucking in the net surplus wealth and net profits into Wall Street to close the loop.'[14] The implication is that the same thing could happen in the future when China is the default banker of the world and suddenly finds itself in trouble.

In spite of the continuous pressure exerted on the system by demand for dollars, Bretton Woods did a hugely important job: preventing a return to the economic crises of the 1930s. But it had also stymied the free flow of capital by maintaining restrictive barriers on trade and currency exchange, and thus held back globalisation. With the collapse of Bretton Woods in 1971, business was widely perceived by economists as the only real engine for future growth. Keeping a lid on the markets had not worked: unrestricted free trade, freed from the straitjacket of regulation, would kick-start a worldwide boom and make globalisation real.

A revolution followed, with people in pin-stripe suits rather than overalls leading it. With deregulation on Wall Street freeing banks to trade as they chose, symbolised by the eventual repeal of the Glass-Steagall Act in 1999, business began taking advantage of floating exchange rates and made hyperglobalisation happen. Even though Wall Street had been working round regulation like Glass-Steagall for years, regulatory control was now officially dead.

According to economist Dani Rodrik at Harvard, by the late 1990s, 'an intellectual framework became established . . . by the World Bank and the WTO [World Trade Organisation], whereby globalisation was seen as the way countries would grow.' If countries opened themselves up to big corporations (by providing attractive employment laws and low corporate tax rates), then they would get payback in the shape of jobs, investment and the chance to attract more business.

This was a not unreasonable assumption to make; indeed, the supply-side economic orthodoxy of the time endorsed this view. But there was a problem, according to Rodrik. 'That narrative failed to see that countries that did well under globalisation did so on their own terms. They maintained strong infrastructure and investment in combination with taking advantage of globalisation. So we only got half the story.'[15]

While big economies like those of the United States and Britain, Rodrik argues, acted like developing countries – desperate to attract global corporations by offering tax cuts and the most attractive cheap labour conditions, yet inevitably being undercut by South America and South East Asia – countries like Germany and Sweden maintained a strong commitment to infrastructure spending, higher levels of corporation tax and state-heavy expenditure on health, retraining and benefits for working parents. In spite of these seemingly antibusiness measures, these countries still managed to attract global corporations looking for higher-paid skilled workers in new technologies and maintained respectable growth rates as a result.

But China, Rodrik says, went one step further when it came to globalisation, behaving as one giant, highly secretive corporation. It protected its own interests while playing hardball on the global stage as ruthlessly as any globalised corporation. 'When you look at how China achieved this feat,' says Rodrik, 'it controlled capital flows, subsidised industries, it required investors to use local content, violated trade agreements, violated property rights. It maintained wide state ownership, largely to protect employment. [China] benefited from all the other countries following the rules of hyperglobalisation.'[16]

While Western nations went for an authentic, free market vision of globalisation, China cunningly had its cake and ate it, too – protecting its own citizens from the tough economic realities that swept across industrial America and Europe, but behaving beyond China as if it were the most ruthlessly competitive company on earth. China held on to pre–Bretton Woods assumptions about investing in infrastructure and subsidising industry at home, while simultaneously joining in the post-Bretton Woods free market free-for-all everywhere else. Jim Yong Kim of the World Bank sums it up neatly when he says, 'Globalisation worked marvellously for Korea, China, and for most of East Asia, but not in Iowa – who voted Trump.'

DOES DEMOCRACY IMPEDE GROWTH?

In 2015, as anti-globalisation placards began to be stencilled and held up at rallies for Trump, Brexit and on anti-TTIP (Transatlantic Trade and Investment Partnership) marches in Britain, America and Europe, something else was going on hidden in the business pages.

More than half of British companies were declared as having foreign shareholders. In 2014, fifty-four per cent of the value of the UK stock market was officially declared as 'owned outside the UK'. In 1998, it was thirty-eight per cent.[17]

In the US, foreign ownership has increased steadily over twenty years. Some of America's biggest companies are now owned by the Chinese and their appetite is growing across a bewilderingly varied array of industries.

In 2013, processed-meat conglomerate Smithfield Foods was bought by Shuanghui International for $7.1 billion. Professor

Minxin Pei at Claremont McKenna College called the deal 'a masterstroke to expand its ability to supply a fast-growing market with premium-brand pork at higher prices ... Shuanghui might (also) use Smithfield as a channel to sell its products in the US.'

In just one year – 2016 – Chinese investors bought:

- Starwood Hotels, incorporating the W Hotel chain, bought by Anbang Insurance in a deal worth $14.3 billion.
- Ingram Micro, a tech company and number sixty-two on the *Fortune* 500 companies, bought by Tianjin Tianhai Investment for $6.3 billion.
- General Electric Appliances, selling toasters and dishwashers, was bought by Qingdao Haier for $5.4 billion.[18]

My old friend Wang at Dalian Wanda bought film company Legendary Entertainment Group, who made *Jurassic Park* and *Pacific Rim*, for $3.5 billion (to go with AMC, America's largest cinema chain, which Wang bought in 2012 for $2.6 billion). So now we know where he spent that $7 billion loose change.

And this only skims the surface of what was bought by Chinese investors in the States in a single year. When one begins to understand who really owns what in any country, talk of a trade war starts to sound a little imbecilic. Trade war with whom? With yourself?

When Bretton Woods collapsed, there was no going back to the old world. Even Yanis Varoufakis, a self-proclaimed 'leftist', is realistic about the options. 'What we don't need is what we did between the mid-1970s and 2008, which is to stabilise global capitalism through an expanding trade deficit by the US. Allowing Wall Street bankers to financialise, creating torrents of speculation on the stream of capital flows. We need a new Bretton Woods: a new managed capitalism just like we had between 1944 and 1970.'[19]

Everyone from Paul Volker to Yanis Varoufakis thinks it should happen. But it won't. 'Of course, this is a new paradigm,'

Varoufakis says, 'we're not going to have fixed exchange rates, or a dominant power like the US, so we better learn how to cooperate at the political level in order to create economic equilibrium that is capable of averting the rise of nationalism.'

Yet we do have the rise of nationalism and a dominant power – China. And as economist Yasheng Huang notes in his book *Capitalism with Chinese Characteristics*, it is China's very dedication to authoritarianism and lack of democracy that has allowed it to grow so dramatically. Huang argues that in the 1980s, entrepreneurial rural China was the engine of capitalist growth for the economy. But in the 1990s, the urban elite that coalesced around the Communist Party began to reverse many of the rural experiments in capitalist enterprise.

In the United States, this may have resulted in a protracted standoff between the powerful farming lobby and the political establishment in Washington, resulting in a compromise. But because this was a command economy, the Communist Party simply did it.

The party even used the promise of capitalist opportunities to the growing urban wealthy to reinforce an anti-democratic agenda across China and quell desires for greater democracy. The party offered prosperity to a growing middle class and achieved growth without a need to make political concessions.

Huang points out that China was not the only populous nation to go through huge economic change in the 1980s and 1990s; so too did India, and India's commitment to secular democracy did not waver as rapid economic growth was achieved. So the 'democracy hinders rapid industrialisation' thesis does not, Huang says, hold true for all countries.

One consequence of China's command economy has been to put huge policy decisions into action fast. Jim Yong Kim of the World Bank gives the example of what China did with mass redundancies, comparing it with what happened in the West. 'When NAFTA [the North American Free Trade Agreement of

1994] and the great trade agreements were made, there was [always] a plan to retrain people with programmes as jobs were lost.' In the US, these programmes were known as Trade Adjustment Assistance (TAA) and have existed in one form or another since 1974. They were designed by federal government to minimise the adverse effects of globalisation by paying for job training and compensating workers who have lost jobs to offshoring.

But TAA has been the subject of controversy as to its effectiveness. A study by Kara Reynolds and John Palatucci of the American University in 2006 concluded that 'the TAA programme is of dubious value to displaced workers.' Reynolds and Palatucci found that TAA scored low when it came to employability following retraining and an average of ten per cent lower wages for workers who found a job after TAA than those who did not take up the scheme.

In effect, they concluded, it remains a scheme that very few people believe works, least of all the politicians who have to sign it off each year.

Now look at China. When two million steel workers were laid off, this is what they did. Retrained them as entrepreneurs running start-ups. A policy decision was made to boost income across the board for these workers in the aftermath of their redundancy, rather than make them accept a pay-cut. Redundancy resulted in a government pledge to maintain rising wages, not the opposite. At the same time, there was an edict to improve working conditions for migrant workers to close any potential gap.

The slogan for this mammoth programme was telling of China's approach to reinvestment in the workforce and thus the economy as a whole: 'Do not leave a single individual behind.'[20]

Yasheng Huang sees China's unswerving commitment to 'not leaving a single person behind' as inextricably bound to its authoritarianism. There is no debate or democratic juggling of conflicting interests. Just a relentless focus on 'The Plan'.

Jim Yong Kim of the World Bank sees this relentless focus most keenly aimed on retraining. 'While Silicon Valley complains there's not enough skilled people for jobs, in Iowa there are people who need jobs, but don't have the right skills because they weren't retrained.' In Asia, even victory is no excuse for complacency. 'In China and South Korea, there's a paranoia about being ready for the next wave. They've perfected the semiconductor business, of going faster and faster, but now they're going "what's next?".'

20,000 ELON MUSKS

GWC is a Sino-Japanese tech company with ambitions that make the Silicon Valley tech giants look modest. With offices in Beijing, Tokyo and in Mountain View, California, where Google are based, GWC are scaling up tech entrepreneurship to industrial grade with the aim of producing twenty thousand Elon Musks.[22]

In 2013, GWC hosted a pitching session in Beijing for budding mobile executives, developers, investors and entrepreneurs at their annual Global Mobile Internet Conference (GMIC). Their aim was fulfilled: twenty thousand budding Elon Musks turned up and began frantically pitching ideas.[23]

The 'G-Summit' is a global competition to find innovations they will back with $1 million. In 2016, winners from Bangalore, São Paulo and Taipei were given the green light to develop ideas with multiplatform potential across the planet.

Silicon Valley is alert to the threat. 'The Valley needs to think more globally,' says Facebook's Vaughan Smith. 'With its focus on Asia, GMIC is among the few tech conferences that's focused on important trends happening outside the US.'

In 2015, Apple's CEO Tim Cook signed up to a social media site: Weibo, China's answer to Twitter. This was not because Apple's boss wanted to post cuddly pictures of pandas. Both

Twitter and Facebook are banned in China and by creating an official presence on China's biggest social network site, millions of Chinese now had access to Apple through the portal of Cook's verified account.

Apple are one of the few tech giants with their feet under the door in China and this is not least because the Chinese have little need for the others. Chinese companies no longer ape Silicon Valley but lead the way, and China does not really need to open the door to Google, Facebook, Uber or Amazon. They have their own versions, innovating by doing everything their Western counterparts do, but doing it bigger, faster and without worrying about what defines their company in a way it might be defined in the West. As a result, they are steaming ahead of their Western progenitors.

Baidu is China's Google, providing the same breadth of service from maps and cloud storage to payment systems, food delivery, healthcare ventures, driverless cars and research into AI, but, according to *Forbes* in November 2017, is already stealing a march on Google, Tesla and the other players in the race to be first with a driverless car. How? Their algorithms are more sophisticated and far-advanced.

Alibaba is China's Amazon. But not just another online payment platform: the largest e-commerce company on the planet. Chief Creative Officer Chris Tung says the West should stop comparing Alibaba to Amazon. 'It's very different from the Amazon model,' he told *Fast Company* in June 2017. 'We don't buy products from brands, we don't sell and take a margin . . . we service as a marketplace, a bridge between the seller and the buyer, through data. $550 billion US gross merchandise value a year. (It's) the largest commerce platform on Earth. Bigger than Walmart. Much bigger than Amazon.'

Tencent is China's Facebook, with WeChat – a clever combination of WhatsApp, Facebook, Apple Pay and Google News – hoovering up over 700 million subscribers.

JD.com is closer to China's Amazon than Alibaba, but as Jason Hiner of tech innovation website ZDNet points out, 'It's racing ahead of Amazon (too).' JD.com have addressed Chinese consumer concern about mass-produced fake goods by authenticating deliveries of global brands and are now offering same-day deliveries to 600 million customers (next-day delivery to the whole of China), working on drones to remote areas.

Didi is China's Uber, with $1 billion investment from Apple. Unlike Uber in the West, Didi have a 'Didi Bus', a driver service that will pick you and your car up if you have had too much to drink. Didi are using big data and machine learning to attempt to solve China's huge traffic congestion and pollution problems in cities by moving cars off the streets at peak hours.[24]

Each of these companies is working on a huge canvas. They combine big data and AI with solving massive social and demographic challenges. In one respect, they're like the Silicon Valley Big Five in that they see no territorial limits on their ambition. But they're certainly not content to stay in Asia, any more than Google was happy to stay in the Bay Area.

Huawei and Xiaomi provide mobile devices and are looking to break into the Samsung and Apple market. Xiaomi hired Google's Android chief Hugo Barra to realise the company's potential, not just in Asia, but across the globe.

These corporations, like GWC with their twenty thousand Elon Musks drive, are not looking for one breakthrough idea, they are looking for twenty thousand. And this industrial scale of entrepreneurialism is down to a cultural preset to think big. Asia does not think big as a grandstanding pose, but because of a fundamental philosophical predisposition.

THE RICE FIELD AND THE HUNTER

In 1999, psychologists Kaiping Peng of Berkeley and Richard Nisbett of the University of Michigan ran a fascinating experiment into the difference between Western and Eastern ways of approaching a problem.[25]

They gave Chinese and American college students a range of scenarios describing conflicts between people and asked for advice on how best to resolve them.

Seventy-two per cent of the Chinese students gave compromise-orientated responses, taking into account the arguments on both sides. Seventy-four per cent of American students found fault on one side or the other, and then sided accordingly.[26]

The Peng–Nisbett 'contradiction' experiment tested a two-thousand-year-old philosophical schism. Western conceptions of the truth are based on the principle of *principium tertii exclusi* – 'the law of the excluded middle' as defined by Aristotle in *Ethics*: 'There cannot be an intermediate between contradictories. But of one subject we must either affirm or deny any one predicate.'[27]

A Western answer to a problem is derived by two people debating. One is exclusively right and the other is exclusively wrong, and the exclusively right 'answer' prevails.

The Chinese, by contrast, follow the 'doctrine of the mean'. In a debate, both parties will be partly right and partly wrong in their argument. The truth will lie somewhere in the middle.[28]

Confucian scholars Li-Jun Ji, Albert Lee and Tieyuan Guo argue that the 'doctrine of the mean' comes directly from Confucius and is thus widely considered the highest ideal of Confucianism.

'Chinese are encouraged to argue for both sides in a debate or to assign equal responsibilities in a dispute. This presents an interesting contrast with the law of the excluded middle in Western philosophies, according to which one ought to eliminate ambiguity or inconsistency by selecting one and only one of the conflicting ideas. Unlike the Chinese tradition, it assumes no merit in the middle ground.'[29]

The middle ground does not mean wishy-washy consensus, but a pooling of knowledge and a preset for the communal good. Psychologist Richard Nisbett ascribes this fundamental difference of approach to landscape.[30]

'The ecology of China, consisting as it does primarily of relatively fertile plains, low mountains and navigable rivers, favoured agriculture and made centralised control of society relatively easy. Agricultural peoples need to get along with one another. This is particularly true for rice farming, characteristic of southern China and Japan, which requires people to cultivate the land in concert with one another.'

The rice field became not merely a place for collaboration, but a metaphor for the nation: people are like grains of rice, both supremely significant and insignificant. Their significance is their contribution to the harvest, their insignificance is the pointlessness of the individual and individual ego.

By contrast, Western individualism grew out of personal struggle. On the barren terrain of the Greek Islands two thousand years before the birth of Christ, survival depended on a solitary hunter outwitting the hunted animal.

When this translated to the Greek *polis* of Plato and Aristotle, the cut and thrust of the hunt became the cut and thrust of debate: the dialectic. The basis for Western philosophy and a cult of individualism that set us down the route of Enlightenment, individualism, property and democracy for the next two millennia. For better or for worse.

THE EMOJI MING VASE

These profound philosophical differences count. In his classic 1975 treatise *On Human Conduct*, Conservative political philosopher Michael Oakeshott makes a profound distinction between two ways a society can be run: one is 'teleocratic' and the other 'nomocratic'.[31]

Teleocratic societies have a declared goal: a higher end. The Enlightenment was teleocratic; it believed greater knowledge would continuously improve society. Communism is teleocratic; it seeks a classless nirvana. Technocracy is teleocratic; it believes in continuing improvement of the human condition through technological advance.

Some teleocratic utopias like communism have an end goal after which history stops. Others seek advance as an end in itself. Progress as a road without destination.

Nomocratic societies, Oakeshott said, are very different. They are bound by rules and tradition, by history and precedent. They have attained if not perfection, a state of lived, empirical best practice. Rules in themselves are the final destination. Oakshott believed conservatism had achieved this state of empirical best-practice in Britain. The rule of law and parliamentary democracy had together delivered unprecedented stability for two hundred years.

When Harold Macmillan resigned as prime minister in 1963, he is rumoured to have been asked what his greatest achievement in office had been. 'Fucking up as little as possible' was his glorious and apocryphal reply. That is nomocratic politics.

In China, there is a winning combination of teleocratic and nomocratic characteristics that co-exist without contradiction. History officially stopped with communism and the realisation of the 'dictatorship of the proletariat'. But Chinese society is underpinned by strict rules and customs dating back to the Ming Dynasty of the fourteenth century.

You can see these rules in operation on a Ming vase. An artefact that reached perfection six hundred years ago, and after which all vases were poor facsimiles of the Platonic Ideal. The Ming Vase embodied China's cultural zenith and in 1450, symbolised China's pre-eminence as the world's most powerful dynastic state.

As Professor Craig Clunas of Oxford and Jessica Harrison-Hall of the British Museum say in their catalogue to the 2014 ceramic exhibition *Ming: 50 Years that Changed China (1400–1450)*: '(Dynastic China) had greater land area, bigger cities (and more big cities), bigger armies, bigger ships, bigger palaces, bigger bells, more literate people, and more religious professionals.'

'Ming' was not a family title, but an adjective meaning 'bright', 'luminous' or 'shining'. It was adopted by Zhu Yuanzhang, the founder of the Ming dynasty at the turn of the fifteenth century as a description of what dynastic China would bring to the world.

The Ming vase was an unimprovable piece of pottery, its perfection dictated by rules going back centuries as to how it would be produced. The vase carried complex messages in its decoration – a meaning understood only by those who understood the rules for reading it. The Ming vase delivered coded signs for those playing power politics in the court of the emperor. When looking at a Ming vase in 1450, the right pair of eyes could spy instructions and even philosophical reflections embedded in the painting and lettering: some subversive, some humorous, others revelatory. Today you look at a Ming vase and see a weeping willow and some pretty blue birds flying over a bridge.

In 1998, a software designer called Shigetaka Kurita was working for Japanese mobile operator NTT DoCoMo, who were in the process of creating a platform with which to access the internet from a handheld device.

They needed something to distinguish their 'i mode' messaging system from everyone else's, and Kurita believed he had the answer. Kurita was obsessed with weather forecasts. A cloud symbol is instantaneously understood by everyone, yet it is actually shorthand for an immensely complex meteorological process unfolding over hours.

The point was not the simplicity of the image, but the fact we accept it as a shorthand for something we know to be far more complex. We do not care that at three o'clock it will be slightly cloudier than at two o'clock, we simply want to know it will be cloudy.

The detail does not matter. It is too much information. We want a shorthand code for the day's overall weather that is easily deliverable.

Kurita then became fascinated by the way manga cartoons had taken stock symbols and used them to express emotions. We might not be interested that a cloud gets darker or lighter throughout the day, but if we are reading a graphic novel, we are interested in the nuance of a character's emotional state and development. The nuance is relevant.

How could a character simultaneously feeling anger, desire and euphoria, have these contradictory, conflicting emotions described by a single icon – a version of the cloud?

Manga cartoons had unwittingly invented the emoji. They distilled the essence of the human condition into a single graphic icon, just as the Ming vase conveyed complex messages in a glazed brushstroke, or the curve of a swallow's tail, five centuries before.

The very first emojis created by Kurita were 172 12-pixel by 12-pixel images based on Japan's *kaomoji* – 'face letter' – culture. They look very different from the ones we use today – a version of a smile, a version of sad, annoyed or crying with laughter.

But they are unmistakably emojis, and they derive not simply from a light-bulb moment by Kurita in 1998, but from a profoundly held Eastern mindset: that any degree of complexity of human life can be distilled and simplified into a language, a set of icons, decipherable to anyone who understands the rules that underpin them.

The emoji, the most widely utilised language of the twenty-first century, has its roots in ancient China. Yet it is not the emoji, but China's most important deal in two millennia – a conscious remapping of Ancient China's dynastic glory – that is on the cusp of reshaping the coming world.

OBOR: THE NEW SILK ROAD

On 13 May 2017, President Xi Jinping signed a cooperation agreement in Beijing with sixty-eight countries, including a delegation sent by President Trump. China, Xi said, would be offering to invest close to a trillion dollars in infrastructure spanning the globe.

The deal was called simply OBOR—One Belt One Road. If realised, it could make China's global ambitions real. The scale was breathtaking: an extraordinary initial $900 billion investment strategy beginning in Asia, encompassing the building of a deep-water port in Gwadar, Pakistan, and a 'port city' in Sri Lanka's Colombo; high-speed rail links in East Africa and from south-west China to Singapore; and gas pipelines across the whole of central Asia. OBOR is, as the *Financial Times* reported at the time, 'arguably the largest overseas investment drive ever launched by a single country.'

OBOR is a conscious recreation of the Silk Road – the network of trade routes from ancient China through central Asia and the Middle East to Europe, and from China to Southeast Asia and East Africa by sea, which effectively globalised the world two thousand years ago. OBOR was first signalled with an announcement by President Xi Jinping in 2013 as a response to the effect slowing growth in Western economies was having on China's own economic wellbeing. For three decades, China's growth had largely depended on exports, such as my Hot Wheels toy cars. Now, to keep Western consumer spending going, China was going to inject phenomenal cash into the equation. In 2015, China launched the Asian Infrastructure Investment Bank (AIIB) with the explicit aim of funding OBOR. That same year, it transferred $82 billion to three state-owned foreign banks for OBOR projects.

Beijing then identified the sixty-five countries along the belt and road that could benefit from OBOR. The plan is not geo-specific to China's neighbours. New Zealand, Britain, even the Arctic, are all on the list. Projects such as the building of the Hinkley Point C nuclear power station in the UK with a Chinese-French consortium are viewed in China as OBOR projects.

Tom Hancock of the *Financial Times* described OBOR as a potential Trojan horse for China's global dominance. 'As China's foreign policy becomes more assertive, OBOR is a geopolitical gambit . . . drawing comparisons with what Edward Luttwak, the military strategist, has called "geo-economics" – when the "logic of conflict" is pursued through "methods of commerce".'

Yet on 11 May 2017, as President Xi Jinping prepared his speech in Beijing to announce OBOR to the world, President Trump made an announcement of his own: a trade deal with China, part of which involved sending a delegation to hear Jinping's speech in two days' time. Trump had, critics said, flip-flopped on China. It was seen by commentators and former supporters of Trump's protectionist rhetoric as a defining moment in his early presidency. The day he became globalist.

As Linette Lopez wrote in *Business Insider* on the day of the announcement: 'This [deal] isn't just a love song for globalisation, it flies in the face of the "Buy American, Hire American" ideology Trump has touted. The entire point, after all, is China helping to build infrastructure in other countries. [It] is clear the tough-on-China Trump we met during the 2016 campaign is no longer with us.'

This was because whatever Trump might say or do (the saying rather different from the actual doing) he knew the deal with China. OBOR was going to change the world, and it would be very unwise to be on the wrong side of the new Silk Road, with little more to offer than a tweet. China had rewritten the rules again, establishing its global dominance, just as it did when it provided the trading infrastructure for globalisation the first time round, one hundred years before the Birth of Christ.

CHAPTER FIFTEEN
THE FUTURE: THINK SMALL

The Deal: Facebook and the OECD/World Bank launch
   the 'Future of Business Research Initiative'
Aim: To identify small to medium-sized enterprises
   (SMEs) as the future driver of world growth
Where: Across the planet
When: 2016

THE RETURN OF GROWTH

In January 2018, against the odds, growth returned. The US, India, Brazil, Russia and Canada were all predicted by the IMF to experience a significant upswing over the coming years: the first prolonged period of growth since the financial crash of 2007/8. However, the picture was far from uniform or even clear. In Europe, things remained 'sluggish' with Brexit casting further uncertainty, even though a weaker pound following the referendum had made British exports more competitive.

China's rapid expansion of credit since 2010 increased risk of a slowdown for the most important economy on the planet – and if that happened – it would cut the legs away from the Chinese economy, and thus everyone else. To add to the caution, interest rates remained low across the world, giving central banks little wriggle-room. The IMF noted that 'weak productivity' potentially undermined it all.

However, one unlikely place provided optimism: manufacturing. And, specifically, small to medium-sized businesses (or SMEs). Manufacturing has declined steadily since the 1970s – the result of globalisation and successive Labour and Conservative governments allowing manufacturing to wither on the vine. As a result, by 2018, manufacturing accounted for barely ten per cent of the UK economy.

But there was a consolation. The manufacturing firms left standing were leaner and more competitive than their foreign competitors, and aided in the export market by a weak pound. Manufacturing may have accounted for only ten per cent of the economy but that ten per cent was booming: back to a level of growth not seen since 1997. People making stuff were not, it turned out, part of an antiquated practice no one wanted, but exactly what the world wanted.

Brandauer was founded in 1862 at 70 Navigation Street, Birmingham, England. The company was originally called Ash & Petit and was part of Birmingham's extraordinary mid-nineteenth-century boom in the manufacture of bespoke steel pens. By 1850, there were over twenty companies based in Birmingham exporting high-end specialist steel pens across the world. The city had cornered the market because one entrepreneur and inventor, John Mitchell, had developed a high-precision machine for producing steel nibs with consistent ink-flow. Mitchell had effectively reinvented the pen, making the medieval quill finally redundant.

In the mid-nineteenth century, Birmingham had the kind of manufacturing specialism that the rest of the world would have killed for. The city had more pen factories than the rest of the planet put together. But what product comes to mind when we think of Birmingham now? Cars. By the mid-twentieth century, a hundred years on from steel nib pens, Birmingham had become Britain's Detroit, with British Leyland's plant at Longbridge the jewel in the crown.

The city had built on its precision specialism in pens in the

Victorian era and passed it on to the manufacture of cars. By 1972, British auto-manufacturing was at its peak, with 1.92 million cars a year rolling off the production line. Then there was the collapse. World-renowned brands like MG Rover, Rolls-Royce and Bentley were bought by foreign giants such as BMW and Ford. Companies including Nissan and Honda took advantage of the downturn to move to a newly 'competitive' Britain.

Now the British car industry is once more booming, under foreign ownership. Aston Martin owned by Ford, then a Kuwaiti finance consortium, and more recently, an Italian equity firm. Bentley and Mini owned by VW. Jaguar and Land Rover by the Indian car giant, Tata Motors.

In 2017, Britain produced nearly as many cars as it had in the supposed heyday of 1972. But this boom was primarily in high-end cars, owned by the foreign companies that swooped in to buy Bentley and Land Rover when they looked likely to go bust. These foreign brands recognised the long-term value of prestigious UK brands, and how that demand would explode with the rise of the super-rich post-2007/8. By contrast, in January 2018, Vauxhall announced 650 job cuts at its factory in Ellesmere Port. The car boom is no return to the 1970s, but a surgical strike at the high end.

These high-end cars are part of a global production line: an exhaust made in Germany, some of the steering wheel made in France, the rest in Spain. A car is not truly made anywhere, it is an assemblage of parts from dozens of countries eventually put together in the most tax-efficient location.

And in Birmingham, the city where British manufacturing kicked off in the nineteenth century with those precision steel nibs made by Ash & Petit, the company that started in 1862 is stronger than ever. Renamed Brandauer, it survived the collapse of British manufacturing in the 1970s and 1980s by sticking with its specialism. Today it makes more than ninety per cent of the switch mechanisms for every kettle on earth. Brandauer makes high-precision components for everything from cars and household goods to aeronautics and medical equipment. There is a tiny bit of their product in everything we use.

Brandauer went on a mini-rollercoaster ride following the Brexit vote in 2016, which dented confidence and led to a plan to lay off staff and cut costs. But the company had a sound platform for the future, no matter where Brexit or the value of the pound took them next: they had global customers, had continually re-invested in cutting edge technology to keep them ahead of the game, and most importantly, held on to their specialism. They were an SME ('small to medium-sized business') and some very big businesses indeed had identified SMEs like Brandauer as the future of all business.

CAMDEN: THE END OF THE EARTH AND THE BEGINNING OF TOMORROW

Camden in New Jersey is the most violent city in America. Avenues of once-prosperous housing are boarded and chained up with the same municipal stamp on the door telling drug dealers this is a 'monitored property'. Gardens are piled high with broken twentieth-century goods: refrigerators, TVs, sewing machines, tyres. I have to swerve my car to avoid a sofa sitting proudly in the middle of the road. Buicks and Cadillacs, once driven by businessmen, now stand tyre-less on bricks in alleyways with makeshift curtains across the windscreen. A place to doss for the night.

Camden's once-great factories producing machine goods and textiles lie derelict, needles and wraps for drugs strewn on the floor. Prostitutes stand bored on street corners, dealers cruise in huge blacked-out Escalades, men high on crack ride children's bikes, cavorting wildly across the road screaming and shouting.

Camden is like a post-apocalyptic movie, and yet it is also one of the most optimistic places I have ever visited in America. Because Camden is not solely the most violent city in America, it is also the city with one of the fastest-growing numbers of start-up companies. On the surface, Camden looks over, but behind this façade, it is alive.

Adam is a big Texan with a broad smile and an infectious laugh. He moved thousands of miles from the Deep South to Camden because he saw it not as a catastrophe, but as an opportunity on the map. Adam had plans to start a handmade printing press and identified Camden as the ideal spot.

He took over a disused car body repair shop. Adam now employs thirty local people with plans to expand into the derelict backyard due to a two-year backlog of orders.

Joe is one of the locals Adam employs. A giant of a man – literally twice my size – Joe turns out sixty or seventy T-shirts a day. Customers range from local pizzerias and colleges to record labels, skate-wear shops and boutique fashion brands. Adam's business has orders stacked up for a year from across the world. 'People like the handmade quality, people even come in to see how we do it. We've spotted a gap in the market and it's booming.'

Joe grew up in Camden in the 1970s and 1980s and remembers it as a thriving and prosperous town to which people aspired to move. 'People would come to the waterfront on Sunday afternoons and dress up and promenade. This was a place people dreamt about moving to!' he says, laughing.

A huge shipyard and countless factories, including Campbell's Soup, the New York Shipbuilding Corporation and RCA Victor Company provided employment for tens of thousands. Then globalisation happened.

In 1950, Camden had 43,267 manufacturing jobs. By 1982, that had fallen to just 10,200. Deindustrialisation in turn accelerated depopulation, across the bridge to Philadelphia and elsewhere. In 1950, Camden had 124,555 residents. By 1980, that number had fallen drastically to just 84,910. And the people who had gone were the professionals and those who ran small and medium-sized local businesses.

In a bid to attract money back to the city in the 1980s, as business was in full flight out of town, Camden's Mayor Randy Primas came up with an idea: he began campaigning to have antisocial business ventures no one else wanted move to Camden instead. In 1985, the Riverfront State Prison was opened, followed by a waste-water sewage facility, given the go-ahead in 1989.

But another rescue plan was also going on behind the scenes. In 1984, a private real estate company called Cooper's Ferry was started by a group of local businesspeople worried by the perception that their city was being handed over to big business uninterested in the welfare of the city, and who would only worsen the city's reputation by relocating prisons and waste facilities there. This kind of investment would be, they argued, a downward spiral destroying any rescue plan they might have.

Cooper's Ferry's strategy for Camden was to hold on to the existing small to medium-sized businesses that had built Camden in the first place by partnering them with other struggling businesses in the area, so pooling expertise and resources. They read 'community' as 'business community', using business to hold the wider community together.

Yet Cooper's Ferry initially struggled to keep Camden afloat, largely because the reputation of Camden as a failing city became a self-fulfilling prophecy. The incineration plant, despite protests from environmentalists and locals concerned about pollution, eventually opened in 1991, offering much-needed employment, but doing little to build the city's image as a hub for innovation.

Then, in 1992, Cooper's had a success. General Electric made an agreement with the state of New Jersey to keep its existing business in Camden rather than leave. In return, the state agreed to build a hi-tech facility on the site of the old Campbell Soup factory. The project ran into difficulties and finally ended up being owned by Lockheed Martin, but proved to be an important step in the city's recovery.

In 2001, Camden's business and community leaders came together to create the Greater Camden Partnership (GCP), which sought a strategic development plan for the city. It targeted the worst affected parts of the city with a 'clean-up' campaign. It then made these cleaned-up downtown areas favourable to SMEs by offering low rents and subsidies with the aim of fostering a new culture of start-up entrepreneurism. Hence the arrival of people like Adam from across America: entrepreneurs keen to get in first on an opportunity.

Since 2014, Camden has been seized on by hundreds of entrepreneurs who have flocked there to start businesses. Part of the reason is the low rents and close access to major metropolitan areas (such as Philadelphia across the river), but the other reason is that the city has managed to rebrand itself as a centre for EdTech and MedTech. As part of the Cooper's Ferry drive to revitalise the city in the 2000s, Cooper University Hospital and the Cooper Medical School of Rowan University became centres of biotech excellence, in the hope this would attract satellite start-ups.

The business upswing for Camden had an unexpected boon. In 2014, car manufacturer Subaru announced it would be relocating its American base to Camden with a new 250,000-square-foot headquarters costing $118 million, and creating five hundred new jobs for local people. Just as the downward spiral for Camden became a self-fulfilling prophecy in the 1980s, so too did the upswing after 2014 in the wake of the Subaru deal, sucking new start-ups into a city declared beyond hope a decade earlier.

Camden got hit as hard as any place possibly could be by the collapse of manufacturing. Luckily, they are turning it around. Not everywhere else in the US has been so lucky. This is the story of twenty-first-century America. Once indestructible brands holding up the economies of entire cities from Portland to New Orleans collapsing overnight. The huge bales of copper wiring and tungsten steel that stood in factories waiting to be turned into gleaming finished goods for foreign markets were exchanged for tumbleweed, blowing across empty factory floors.

This is the America that logically voted Trump – a nation that increasingly looks to be on its way out. If it is true that you get the leaders you deserve, then Trump was an extraordinary indicator of how bad things had got. A nation retreating into the past: religious fundamentalism, fear and distrust of not only foreigners, but any kind of difference, and the depressing backwoods certainties of homebrew racism. A country continually rebuilt on immigration, now hating itself.

In the late 1980s, I travelled to both the US and to communist Eastern Europe for the first time. America seemed impossibly exciting in those days: the bright shining future pulling itself out of recession. The United States was less a nation than the planet's most powerful centrifuge, sucking the rest of the world into its dynamic vortex.

In Poland and the Soviet Union, by contrast, you could sense it was over. The lights were on half power at night, casting a sickly, yellow glow over the cities. The people were demoralised. Even the police did not bother to check anyone's papers. They knew the game was up.

Now the US is starting to feel like those communist countries once did: a crumbling infrastructure, a sense of disillusionment with the political 'elite', and streets populated by the homeless and mentally ill, whom no one can afford to look after. The future, for the first time in a century, is elsewhere.

Trump promised to make America great again, but in Camden, there are people on the ground already doing it for themselves. In America's most violent city, there is a miracle going on. Camden's very destitution has been seized on by the hundreds of entrepreneurs piling in.

Down the road from Adam's printing press is a tech start-up, a shoe business and a whisky distillery run by two twenty-three-year-olds from New York. They have orders from across the world and part of their brand is that they are proud to come from Camden.

In 2013, Paymon Rouhanifard, a one-time financial analyst on Wall Street, was appointed to turn around Camden's schools. In

2016, they returned surprising results. The bedrock of poverty in Camden, he says, underscores everything they try to achieve, but the schools are now in turnaround and, most importantly, kids are turning up in the morning.

Joe, who works for Adam at the printing press, says that if he was not working there he would 'one hundred per cent' be selling drugs, and after a couple of years of that 'probably dead'.

'A kid can earn two hundred bucks a day on the street and what could I earn on mimimum wage – fifty? Sixty? What are you going to choose when that legitimately earned money can't feed a family? Those kids selling drugs are putting their lives at risk, but they're smart. They know how to turn cocaine into crack. That makes them chemists. They need to put those skills to something legal. They're also the sharpest business people on this street, because they've survived and grown their business. That skill needs to be channeled properly.'

Beneath the crumbling city is a real community. The kind of community that has disappeared from once-destitute areas that have become revitalised and then gentrified thanks to outliers like Adam.

In Brooklyn, in East Berlin and in East London, the life that was breathed back by artists and young alternative businesses, seizing an opportunity to work somewhere cheap, was snuffed out once a tipping point was crossed from 'actually dangerous' to 'fashionably edgy'. It happens time and time again.

Serious money arrives with its tinted-glass cars and gentrified gates, and the shutters on a genuinely connected community come down. This is not inverted snobbery, it is purely the way it is. Camden does not yet have the luxury of turning away the well-to-do who want to live somewhere edgy. They still have community, because the community needs to work to survive for now.

People call out to each other across the street to ask how they are; young and old neighbours who have known each other for decades look out for each other, and protect their community from petty crime such as burglary as best they can. In spite of the crime, they get on with it. The place feels alive and loved, not killed by new money.

The new entrepreneurs in Camden sense the value of what they are joining. They do not see themselves on a mercy mission, but proud of what Camden is.

As Adam explains, 'We feel like we are re-inhabiting what lost empire has deserted. I could come here and start any business. It's not what I do that even matters, it's the place we are investing in. I think the people who have come here – sure they have come here because of cheap rents, but the difference is they see what the place has – its incredible vibrancy and community – and they want to stay and be part of it.'

Camden's new business outliers reminded me of what Tom Peters, the man who remade the workplace with his vision of self-determined work back in the late 1970s, told me when we met in Boston. 'Whoever you are, however safe you think your job is, and well insulated your future looks, forget it. It's over.'

Reading this, you might think Camden has little to do with your town or your job – but you would be wrong. Camden is not an interesting, picaresque diversion into underclass America that has somehow turned it around, it is both a warning and a message of hope to everyone. This is what the world is fast becoming. Everywhere. But it needn't mean game over.

The old certainties – the mental factory you travel to every day in your mind – is about to shut down. The town, suburb or village you live in might not end up looking like Camden did when the money began to leave, but the same economic principles apply. Prepare yourself for change and get the right mindset to deal with it.

Walking down the battered streets of Camden, New Jersey, is no different from walking down the High Street in Camden, London. It is no different from the street markets in Nairobi, the sprawling food stalls in São Paulo or Bogotá, or impromptu markets that spring up anywhere in the world where there is a dusty road and people to sell to. Each delivers the same epiphany of hope and energy.

I mentioned this to Tom Peters and he exploded with enthusiasm. 'Yes! Precisely! Exactly!'

To me, I said to Tom, if you walk down any street anywhere in the world, what do you see? You see people who have had an idea. They have taken that stupid, crazy notion to run a shop selling coffee, old furniture, umbrellas, psychotherapy, carrots or dry cleaning, and turned it into a reality.

After a year, two years, five years, that business has either gone under or thrived. The people have either made a go of it or they have moved on to another stupid, crazy idea that has either thrived or gone bust.

To look at a high street is to see human endeavour and capitalism at its purest. The high street is a rolling conveyor belt of human beings forever striving, each with their own individual epiphany made real through business. The primal, human engine of the mind, pumping out ideas. We as humans cannot help it: we see an opportunity and go for it.

WHY THE SME NOT GLOBAL CORPORATIONS COULD OWN THE FUTURE

In April 2017, Ciaran Quilty, Facebook's Regional Director of SME for EMEA, declared that 'SME's are the undisputed engine of economic growth.' The world may be preoccupied with global corporations taking over but these corporations, most notably Facebook, believe the future belongs to the small business.

In 2016, Facebook, the OECD and World Bank launched a research initiative. The FoBS (Future of Business Study) analysed 140,000 SMEs in thirty-three countries to understand the forces underlying the dynamics of the global economy, and the key role of the SME.

The Future of Business Study uncovered an extraordinary fact. In 2016, the IMF announced a global slowdown, a stuttering Chinese economy, geopolitical instability in the wake of the election of Donald Trump and business uncertainty in Europe following Brexit. But for small to medium-sized enterprises, things were looking good. Sixty-six percent of SMEs across the world said they felt 'optimistic' about not only their own business's performance, but the economy as a whole. Brandauer in Birmingham, who had ploughed on doggedly making kettle switches even when the rest of manufacturing was collapsing around them, were a classic SME. Optimistic about their future, regardless of what else was going on, because they had maintained their focus and hence were flourishing.

These SMEs are not an add-on to capitalism. They are capitalism. SMEs account for over ninety-five per cent of firms and up to seventy per cent of all employment. As larger firms downsize and outsource, the weight and dependency of the Western industrialised economy on SMEs is increasing. According to the OECD, up to sixty per cent of new SMEs in the last five years are involved in either 'innovative' product – creating products or services that have never be seen before – or employ dynamic and unorthodox business structures. SMEs are genuinely 'disruptive' and risk-taking, not through choice but because they need to be. Over half of SMEs go bust within five years, but eighty per cent of those involved go on to start new SMEs.

And this approach to business gets results. The five per cent fastest growing companies on earth are dominated by SMEs in the technology sector, and with a job creation rate that exceeds larger corporations. High-growth small firms spend less on R&D than these big companies, but innovate in literally everything else they do and often, because the nature of their business is innovation, they do not see a distinction between what the company does and the need to innovate. It is simply, to use an overused business cliché, part of their DNA.

Interestingly, R&D is now viewed by bigger companies as an extraneous cost. Tim Cook of Apple has said that companies like his can learn from SMEs: the low-cost R&D approach taken by digital start-ups, who will spend short bursts of time working on hundreds of ideas, rather than a long time working on one. A useful strategy when ideas are now out of date so quickly.

The digital revolution has connected businesses with customers across the world and means being in a low-rent location like Camden, New Jersey, is no longer a disadvantage. Location is suddenly irrelevant. Globalisation has been good for the digital SME. Seventy-five percent use online tools to attract customers from across the world. But technology has also dramatically reduced start-up costs, as well as advertising costs. This has been one of the most important reasons for the rise of the small business. You literally need just a phone and something to sell, and you're in business. As Facebook's Ciaran Quilty observed, 'Today, small businesses are finding that all they need is a mobile phone and a few dollars budget to experiment with.'

THE SME GENDER REVOLUTION

Facebook's most important discovery was that SMEs closely shadow the gender shift from male to female bosses. Women rather than men were the most enthusiastic users of digital tools when it came to running a small business. And women in some of the most patriarchal and repressive countries across the world are the ones with some of the fastest growing businesses. In Africa and the Middle East, women are starting businesses at an incredible rate and growing them fast. Nigeria had the highest percentage of women anywhere in the world with the strongest can-do attitude to starting and scaling up a successful business.

In a study of the global picture for women entrepreneurs by Dr Ruta Aidis for Dell Computers in June 2015, it was Western countries that needed to reconsider their definition of repressive. In advanced Western democracies with a two-hundred-year-old business and banking structure, women are held back from starting their own business by long-established constraints of practice that are less calcified elsewhere.

This was because, Aidis discovered, women have the double-whammy of building the business in the West, whilst fighting a male-dominated financial infrastructure. If women are ever to break this control, she concluded, owning and building the business from the start is key.

Lack of ambition, Aidis noted, was a Western phenomenon, too. Only twenty-one per cent of women entrepreneurs in the West who were interviewed, said they intended to grow their companies by fifty per cent. 'We've identified that there is a gender growth gap. If we don't have women participating in the innovation of starting and scaling a business, (women) are going to miss out.'

In India and Pakistan, two nations with a high percentage of women entrepreneurs working with microbusinesses, the problem is not just the male hierarchy and cultural bias against women running businesses, but a physical restriction to resources. In Pakistan, only ten per cent of women have access to the internet and only three per cent a bank account.

SMEs run by women could prove as important to the second half of the twenty-first century as Silicon Valley did, the first. By running SMEs, women could potentially drive huge social and cultural change in a way unimaginable to political and civil rights reformers. Not by doing anything more than simply existing and showing it can be done.

When business is dynamic in this way, it can be like a bushfire through a dead forest. But this gender revolution in the running of SMEs requires two things in place, especially in the developing world, both enabled by technology: mobile money to circumvent the banks, and access to the internet. The first is already happening, and the second is about to.

THE RETURNABLE ROCKET

On 30 March 2017, I was standing in Peter Thiel's office in San Francisco, when something happened. Elon Musk's SpaceX, looking to land the first rocket on Mars, and in which Thiel and his partner Jack Selby have invested 'significantly', flashed up on the news.

After five years of relentless testing and retesting, the SpaceX Falcon 9 rocket had taken off hours earlier from Cape Canaveral in Florida and successfully launched a communications satellite into orbit, before touching back down on a drone ship floating in the Atlantic Ocean.

It was an extraordinary moment and made me think that these tech billionaires may look like humble guys in T-shirts, but they are in the mould of the great, eccentric, visionary business leaders of the past: Howard Hughes with his flying boat and William Randolph Hearst with his castle full of tigers and giraffes.

Musk appeared immediately on the company's live stream: '(This) means you can fly an orbital-class booster, which is the most expensive part of the rocket. This is going to be, ultimately, a huge revolution in spaceflight.'

Jack Selby smiled and chuckled to himself. I asked him what was so funny. 'That's not why this is so important. Of course, yes. A returnable rocket, colonisation of space eventually and saving Earth, sure.' But? 'But the reason this is important is because of what space is really a platform for.'

Which is? 'How do you get the internet on your phone?' I turn on my phone. 'And how does it get to your phone?' Via a satellite signal, so what's your point? 'Exactly. And how quickly does that happen?' It depends where I am. 'Precisely.'

The returnable rocket Elon Musk landed on a postage stamp in the middle of the Atlantic Ocean is going to change the world, but the most immediate way is also the least immediately apparent.

By owning space, you own the platform for beaming the internet directly back to Earth without the time lag. Internet access currently depends on satellites, but the 'latency' – the time it takes receiving a request and responding – limits everything.

It is not only impractical for the ocean of real-time applications: everything from online gaming to live streaming and teleconferencing, such as Skype or FaceTime, it puts the brakes on the realisation of the 'Internet of Things'. The inter-connectedness of everything we do and use.

For five years, Musk had been in a race with Greg Wyler, founder of OneWeb, backed by Richard Branson's Virgin Galactic. But Musk was backed by another player: Google.

High-speed satellite internet connection changes everything. Speed will no longer be measured by an evolution of Gs – from 4G to 5G to 6G – with success defined by incrementally less buffering time. It will mean you will be able to stream anything immediately. Boom. Like that.

High-speed internet connection anywhere in the world amplifies the SME revolution in the developing world in the way that the laying down of railway track across Africa and Asia did in the nineteenth century. Except this time, it won't be a handful of industrialists who will benefit, but the millions of people who will be able to run their own business with the device they hold in the palm of their hand.

Google have invested in SpaceX, but Google will no longer call the shots on the internet. Elon Musk will. Oh, and his friend Jack Selby, smiling in the corner. They will not simply be the new Verizon or Comcast, they will control internet access to Mars and the Moon when SpaceX's returnable rockets ferry people back and forth from Earth, having colonised them, too.

In the immediate future, the returnable rocket changes life on Earth for one very simple reason. It will allow low-orbit satellites, approximately 100 miles above the planet, to do the job satellites currently do with a fraction of the lag. In 2015, *Wired* calculated the increased internet speed from low-orbit satellites and estimated they would cut a 500-millisecond lag to 20 milliseconds: the same speed of delivery as a fibre-optic, home internet connection now. No wonder Jack Selby kicked back in his chair that day and slicked back his hair.

THE GIANT LEAPFROG

Instantaneous internet connection from space suddenly eradicates the need for terrestial infrastructure: so where that infrastructure has collapsed, or was never there to begin with, there will no longer be a problem. What was once considered the modern world is no longer the modern world: it will have been leapfrogged and the business playing field flattened.

Time and time again, tech entrepreneurs have told me that the greatest hindrance to their coming revolution is the outdated twentieth-century infrastructure they have to deal with. If all this was gone, they say, we could have singularity and the Internet of Things in a heartbeat.

Decrepit roads and run-down transport networks, crumbling buildings and public amenities, pre-internet laws and regulations governing how things should be moved in the internet age, how people should be employed in the internet age, how the internet itself should operate in the internet age. These laws and rules, they say, were invented for a different industrial revolution.

Look at the world waiting to have the go button pressed: drone deliveries, driverless cars, flying cars, space habitation, everything from pre-fab 3-D printed houses to 3-D printed organs for operations, or climate change solutions like fake clouds and orbiting solar panels to save the Earth.

Then there is the stuff on the ground and in the body: MedTech and gene editing, EdTech and the school in a box, the robot/human interface, work surveillance, bio-policing of the body, vertical farming, predictive policing and pre-crime arrests, iPhone technology on a contact lens, as if any of us wanted it.

Not to mention Elon Musk's other pet project: the 'hyper loop' – a frictionless pod levitating at 800 miles per hour inside a giant metal tube – a 'cross between Concorde, a rail gun and an air-hockey table' – taking you from London to Edinburgh or LA to San Francisco in thirty minutes. These are the myriad facets of singularity waiting for the lawyers to catch up.

This revolution, they say, is being held up by vested interests tied into protecting an outdated infrastructure from being dismantled. Politicians and bureaucrats holding on to what little legislative and bureaucratic power they still have left.

But once the internet is beamed from space, physical and legal obstacles on Earth to these transformations melt away. And places like Camden – whether those places be in Tasmania or Tajikistan – could be in poll position to take advantage fastest.

SMEs are the future, because they are a chance to reset capitalism using the digital revolution. A revolution in which we will all be a dynamic corporation of one.

This is the twenty-first-century twist of fate. The cities that built a deep, complex infrastructure for the first industrial revolution, and then extracted further power and resources for themselves in the late twentieth century by allowing places like Camden to fall prey to globalisation, are now going to get their comeuppance.

Once London, Paris, Nairobi, Shanghai or New York could suck the life from the hinterland around them, but there was a price to pay: they saddled themselves with an unwieldy infrastructure. They believed themselves indispensable and all-powerful. But then the twenty-first century happened.

The tech revolution offers a new paradigm. The very places where the infrastructure was either wiped out or never happened – rural Malawi, rural Wales, the Rust Belt of the American Midwest, the Australian outback – suddenly have the advantage. In one technological jump, they can leapfrog the twentieth-century mega-cities held back by cumbersome twentieth-century infrastructure and complacent twentieth-century thinking.

One word will enable a company, an individual, a city, to survive this coming revolution: adaptability. The obstacles preventing adaptation are not simply physical, but mental. The enemy is not robots or the tech companies, immigrants or the Chinese, it is complacency and the sense that you either do not need to change because you are safe from change, or cannot change because you don't know how.

To anyone saddled by this thinking, Camden – and anywhere like Camden deemed 'the past' – is not the past, it is the future, and with a lesson for all of us. Here, as elsewhere across the globe, the deals being made are not the deals of the twentieth century, those made between the CEOs of huge multinationals. These new deals are the deals of the twenty-first century, deals made by two people no one has yet heard of.

Entrepreneurs with a business idea that falls outside the categorisations of this book, because it hasn't been invented yet, who took the initiative to start their business in a place no one would dream of starting a business, and will in twenty years' time be hailed as the new Steve Jobs and Mark Zuckerberg . A big future – in short – that will start small.

WE ARE ALL BUSKERS NOW

On my last evening in Camden New Jersey, I took a walk. As darkness fell on a street corner, I passed a busker playing a smashed guitar fixed up with gaffer tape, banging the splintered wood with a lollipop to create his own rhythm section.

Buskers were once outsiders. You would walk past and try to work out their story. Were they a genius musician who never got the breaks? A loser with nothing better to do than beg for money? Was this a lifestyle choice: to stay outside society's rules by deciding they would do their own thing?

Suddenly society stopped having rules. Jobs were no longer for life. Savings could disappear in a blink. The whole economy could go belly-up in an instant if banks bet the wrong way. Hard work and diligence were not enough to be rewarded with a decent life.

Nothing made sense anymore and in this new world being remade before our eyes, the busker stopped looking like a loser or an outsider and started to look like an entrepreneur. Someone with initiative going out on a limb, no matter what anyone else thinks of them.

We all need to be buskers now. Using what talent and guile we have to forge a means to make a living. That busker was not performing on the same street I was looking at. To me, it looked like a desolate post-industrial landscape without hope. To him, it was a business opportunity, and I was a potential punter willing to throw some money in his tin.

That busker in Camden has become my role model. When I lie at night thinking in dread about the future and what is required to survive, I remember that busker, and it fills me with optimism. Here was a man in the most violent city in America prepared to stand on a street corner as night fell. Tune his guitar, straighten his hat, look up to see who's listening, and begin to go to work.

NOTES ON SOURCES

1. CASH: WHO IS KILLING IT AND WHY

1 UK Payment Methods 2016 report, Payments Council, 20 May 2016: www.paymentsuk.org.uk/industry-information/annual-statistical-publications.
2 'Brother, can you spare a contactless payment? Homeless go hi-tech', IBTimes, 1 March 2017.
3 Bill Maurer, *How Would You Like to Pay? How Technology Is Changing the Future of Money*, Duke University Press, 2015.
4 eCorner.stanford.edu, 21 January 2004. Thiel and Levchin discuss their first meeting.
5 Ibid.
6 Drazen's interview with MIT magazine *Spectrum*, Winter 1999. I interviewed Drazen for my 2014 BBC series *The Men Who Made Us Spend* (Ep. 3) in which he tells the story of the experiment in full.
7 Ashlee Vance, *Elon Musk: Tesla, SpaceX and the Quest for a Fantastic Future*, Ecco, 2015.
8 MIT *Spectrum*, Winter 1999.
9 'Credit Card Debt: Average US Household Owes $16,000', *Time* magazine, 20 December 2016.
10 For a full account of how debt window-dresses the figures on growth, see interview with Matt Whittaker, Resolution Foundation in my series *The Super-Rich and Us*, BBC, 2015.
11 eBay media centre, 8 September 2014.
12 Interview with Benjamin Barber in *The Men Who Made Us Spend* (Ep. 3), BBC, 2014.

13 'Customer Data: Designing for Transparency and Trust', *Harvard Business Review*, May 2015.

14 *New York Times*, 11 September 2014.

15 'Banks Did It Apple's Way in Payments by Mobile', *New York Times*, 11 September 2014.

16 Bill Maurer, *How Would You Like to Pay?*

17 Kenneth Rogoff, *The Curse of Cash*, Princeton Press, 2016.

18 'How Big Is the Black Market?' Freakonomics.com, 25 June 2012.

19 'Drug Money Saved Banks in Global Crisis, Claims UN Advisor', *Guardian*, 12 December 2009.

20 'The Defence Advanced Research Projects Agency (DARPA) awards $1.8 million contract to research blockchain for military security', *Quartz* magazine.

2. RISK: HOW CHAOS CAME TO WALL STREET

1 There are many accounts of Bouazizi's death, but the most detailed are in 'The Real Mohamed Bouazizi', *Foreign Policy*, 16 December 2011, which pieced events together one year on, and 'How A Man Setting Fire to Himself Sparked an Uprising in Tunisia', *Guardian*, 28 December 2010, for a report in the immediate aftermath.

2 'The Tragic Life of a Street Vendor', Al Jazeera, 20 January 2011. Yasmine Ryan's investigation discovered that Hamdi was subsequently dismissed.

3 This specific quote has been widely repeated in reports of Bouazizi's death. In the myth-making of the Arab Spring that followed his suicide, Bouazizi was alleged to have also threatened the officials with setting himself alight.

4 Professor Jane Harrigan, *The Political Economy of Arab Food Sovereignty*, Palgrave Macmillan, 2014.

5 'Not A Game: Speculation Versus Food Security', Oxfam report on financialised food markets, 3 October 2011.

6 *Fat Land* by Greg Critser, Houghton Mifflin, 2004, on the backstory of the power wielded by the farming lobby and corn producers in 1970s American politics.

7 Professor Jane Harrigan's inaugural lecture at SOAS, 28 April 2011: 'Did Food Prices Plant the Seeds of the Arab Spring?' puts the rise in wheat prices in the wider context of the fragile food system of North Africa.

8 Professor Rami Zurayk, 'Use Your Loaf: Why Food Prices Were Crucial in the Arab Spring', *Guardian*, 16 July 2011.

9 Ibid.

10 Interview with Robert Dall in *The Super-Rich and Us*, BBC, 2015.

11 Ibid.

12 *Der Speigel*, 8 February 2010; 'Greek Debt Crisis: How Goldman Sachs Helped Greece to Mask Its True Debt', *Independent*, 10 July 2010, on the plan to sue Goldman Sachs for massaging Greece's accounts; and BBC News, 20 February 2012, with an account on the history.

13 Michael Sandel, *What Money Can't Buy: The Moral Limits of Markets*, US Macmillan, 2012, for the context of viaticals and the 'death futures' market.

14 'Physician pleads guilty in massive securities fraud', *Orlando Sentinel*, 28 December 2006.

15 US District Court notes: Southern District of Florida. Case no. 04-60573– CIV–Moreno/Simonton.

16 'The subprime mortgage is back. It's 2008 all over again': Tyler Durden article for Zerohedge.com, 15 June 2016.

17 Ibid.

18 'Chinese Shadow Banking', *Financial Times*, 29 April 2016.

19 'China: The power behind the $700 billion bailout', *Wall Street Journal*, 10 December 2008.

20 William Pesek, Barrons.com, 6 July 2016.

21 *Financial Times*, 29 April 2016.

22 George Monbiot, *Guardian*, 25 March 2015.

23 Ibid.

24 'Why Trading Water Futures Could Be in Our Future', CNBC, 2 July 2014.

25 Ibid.

26 'California drought spurs protest over "unconscionable" bottled water business', *Guardian*, 19 April 2015.

27 'Forest Service: Expired Nestlé Water Permit a Priority', *Desert Sun*, 11 April 2015.

28 'A 280,000% mark up for . . . water. A look inside the bottled water industry', Zerohedge.com, 29 July 2013.

29 'California water prices set to rise next year: Fitch', Reuters, 18 August 2015.

30 'The Anthropocene Epoch: scientists declare dawn of human-influenced age', *Guardian*, 29 August 2016.

31 Ibid.

32 Ibid.

3. TAX: WHY EVERYWHERE WANTS TO BE THE CAYMAN ISLANDS

1 *Britain's Trillion Pound Island – Inside Cayman*, BBC, 2015.
2 Richard Stott, *Daily Mirror* archive.
3 For a full account of Rossminster: Nigel Tutt, *The Tax Raiders: The Rossminster Affair*, Financial Training Publications, 1985.
4 'Taxman', George Harrison, © 1966, 1967 Northern Songs Ltd.
5 *The Super-Rich and Us*, BBC, 2015: Ex-tax inspector Richard Brooks gives a detailed account of Rossminster's business practices.
6 Jan Fichtner, *The Anatomy of the Cayman Islands Offshore Financial Center: Anglo-America, Japan, and the Role of Hedge Funds*, Amsterdam Institute for Social Science Research, University of Amsterdam, 2016.
7 Nicholas Shaxson, *Treasure Islands: Tax Havens and the Men Who Stole the World*, Bodley Head, 2011, gives a full account of George Bolton and the key role of the eurodollar in the offshore story.
8 Ibid.
9 *The Super-Rich and Us*: my interview with Arthur Laffer.
10 Ibid., interview with Richard Brooks.
11 Richard Brooks, *The Great Tax Robbery*, Oneworld, 2014: A full account of Brooks's investigation into the tax system.
12 Jan Fichtner, *Anatomy of Offshore*, University of Amsterdam, 2016.
13 Ibid.
14 Financialsecrecyindex.com, Review, 2015.
15 *Britain's Trillion Pound Island*, op. cit.
16 Jan Fichtner, op. cit.
17 *Britain's Trillion Pound Island*, op. cit.

4. WEALTH: INEQUALITY AS A BUSINESS OPPORTUNITY

1 Melanie Kramers, 'Eight people own same wealth as half the world', Oxfam pre-Davos report, 16 January 2017.
2 'Never Mind the Gap: Why We Shouldn't Worry About Inequality', Institute of Economic Affairs, 23 May 2016.
3 Arnold Schwarzenegger, 'I Don't Give a Damn' (about climate change deniers), Fortune.com, 8 December 2015.
4 'Revisiting Plutonomy: The Rich Getting Richer', Citigroup Equity Strategy, 5 March 2006.

5 Thomas Piketty interviewed in *The Super-Rich and Us*, BBC, 2015.

6 'Mothers campaign group to leave Newham flats', BBC News, 2 October 2014.

7 Robin Wales of Newham Council subsequently apologised: 'I apologise to the Focus E15 families but this is a London housing crisis', *Guardian*, 6 October 2014.

8 Friedrich Engels, *The Condition of the Working Class in England*, Otto Wigand, 1845.

9 Mike Davis, *Planet of Slums*, Verso, 2006.

10 ONS statistics quoted in *The Super-Rich and Us*.

11 Ibid.

12 Ibid.

13 Robert Frank, *Richistan: A Journey Through the American Wealth Boom and the Lives of the New Rich*, Crown, 2007, gives a detailed description of this sealed-off world.

14 NASA's Goddard Space Flight Center and the US National Science Foundation modelling inequality research project, March 2014.

15 'Monitoring Poverty and Social Exclusion', Joseph Rowntree Foundation and New Policy Institute, 2015.

16 Richard Baldwin, *The Great Convergence*, Harvard Press, November 2016.

17 David Graeber interviewed in *The Super-Rich and Us*.

18 Simon Jenkins, 'We should cash-bomb the people not banks', *Guardian*, 26 November 2014.

19 David Graeber, *Debt: The First 5000 Years*, Melville House Publishing, 2013. For the historical context to the ideas outlined by Graeber in *The Super-Rich and Us*.

20 Thomas Piketty in *The Super-Rich and Us*.

21 Zoe Williams, 'Housing: are we reaching a tipping point?', *Guardian*, 29 March 2015.

22 Nick Hanauer interviewed in *The Super-Rich and Us*.

23 The DCDC Global Strategic Trends Programme 2007–2036, 23 January 2007.

24 *Weekend World*, LWT, 12 p.m., 6 January 1980. A transcript of the whole programme can be found on margaretthatcher.org

25 Nick Hanauer, op. cit.

26 For a full account of trickle-down and the Laffer Curve from a Keynesian perspective: Ha-Joon Chang, *Twenty-Three Things They Don't Tell You About Capitalism*, Penguin, 2010.

27 DCDC Report, 23 January 2007.

28 Edmund Burke's letter to Charles Fox, 8 October 1777.

5. FOOD: OWNING FAT AND THIN

1 Newarke Houses Museum: http://www.leicester.gov.uk/your-council-services/lc/leicester-city-museums/museums/newarkehouses/.
2 Daniel Lambert: http://www.bbc.co.uk/leicester/content/articles/2009/06/23/daniel_lambert_feature.shtml.
3 Obesity rates: http://www.telegraph.co.uk/health/healthnews/7307756/obesity-rates-20-per-cent-higher-now-than-in-the-1960s.html.
4 Greg Critser, *Fat Land: How Americans Became the Fattest People in the World*, Houghton Mifflin Harcourt, 2003.
5 John Yudkin, *Pure, White and Deadly*, Viking, 1986.
6 Professor Philip James: http://www.iaso.org/about-iaso/iasomanagement/experts/wptjames/.

6. DRUGS: THE MEDICATION OF MODERN LIFE

1 Centers for Disease Control and Prevention (CDC), Therapeutic drug use US overview, 19 January 2017.
2 'The Hispanic Paradox', *Lancet*, 16 May 2015.
3 For a full account of Gadsden's interview and its ramifications: Ray Moynihan and Alan Cassels, *Selling Sickness: How the World's Biggest Pharmaceutical Companies Are Turning Us All into Patients*, Douglas & McIntyre, 2006.
4 *Daily Telegraph*, 16 December 2016.
5 Moynihan and Cassels, *Selling Sickness*.
6 R.D. Laing, *The Divided Self: An Existential Study in Sanity and Madness*, Harmondsworth Penguin, 1960.
7 Philip K. Dick, *A Scanner Darkly*, Granada, 1978.
8 Howard Markel, 'Patents, Profits and the American People: The Bayh-Dole Act of 1980', *New England Journal of Medicine*, 29 August 2013.
9 Peter Rost, *The Whistle Blower: Confessions of A Healthcare Hitman*, Soft Skull Press, 2006.
10 John Abramson, *Overdosed America: The Broken Promise of American Medicine*, HarperCollins, 2004.
11 Ibid.
12 Vince Parry, 'The Art of Branding a Condition', *Medical Marketing & Media*, Vol. 38, Issue 5, May 2003.
13 'Why your workplace wellness program isn't working', *Business Journal*, 13 May 2014.

14 '80% of American adults don't get recommended exercise', CBS News, 3 May 2013.

15 'Quantified self: self-knowledge through numbers': quantifiedself.com.

16 'Could brain-altering nootropic drugs make you smarter?' ABC 7, 16 November 2016.

17 'Facebook blocks Admiral from using profiles to price car insurance', *Daily Telegraph*, 2 November 2016.

18 US Health Insurance Cover – CDC FastStats: www.cdc.gov.

19 Vince Parry, 'The Art of Branding a Condition', op. cit.

20 David Healy, *Let Them Eat Prozac: The Unhealthy Relationship Between the Pharmaceutical Industry and Depression*, NYU Press, 2006.

21 Data and Statistics: ADHD – CDC FastStats: www.cdc.gov.

22 David Rosenhan, 'On Being Sane in Insane Places', *Science*, 19 January 1973.

23 Robert Spitzer obituary, *New York Times*, 26 December 2015.

24 Allen Frances, *Saving Normal: An Insider's Revolt Against Out-of-Control Psychiatric Diagnosis, DSM 5, Big Pharma, and the Medicalization of Ordinary Life*, William Morrow, 2014.

25 Ibid.

26 Moynihan, Cooke, Doust, Bero, Hill, Glasziou, 'Expanding Disease Definitions in Guidelines and Expert Panel Ties to Industry: A Cross-sectional Study of Common Conditions in the US', *PLOS Medicine*, 7 February 2013.

27 Erin White, 'Behind the Boomer Coalition: A Heart Message from Pfizer', *Wall Street Journal*, 10 March 2004.

28 Howard Wolinsky, 'Disease Mongering and Drug Marketing', EMBO report: www.ncbi.nlm.nih.gov.

29 Barbara Ehrenreich, *Smile or Die: How Positive Thinking Fooled America and the World*, Granta, 2010.

7. WORK: FROM WHAT WE DO TO WHO WE ARE

1 Dr Nerina Ramlakhan, 'Tech-free bedroom for a peaceful sleep', Silentnight/Ofcom 2014, 5 March 2015.

2 'Cellphones can damage romantic relationships, lead to depression', Baylor Study, 29 September 2015.

3 Dr Nerina Ramlakhan, op. cit.

4 Daniel Nelson, ed., *A Mental Revolution: Scientific Management Since Taylor*, Ohio State University Press, 1992.

5 Matthew Stewart, *The Management Myth: Why the Experts Keep Getting It Wrong*, W.W. Norton & Company, 2009.

6 Frederick Winslow Taylor, *The Principles of Scientific Management*, Harper and Brothers, 1911.

7 'Guru: Frederick Winslow Taylor', *The Economist*, 6 February 2009.

8 Joseph Raynus, *Improving Business Process Performance*, Auerbach Publications, 2011.

9 Richard Sennett, *The Culture of the New Capitalism*, Yale University Press, 2007, is a superb overview of the development of the ideas underpinning corporate belief systems.

10 John Hayes, *The Theory and Practice of Change Management*, Palgrave MacMillan, 2014.

11 Tom Peters and Robert Waterman, *In Search of Excellence: Lessons from America's Best Run Companies*, Warner, 1984.

12 'Join the cult and give up any free time in your life', former recruitment coordinator for Airbnb in Dublin, Glassdoor App.

13 'The Impact of EU Enlargement on Migration Flows', Home Office Online Report, 3 March 2003.

14 Tom Peters, 'Tom Peters's True Confessions', *Fast Company*, 30 November 2001.

15 My interview with John Bennett in *Who's Spending Britain's Billions?*, BBC2, October 2016.

16 Rachael Orr, 'How to Close Great Britain's Great Divide: The Business of Tackling Inequality', Oxfam, September 2016.

17 'Uber CEO caught on video arguing with driver about fares', Bloomberg, March 2017.

18 Marc Levinson, *The Box: How the Shipping Container Made the World Smaller and the World Economy Bigger*, Princeton University Press, 2008, tells the story in forensic detail.

19 My interview with Steve Howard in *The Men Who Made Us Spend*, Ep. 1, BBC2, September 2014.

8. UPGRADE: ENGINEERING DISSATISFACTION

1 I visited Livermore fire station in 2014. For the full history, their website is 'Home of the World's Longest Burning Light Bulb': www.centennialbulb.org.

2 Cosima Dannoritzer's 2010 documentary *The Light Bulb Conspiracy* examines the evidence for planned obsolescence extensively, interviewing key protagonists.

3 'Does the UK have a problem with old sofas?' BBC News, 11 December 2015.

4 'Death of the Seven Year Itch: average relationship is now just 2 years 9 months', *Daily Mail*, 4 February 2014.

5 Cosima Dannoritzer, *The Light Bulb Conspiracy*, op. cit.

6 *The Men Who Made Us Spend*, Ep. 1, BBC2, September 2014.

7 Ibid.

8 'Smart Africa: smartphones pave way for huge opportunities', *Financial Times*, 26 January 2016.

9 Ibid.

10 Glenn Adamson, *Industrial Strength Design: How Brooks Stevens Shaped Your World*, MIT Press, 2003.

11 Alfred. P. Sloan Jr, *My Years with General Motors*, Bantam Doubleday Dell, originally published 1964, reprinted 1998.

12 *The Men Who Made Us Spend*, op. cit.

13 Ibid., Ep. 3.

14 Steve Jobs – iPhone Introduction, 9 January 2007, YouTube.com.

15 'Bottled air started as a joke. Now China can't get enough', Mashable, 12 May 2016.

16 Ibid.

17 Ibid.

18 Ian Sample, 'Body upgrades may be nearing reality, but only for the rich', *Guardian*, 5 September 2014.

9. POWER: THE FIRM WHO KNOW EVERYTHING

1 James Ledbetter, *Unwarranted Influence: Dwight D. Eisenhower and the Military-Industrial Complex*, Yale University Press, 2011, explains Eisenhower's speech in the context of an escalating Cold War.

2 James Ledbetter, 'What Ike Got Right', *New York Times*, 13 December 2010.

3 Ronald C. White, *American Ulysses*, Random House, 2016, is an exhaustive biography of the president including his early military career.

4 Barry Popik, 'Origin, Myth of the "Lobbyist"', RedState, 31 January 2010, delves into the first historical references for the term.

5 'Powell Memorandum: Attack on American Free Enterprise System', Washington and Lee University School of Law: https://law2.wlu.edu/powellarchives/.

6 Confidential Memorandum, 'Attack on American Free Enterprise', 23 August 1971. To: Mr Eugene B. Sydnor, Chairman Education Committee, US Chamber of Commerce. From: Lewis F. Powell, PBS Supreme Court Primary Sources.

7 Lee Drutman, *The Business of America is Lobbying: How Corporations Became Politicized and Politics Became More Corporate (Studies in Postwar American Political Development)*, OUP USA, 2015.

8 Jane Mayer, *Dark Money: The Hidden History of the Billionaires Behind the Rise of the Radical Right*, Knopf Doubleday, 2016.

9 F.A. Hayek, *The Road to Serfdom*, Routledge, 1944.

10 Adam Smith, *The Wealth of Nations*, Penguin Classics, first published 1776.

11 *Come and See*, directed by Elem Klimov, Mosfilm/Belarusfilm, Soviet Union, 1985.

12 Lee Drutman, *The Business of America is Lobbying*, op. cit.

13 Malcolm Moore, 'Ancient Chinese "cheat sheets" discovered', *Daily Telegraph*, 15 July 2009.

14 Duff McDonald, *The Firm: The Story of McKinsey and its Secret Influence on American Business*, Simon & Schuster, 2014.

15 Ibid.

16 'War for Talent', the McKinsey survey: https://Invosights.wordpress.com.

17 *The Super-Rich and Us*, Ep. 2, BBC2, 2015.

18 'McKinsey's close relationship with Enron raises question of consultancy's liability', *Wall Street Journal*, 17 January 2002.

19 Ben Chu, 'McKinsey: How does it always get away with it?', *Independent*, 7 February 2014.

20 Ibid.

21 George Monbiot, 'The great free market experiment is more like a corporate welfare scheme', *Guardian*, 4 September 2007.

22 Ibid.

23 Allyson M. Pollock, *NHS plc: The Privatisation of Our Healthcare*, Verso, 2005.

24 Ibid.

25 *Who's Spending Britain's Billions?*, BBC2, 2016.

26 Ibid.

27 Ibid.

28 Harriet Agnew, Miles Johnson and Patrick Jenkins, 'Inside McKinsey's private hedge fund', *Financial Times*, 6 June 2016.

29 Ibid.

30 *Who's Spending Britain's Billions?*, op. cit.

31 Walter Kiechel, *The Lords of Strategy: The Secret Intellectual History of the New Corporate World*, Harvard Business School Press, 2010.

32 Josh Marshall, http://talkingpointsmemo.com, http://talkingpoints-memo.com/11 April 2006.

10. BUSINESS: WHY
CORPORATIONS TOOK OVER

1 For an excellent account of Abs and his early career: Harold James, *The Nazi Dictatorship and the Deutsche Bank*, Cambridge University Press, 2004.

2 Ibid.

3 Claire Provost and Matt Kennard, 'The obscure legal system that lets corporations sue countries', *Guardian*, 10 June 2015.

4 Antonio Parra, *The History Of ICSID*, OUP Oxford, 2012.

5 Provost and Kennard, 'The obscure legal system', op. cit.

6 'Investor-State Dispute Settlement: The Arbitration Game', *The Economist*, 11 October 2014.

7 Provost and Kennard, op. cit.

8 Ibid.

9 Ibid.

10 Kathleen Chaykowski, 'Mark Zuckerberg's Manifesto is Facebook's State of the Union', *Forbes*, 16 February 2017.

11 *Who's Spending Britain's Billions?*, BBC2, October 2016.

12 Tamasin Cave and Andy Rowell, *A Quiet Word: Lobbying, Crony Capitalism and Broken Politics in Britain*, Bodley Head, 2014.

13 Tamasin Cave and Andy Rowell, 'The truth about lobbying: 10 ways big business controls government', *Guardian*, 12 March 2014.

14 Business Insider report on Oxfam infographic, 'These ten companies control everything you buy', 28 September 2016.

15 Fred Siegel, *The Revolt Against the Masses: How Liberalism Has Undermined the Middle Class*, Encounter Books, 2014.

16 John Carey, *The Intellectuals and the Masses: Pride and Prejudice Among the Literary Intelligentsia, 1880–1939*, Faber & Faber, 1992.

17 'FBI breaks into San Bernardino gunman's iPhone without Apple's help, ending case', Fox News, 29 March 2016.

18 'Tim Cook says Apple's refusal to unlock iPhone for FBI is a "Civil Liberties" Issue', *Guardian*, 22 February 2016.

19 Thomas Mann, *The Magic Mountain*, Secker & Warburg, 1945.

20 'Unilever boss Paul Polman slams capitalist obsession with profit', *Daily Telegraph*, 28 January 2015.

21 Marion Nestle, 'Pepsi to reduce sugar in its drinks? Really?', FoodPolitics.com, 18 October 2016.

22 Alex Berenson, *The Number: How the Drive for Quarterly Earnings Corrupted Wall Street and Corporate America*, Random House, 2004.
23 Jason Trennert, 'Remembering the Reagan Bull Market', *Wall Street Journal*, 13 August 2009: www.jasontrennert.com.

11. NEWS: WHY THE FACTS DISAPPEARED

1 Dan M. Kahan, Ellen Peters, Erica Cantrell Dawson and Paul Slovic, 'Motivated Numeracy and Enlightened Self-Government', Yale Law School, Cultural Cognition Project Working Paper No. 116, 8 September 2013.
2 'The New World: Nothing But the Truth', BBC Radio 4, 2 January 2017.
3 'Four more years attributed to Rove's strategy', *Washington Post*, 7 November 2004.
4 'How Jared Kushner won Trump the White House', *Forbes*, 22 November 2016.
5 Brendan Nyhan et al., 'When Corrections Fail: The Persistence of Political Misrepresentations', Dartmouth.edu, cited in: Brendan Nyhan and Jason Reifler, 'Misinformation and Fact-Checking', Media Policy Initiative Research Paper, New America Foundation, February 2012.
6 'The New World: Nothing But the Truth', op. cit.
7 Rosser Reeves, *Reality in Advertising*, Widener Classics, originally published in 1961.
8 'Smoke Gets in Your Eyes', written by Matthew Weiner, *Mad Men*, season 1, Ep. 1, 2007.
9 *The Men Who Made Us Spend*, Ep. 2, BBC2, September 2014.
10 Ibid.
11 Ibid.
12 Ibid.
13 Ibid.
14 'Pictures raise news issue', *New York Times*, 23 January 1987.
15 *Honest Man: The Life of R. Budd Dwyer*, directed by James Dirschberger, Eighty Four Films, 2010.
16 Catherine Taibi, 'Biggest media screw-ups of 2013', Huffington Post, 23 January 2014.
17 John Ioannidis, 'Why most published research findings are false', PLOS Med 2 (8) e124.doi: 10. 137/journal.pmed 0020124, 30 August 2005.
18 Richard Smith, 'Time for science to be about truth rather than careers', *BMJ*, 9 September 2013.

19 Ibid.

20 Ibid.

21 'Beyond Distrust: How Americans View Their Government: 1958–2015', Pew Research Center, 23 November 2015.

22 James Curran and Jean Seaton, *Power Without Responsibility*, Routledge, 2003.

23 David McKie, 'Rupert Murdoch is not the first press baron with a thirst for power', *Guardian*, 14 July 2011.

24 Ibid.

25 Peter Jackson and Tom de Castella, 'Clash of the Press Titans', BBC News, 14 July 2011.

26 *Outfoxed: Rupert Murdoch's War on Journalism*, directed by Robert Greenwald, MoveOn.org/Ryko Distribution, 2004.

27 Ibid.

28 Ibid.

29 *Loose Change 9/11: An American Coup*, directed by Dylan Avery, distributed by Microcinema International, 2005.

12. ROBOTS: THE HUMAN MACHINES

1 Alan Turing, 'Computer Machinery and Intelligence', University of Manchester, 1950, and Jack Copeland, *The Essential Turing: The Ideas That Gave Birth to the Computer Age*, Oxford University Press, 2004.

2 Ibid.

3 'Computer AI passes Turing Test in "world first"', BBC News, 9 June 2014.

4 'Eugene the Turing Test-beating "human computer" in "his" own words', *Guardian*, 9 June 2014.

5 John Markoff, 'Computer wins on *Jeopardy!* Trivial, it's not', *New York Times*, 16 February 2011.

6 Stephen Baker, *Final Jeopardy: Man vs. Machine and the Quest to Know Everything*, Houghton Mifflin, 2011.

7 Ibid.

8 Elizabeth Kolbert, 'Our Automated Future', *New Yorker*, 19 December 2016.

9 Ibid.

10 Ibid.

11 'Japanese insurance firm replaces 34 staff with AI', BBC News, 5 January 2017.

12 'Safe human robot interaction with industrial and service robots', Eurobotics Forum, 6 March 2012.

13 Carl Benedikt Frey and Michael A. Osborne, 'The future of employment: How susceptible are jobs to computerisation?', Oxford Martin School, University of Oxford, 17 September 2013.

14 Elizabeth Kolbert, 'Our Automated Future', op. cit.

15 Martin Ford, *The Rise of the Robots: Technology and the Threat of Mass Unemployment*, Oneworld Publications, 2016.

16 'Artificial Intelligence, Automation and the Economy', Executive Office of the President of the United States, Washington DC 20502, 20 December 2016.

17 Daron Acemoglu and Pascual Restrepo, 'The Race Between Machine and Man: Implications of Technology for Growth, Factor Shares and Employment', MIT, 2016.

18 Sugata Mitra, 'The Hole in the Wall Project and the Power of Self-Organized Learning', Edutopia, 3 February 2012.

19 John Chubb and Terry Moe, *Politics, Markets and America's Schools*, Perseus, 1990.

20 John Chubb and Terry Moe, *Liberating Learning: Technology, Politics and the Future of American Education*, Jossey-Bass, 2009.

21 Tamasin Cave and Andy Rowell, *A Quiet Word: Lobbying, Crony Capitalism and Broken Politics in Britain*, Bodley Head, 2014.

22 Ibid.

23 Ibid.

24 'UK wage growth outpaces inflation', BBC News, 15 February 2017.

25 Paul Mason, 'Our problem isn't robots, it's the low-wage car-wash economy', *Guardian*, 12 December 2016.

13. TECHNOLOGY: FIVE COMPANIES TO RULE US ALL

1 Michael Lewis, *The Big Short: Inside the Doomsday Machine*, Penguin, 2011.

2 David Graeber, *Debt: The First 5,000 Years*, Melville House Publishing, 2013.

3 Gilles Deleuze and Felix Guattari, 'A Thousand Plateaus: Capitalism and Schizophrenia', Les Editions de Minuit, 1980; University of Minnesota, 1987; Bloomsbury Academic, 2013.

4 Bill Gates, *The Road Ahead*, Viking, 1995.

5 Dave Eggers, *The Circle*, Penguin, 2014.

6 Dominic Rushe and Sam Thielman, 'Inside Alphabet: why Google rebranded itself and what happens next', *Guardian*, 11 August 2015.

7 Larry Page, 'Larry's Alphabet Letter: G is for Google', Google Founder's Letter, 2015, abc.xyz.

8 Sean Keeley and Sarah Anne Lloyd, '25 Facts About Bill Gates's Medina Mansion', Seattle.curbed.com, 16 February 2017.

9 Douglas Coupland, *Micro-serfs*, Harper Collins, 1995.

10 Farhad Manjo, 'Tech's "frightful 5" will dominate digital life for foreseeable future', *New York Times*, 20 January 2016.

11 Ibid.

12 Ibid.

13 Ibid.

14 Natt Garun, 'Amazon just launched a cashier-free convenience store', The Verge, 5 December 2016.

15 Berkeley Dietvorst, Joseph Simmons and Cade Massey, 'Algorithm aversion: People erroneously avoid algorithms after seeing them err', publicly accessible Penn dissertation, University of Pennsylvania, 2016.

16 Ibid.

17 Yuval Noah Harari, *Homo Deus: A Brief History of Tomorrow*, Harvill Secker, 2016.

18 Ibid.

19 'Shane Legg Q and A on Risks of AI', Less Wrong Community Blog, 2011.

20 Mike Schuster, 'Zero-Shot translation with Google's multilingual neural machine', http://research.googleblog.com, 22 November 2016.

21 Ibid.

22 Ibid.

23 Hal Hodson, 'Revealed: Google AI has access to huge haul of NHS patient data', *New Scientist*, 29 April 2016.

24 Julia Powles and Hal Hodson, 'Google DeepMind and healthcare in an age of algorithms', *Health and Technology*, 16 March 2017.

25 Matt Burgess, 'DeepMind's Streams app is reportedly saving NHS nurses two hours a day', *Wired*, 27 February 2017.

26 Alex Hern, 'Google's DeepMind plans bitcoin-style health record tracking for hospitals', *Guardian*, 9 March 2017.

27 'The CIA-backed start-up that's taking over Palo Alto', CNBC, 12 January 2016.

28 Ibid.

29 Ibid.

30 Matt Burns, 'Leaked Palantir doc reveals uses, specific functions and key clients', TechCrunch, 11 January 2015.

31 Ibid.

32 'Responding to crime in real time at the LAPD', https://www.palantir.com.

33 Darwin Bond-Graham and Ali Winston, 'Forget the NSA, the LAPD spies on millions of innocent folks', *LA Weekly*, 27 February 2014.

34 TechCrunch, op. cit.

35 *LA Weekly*, op. cit.

36 Ibid.

37 Ibid.

38 TechCrunch, op. cit.

39 Mike Isaac, 'Uber's CEO plays with fire', *New York Times*, 23 April 2017.

40 Ibid.

14. GLOBALISATION: HOW ASIA REWROTE THE RULES

1 Jan Wong, *Red China Blues: My Long March from Mao to Now*, Doubleday Canada, 1997.

2 'Visions of China: Reformer with an Iron Fist', CNN, 2001.

3 Ibid.

4 Frank Dikötter, *The Cultural Revolution: A People's History: 1962–76*, Bloomsbury, 2016.

5 Joseph Nye, 'Global Power Shifts', TED talk, October 2010.

6 Jim O'Neill, 'The New World: Fixing Globalisation', BBC Radio 4, 6 January 2017.

7 Peter Navarro, *Death by China: Confronting the Dragon – A Global Call to Action*, Pearson FT Press, 2011.

8 Yi Wen, 'China's Rapid Rise: From Backward Agrarian Society to Industrial Powerhouse in Just 35 Years', Federal Reserve Bank of St Louis, April 2016.

9 Jim O'Neill, 'The New World', op. cit.

10 'Wolverhampton Goodyear factory work to stop by Christmas', BBC News, 30 November 2016.

11 'Goodyear Closure: Wolverhampton factory shuts gates for last time after 89 years', *Express & Star*, 20 December 2016.

12 Dani Rodrik interviewed for O'Neill, 'The New World', 6 January 2017. For more on the roots of globalisation: Dani Rodrik, *The Globalization Paradox*, Oxford University Press, 2012.

13 Paul Mason, *PostCapitalism: A Guide to our Future*, Allen Lane, 2015.

14 O'Neill, 'The New World', op. cit.

15 Ibid.

16 Ibid.

17 'Ownership of UK Quoted Shares: 2014', ONS, 2 September 2015.

18 Stephen Gandel, 'The biggest American companies now owned by the Chinese', *Fortune*, 25 March 2016.

19 'The New World', op. cit.

20 Ibid.

21 Ibid.

22 GWC, 'Mission & History', en.gwc.net.

23 Ibid.

24 Jason Hiner, 'Chinese companies that will shape the future of the Tech industry: My week in Beijing', ZDnet.com, 22 May 2016.

25 Kaiping Peng and Richard E. Nisbett, 'Culture, dialectics and reasoning about contradiction', *American Psychologist*, September 1999.

26 Drake Baer, 'The fascinating cultural reasons why Westerners and East Asians have polar opposite understandings of truth', Business Insider, 21 May 2015.

27 Aristotle, *Ethics*, OUP Oxford, World Classics, 2009.

28 Drake Baer, 'The fascinating cultural reasons', op. cit.

29 Michael Harris Bond (ed.), *The Oxford Handbook of Chinese Psychology*, OUP, 2015.

30 Richard E. Nisbett, *The Geography of Thought: How Asians and Westerners Think Differently and Why*, Free Press, 2004.

31 Michael Oakeshott, *On Human Conduct*, OUP, 1975.

ACKNOWLEDGEMENTS

I want to thank everyone who took the time and effort to be interviewed. Robert, Kate and everyone at UA. Rupert, who got the idea in an instant and helped shape the book so deftly. Cameron, Ben and everyone at Hodder. Nicola at Keystone Law. Nick, Andrew, Kaitlyn and co. at Harper US. Jonathan at Curtis Brown NY. Everyone at the BBC I've worked with on the films including Janis, Martin, Mike, Fiona, Charlotte, Tom, Mac, Fatima, Kim, Patrick, Adam, Don, Gian and Clive. Everyone at Pulse: Will, Stu, Ed, Tom, Annabel, Izzy, Emma, Claire, Marisa and Thomas. Everyone who shot, researched and edited the series: Johan, Andy, Ariel, Adam, Jay, Brendan, Tim, Petra, David, Alex and the legion of other dedicated professionals who had to put up with me. Everyone at the *Guardian*, including Malik, Tim, Nicole and my old friend Ian. Melanie and Rachel at Oxfam. Liz and everyone at the OU. Jo, Gudren, Holly and everyone I worked with at Fresh One. Roy who pushed me to do it in the first place and has been a constant friend throughout. David G and Helen. Lucy and Victoria for their generosity in pointing and repointing me in the right direction. Tamasin at Spinwatch. Gerard, Janet, Fenton, Guy, Sean and Dave. Hannah who was there from start to finish, and without whom I couldn't have done it. Mr. Williams for persuading me to do GCSE Politics and Economics. My mum and dad, Alina and Peter, and my brother Andreas, for all their unwavering love and encouragement.